*Woodland Period Systematics
in the Middle Ohio Valley*

A Dan Josselyn Memorial Publication

WOODLAND PERIOD SYSTEMATICS IN THE MIDDLE OHIO VALLEY

Edited by Darlene Applegate
and Robert C. Mainfort Jr.

THE UNIVERSITY OF ALABAMA PRESS
Tuscaloosa

The University of Alabama Press
Tuscaloosa, Alabama 35487-0380
uapress.ua.edu

Copyright © 2005 by the University of Alabama Press
All rights reserved.

Inquiries about reproducing material from this work should be addressed to the University of Alabama Press.

Typeface: Bembo

Cover image: Courtesy of the William S. Webb Museum of Anthropology, University of Kentucky
Cover design: Paul Moxon

E-ISBN: 978-0-8173-8306-0

Cataloging-in-Publication data is available from the Library of Congress.
ISBN: 978-0-8173-1465-1 (cloth)
ISBN: 978-0-8173-5237-0 (paper)

Contents

List of Figures   vii

List of Tables   ix

Preface   xi

1. Woodland Taxonomy in the Middle Ohio Valley: A Historical Overview
   Darlene Applegate   1

2. Adena and Hopewell in the Middle Ohio Valley: To Be or Not To Be?
   N'omi B. Greber   19

3. Archaeology at the Edges of Time and Space: Working across and between Woodland Period Taxonomic Units in Central Ohio
   Jarrod Burks   40

4. The Bullock Site: A Forgotten Mound in Woodford County, Kentucky
   Eric J. Schlarb   52

5. Walker-Noe: An Early Middle Woodland Adena Mound in Central Kentucky
   David Pollack, Eric J. Schlarb, William E. Sharp, and Teresa W. Tune   64

6. Middle Woodland Ritualism in the Central Bluegrass: Evidence from the Amburgey Site, Montgomery County, Kentucky
   Michael D. Richmond and Jonathan P. Kerr   76

7. Adena: Rest in Peace?
   R. Berle Clay   94

8. Reflections on Taxonomic Practice
   James A. Brown   111

9. Learning from the Past: The History of Ohio Hopewell Taxonomy and Its Implications for Archaeological Practice
   Lauren E. Sieg and R. Eric Hollinger   120

10. Rethinking the Cole Complex, a Post-Hopewellian Archaeological Unit in Central Ohio
William S. Dancey and Mark F. Seeman   134

11. The Many Messages of Death: Mortuary Practices in the Ohio Valley and Northeast
Sean M. Rafferty   150

12. Taxonomic Homogeneity and Cultural Divergence in the Midcontinent
David S. Brose   168

13. Valley View: Hopewell Taxonomy in the Middle Ohio Region
Lauren E. Sieg   178

14. Building Woodland Archaeological Units in the Kanawha River Basin, West Virginia
Patrick D. Trader   197

15. Some Comments on Woodland Taxonomy in the Middle Ohio Valley
Robert C. Mainfort Jr.   221

References Cited   231

Contributors   271

Index   275

Figures

Figure P.1. Key archaeological sites mentioned in text   xii

Figure 2.1. Draft map of Ephraim Squier and Edwin Davis   26

Figure 2.2. Carriage Factory/Miller Mound   27

Figure 2.3. Unique effigy flared-end tubular pipe   32

Figure 3.1. Barricaded, nucleated settlements in the central Ohio study area   42

Figure 3.2. Early nucleated Woodland period sites in central Ohio   47

Figure 3.3. Late (post–A.D. 1000) "Adena" sites in central Ohio   49

Figure 4.1. Location of Woodland period mound and village sites in the Elkhorn and Stoner Creek drainages   54

Figure 4.2. Submound post pattern and associated features in the Bullock Mound   56

Figure 5.1. Location of Walker-Noe and some related sites   65

Figure 5.2. Plan view of Walker-Noe Mound   67

Figure 6.1. Map of the Middle Ohio Valley showing location of the Amburgey site and select Middle Woodland ritual sites   77

Figure 6.2. Plan view of the Middle Woodland component at the Amburgey Site   79

Figure 6.3. Middle Woodland artifacts recovered from the Amburgey site   82

Figure 6.4. Maximum calibrated date ranges from select Middle Woodland sites in central Kentucky   93

Figure 10.1. Locations of select sites referred to in the text   136

Figure 10.2. Time-space chart of significant Woodland and Late Prehistoric period sites in central and eastern Ohio   145

Figure 10.3. Typical Cole Cordmarked rims   147

Figure 11.1. Adena mound sites used in analysis   155

Figure 13.1. Regions along the Ohio River   182

Figure 13.2. Localities in the Middle Ohio Valley region   183

Figure 14.1. Map of the Kanawha River basin showing locations of important sites   198

Figure 14.2. Comparison of Woodland period phases in the Kanawha River basin   200

Tables

Table 3.1. Selected Woodland period taxa in use predominantly in southern Ohio   41

Table 3.2. Radiocarbon assays mentioned in the text   48

Table 6.1. Artifacts recovered from features at the Amburgey site   78

Table 6.2. Quantitative and qualitative attributes of copper ear spools   86

Table 6.3. Radiocarbon dates from the Amburgey site and selected late Middle Woodland period sites in central Kentucky   92

Table 10.1. Radiocarbon dates from central Ohio Cole Complex sites   143

Table 11.1. Regional Adena traditions   166

Table 13.1. Site location and architectural forms in the Little Miami locality   185

Table 13.2. Radiocarbon dates from sites in the Little Miami locality   187

Table 13.3. Embankment wall fill, mound fill, and burial types in the Little Miami locality   189

Table 13.4. Use of stone, other architectural elements, and evidence for habitation at sites in the Little Miami locality   190

Table 14.1. Radiocarbon assays mentioned in the text   204

Preface
The Good Servant and Bad Master

Historical Context

This volume on Woodland-related systematics in the Middle Ohio Valley is based on two symposia held in 2002 and 2003. The idea for the symposia originated over breakfast at the Society for American Archaeology meeting in 2002. As they discussed their research on Woodland period sites in the "periphery" of the Ohio Valley Adena/Hopewell "core," Darlene Applegate and Jarrod Burks lamented about the problems they had in applying traditional formal and temporal units to the archaeological records in south-central Kentucky and eastern Ohio, respectively. Of course, these concerns were not new revelations about the state of Woodland period systematics in the Ohio Valley; many researchers before (e.g., Clay 2002; Fitting and Brose 1971) had expressed similar dissatisfaction. Nor were they limited to the Ohio Valley, as recent conferences on regional taxonomy attest (e.g., Williamson and Watts 1999). Nevertheless, the concerns were pressing enough to warrant organization of symposia.

The first symposium on Woodland taxonomy in the Middle Ohio Valley was held in October 2002 at the Forty-eighth Annual Meeting of the Midwest Archaeological Conference in Columbus, Ohio. Seven papers, six of which are included in this volume (Brown, Burks, Clay, Schlarb, Sieg, and Sieg and Hollinger), were presented at the meeting. Applegate and Robert Mainfort served as discussants. The second, similarly titled symposium was held in April 2003 at the Sixty-eighth Annual Meeting of the Society for American Archaeology in Milwaukee. Five of the eight presentations were new, and four of these are included here (Applegate, Brose, Pollack et al., and Rafferty). Mainfort, R. Barry Lewis, James Stoltman, and N'omi Greber served as discussants.

Both symposia were very well received, prompting Applegate and Mainfort to assemble the present volume. To expand geographic and temporal

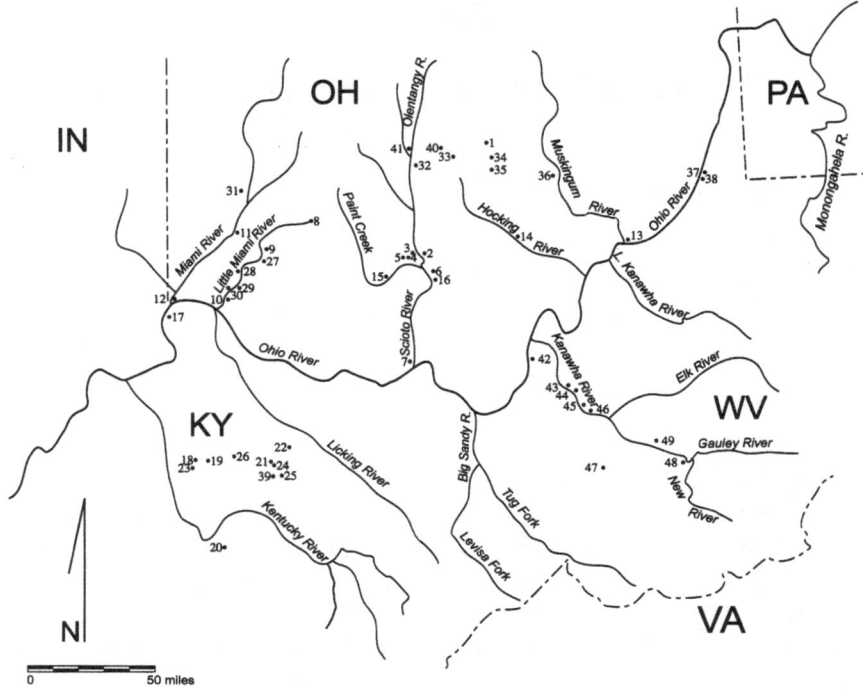

Figure P.1. Key archaeological sites mentioned in text. 1, Newark; 2, Hopeton; 3, Mound City; 4, Anderson; 5, Hopewell; 6, High Bank; 7, Tremper; 8, Pollock; 9, Fort Ancient; 10, Turner; 11, Miamisburg; 12, Miami Fort; 13, Marietta; 14, The Plains; 15, Seip; 16, Harness; 17, Robbins; 18, Drake; 19, Peter Village; 20, Walker-Noe; 21, Wright; 22; Morgan Stone; 23, Bullock Mound; 24, Camargo Earthworks; 25, Amburgey; 26, Auvergne Mound; 27, Stubbs; 28, Fosters; 29, Milford; 30, Camden Works; 31, Lichliter; 32, Scioto Trail; 33, Ety; 34, Strait; 35, Swinehart Village; 36, Linn 7; 37, Cresap; 38, Natrium; 39, Ricketts; 40, William Davis; 41, Toephner; 42, Woods and Childers; 43, Winfield Locks; 44, Parkline; 45, Murad Mound; 46, Charleston Mound Group; 47, Coco Station; 48, Mount Carbon Village; 49, Buck Garden.

coverage, they solicited additional papers, resulting in the chapters by Dancey and Seeman, Greber, Richmond and Kerr, and Trader.

The Middle Ohio Valley

The Middle Ohio Valley includes the intermediate stretch of the Ohio River in northwestern West Virginia, southern Ohio, northeastern Kentucky, and southeastern Indiana between the confluences with the Muskingum and Kentucky rivers (Figure P.1). Other major tributaries are the Little Kanawha, Hocking, Kanawha, Big Sandy, Scioto, Licking, Great Miami, and Little Miami rivers. The region encompasses four major physiographic zones: the Unglaciated Allegheny Plateau section of the Appalachian (Cumberland) Plateau province in eastern Ohio, northwestern West Virginia, and eastern Kentucky; the Glacial Till Plain section of the Central Lowland province in central and western Ohio and southeastern Indiana; and the Bluegrass (Lexington Plain) and Knobs sections of the Interior Low Plateau province in north-central Kentucky (Fenneman 1938; Hunt 1967). As noted by Maslowski and Seeman (1992:12):

> The mid-Ohio Valley region presents a distinctive environmental context when compared to other regions of the mid-continent. It evidences a moderately stressful cold season, a limited complement of aquatic and/or "floodplain" resources, but diverse and considerable nut and animal productivity. Within the region, environmental comparisons suggest that there are important disparities with regard to the distribution of large terrace surfaces, the length of the growing season, and flood potential. Differences in biological resources represent differences of degree rather than kind.

A volume devoted to systematics in Middle Ohio Valley archaeology makes sense because the prehistoric record of the region has figured prominently in the development of Eastern Woodlands archaeology and likely will influence the course of future growth. For instance, previous archaeological research in the region contributed substantially to the construction of archaeological units and concepts used by Eastern Woodlands prehistorians today. Of these, "Adena" and "Hopewell" are viewed by many archaeologists as the most significant, pervasive, and problematic, as is illustrated by most contributors to this volume. Greenman's research in central Ohio, Webb's work in north-central Kentucky, and Dragoo's investigations in West Virginia provided much of the data used to define "Adena," and the research of Mills, Shetrone, Moorehead, and others in southern Ohio produced data critical to the formulation of "Hopewell." Because units are the foundation of explanation in any scientific endeavor, it is appropriate and proper to present a comprehensive examination of systematics, classification, unit evaluation, and unit construction in Middle Ohio Valley Woodland period archaeology.

Archaeological Systematics

Scientific research requires the creation and application of units that organize individual pieces of data in meaningful ways. These units are used in collecting scientific data and in developing scientific explanations about the world around us. Unit creation is an intentional process, guided by the nature of the data and the goals of the research.

The term "systematics" refers to "the set of propositions, concepts, and operations used to create units for any scientific discipline" (Dunnell 1971:7) or "the procedures for the creation of sets of units derived from a logical system for a specified purpose" (Dunnell 1971:25). Thus, systematics is the theoretical process of identifying, defining, and describing the units that are used in scientific research. Whereas systematics encompasses the *conceptual* framework for unit construction, there are several *operational* approaches to unit construction in science, including classification and grouping.

Classification is an idea-based endeavor that creates and defines universal (ahistorical and aspatial), subjective, a priori units referred to in general terms as "classes" (Dunnell 1971). Type, horizon, tradition, locality, and period are examples of class units used in archaeology. There are two approaches to classification: paradigms and taxonomies. Paradigmatic classification involves the creation of unique classes based on one set of equally weighted dimensions or criteria, and taxonomic classification involves the creation of classes (taxa) based on multiple sets of weighted or nonweighted dimensions or criteria. Paradigms are permutable, meaning the positions of classes in the classification are arbitrary. In contrast, taxonomies are nonpermutable, meaning the structure of the classification is dependent on the relative positions of taxa. There are advantages and disadvantages to both classification approaches. Paradigms are unambiguous and parsimonious, but may include more classes than needed. Taxonomies allow one to display more complex relationships among classes, though they can be ambiguous and nonparsimonious.

Grouping is a phenomenon-based endeavor that creates and describes particularistic (temporally and spatially bounded), objective, *a posteriori* units referred to in general terms as "groups" (Dunnell 1971). Because they were formulated on the basis of recovered artifactual remains and they applied to actual archaeological materials from specific sites and time periods, Hopewell and Adena trait lists are examples of group units used in archaeology. The particularistic nature of groupings can be problematic if the group units are used outside their particular temporal and spatial contexts. As subsequent chapters will reveal, this has certainly been the case for Adena and Hopewell trait lists. "Because grouping counts and thus requires actual phenomena [objects or events], the products are groups restricted in their organizing capacity to the data upon which they are based" (Dunnell 1971:91).

It is important to note that classification and grouping provide organizational units (classes and groups) rather than explanatory devices (models). As such, classes and groups are tools for explanation, not explanations in and of themselves. Particular class and group units will not be appropriate for developing all manner of archaeological explanations. Class units must be evaluated with respect to the explicit goal of the classification in terms of logical consistency, validity, parsimony, and relevance. Group units can only be evaluated with respect to the objects or events from particular times and locations on which they are based (Dunnell 1971; Ramenofsky and Steffen 1998; Stothers 1999). Unit evaluation must be an explicit and intentional component of archaeological systematics.

Volume Overview

This volume is concerned with archaeological units used to organize data about those portions of the prehistoric record in the Middle Ohio Valley dated from about 1000 B.C. to A.D. 1000. On the most general level, one goal of the volume is to consider the role of systematics in archaeology. To what extent do scales of archaeological data coincide appropriately with scales of archaeological research questions? Should the "culture" unit be applied in archaeological research, and, if so, how can this be best accomplished? What is the relationship between formal similarities in the material record and historical continuities of past human groups? Given recent advances in absolute dating methods, is it still desirable to use chronological units to temporally order the archaeological record? Fundamental issues such as these are relevant for archaeologists working in any geographic region of the world.

The more specific goal of the volume is to critically examine archaeological units devised by and used by Middle Ohio Valley archaeologists. Central to this goal is consideration of two taxa that are cornerstones of Woodland archaeology not only of the Middle Ohio Valley but also of the Midwest and Midsouth: Adena and Hopewell. How were these taxa originally developed and applied? Why, after more than a century of research, are these taxa so problematic? Are they still effective constructs given our current research questions and our current understanding of the archaeological record? If not, what alternative units might be used? If so, how are these taxa best defined—are they horizons, traditions, phases, aspects, cults, or cultures? Over what geographic ranges and to what parts of the archaeological record can the taxa be appropriately applied?

In addition to Adena and Hopewell, contributors consider other archaeological units that have implications beyond the Middle Ohio Valley, namely, the Early Woodland, Middle Woodland, and Late Woodland periods. What criteria are useful in defining the periods, and over what temporal-spatial boundaries do those criteria hold? How can we accommodate regional variation in the development and expression of traits used to delineate these periods? Is it prudent to equate these chronological units with cultural types?

Finally, several archaeological taxa specific to the Middle Ohio Valley are evaluated in the volume. These include the Cole Complex of central Ohio and the Kanawha Tradition of West Virginia. General lessons learned from these historical reviews and critical analyses can be applied to other Woodland units in the Middle Ohio Valley, such as the Intrusive Mound complex and the Newtown phase.

The chapters are organized according to three central themes: unit application, unit evaluation, and unit construction. Applegate's introductory chapter lays out some fundamental issues in the construction of formal, synthetic, and chronological units, illustrating these with examples from the Middle Ohio Valley. McKern's (1939) Midwestern Taxonomic Method, the integrative approach of Willey and Phillips (1958), Ford and Willey's (1941) stage approach and Griffin's (1946, 1952a, 1967, 1978a) period scheme are summarized. The manner in which these classificatory systems have been applied in the Middle Ohio Valley—especially in reference to Adena, Hopewell, Woodland, Early Woodland, Middle Woodland, and Late Woodland—are considered.

Five chapters concerned with unit application follow. Greber provides an incisive comparison of Adena and Hopewell, using the type sites as a point of departure. Recognizing the legitimacy of calls for the abandonment of these taxa, Greber argues that they can be employed fruitfully when defined spatially and temporally in a manner suitable to consider questions appropriate for the data available. To this end, Greber suggests the use of central Scioto Hopewell and central Scioto Adena taxa for the Ross County, Ohio, area, where the type sites are located. Furthermore, Greber contends that in order to define units that can be useful in seeking answers to specific questions related to specific research goals, archaeologists must organize the diversity seen in the archaeological cultural remains in local, regional, and wider contexts in a manner that retains more than trivial distinctions. To illustrate this point, Greber suggests that archaeologists develop a new classificatory system that combines spatial terminology (e.g., Middle Muskingum, Central Bluegrass) with formal terminology (e.g., Adena, Hopewell).

Burks argues that use of the Adena and Hopewell concepts outside the traditional core areas has masked data critical to understanding diachronic changes in settlement patterns in central Ohio. Research from regions that express the more classic taxonomic characteristics as defined in the literature has, over the years, eclipsed much of the variability from more peripheral areas. Loss of this variability has resulted in island-like concepts such as "Adena" and "Hopewell" with little linkage through time and space. Burks demonstrates that continuing research at the edges of taxonomic units of time and space shows that important changes in Woodland period community organization, such as household aggregation, began in areas thought to be peripheral. Furthermore, these changes began well before the decline of the Hopewell phenomenon, to which they are commonly linked.

Three case studies (Schlarb, Pollack et al., and Richmond and Kerr) bring to the fore the difficulties that arise when attempting to apply the traditional concepts of Adena and Middle Woodland to previously unpublished and new data from sites in central Kentucky. Schlarb's examination of the Bullock site reveals that a traditional trait list approach to the site made it difficult to assign cultural affiliation, because the site contained traits that are diagnostic of both Adena (Adena Plain pottery) and Hopewell (rectangular submound structure). Schlarb concludes that the Bullock Mound is a late Adena site that reflects interaction with Hopewellian groups north of the Ohio River.

Pollack et al. describe recent archaeological investigations at Walker-Noe, a small mound that lacks a submound structure and burial tombs or pits but contains a centrally located area of intensive burning surrounded by cremations. Noting that the site reflects variability in Middle Woodland mortuary practices and mound construction on a local level, Pollack et al. argue that at a regional level Walker-Noe reflects problems in using broad taxonomic units, such as Adena and Hopewell, to characterize all Middle Woodland sites in the Middle Ohio Valley.

Richmond and Kerr describe a Middle Woodland component at the Amburgey site, where a Connestee Series tetrapodal vessel, copper ear spools, a copper celt, and a possible circular structure recently were discovered. Based on comparisons of the artifact content, site structure, and radiometric assays from the site with contemporaneous sites in the immediate vicinity and region at large, Richmond and Kerr conclude that the site represents a regional Hopewellian variant. The presence of Hopewell artifacts in a nonmound context and in an area traditionally associated with Adena, the absence of inhumations at an apparent ritual facility, and the unusual post mold pattern illustrate the types of variability that make it difficult to use traditional systematics to describe sites outside the core.

The next six chapters in the volume focus on unit evaluation. Clay and Brown deal with Adena from different but complementary perspectives. Clay specifically addresses the expropriation of the Adena concept by influential Washington-based archaeologists advocating migrationist views of culture change in eastern North America. His historical review of the Adena concept—its development and its use—coupled with his long involvement in Adena research leads him to propose that archaeologists "deconstruct" Adena and replace it with localized Woodland culture sequences.

Brown considers the historical development of the "Adena Culture" unit, arguing that the underlying conceptual propositions—the age-area view of culture—and the inconsistent content of this unit make it invalid and in urgent need of reformulation. Brown sees in this taxon a prime illustration of the problems in archaeologically identifying "cultures." Another taxonomic issue Brown addresses is the relationship between formal similarities and temporal units. Using the Late Woodland period as an example, he cautions against the definition of temporal units on the basis of formal similarities that are time-transgressive and lack evolutionary significance.

The history of Hopewell taxonomy is considered by Sieg and Hollinger, who propose strict adherence to the systematics of Willey and Phillips (1958) as one means to untangling the current morass. Historically, Hopewell has been considered a culture, complex, horizon, phase, period, style, trading system, mortuary and religious system, symbolic system, and interaction sphere. Sieg and Hollinger argue that the Hopewell taxon has become problematic because it was defined without any theoretical taxonomic context; it was defined largely on the basis of mortuary and ceremonial objects to the exclusion of other types of artifacts; it includes such a large list of diagnostic traits that its archaeological visibility may not be justified; and it has been used inconsistently by archaeologists. They conclude that, at a broad geographic scale, Hopewell is most productively and appropriately classified as a horizon as defined by Willey and Phillips.

Dancey and Seeman discuss a post-Hopewellian taxonomic construct in central Ohio, presenting a valuable summary of data and refreshingly arguing against further formulation of the Cole Complex until more data are available. Originally formulated to describe the reemergence of a local, nonagricultural tradition following the Hopewell "collapse," the Cole Complex was defined largely on the basis of ceramic assemblages. Due to inadequate empirical support for the taxon, Dancey and Seeman propose to replace the Cole Complex with a systematics that is grounded in time-space distributions of artifact styles and geocultural deposition units and that uses the concepts of horizon (at various scales), tradition (at various scales), and style zone to estimate the broad outline of human history along with the size, shape, and local histories of interacting populations.

A multiscalar approach to regional Woodland diversity is advocated by Rafferty, who focuses on mortuary data and its messages. Using data from six sites in the Middle Ohio Valley, Rafferty demonstrates that, rather than being a monolithic construct with a single characteristic mortuary program, Adena encompasses distinct regional mortuary patterns that vary in terms of mound structures, burial modes, and grave goods. These differing patterns are indicative of significant regional differences in the ritual practices associated with death.

Brose argues that the study of the human past can succeed not only to the degree that the scales of data and questions are similar but also to the extent that our descriptions of past and present scales are critically rethought, for we cannot know whether the scales of the problems are comparable if we have no comparability between the tools with which to measure the scales. He recommends replacing sociopolitical models inferred from ethnographic simulations of distant archaeological contexts with those based on appropriately bounded taxonomic structures of archaeologically recoverable indices of economic and social complexity. Emphasizing the importance of scale, Brose argues that this approach demands justifying the criteria used for defining each and every cultural/chronological system and that it succeeds only to the extent that it explicitly describes the boundary conditions over which such defined taxonomic units may be valid or useful.

Two chapters in the volume focus on unit construction. In her chapter on Ohio Hopewell, Sieg, like Rafferty, argues against monolithic views of archaeological taxa. Using data from domestic and ceremonial sites in southern Ohio, Sieg identifies local distinctions in site age, architecture, artifacts, and geographical proximity while at the same time recognizing horizon-like Hopewell influences that were part of a broader Middle Woodland cultural landscape. She proposes a potentially useful series of regional Hopewellian phases that, whatever their final form, call attention to diversity within individual river drainages that often is masked by the overarching Hopewell construct.

The history of Woodland period classification in the Kanawha River basin of West Virginia is summarized by Trader, who also provides important new data that lead to a call for Woodland unit revisions. Trader recognizes the fundamental contributions made by Edward McMichael to the development of formal and chronological units for the Kanawha Woodland while at the same time noting the shortcomings of McMichael's formulations in the light of recent archaeological research. Trader uses data—including radiocarbon dates, faunal and floral remains, and settlement patterns—from more than a dozen domestic and ceremonial sites to formulate a revised taxonomic scheme for the Kanawha Woodland.

The volume concludes with an overview by Mainfort, whose perspective has been shaped by experience in the lower Mississippi Valley. He emphasizes that archaeologists tend to forget that their taxonomic units are arbitrary constructs that should be retained only so long as they prove useful for explaining the archaeological record. As tools, they are subject to modification and refinement and, if no longer useful, to discard. Following the other contributors, Mainfort argues that research questions should dictate appropriate taxonomy and that existing taxonomy should not constrain research questions. In this regard, both flexibility and awareness of appropriate geographic scale are critical to the utility of taxonomic units at any level.

Acknowledgments

This volume represents a herculean effort on the part of the contributors to synthesize recent Woodland period research in the Middle Ohio Valley and to evaluate and, in some cases, to reformulate the archaeological units used to measure variability in that data. Certainly this volume would not have been possible without their dedication to the discipline and their willingness to "think outside the box." We greatly appreciate the time and effort they put into their contributions and the timely manner with which they submitted drafts for review.

Mary Lynn Kennedy (Arkansas Archeological Survey) was instrumental in producing several graphics. Tom Green, director of the Survey, provided encouragement and support throughout the production process. Lynne Sullivan and David Anderson provided insightful reviews of the manuscript.

The title of the preface is drawn from Trigger's statements, "Yet if typology is a good servant, it can be a very bad master" (1999:303) and "We must welcome the creation of new typologies and be prepared to evaluate both old and new ones on their merits. In this way we do our best to ensure that classifications, which we cannot get along without, remain our servants and do not become our masters" (1999:322).

*Woodland Period Systematics
in the Middle Ohio Valley*

I
Woodland Taxonomy in the Middle Ohio Valley
A Historical Overview
Darlene Applegate

The long history of archaeological investigations in the Middle Ohio Valley has influenced considerably the development of Eastern Woodlands archaeology. "Adena" and "Hopewell," for example, are taxa that developed in the Middle Ohio Valley and are now fixed in Americanist archaeology. Unfortunately, conceptual thinking about these and related taxa has not kept pace with the flurry of archaeological discoveries made over the last century in the Middle Ohio Valley. Our understanding of the Woodland period archaeological record has changed dramatically as archaeologists have documented a great deal of formal and temporal diversity in what previously were considered fairly monolithic and chronologically sequential lifeways. As the chapters in this volume illustrate, our ability to communicate effectively about this variation has been hampered by the use of outdated and ambiguous archaeological units that now have multiple meanings or lack empirical basis.

The scientific study of the human past using the archaeological record requires appropriately constructed and consistently applied units of measurement. Broadly defined, units are "divisions of variation" in archaeological phenomena and "the means by which we partition and specify a range of variability that is relevant for particular research interests" (Ramenofsky and Steffen 1998:3). Archaeological units are developed to measure variation in three dimensions: form, time, and space (Spaulding 1960; Willey 1953; Willey and Phillips 1958). They differ in terms of inclusiveness, resolution, measurement scale, and content (Dunnell 1971; Ramenofsky and Steffen 1998).

Unit construction involves creating new units or selecting existing units and evaluating those units relative to a specific research agenda (Ramenofsky and Steffen 1998; Stothers 1999). "The evaluation process begins with a clear identification, or *description,* of the unit structure and then proceeds with an *assessment* of the performance and the relevance of those units within a particular research structure" (Ramenofsky and Steffen 1998:8; emphasis added). Archaeological unit evaluation and construction are the general goals of this volume. More specifically, authors consider the development and application of archaeological units related to Woodland research in the Middle Ohio Valley. In this chapter I begin the evaluation process by describing existing unit structures used in the Middle Ohio Valley, focusing on formal and chronological units. Formal units are based on similarities or differences in the formal properties of artifacts and assemblages, and chronological units are used to partition the time continuum.

Formal Units

HISTORICAL CONTEXT

One early attempt by archaeologists to develop formal units resulted in the Midwestern Taxonomic Method (MTM), which was formalized by McKern (1939). Ignoring temporal and spatial dimensions, archaeologists used formal similarities in artifact assemblages to delineate five hierarchically arranged units (from least to most inclusive): focus, aspect, phase, pattern, and base. Lists of formal artifact types from individual site components were compared, and similar components were grouped as a focus. Foci that shared similar artifact types were grouped as an aspect, similar aspects as a phase, similar phases as a pattern, and similar patterns as a base. Formal traits that delineated a particular group were referred to as diagnostics, and formal traits that distinguished among groups were referred to as determinants.

An apparently straightforward scheme, the MTM proved problematic. Some units (e.g., focus) were unreliable, meaning they were not consistently applicable, partly because of the subjectivity involved in identifying how many and which similar traits were needed to group components as a focus. All units were empirically invalid, meaning they did not perform as intended within a given research context, largely because the units were intended to partition formal variation only but necessarily considered time and space as well (Lyman et al. 1997; Ramenofsky and Steffen 1998). The MTM "now can be seen as a highly formalistic misapplication of the taxonomic approach to the classification of archaeological cultures" (Trigger 1978:102). Nonetheless, subsequent unit schemes drew from the MTM (Lyman et al. 1997). For example, archaeologists have used or recast "component" and "phase" (e.g., Willey and Phillips's integrative approach), trait lists (e.g., Greenman's and Webb's definitions of Adena), and determinant traits (e.g., Willey and Phillips's horizon markers).

Following a different tack, Willey and Phillips's (1958) integrative approach explicitly considered the dimensions of time and space as well as form in the construction of archaeological units. Components and phases were integrated using two intra-area units, tradition (similar phases covering a small geographic area but a long temporal interval) and horizon (similar phases covering a large geographic area but a short temporal interval), which in turn were integrated using one interarea unit, stage. Formulated for use in describing diachronic patterns of culture change, the units were "historical constructs concerned primarily with the occurrences of styles or technical features in space and time and in the establishment of diffusional or genetic connections between such forms" (Willey and Sabloff 1974:148), a telling statement about the systematics of Willey and Phillips.

Although Willey and Phillips's scheme was more reliable and empirically valid than the MTM, it was abstractly invalid, meaning it lacked "conceptual coherence between research goals and unit concepts" (Ramenofsky and Steffen 1998:9). Specifically, in their attempt to imbue culture history with ethnographic character (Lyman et al. 1997), Willey and Phillips (1958:48) conflated their archaeological units with sociocultural meaning to describe "the maximum units reflecting the major segmentations of culture-history," namely, cultures and civilizations. Furthermore, the integrative approach assumed rather than demonstrated that formal similarity and spatial-temporal similarity indicated historical relatedness.

Despite these problems, Willey and Phillips's intra-area integrative units (tradition and horizon) are still commonly used in American archaeology. And the misguided effort to link archaeological cultures with sociocultural units such as ethnographic cultures continues. As Lyman et al. (1997:1) observed, many of the archaeological units developed in the culture history paradigm "remain so ingrained in our thinking today that we often fail to acknowledge them or to realize that we use them" daily in student training, contract work, and research projects. Yet, with this continuity also came innovation in unit construction as the "new" archaeologists created qualitative and quantitative archaeological units.

The diverse systematics of post–culture history paradigms guided the process of archaeological unit construction. Attempts by processual archaeologists to explain cultural change from a positivistic, essentialist, evolutionary perspective are accomplished with a focus on function, technico-economic factors, adaptation, ecology, systems, and middle-range laws using a deductive approach (Ramenofsky and Steffen 1998; Trigger 1978, 1989; Willey and Sabloff 1974). "Definition of archaeological units has been seen as the identification of specific adaptations to local and regional environments" (Muller 1986:24). Behavioral archaeologists seek to identify middle-range, nomothetic laws that link human behavior and artifactual remains (Schiffer 1976; Trigger 1989) by constructing units related to formation processes, ethnoarchaeology, and experimental archaeology (Ramenofsky and Steffen 1998). Interactional archaeologists use a more particularistic, inductive approach to consider how intersocietal contact and competition cause cultural change (Trigger 1989). They construct units within the domain of social interactions. Settlement archaeologists are concerned with the distribution of humans at various scales on the landscape, constructing units related to settlement patterns and settlement systems.

Out of the paradigmatic reorientation were constructed archaeological units such as system (Flannery 1968), focal-diffuse (Cleland 1976), c- and n-transforms (Schiffer 1976), systemic and archaeological contexts (Schiffer 1976), interaction sphere (Caldwell 1964; Seeman 1979; Struever and Houart 1972), peer polity (Braun 1986; Renfrew and Cherry 1986), core-periphery (Pacheco, ed. 1996; Seeman 1979), scatters (Wandsnider 1998), and hamlets (Dancey 1992; Dancey and Pacheco 1997; Fuller 1981; Pacheco 1997; Prufer 1964a). Some of the new units are groups (particularistic, objective, a posteriori units based on actual phenomena), but most are classes (universal, subjective, a priori units based on ideas) (preface, this volume).

Unit evaluation in the post–culture history era has varied. Generally speaking, assessments of unit reliability and empirical validity have been considered more often than assessments of abstract validity. A notable exception to the latter is the "clear integration between behavioral goals and units" in behavioral archaeology (Ramenofsky and Steffen 1998:14).

In summary, culture historians developed some formal units that have been largely abandoned (e.g., focus) and others that continue to be used by Americanist archaeologists (e.g., phase, tradition, horizon). Following the era of culture history, archaeologists constructed formal units to measure archaeological variation related to adaptation (e.g., system), formation processes (e.g., c- and n-transforms), social interactions (e.g., interaction sphere), and settlement (e.g., hamlet). How are these units used in Middle Ohio Valley archaeology?

Formal Units for the Middle Ohio Valley

Traditionally, existing formal and synthetic units have been used in Middle Ohio Valley archaeological research by qualifying the units with terms deriving from "type" sites (e.g., Hopewell, Adena), geographic or physiographic locations (e.g., Woodland, Glacial Kame, Newtown), or cultural traits (e.g., Intrusive Mound). This produces a binomial designation such as Woodland Culture, with the first term serving as a modifying adjective to the second term specifying the unit. The approach is not unlike that developed for artifact typologies, such as the Southeastern Ceramic Typology (Ford and Griffin 1938). This procedure makes sense in principle. In practice, however, the approach has created much confusion and has limited archaeological investigations, primarily because of recycling of modifiers, inconsistent use and misapplication of units, conflation of group and class units, and conflation of archaeological and sociocultural units. A cursory review of one century of archaeological literature on Woodland research in the Middle Ohio Valley makes these problems readily apparent, particularly with respect to "Woodland," "Hopewell," and "Adena."

Woodland

Consider the term "Woodland," which plays a central role in archaeological interpretation in the Middle Ohio Valley. Early references to Woodland appeared in the 1930s. According to Griffin (1986), in 1935 the term was appropriated from the "Eastern Woodlands culture area" to describe non-Mississippian archaeological complexes in eastern North America. Deuel (1935) identified the Woodland Basic Culture as one of two pottery-bearing cultures of the Mississippi Valley. McKern (1937, 1939) defined the Woodland Cultural Pattern or Woodland Pattern as a complex of phases exhibiting determinant traits related to artifact types, mortuary treatment, and, to a lesser extent, settlement. Cole and Deuel (1937) recognized the Woodland Pattern, and Jennings (1941) referred to the Woodland Basic Pattern or Basic Woodland. A list of 81 traits for the Woodland Pattern was compiled at the first Woodland Conference in Chicago (Baker et al. 1941).

Other culture historians viewed Woodland as a part of a developmental stage, the Formative (Willey and Phillips 1958). Willey (1966) classified Woodland as a major cultural tradition characterized by pottery, mounds and other earthworks, and agriculture. Others (e.g., Caldwell 1962; Yerkes 1988) used a more diverse set of traits that incorporated an ecological-adaptation approach in defining a Woodland (or Northern) Tradition. Using Willey and Phillips's (1958) tradition concept, Silverberg (1968) referred to three Woodland traditions (though he also used the term "phases") in the Ohio Valley: Early Woodland, Middle Woodland, and Late Woodland. Seeman (1992b) also discussed Woodland traditions.

In the literature, then, there are references to Woodland, Woodland Culture, Woodland Pattern, and Woodland Tradition, sometimes in combination in the same article. A similar history of multiple formal unit use exists with the Hopewell concept.

Hopewell

In the late nineteenth century, Putnam, Moorehead, and Fowke recognized that earthworks, skeletal remains, and associated artifacts at such Ohio sites as Turner and Hopewell represented one of two distinct mound-building groups in the Middle Ohio Valley (Shetrone 1920). Mills (1906) and Moorehead (1909) used the designation "Hopewell culture" in an ethnographic sense, akin to tribes or nations, to classify prehistoric groups represented at Hopewell and similar sites, being among the first of many archaeologists (Dragoo 1976b:18; Ford 1974:402; Shetrone 1920:156; Silverberg 1968) to refer to Hopewell with an invalid unit. Other references to Hopewell as a culture (e.g., Henderson et al. 1988; Railey 1996; Shetrone 1930a) are not ethnographic and instead imply Trigger's (1978:76) materialistic definition of archaeological cultures: "a geographically contiguous set of artifact types that may occur in differing combinations in different functional contexts and that together form the surviving material expression of a distinctive way of life sufficiently comprehensive to permit its bearers to perpetuate themselves and their behavioral patterns over successive generations."

Hopewell has been designated a phase by several archaeologists. Cole and Deuel (1937:20) identified Hopewell as "a specialized phase of the Woodland pattern." McKern (1936:330) recognized a Hopewellian Phase that subsumed three unlisted aspects and was one of two phases that made up an unnamed pattern in the Midwest. In their summaries of Ohio and Scioto River valley (Ohio) archaeology, respectively, Morgan (1952:88) and Prufer (1975:316) identified Hopewell as a phase in the MTM sense. Similarly, Griffin (1943b:307) referred to Hopewell as "an archaeological unit equivalent to a phase" with "a basic Woodland background." Griffin also referred to "the Hopewell culture" in the same article and in two other publications (1967, 1996). Willey and Phillips (1958) identified Ohio Hopewell as a phase.

Another unit associated with Hopewell is interaction sphere (Blosser 1996; Richmond and Kerr, this volume). Caldwell (1964) considered the Hopewell Interaction Sphere as the geographic area within which a system of artifact styles and mortuary customs reflecting ideological commonality was shared among regional societies. Struever and Houart (1972) viewed the Hopewell Interaction Sphere in economic terms as the geographic area within which a redistributive system operated, circulating raw materials and finished goods. Similarly, Brown (1977) referred to a "Hopewellian network" of interregional exchange connecting regional traditions.

Numerous archaeologists (e.g., Brown 1977; Caldwell 1962; Willey 1966; Willey and Phillips 1958) referred to Hopewell as a climax, which implies Hopewell is a horizon, tradition, or culture depending on how "climax" is defined. Sieg and Hollinger (this volume) classify Hopewell as a horizon, according to the systematics of Willey and Phillips (1958). Others view Hopewell as a tradition (Caldwell 1964; Hall 1979; Shane 1975; Shane and Murphy 1975). Additional units associated with Hopewell are complex

(Cochran 1996; Rafferty, this volume) and cult, the latter referring to mortuary ceremonialism exhibited by a small group of elites who controlled interregional exchange networks (Prufer 1964b; Rafferty, this volume).

Other archaeologists have opted to omit units altogether, referring simply to "Hopewell" or "Hopewell phenomenon" (e.g., Dancey and Pacheco 1997; Hawkins 1996; Pacheco 1997; Railey 1990; Riordan 1996; Vickery 1996; Pollack et al., Schlarb, this volume), "Ohio Hopewell" (Connolly 1996; Genheimer 1996; Lepper 1996; Pacheco 1996), or "Hopewell peoples" or "Hopewell populations" (Greber 1996, this volume; Wymer 1996). A more detailed historical examination of the Hopewell concept is provided by Sieg and Hollinger (this volume).

Adena

In contrast to Hopewell, since the early twentieth century Adena consistently has been identified as a culture (in ethnographic terms) and defined in terms of trait lists. Adena was classified by Mills (1917) as a developmentally early subgroup of the Hopewell culture. Shortly thereafter Shetrone (1920, 1930a) summarized the artifacts, earthworks, and mortuary traits that distinguished the Adena culture, with culture designating "a specific social group" (Shetrone 1920:144).

On the basis of his study of 70 mounds in the Ohio Valley, Greenman (1932) identified 59 cultural traits diagnostic of the Adena culture, creating a foundation for defining Adena in subsequent decades. Webb and Snow (1945) also designated Adena a culture on the basis of formal similarities evidenced at more than 170 sites; their trait list later ballooned to 218. Solecki (1953) added eleven traits on the basis of excavations at Natrium Mound in West Virginia. In 1957 Webb and Baby outlined a revised list of 241 diagnostic Adena traits on the basis of more than 200 earthwork sites, but they also evaluated the occurrence of Adena traits at eastern Kentucky rockshelters. Although a discussion of Adena culture subsistence (Goslin 1957) was included in their updated Adena volume, Webb and Baby (1957) did not add subsistence-related traits to the complex. Webb and Baby (1957) and Ritchie and Dragoo (1960) identified chronological divisions of Adena culture.

Dragoo (1963, 1976b) also classified Adena as a culture in the ethnographic sense and approached Adena cultural studies from the trait-list approach. However, he attempted to consolidate the list and identify the most salient traits, arguing that many of the traits in the Adena trait list "are so general in nature and distribution as to make them useless in seeking cultural and temporal differences among the various Adena components"

(1963:176). Dragoo also reorganized Adena chronology on the basis of his research at the Cresap Mound in West Virginia.

Silverberg (1968:226) identified the materialistically distinct Adena culture as "a representative of the Early Woodland Tradition" in the Ohio Valley. Haag's (1974) discussion of the Adena culture followed the diagnostic trait-list approach that by then was entrenched in Adena archaeology. However, he recognized that "up to this time our thinking about Adena had been almost completely material culture–oriented" (Haag 1974:142). Ford (1974:401) referred to "Adena societies" in his summary of northeastern archaeology, but from an ecological rather than a material culture perspective.

In contrast with the mainstream, a divergent view of Adena was offered by McKern (1936), Griffin (1943b),[1] and Caldwell (1962), who tentatively classified Adena as an aspect in the MTM sense. Other archaeologists associated Adena with the phase unit, following the systematics of Willey and Phillips (1958). McMichael and Mairs (1969) identified an Adena Phase of the Kanawha Tradition in West Virginia (Trader, this volume). Adena was defined as a phase of the Scioto Tradition in Ohio by Shane (1975) and Shane and Murphy (1975). Seeman (1992b) recognized Early Adena and Late Adena phases in Ohio. Other archaeologists identify Adena as a complex (Greber, Rafferty, this volume) or a cult (Rafferty, this volume).

In summary, Adena typically has been identified as a culture and defined using a trait-list approach; aspect, phase, complex, and cult units have been employed less frequently. As with Hopewell, recently there has been a trend to refer to Adena without reference to a particular unit (e.g., Clay 1986; Jefferies 1991; O'Malley 1988; Railey 1990; Seeman 1986; Pollack et al., Richmond and Kerr, Schlarb, this volume). Clay (this volume) argues for abandoning the Adena concept altogether.

Evaluation

The preceding review of formal unit usage in Middle Ohio Valley archaeology illustrates four problems. First, as data accumulated and paradigms shifted, the same modifiers were combined with different units—units created for use in quite different conceptual frameworks. There is a long history of recycling terms such as Woodland, Hopewell, and Adena, among others, by tacking on different units. This is a problem of abstract validity. Theoretically, the same modifier could be used in combination with different units depending on the systematics employed, but I seriously question the wisdom in doing so because this practice creates a great deal of confusion. Consider other sciences. Geologists use units such as biofacies and lithofacies to delineate facies variability and units such as member, formation, and series to delineate lithostratigraphic variability. They typically do not use the same modifier in combination with different units within or among classificatory schemes. Thus, there are no references to the Cincinnati biofacies and Cincinnati series or to the Meramec member of the Meramec formation. Instead, there are references to the Garrard biofacies and Cincinnati series or to the Lost River member of the St. Louis formation of the Meramec series. A further complication is the fact that some terms (e.g., Adena and Hopewell) used today as modifiers to class units (e.g., phase, horizon, tradition) were initially conceived as group units, so that what began as a group is now a class; this point is considered in more detail below.

Another problem is the inconsistent use or misapplication of units. The culture and phase units are the best illustrations of the inconsistency problem. In Middle Ohio Valley Woodland research, "culture" has been defined as an ethnographic group or society, as the archaeological traces of a distinctive way of life, and as a collection of phases linked by common tradition. Each definition conveys distinctly different information about the particular modifier being designated as a culture. "Phase" is a unit with different definitions in different classification schemes (McKern 1939; Willey and Phillips 1958), yet archaeologists use the unit without delineating the manner in which it is employed. The unit component of binomial designations is very significant. It conveys considerable, important information, and it allows the researcher to address different kinds of research questions from different theoretical perspectives. It cannot be taken lightly, and it must be used consistently. This inconsistency is another source of considerable confusion. Inconsistent use of units makes units unreliable and potentially invalid.

Adena provides an excellent example of the misapplication of units. For instance, Fitting and Brose (1971) observed that Adena was intended to measure variability in archaeological sites, but it measures variability in artifacts. Many traits deemed diagnostic of Adena are too general, making it difficult to measure temporal and spatial variability in the archaeological record (Dragoo 1963; Fitting and Brose 1971; Griffin 1971; Clay, this volume). As currently defined, Adena culture measures variability in the material remains of a limited range of human behavior, namely, mortuary and ritual behavior. Therefore, "Adena as a mortuary complex must be separated from Adena as a settlement system and Adena as a nonmortuary style zone" (Fitting and Brose 1971:45). The concept "obscured our knowledge, or at least our awareness, of a variety of other things that characterize the Adena culture," such as subsistence and settlement strategies (Haag 1974:143), and it "inevitably narrows the kinds of social and cultural inferences that may be drawn from its remains" (Callender 1971:180).

A third and related problem with Middle Ohio Valley Woodland formal units is conflation of group and class units. For example, as originally conceived, Adena and Hopewell are groups, or phenomenological units, that describe specific artifact assemblages from particular times and places. As such, they are units in and of themselves—the problematic ways in which they were described notwithstanding—and they can be used only to organize the data on which they are based. However, Adena and Hopewell have been appropriated for use as modifiers in class designations. A group should not be used as a class. As noted in the preface, grouping and classification are two distinctly different approaches to constructing units, resulting in distinctly different types of units.

Conflation of archaeological units with sociocultural units is the fourth problem with Middle Ohio Valley Woodland formal units. Archaeological units that measure variability in material remains do not and cannot measure variability in people (Trigger 1999). "The assumption that similarities in traits of material culture imply an ethnic identity is only a game that archaeologists play and don't play too well at that" because "race, language, social organization, and material culture do not vary coterminously today and probably did not do so at any time in the past" (Brose and Fitting 1971:30). "There is a significant problem with associating artifacts with ethnicity" (Sanger 2002:7).

The development, application, and problems of formal units in Middle Ohio Valley Woodland research are considered in more detail by other contributors to this volume. Beyond formal units, equally important to Middle Ohio Valley Woodland archaeology are chronological units.

Chronological Units

HISTORICAL CONTEXT

Time is one of the three dimensions of interest to archaeologists. Chronologies are measurements of the time dimension, or "the archaeological units that slice up time, making the concept into usable, archaeological products" (Ramenofsky 1998:74). "The construction of chronologies is a methodological endeavor" (Ramenofsky 1998:78) that involves partitioning the time continuum into units (Stoltman 1978). Chronological unit construction involves specifying the geographic boundaries of the model, the purpose of the model, and the unit boundary criteria, which typically are arbitrary (e.g., 200-year intervals), natural (e.g., climatic changes), or cultural (e.g., technological developments), the cultural corresponding to trait complexes, not formal assemblage properties (Stoltman 1978). As with formal unit construction, chronological unit construction typically results in the designation of a binomial term (e.g., Stone Age), with the first term being a descriptive modifier and the second term being the unit. The two most commonly used chronological units in Americanist archaeology are stage and period.

Constructing chronologies was "the heart of culture history" (Ramenofsky 1998:74). Early culture historians such as Alfred Kidder and Nels Nelson viewed time as continuous; they developed chronological units that derived from the direct historical method and were tested through stratigraphy. After the 1920s culture historians viewed time as discontinuous; they developed chronological units that derived from stratigraphically ordered artifact types (Dunnell 1971; Lyman et al. 1997). Following the advent of such dating methods as radiocarbon dating and dendrochronology, absolute estimates were incorporated into chronological unit construction.

One system for measuring time in the Eastern Woodlands was proposed by Ford and Willey (1941). Their chronological unit was the stage, and they identified five stages in Eastern Woodlands prehistory: Archaic, Burial Mound I, Burial Mound II, Temple Mound I, and Temple Mound II. Boundary criteria included pottery and pipe types, burial practices, subsistence strategies, and earthwork types. Ford and Willey's (1941) scheme was revised by Willey (1966), who switched the unit from stage to period and stipulated absolute dates for each period. He added an additional division, the Paleoindian Period, and subdivided the Archaic into Early, Middle, and Late periods.

Another chronological scheme for the Eastern Woodlands was devised by Griffin (1946, 1952a, 1967, 1978a). In the early phases of development, Griffin's (1946:39; emphasis added) scheme sought to identify "successive cultural *stages* . . . on the basis of local stratigraphy, the interchange of specific cultural items and the common possession of definite cultural concepts at specific chronological *periods*." For example, Transitional, Early, and Middle periods of the Woodland pattern were designated. In 1952 Griffin constructed five periods: Paleoindian, Archaic, Early Woodland, Middle Woodland, and Late Woodland-Mississippi. Griffin's 1967 formulation specified absolute dates for the Fluted Point, Early Archaic, Middle Archaic, Late Archaic, Early Woodland, Middle Woodland, Late Woodland, and the Mississippi periods. (Therefore, "Woodland" was used by archaeologists as both a formal unit and a chronological unit [Anderson and Mainfort 2002a].)

Unfortunately, several problems emerged with the chronological schemes. In an attempt to make their research more anthropological, culture historians conflated chronological units with formal units (Lyman et al. 1997; Stoltman 1978). This created a serious problem as "determinant" or "marker" artifact types were used to measure variability in two dimensions, time and form, simultaneously (Lyman et al. 1997). To improve the resolution, and therefore the reliability, of chronological units, culture historians employed the type-variety system, in which variations of a determinant or marker artifact type were used to measure variation in time and space at a finer scale. Unfortunately, this approach, too, became conflated with sociocultural meaning (Lyman et al. 1997). The discontinuous, anthropological view that culture change "involved the transformation of one kind of culture through a series of abrupt steps" into another kind of culture created an invalid means of measuring time and constructing chronological units (Lyman et al. 1997:11). Finally, an essentialist view of time plagued culture history. "Culture historical units are empirical generalizations derived from stylistic analyses of artifacts, stratigraphy, and seriations. Once established, the units are often accepted as natural, and traits that define those units are tangible evidence of the reality" (Ramenofsky 1998:83). This view confuses time and chronology, and it results in tautological arguments.

Although there have been few attempts to develop new chronological units for the Eastern Woodlands since the collapse of the culture history paradigm, two were published by Stoltman (1978) and Yerkes (1988). Stoltman sought to develop a descriptive, "pan-Eastern temporal framework" (1978:707) "to facilitate comparative analysis of local and regional culture sequences, histories, and processes within the East" (1978:711–712). Using cultural criteria to mark unit boundaries, Stoltman (1978) used two chronological units (era and period) to delineate five major divisions: Paleo-Indian Era, Transitional I Period, Meso-Indian Era, Transitional II Period, and Neo-Indian Era. The Neo-Indian Era was subdivided into three periods, Developmental, Intermediate, and Florescent, and each of these was further partitioned into Early and Late subperiods. Absolute dates were given for each division.

In order to examine the Woodland and Mississippi traditions in the Midwest, Yerkes (1988) used periods to designate three chronological divisions for the interval between 5000 and 400 B.P. The Transitional Period, Middle Woodland Period, and Late Prehistoric Period were bounded by cultural criteria including subsistence, settlement and exchange strategies, diagnostic artifacts, earthwork types, mortuary behavior, and sociopolitical organization. Absolute dates were given for each period.

Generally speaking, archaeologists have been more concerned with reliability than with validity in their use of chronological units. In terms of reliability, chronologies resulting from relative dating methods have coarse resolution because the duration of each chronological unit is unknown (Ramenofsky 1998). But this is not to say that such units are invalid, because the units may be useful in addressing many archaeological research questions. Chronologies resulting from absolute dating methods have fine resolution because numbers are used to "create the divisions between units" (Ramenofsky 1998:80). Unfortunately, the improved resolution afforded by absolute dating methods has lulled archaeologists into a false sense of security because "exactness . . . does not guarantee that an estimate is free of systematic error nor that the estimate will work for the purpose at hand" (Ramenofsky 1998:81). In terms of validity, "there has not been much discussion of whether there is a conceptual fit between chronological units and temporal research goals" because it is assumed that "the events described by cultural historical sequences are correct" and that "the units describing the sequences are real and have been discovered" (Ramenofsky 1998:75).

Chronological Units for the Middle Ohio Valley

Today most archaeologists working in the Middle Ohio Valley continue to use a chronological scheme derived from the culture history paradigm, namely, Griffin's (1952a, 1967, 1978a) four-period scheme. The following discussion, then, considers how Early Woodland, Middle Woodland, and Late Woodland period units have been and are used by Middle Ohio Valley archaeologists.

Early Woodland Period

Although the Early Woodland period was conceived as a stage of cultural development in the past, few archaeologists espouse this perspective today. The prior view that the Early Woodland period everywhere marked a sudden and radical shift in cultural development, which often was explained by diffusion or migration, has been replaced with the view that events in the Early Woodland period represent indigenous continuations from earlier times. "Hence the period marks the passage of time more than the appearance of some distinctive process or stage" (Brown 1986:599).

Previous views of the Early Woodland period identified as significant lower boundary criteria at least four cultural traits: pottery manufacture, earthwork construction, elaborate mortuary ceremonialism, and food production (e.g., Griffin 1952a, 1967). Of these, the introduction of pottery was considered most diagnostic and still is by many archaeologists today (Anderson and Mainfort 2002a). However, as evidence of these traits was increasingly noted at earlier Archaic sites, the traits have been "qualified to the point that they have lost their original significance" (Lewis 1986a:171). A major problem, which has been noted by many archaeologists (Brown 1986, this volume; Greber, this volume; Stoltman 1978; Yerkes 1988), is that these traits tend to be time transgressive, meaning they develop at different times in different places.

This transgression has made it difficult to establish a universal date for the lower boundary of the Early Woodland period, so the boundary dates for the unit vary across the Eastern Woodlands and throughout the Ohio River drainage, though in the Middle Ohio Valley apparently there is less variability in the *earliest* evidence of pottery within the region (see Seeman 1986:564). Hence, in the Middle Ohio Valley the lower boundary of the Early Woodland period consistently is dated at 1000 B.C. (e.g., Railey 1996; Burks, Schlarb, this volume). This consistency may reflect automatic use of acquired wisdom rather than the facts of the archaeological record. Evidence of pottery as old as 1500 B.C. is recorded for the Hocking Valley in southern Ohio (Keener and Pecora 2003; Murphy 1989) and Trader (this volume) reports the discovery of pottery as old as 1375 B.C. in the Kanawha Valley of West Virginia; on the other hand, pottery is not documented until 800 B.C. in other portions of the Middle Ohio Valley (Wilkins 1979).

Middle Woodland Period

The Middle Woodland period often is defined with reference to the Hopewell manifestation, not only in the Middle Ohio Valley but also throughout the Eastern Woodlands (Griffin 1967:183; Seeman 1986:566). Thus, the boundary criteria for the Middle Woodland period are cultural assemblages associated with Hopewell. These traits include Hopewell wares such as zoned and rocker-stamped pottery, bladelets, platform pipes, obsidian artifacts, mica and copper cutouts, Copena bifaces, conjoined geometric enclosures, hilltop enclosures, and horizontal cemeteries. Although many of the diagnostic cultural items typically are associated with ceremonialism, Struever and Houart (1972) and Greber (1997) noted that some occur in nonritual contexts. Maize agriculture (Dragoo 1976b; Prufer 1965) is no longer considered a boundary criterion for the Middle Woodland period (Anderson and Mainfort 2002a; Railey 1996).

Griffin (1967) was among the first to observe that Middle Woodland sites in different parts of the Eastern Woodlands exhibit diagnostic Hopewellian traits to varying degrees (see also Anderson and Mainfort 2002a). This observation has been echoed by archaeologists in reference to the Middle Ohio Valley (Railey 1996; Burks, this volume). Correspondingly, time transgression in the boundary criteria makes it difficult to establish universal dates for the Middle Woodland period in the Middle Ohio Valley. The lower bracket is often placed at 200 B.C. (Griffin 1967; Railey 1996; Burks, Pollack et al., Sieg, this volume), but has been dated as early as 400 B.C. (Clay and Niquette 1992; Richmond and Kerr, Trader, this volume) or as recently as A.D. 1 (Seeman 1986; Schlarb, this volume) or A.D. 100 (Murphy 1989). The upper bracket is placed at A.D. 300, 400, or 500.

Late Woodland Period

Like the Middle Woodland period, the Late Woodland period has been conceived in reference to the Hopewell manifestation. The collapse of Hopewell, referring to the decline in mortuary ceremonialism and associated material culture, marks the beginning of the Late Woodland period in the Eastern Woodlands (Dragoo 1976b; Griffin 1967) and in the Middle Ohio Valley (Railey 1996). The beginning of the Late Woodland period "is most clearly observed where the more showy Hopewellian cultures had existed before" (Griffin 1967:187), such as in southern Ohio.

Boundary criteria for the Late Woodland period combine material culture and subsistence-settlement lifeways. Criteria for the lower boundary include reduction in earthwork construction and interregional exchange activities, production of cordmarked cooking pots, occupation of nucleated circular villages (Dragoo 1976b; Railey 1996; Burks, this volume), and Chesser Notched points (Seeman and Dancey 2000). The upper boundary criterion is consistently identified as the widespread adoption of maize agriculture or horticulture, but other criteria are complex village societies, platform mound construction, elaborately decorated pottery, shell-tempered pottery, and social ranking (Dragoo 1976b; Ford 1977; Griffin 1967; Railey 1996).

As with the Early and Middle Woodland periods, diagnostic traits of the Late Woodland period are time transgressive. As such, the dates that bracket the Late Woodland period vary across the Eastern Woodlands and in the Middle Ohio Valley. The Late Woodland period has been dated at A.D. 400 to 1000 (Burks, this volume) or A.D. 541 to 1005 (Seeman and Dancey 2000) in Ohio, A.D. 400 to 1000 in West Virginia (Clay and Niquette 1992; Trader, this volume), and A.D. 500 to 1000 (Railey 1990, 1996; Pollack et al., Schlarb, this volume) or A.D. 400/500 to 900/1000 (Pollack and Henderson 2000) in Kentucky.

Evaluation

The "period" is the chronological unit most commonly used by archaeologists working in the Middle Ohio Valley, as is Griffin's (1952a, 1967, 1978a) four-period scheme for subdividing prehistory. The identification of "Woodland" as a chronological unit, a period, originates largely with Griffin. In the Middle Ohio Valley, as in many parts of the Eastern Woodlands, three subdivisions of the Woodland period are recognized. Regardless of research interest, archaeologists almost reflexively use Early, Middle, and Late Woodland periods as the chronological units for dividing the time continuum between the adoption of pottery and the adoption of maize agriculture.

This may not be a prudent enterprise in all cases, considering Ramenofsky's (1998) argument that there is no "one-size-fits-all" chronological scheme that will be appropriate for all archaeological research questions.

The reliability and validity of existing chronological units must be evaluated with respect to one's research questions (Ramenofsky 1998; Stoltman 1978). If judged unreliable or invalid, new chronological units must be constructed, or existing units must be reformulated. Assessment of chronological unit reliability is accomplished with cross-dating using multiple criteria such as absolute dates and chronologically diagnostic artifacts (Ramenofsky 1998; Seeman and Dancey 2000). Assessment of chronological unit validity focuses on the ability to investigate certain research questions using the chronological divisions. "Chronological units are task-specific tools and, conceivably, there are as many chronologies as there are research questions" (Ramenofsky 1998:75). Archaeologists need a more diverse arsenal of chronological units to use in addressing different research questions (Brew 1946; Ramenofsky 1998; Brown, this volume). Given the previous discussion, it is of vital importance that we work more vigorously on chronological unit construction in the Middle Ohio Valley. Until we do, we will continue to be haunted by the types of problems summarized briefly below and discussed further by other contributors to this volume.

One widely recognized problem is the use of time-transgressive boundary criteria (Brown, Greber, this volume); this is a problem of unreliability. Time-transgressive criteria make it difficult to designate beginning and ending dates for chronological units applied over large geographical areas, such as the Middle Ohio Valley. Although a difference of one or several hundred years in bounding chronological units will not have significant negative implications for the investigation of some research questions, it will for others. Furthermore, if sites are assigned to chronological units on the basis of the presence or absence of boundary criteria rather than absolute dating, sites of an appropriate age but lacking in boundary criteria artifacts (e.g., an aceramic Early Woodland period site) due to function, preservation, or other reasons will be misclassified (Lewis 1986b; Stoltman 1978). Perhaps Tiffany (1986) was correct, at least for some archaeological research, that current period units are significant only at the local level.

A second problem with the prevailing chronological scheme is the misuse of terms, which is an issue of invalidity. "Unfortunately, in archeology the terms . . . 'Early Woodland,' and 'Middle Woodland' situationally serve different classificatory purposes. Some archaeologists use them as units of a time stratigraphy, others would have them reflect locally significant temporal shifts in diagnostic artifacts, and yet others have regarded them as stages in an evolutionary trajectory of increasing cultural complexity" (Farnsworth and Asch 1986:329). The same modifiers are used in combination with different types of units, or there are different interpretations of what the units mean (Greber, Sieg and Hollinger, this volume).

One final and related problem with the current temporal model is the tendency to equate chronological units with formal units, which is invalid. It has become common practice to link the Early Woodland period with Adena, Middle Woodland with Hopewell, and Late Woodland with Cole, Intrusive Mound, or Newtown in the Middle Ohio Valley (Clay 2002; Dancey and Seeman, Greber, Sieg and Hollinger, this volume). Such statements as "the Hopewell culture, which is nearly a synonym for the Middle Woodland period in the minds of many archaeologists" (Railey 1996:79) say it all. At the least, this approach implies a sequential, stagelike view of cultural development, whereby one lifeway transforms into the next at the same time across some geographic space. This approach conflates different types of units, makes it impossible for coexistence of different groups, and ignores variability in the archaeological record. Equation of different units has proved problematic in the case of Adena, for example, because it is associated with the late Early Woodland period in Ohio (Seeman 1986; Greber, this volume) but with the early Middle Woodland period in Kentucky (Railey 1996; Richmond and Kerr, Schlarb, this volume).

Conclusions

The conclusion I draw from the preceding review of Woodland systematics, classification, and grouping in the Middle Ohio Valley mirrors that drawn by several archaeologists (e.g., Griffin 1971; Clay, this volume) regarding Adena and by others (e.g., Anderson and Mainfort 2002b; Dunnell 1971; Lyman et al. 1997; O'Brien et al. 2002; Ramenofsky and Steffen 1998) regarding archaeological systematics and classification in general: there is much work to be done. Archaeological classification in the Middle Ohio Valley must become a more intentional activity. Major hurdles to overcome relate to invalidity in unit construction and application. In terms of formal unit schemes, current practice is problematic because modifiers are recycled in combination with different units, units are used inconsistently or misapplied, group and class units are conflated, and archaeological and sociocultural units are conflated. In terms of chronological unit schemes, current practice is problematic because boundary criteria are time transgressive, modifiers and units are misused, and chronological units are equated with formal units. When existing taxonomies are found inadequate for any reason, new units must be constructed, or existing units must be clearly and appropriately reformulated.

When existing units are used, at least three things must be considered.

First, archaeologists must be crystal clear about defining formal or chronological units in their research. It is very frustrating to try to decipher poorly defined unit classifications; this greatly impedes effective communication. Second, the important process of unit evaluation cannot be ignored. Researchers must consider the reliability and validity of formal or chronological units with respect to their specific research questions. Third, archaeologists must not compare apples and oranges. As researchers move beyond their own study areas to compare their findings with those of other archaeologists, they must compare data classified according to similar formal and chronological unit schemes and for similar research purposes. For example, the concepts of Adena and Hopewell, as currently conceived by most archaeologists, should not be used as part of unit designation when classifying assemblages from nonceremonial contexts or testing hypotheses about nonritual behaviors such as settlement. Similarly, sites assigned to chronological units on the basis of cultural boundary criteria (e.g., presence or absence of pottery) should not be compared with sites assigned to chronological units on the basis of other criteria (e.g., climatic changes).

Note

1. In contrast, in his summary of Eastern Woodland prehistory, Griffin (1967: 183) classified Adena as a culture, describing it as one of several "regional 'tribes'" of the "latter half of the first millennium B.C."

2

Adena and Hopewell in the Middle Ohio Valley
To Be or Not To Be?

N'omi B. Greber

> Our aim here will be to achieve generality along with simplicity, and this largely because of the aesthetic satisfaction which success will yield. . . . To a non-mathematician it often comes as a surprise that it is impossible to define explicitly all the terms which are used. This is not a superficial problem but lies at the root of all knowledge; it is necessary to begin somewhere, and *to make progress one must clearly state those elements and relations which are undefined and those properties which are taken for granted.*
>
> —Gilbert de B. Robinson, 1946

Archaeology is an artistic science. Its practitioners work within their own culture. The use of a framework, that is, words that describe what we are talking about, to organize one's own thinking and to aid in communicating with others is not unique to the discipline. It is part of being human. In the particular instance of archaeology, we wish to organize space, time, and archaeological material remains including human-caused changes in a natural environment. A wide range of methods and viewpoints have been used "to make sense of the archaeology of North America" (Hegmon 2003:214). This is not in itself unproductive. Frameworks are arbitrary, and equally *useful* systems based on diametrically opposed assumptions can exist side by side. The term "useful" is defined as adding insight to the particular questions being considered in a manner intelligible to others.

Provided the elements are clearly set out, arbitrary units can be set up that listeners or readers can then judge for themselves to be useful or not. As phrased in an editorial decision, "We have not sought to resolve artificially the real distinctions among their [the volume authors] approaches, but highlight them all as contributions to a larger whole" (Knapp and Ashmore 1999:4). Appreciation of the contributions of varying approaches does require clarity in communication. The use of the same word to refer to different elements of the basic dimensions of time, space, and form creates difficulties in communication that are not unique to Middle Ohio Valley studies. For example, in eastern North American archaeology the word "Woodland" has specified both time and archaeological cultural remains. Suggestions to avoid this confusion have been made (e.g., Stoltman 1978) but as yet have not been generally accepted.

A common practice that requires additional words but adds clarity is appending modifiers such as "Woodland time period" or "Woodland culture." With the use of the Woodland as a temporal distinction, another recurrent problem arises when an entity called "Adena" is equated with an "Early Woodland" time period and when another labeled "Hopewell" is equated with "Middle Woodland." In the Middle Ohio Valley these entities overlap in space, in form, that is, some archaeologically recovered material remains, and, as is becoming more evident, in time. The task of defining appropriate units of time and space to organize the overlap and diversity seen in the archaeological cultural remains in local, regional, and wider contexts is a long-term and difficult one. This chapter discusses one framework proposed as part of this task. It is based on a comparative analysis of the type sites located in the central Scioto valley. Portions of this framework suggest attributes for evaluating the usefulness, or not, of the concepts of "Adena" and "Hopewell" when viewing sites found throughout the Middle Ohio Valley.

Background

Terminology

For both "Adena" and "Hopewell," my units of thought are peoples and groups of peoples. Within and among groups, individuals participate in a range of social organizations centered on political, ritual-ceremonial, economic, religious, and social aspects of life. Recognizing the differences among these aspects is not an attempt to make trivial distinctions; instead, it can be useful, as pointed out by Hegmon (2003:226). The patterns that arise in combinations of these aspects were and are the reality for people and may, but need not, correspond to any patterns seen in the present or in the ethnohistoric past. I assume that any and all of these elements might be reflected in archaeological remains, including interments. With respect to interpreting burial practices and artifacts found in tombs, I assume that the physical aspects of both are accomplished by the living, informed by the dead. I take as an established fact that the existence of features and objects identified as ritual, symbolic, and so on, does not require an interpretation of mortuary camp or of only funeral events (Buikstra and Charles

1999:220–222; Greber 1983:92, 1996). "Caches of artifacts not directly associated with burials bear witness to the fact that social rituals were not the exclusive provenance of mortuary behavior" (Buikstra and Charles 1999:208–209; see also Richmond and Kerr, this volume).

History

The origin and history of the Adena label have been well detailed elsewhere (e.g., Swartz 1971; Clay, Brown, this volume). Briefly, relationships between the entities "Adena" and "Hopewell" have been variously characterized since Mills (1906:135–136) first used these designations. A seminal Adena synthesis by Greenman (1932) was initiated by his excavations in the Hocking Valley. By 1957 Webb and Snow (1945), and later Webb and Baby (1957), expanded the range of attributes and sites to be included. Dragoo's later work (1963, 1976a) encompassed all these and added sites on the East Coast. Among the relationships proposed, Adena was more frequently considered ancestral to Hopewell, but other views emphasized a chronological overlap (Murphy 1975; Otto 1979).

Some suggested that "Adena" has no true identity. Valuable discussions of the conundrum, but no one choice, came from a conference at Ball State (Swartz 1971). More recently, I have suggested a scenario in which I think all descriptions can fit the known data *if* the question of relationships is appropriately phrased (Greber 1991a). That is, when making comparisons, strong consideration should be given to appropriate geographic boundaries. The need to study restricted but ecologically meaningful areas had been noted at Ball State (Swartz 1971:142 [Shane], 158 [Griffin]). Many studies do compare sites from relatively wide-ranging areas (e.g., Webb and Snow 1945:132–252; Rafferty, this volume). In these, it can be difficult to separate the effects due to space and time and to find the dimensions and scale of time suitable for the questions being asked. For many questions, such as those concerning local ancestry and causes of change in the local physical and social world, interregional contacts, or the existence and direction of diffusion, a time scale in terms of human generations is usually needed. Data available from the Middle Ohio Valley provide no absolute time scale such as might come from dendrochronology to provide such a scale. It is difficult to impossible to identify truly contemporaneous sites when considering separated geographic areas such as the Big Sandy and the central Scioto valleys, and it is not easy in local areas (Greber 2003).

Radiocarbon assays are a valuable tool for understanding the changes that took place in human activities through time. They can be used to define eras and provide large-scale order. For example, the assays completed early in the development of the technique demonstrated that Hopewell peoples were not the last pre-Columbian residents in the Ohio Valley (Griffin 1958). Prior to the availability of radiocarbon dating, on the basis of an assumption that human activities change in a linear fashion from simple to complex, some researchers had placed "Hopewell" near A.D. 1400 (e.g., Ford and Willey 1941:343).

On a finer scale, there is as yet no direct link between the solar year during which a particular event occurred and the means and standard deviations of the statistical process that yields a single radiocarbon determination on the basis of organic remains associated with the event. When evaluating possible models in considering the interactions of actual people, it is not practical, for example, to marry someone who died two generations ago (the length of the standard deviation of many accepted radiocarbon dates), but one might present a gift. In addition, the time-transgressive nature of attributes describing the archeological remains is of importance when forming comparative models. On the basis of easily recognizable but rare (e.g., obsidian) or relatively rare (e.g., rocker stamped ceramics) elements of Ohio Hopewell remains, the chronological boundary between Hopewell and Adena has been described as one of the best defined in North American prehistory (Griffin 1958; Seeman 1986; Stoltman 1978).

Stoltman (1978) noted that even these relatively fixed boundaries have accuracy limits in most *geographic areas* of at least one and more likely several centuries. This span of years can easily encompass four generations of humans who lived in the Central Ohio Valley, some of whom apparently accepted major changes in their worldview while others maintained the stability of "the way things are always done" (Stark et al. 1998:211) not only in everyday matters but also in ritual-ceremonial ways of using portable objects and fixed elements of the landscape such as wooden structures and mounds. Placing these changes onto a civil calendar for each tributary is a more daunting task than I can attempt. Recognizing that such changes did occur in a particular valley is a more reasonable goal. Early researchers sought unity within the diversity exhibited across the Middle Ohio Valley. Today more research centers on exploring local diversity rather than on looking at the unity emphasized by Webb and others. Even without a strict control of time across the entire area, of paramount importance in understanding possible connections between "Adena" and "Hopewell," described by overlap and diversity, is the fact that in the Middle Ohio Valley, Hopewell peoples occupied a smaller territory than did Adena peoples. Webb and Snow (1945:Map facing 132) pictured the Adena occupation in the Ohio River Valley as concentric rings centered on Chillicothe. This picture illustrates the influence of the historical archaeological precedent provided by excavation of *the* Adena Mound early in the twentieth century. But it is not a good a representation of the cultural relationships among the many local regions within the Central Ohio Valley.

Lifeways in the Homelands

Ohio Hopewell peoples lived along portions of the major southward-flowing river valleys from the Great Miami to the Muskingum, except in the Hocking (Figure P.1). Elements of a common worldview appear across the region, although some differences in materials, design, and treatment of artifacts, structures, and enclosures reflect local customs and ways. One signature of Ohio Hopewell is the acquisition of exotic raw materials and, to a lesser extent, exotic objects. These probably were acquired through a mix of contacts, including personal travel, formal and informal gifts, direct and indirect barter, and other personal and group activities. Copper, mica, and marine objects formed a basic trio. Obsidian, silver, tiny bits of gold, galena, and a variety of exotic cherts were among imports added to the more local materials that formed everyday and special objects. The greatest quantity of objects has been recovered from sites concentrated in the central Scioto and the lower Little Miami valleys. Some also came from Tremper, the outlier in the lower Scioto valley, and unknown amounts came from the Cherry Valley Mounds associated with the Newark Earthworks in the upper Licking valley. The organization in the placement of artifact deposits recorded by archaeologists reflects design criterion also seen in wooden structures and earthwork walls (Greber 1996).

Recent work has firmly placed representative wall construction in the Hopewell era (circa 2000–1500 B.P.) at hilltop sites Fort Ancient (Sieg 1999; Sieg and Connolly 1997), Miami Fort (Maslowski et al. 1995:34), and Pollock (Riordan 1995) and at geometric works including Anderson (Pickard and Pahdopony 1995), High Bank (Greber 2002), Hopeton (Lynott 2004; Ruby 1997), and Newark (Lepper 1998:126, Maslowski et al. 1995:27, 34) (see also Greber 2003:Figure 6.5 and Mainfort and Sullivan 1998:Figure 1.1). Monumental enclosures occur in all the Hopewell valleys, encompassing a wider area than that where major deposits of portable objects occur. This extension adds the Great Miami on the west and the lower Muskingum on the east (Greber 1991b, 2000). The majority of Hopewell sites fall along the streams and rivers in the glaciated parts of Ohio, with the exception of the Scioto south of Chillicothe and the "hinterlands" (Carskadden and Morton 1997:368–369) of the middle Muskingum. Due at least in part to Pleistocene events, this latter area contains more environmental diversity than other nearby unglaciated areas. Here, "Hopewell" is less dramatic than in the nearby Newark region, located in the Licking Valley, a Muskingum tributary.

The subsistence base included gathering wild flora and fauna, hunting, and gardening. The percentage of cultivated versus gathered food likely varied by region and through time. The local settlement pattern is still debated, specifically as to the degree of mobility. At least in Ross County, which holds the greatest number of varied ecological niches in the central Ohio River valley, small Hopewell occupations are commonly found as part of multicomponent sites along old oxbow levees or other similar locations.

In contrast to "Hopewell," archaeological remains identified as "Adena" occur in a wider swath of the Ohio Valley, extending outside Ohio—west and south into Indiana and Kentucky and eastward into West Virginia and the southwestern corner of Pennsylvania (Figure P.1). The environmental settings have a correspondingly wider range that includes the bluegrass area of Kentucky and the mountains of southwestern Pennsylvania. As with "Hopewell," the general type of "Adena" identifiers includes mounds, enclosures, and the exotic materials, special artifact forms, and features found under, about, and within mounds (Clay 1998b; Seeman 1986:566; Webb and Snow 1945:12–28). Also, as with Hopewell, limited data are available from habitation sites. Hunting, gathering, and gardening formed the subsistence base. The amount of gardening is still uncertain and likely varied through time and space. Although sparse, "settlement data suggest low population density, mobility, and an absence of settlement nucleation. The critical Adena addition to the earlier Archaic way of life was a greater emphasis on mortuary ritual" (Clay 1998a:6).

Sites are not limited to river floodplains. In areas such as the Central Kentucky Bluegrass, concentrations occur in uplands. An important aspect of the settlement pattern is the general spatial separation of domestic and ritual sites among the autonomous groups of Adena peoples in the Central Ohio Valley who shared "a common repertoire of symbols and ritual beliefs" (Hays 1994:41). Some aspects of these beliefs were reflected in objects made of local and imported materials placed in tombs and occasional caches. An overlap exists in the types of materials and artifact forms found in Adena and Hopewell contexts and in the chronological time of their disposition. The specific collection of attributes that distinguish one or the other entity has been debated extensively. Herein, I begin at the beginning with the sites named Hopewell and Adena.

The Type Sites

In an attempt to minimize differences due to geographic separation, I compared the two type sites, both located in the central Scioto region. Although all investigators, myself included, agree that information from a wider range of features would be desirable, most of the present data set comes from mounds and enclosures. Optimally the data set should include information for the ground covered by the mound, as well as materials within and about it. Using the variables from such an idealized data set and acknowledging much missing data, I established a formal description of each type site as an example of the manner in which central Scioto Adena and Hopewell peoples used artifacts and space. The strategy was not entirely new, but related schemes have not usually been applied to a closely restricted geographic area (e.g. Webb and Snow 1945:132–219). A brief summary of the results follows; details have been presented at length elsewhere (Greber 1991a).

THE SITES

The Hopewell site covers extensive areas of two terraces above the active floodplain of the north fork of Paint Creek, a major tributary of the Scioto (Greber and Ruhl 2000; Moorehead 1922; Shetrone 1926). At least 40 mounds were constructed within and beyond the main enclosure walls, which are both geometric and hilltop in ground plan. The mounds ranged from several 30 cm high and 3 m across to the outsized Mound 25, composed of three conjoined sections that stretched more than 150 m. Both large and small mounds, mantles of carefully chosen sands, gravels, and colored soils, covered a variety of civic/ceremonial/ritual remains including prepared floors, distinctive clay hearths, wooden structures, large and small artifact deposits, and sometimes groups of tombs. Ongoing work has identified additional, nonmounded features and a previously unrecorded small circular enclosure among the mounds (Pederson et al. 2002). A day's walk away, numbers of the same types of remains were scattered across the terrace about the Adena Mound (Mills 1901–1902), but not in the quantity found at the Hopewell site.

The Adena Mound was the northernmost of the Chillicothe Northwest Group of 12 mounds located along the west side of the Scioto, from the northwestern edge of the A.D. 1840 limits of Chillicothe to the small Lake Ellensmere (Figure 2.1). This is a shorter walk than circumnavigating the Hopewell site. Other mounds and two simple enclosures were scattered for a similar distance on the same terrace toward the north between the lake and Mound City, a simple enclosure associated with approximately two dozen mounds.

The Chillicothe Northwest Group included small conical mounds, intermediate-sized mounds, a conjoined set, and, surprisingly, a large elongate mound similar in size to Seip-Pricer, the second largest recorded Ohio Hopewell mound. An 1890s photograph of Moorehead's excavation tunnels

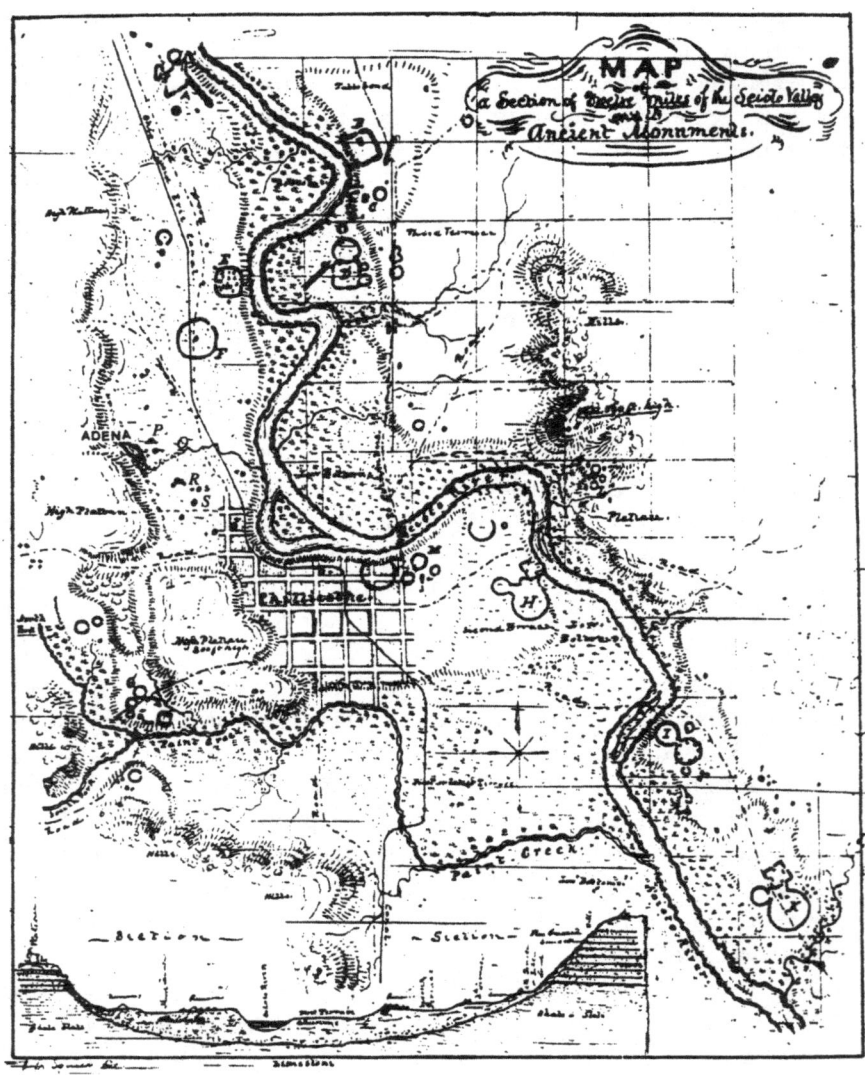

Figure 2.1. Draft map of Ephraim Squier and Edwin Davis, now in the Library of Congress Archives. A, Dunlap; B, Cedar Banks; D, Hopeton (also Hopetown); E, Mound City; F, Shriver Circle; G, Junction; H, Works East (also Prairie Works); I, High Bank; K, Liberty (also Harness); L, unnamed; M, Chillicothe. The designation "P" has been added for the Adena Mound, as have Q, R, and S for the approximate locations of Story Mound, Worthington Mounds, and the Carriage Factory/Miller Mound, respectively.

Figure 2.2. The Carriage Factory/Miller Mound showing the entrances to the three tunnels excavated into the mound in May 1897 (Moorehead 1898–1899:Figure V). The outer strata at the side of the mound containing rich black soil had been previously removed, apparently by local people. Moorehead describes the mound as 35 feet high and 225 feet long.

documents the existence and size of this mound, the Carriage Factory/ Miller Mound (Figure 2.2). His limited and inconsistent report gives believable and spectacular, but culturally unassignable, details (Moorehead 1898–1899:126–132). The mound vanished, apparently by 1905. Possibly it was used as a borrow area for railroad construction, as occurred in more recent times at the G. E. Mound, a.k.a. the Mount Vernon site, in Indiana (Tomak and Burkett 1996). The four conjoined Worthington Mounds (Moorehead 1892:Mounds 40–43) repeat the common pattern for such sites in southern Ohio, including mounds at the Hopewell site. Each mantled a distinct horizontal space. They varied in size and in the type and complexity of features built on the floors. In Mound 43, the largest mound, complex strata covered the remains of a 15-m dismantled and burned structure, clay deposits, burials, and such. Under Mound 42 nothing was found except a "small animal bone, four mussel shells, and about a pint of ashes" in a small pit or hole at the center of the base floor (Moorehead 1892:167). The more common single conical mounds include the Adena Mound, the R. P. Swartz Mound that covered the Spetnagel Cache of some two hundred turkey-tail blades of Wyandotte chert (Shetrone 1923), and the extant Story Mound. The remaining mounds of the group apparently were smaller.

At the Adena Mound, the original use of the space was centered around a large subfloor tomb flanked by a bark-covered floor and two large hearths. Evidence for a wooden structure is seen in a field photograph of a line of postholes, but its exact location and floor plan are not known. The excavation technique limited the amount of floor exposed at one time (Greber 1991a:3–6). Most tombs were built above the original prepared floor (Greber 1991a:Figures 4 and 5). The distinctive dark sand used for the first major stage came either from the bottom of Lake Ellensmere or from some other subsurface stratum. Surface soils and gravels were used for the second stage. A majority of the Chillicothe Northwest Group had two such stages, suggesting some continuity in an accepted design, process, or both, for completing mound construction. Overlap in burial practices and submound features among mounds also occurred.

Overall, the limited data available from the total range of mound morphology, features, and artifacts found near the Adena Mound represent a significant portion of the range found in the wider geographic areas of Ross County and southern Ohio. I interpret this limited evidence as indicating that changes in the organization of ceremonial/ritual events occurred through time in the area about the Adena Mound and that people(s) associated with the mound participated in some phase of these changes. Differences in ceremonial/ritual activities and organization, mantled by separate mounds, occurred in *this small area*. We do not yet know the exact chronological order. We did determine that, on the basis of an assignment of turkey-tail bifaces to 1200–800 B.C. (Seeman 1986:570), the R. P. Swartz Mound was an early construction. It is likely that the Carriage Factory/Miller Mound is at the later end of the sequence, perhaps some 10 centuries later.

INTERMENTS

A total of 23 individuals were interred in the first stage of Adena Mound construction and 13 in the second (Greber 1991a:Figures 4 and 5). I was not able to reconstruct any stratigraphy in the second stage. From the Hopewell site I chose for detailed analysis a similar number of individuals apparently associated with a separately mantled circular structure that was part of the set of structures mantled by the central mound of Mound 25 (Greber 1991a:Figure 7; Greber and Ruhl 2001:Figures 2.14, 2.15, and 2.16, Group C). The majority of the interments were extended primary burials sharing a horizontal space similar in size to the first activity space at Adena. This contrast in the use of vertical and horizontal space has been noted before (e.g., Clay 1986). Although the subfloor tomb apparently was reopened, because only one-quarter of the Adena interments were on the floor, this space was likely not in active use as long as the Hopewell floor. A chi-square test demonstrated that the greater number of cremations in the Hopewell space is statistically significant ($\chi^2 = 9.82, p < 0.01$, see Greber 1991a:12, Table 1). Cremated and noncremated individuals were not distinguished by artifact distribution, suggesting that the time of death, the distance from the Hopewell site where the death occurred, or both prevented a primary interment. That is, those who used the Hopewell building likely lived farther from the building than the comparable group(s) lived from the Adena Mound site. The percentage of cremations within a burial population has been used to order "Adena" and "Hopewell" chronologically, but interpretation of the practice needs to be made on a case-by-case basis.

Artifacts

I assume some usefulness in interpreting relationships within a group by comparing objects associated with human remains. In this case, nonparametric statistics were used to compare the nonperishable raw materials and quantity of associated objects (Greber 1991a:12–14, Tables 1 and 2). Briefly, continuity is seen in the occurrence in both groups of the three basic exotic materials: copper, mica, and marine objects. The distribution pattern of copper objects is similar for the two groups, whereas mica objects were more commonly found with the Hopewell individuals. Although the most frequently illustrated mica cutouts of effigy raptor claws and a human hand were found within Group C, mica pieces were distributed among the other groups sharing the central main floor at Mound 25. That is, the contrast apparently reflects a true difference between "Adena" and "Hopewell" mica use. A definite contrast occurs in the wider range of forms made from the three basic materials found within Group C. Copper ear spools, plaques, celts, two-dimensional effigies, and an elaborate headdress from Hopewell contrast with rings and bracelets from Adena. Another contrast is seen in the greater number of flint types found within the Adena group. Among the tools from both sites are groups of implements that likely were used in making or decorating fabrics, leather, or furs. An overlap in artifact forms occurs, for example, in pulley-shaped ear ornaments, "expanded center" stone gorgets, large shell beads, and mica crescents.

An overlap in artifact form does not mean there is no justification for an archaeological construct identifying two separate cultural entities in Ross County. It is a problem when a single object must be used to determine cultural affiliation. As noted by Greenman (1932:493), "To a large extent, it is a different numerical predominance of the same or similar traits which constitutes the difference between Adena and Hopewell." The time-transgressive use of objects, particularly ones used in ceremonial or ritual context that may be held as heirlooms, can be seen in the distribution of copper ear spools (Ruhl 1992, 1996; Ruhl and Seeman 1998). The relative order in Ruhl's similarity seriation of 395 ear spools found in Ohio Hopewell contexts corresponds to the limited stratigraphic and radiocarbon data available for the sample (Greber 2003:93, 109–110, Figure 6.3, Table 6.2). Dates corresponding to Ruhl's rank order extend from circa 1950–1200 B.P. The rank order of ear spools placed together in single deposits shows a significant range within the seriation (Greber 2003:Figure 6.1). Although this range cannot yet be firmly translated into specific calendar years, it demonstrates the heirloom nature of the ear ornaments.

The context in which such objects are found can aid interpretations. For example, circular copper bracelets were found with other clearly Hopewell objects at the Hopewell site and also were found within the Adena Mound, apparently used as individual jewelry. The mound located within the Shriver Circle, an enclosure located between the Adena Mound and Mound City, has been labeled "Adena" apparently on the basis of the occurrence of circular copper bracelets. The mound mantled an "altar" paved with fitted stones. Inside the altar was a burnt deposit containing calcined bits of bone and two "heaps" of five "extremely well wrought" circular copper bracelets; "a couple of thick sheets of mica" had been placed on the western side of the altar and the entire feature carefully covered by a sand layer (Squier and Davis 1848:156–157, 204, Figure 88). The total number of bracelets, the fine workmanship, and the design of the deposit indicate to me behavior closer to Hopewell than Scioto Adena.

DISCUSSION

Although the type sites are not modal, they do form classic nodes in cultural variation. The uniqueness of Mound 25 and the rarity of sites such as Seip-Pricer, Edwin Harness, and perhaps Carriage Factory/Miller Mound make a logical break appropriate between the peoples who built these and their ancestors. As seen in the framework discussed here, a break can be seen in four aspects of cultural activities: a basic change from a single group's use of vertical space to a multigroup use of a shared horizontal space for interments and other ceremonial/ritual/civic activities; a great increase in both the quantity and forms of artifacts produced in mica, copper, and marine materials; the addition of other exotic and local raw materials used for symbolic objects; and a significant increase in the size and complexity of archaeologically recoverable civic/ceremonial/ritual remains.

If multiple autonomous groups were associated with the layering of interments at the Adena Mound, as has been suggested by Clay (1991b) for other "Adena" mounds, then a rearrangement rather than a major change in organization would have defined the break. Primarily because of the patterning of conjoined mounds, I consider such a sequence less likely in the central Scioto area, but possibly more applicable elsewhere (viz., Clay 1998b: 6–7). I will return to this point again. In Ohio beyond the central Scioto valley, there may not have been a local antecedent that looked like the Adena Mound for sites such as Turner and Fort Ancient in the Little Miami Valley or Newark in the Muskingum Valley. The 65-foot-tall "Adena" Miamisburg Mound in the Great Miami Valley would tower over Hopewell Mound 25. When and how does its construction fit in with its neighbors? The progression of cultural change through time need not be, and likely was not, the same in all the Ohio Hopewell regions.

The Lower Hocking Valley

INTRODUCTION

In Ohio Hopewell many artifact forms cross media, thus emphasizing qualities of the raw material itself in addition to the symbolic nature of the form. Copper and mica were used to fashion human faces, hands, and torsos and similar elements of more abstract designs. Boat stones and celts appear in copper and stone. The widespread use of copper for symbolic forms and the contrast seen in the range of forms in Ross County sites suggest that it is reasonable to use the range of forms found in another limited geographic area as part of an Adena-Hopewell comparative framework for that area. The Ross County comparison also dealt with the architectural complexity of ritual/ceremonial/civic remains. These two attributes are used to study sites in the lower Hocking Valley, where large "Hopewell" sites are not recorded. This absence, seen in an area with the Marietta and Newark works in the next eastern valley and the Scioto sites to the west, has been interpreted by some as indicating that the valley was abandoned during the Middle Woodland era (Black 1979:25; Seeman 1986:567).

THE PLAINS

More than 200 mounds occurred in the lower Hocking Valley. On the plains, an unusually wide section of relatively flat land in the mature and narrow lower Hocking was a group of 7 to 9 circular enclosures and more than 20 mounds, frequently considered to be classic Adena (Greenman 1932; Squier and Davis 1848:Plate 33, no. 2; Webb and Snow 1945). As in Ross County, the data are checkered. Excavations began early in the nineteenth century and continued intermittently. Within this group one can trace a range of elaboration in the construction of features and mounds. Also, cop-

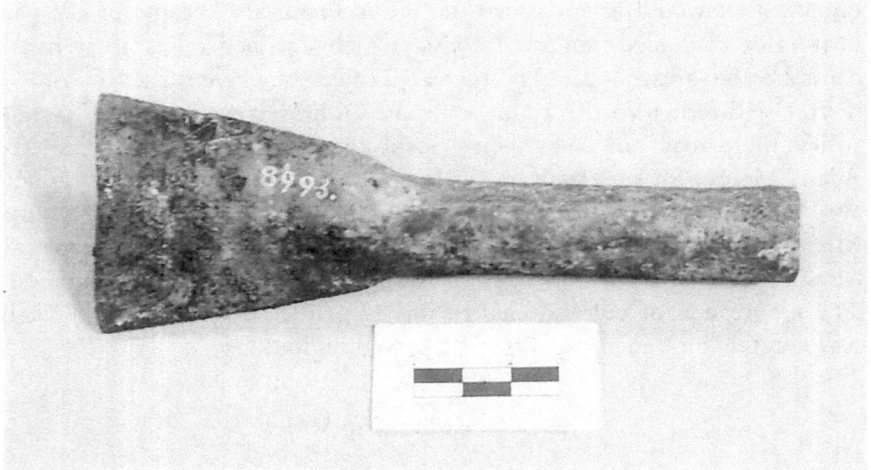

Figure 2.3. A unique effigy flared-end tubular pipe recovered in 1877 by E. B. Andrews from a log tomb in Connett Mound 7, The Plains. Andrews recovered a stone pipe of the same shape from a redeposited cremation in Connett Mound 6. Peabody Museum of Archaeology and Ethnology catalogue number 76-7-10/8993. Photograph copyright President and Fellows of Harvard University.

per was used to make forms, some of which, to my knowledge, have not been recovered in central Scioto Adena mounds.

From a log tomb in Connett Mound 7, Andrews (1877) recovered a unique hollow object made of sheet copper and shaped as a tubular pipe with a flared end (Figure 2.3; Putnam 1882:Figure 17, PMAE 76-7-10/8993). More than 450 rolled copper beads were found in a line about the burial in a manner reminiscent of the surrounding pearls or, in one instance, copper ear spools in several central Scioto Hopewell burials. The mound structure showed an east-west color differentiation also found in many Hopewell sites. With a redeposited cremation in Connett Mound 6, Andrews recovered a stone flared-end tube pipe and two copper objects. One is a fragment of a thin copper plate with scalloped edges and interior holes, possibly for hanging. The second (PMAE 76-7-11016) has been identified as a panpipe cover (Turff 1997:A103). It is similar to a copper band from the Hopewell site (FMNH 56006) that also has been identified as a panpipe cover (Greber and Ruhl 2001:Figure 2.2; Leader 1988:99, 248) and to another from Turner that was found on the chest of an extended interment (86-32-NA379) in the Burial Ridge (Willoughby and Hooton 1922:18, Plate 7a, PMAE 86-32-A743); with the remains were two copper ear spools, shell beads, and 12 bladelets (one found near the shoulder, the others in a deposit in the northeast corner of the grave). In contrast, from Connett Mound 3, Skinner and

Norris (1981, 1984b) reported two fragmentary sheet copper plates that had been hit by both a sharp and a blunt instrument and bent before deposition. The shape is not that of the typical Scioto copper plaques, but more closely resembles specimens found at Natrium and Cresap mounds in West Virginia (e.g., Dragoo 1963:Plates 12, 13). As an example of simple copper forms found within the mound group, simple circular bracelets were the only copper objects recovered from Coon Mound.

I would not suggest assigning Connett Mound 6 to classic "Hopewell" because of the apparent occurrence of a single panpipe cover. Small numbers of bladelets, another Hopewell diagnostic, have also been found in the lower Hocking (Greber 1991a:21). These objects were used as tools, but they had a strong degree of social choice ascribed to them. They are one of the few artifacts made of Ohio raw materials found, in small quantities, in sites of the Hopewell era outside Ohio (Chapman and Keel 1979; Mainfort 1986). The limited number of radiocarbon dates from the Connett Mounds and the Armitage Mound (Abrams 1992a) fall within the traditional Hopewell era. The calibrated average of two radiocarbon assays from Connett Mound 4 is cal A.D. 28 (129) 317 (1869 ± 50 B.P.) at two sigma; four from Armitage produced a calibrated average of cal A.D. 28 (236) 414 (1810 ± 80 B.P.), and the one assay from Connett Mound 3 calibrates to cal A.D. 141 (263, 275, 338) 429 (1720 ± 55 B.P.) (see Maslowski et al. 1995:31–33; calibrations performed with CALIB 4.3).

I interpret the elaboration of copper forms and mound structure, bolstered by a few dates, as indicating changes through time in an area where an apparent elaboration in cultural choices did not produce classic Hopewell flamboyance but instead remained closer to the more widespread culture found in the valleys on the south side of the Middle Ohio and in the Upper Ohio itself. The apparent occurrence of a panpipe cover in the plains is a demonstration that the use of objects can be not only time transgressive but also space transgressive. We recognize that a single glass bead found in a seventeenth-century aboriginal site in the Ohio Valley does not place the site into a European culture, but rather signifies some type of direct or indirect contact. It is likely that the contacts that brought the bladelets and a panpipe cover into the lower Hocking, quite possibly from some relatively nearby valley, were not of the same form as those that brought Flint Ridge bladelets to the group of great mounds and earthen enclosure at Pinson Mounds, Tennessee (Mainfort 1986, 1988).

On the South Bank

As in the valleys of the rivers that join the Ohio River on the north bank, a diversity of environments and archaeological remains are found south of

Ohio in Kentucky. Sites that formed the basis for Webb's definition of the Adena Complex of Kentucky are located in different environments and separated from each other by as much or greater distances than is found between regions in the Ohio Hopewell area. There is a common thread in archaeological remains from the Kentucky mounds, yet, not unexpectedly, diversity also exists, apparently due to both space and time. As fieldwork continues, the sense of local developments in cultural change emerges as suites of local sites are compared (e.g., Richmond and Kerr, this volume). In a repeat of my comments for Ohio sites: each site is part of a local sequence of social events and interactions that formed the local cultural remains. The patterns of each sequence are unlikely to be the same as those found in the Chillicothe Northwest Group in Ohio and need not duplicate other Kentucky sequences.

Traditionally these sites are "positioned in a geographic area normally associated with Adena" (Richmond and Kerr, this volume), and this "Adena" has been assumed to occur in Early Woodland times. Recent work is adding to the chronological data that places use of some Kentucky sites in Middle Woodland times. A good example of this is the Amburgey site, a multicomponent, apparently nonmound site located in Montgomery County. Well-documented and carefully analyzed artifacts diagnostic of classic Hopewell, including copper ear spools and a Connestee Series tetrapodal vessel, were recovered. Copper ear spools, in relatively small quantities, have a wide distribution that includes sites in the southeast. Richmond and Kerr (this volume) report that the Connestee vessel is an apparent import from the Appalachian area of eastern Tennessee and western North Carolina, but not from the same source(s) as pieces found in Ohio Hopewell sites (Chapman and Keel 1979). The calibrated average of two radiocarbon assays from Amburgey is cal A.D. 81 (136, 152, 176, 192, 211) 318 at two standard deviations. The Camargo site complex, as well as the Ricketts and Wright mounds, is located in the region. Another Connestee Series tetrapodal vessel was recovered from Camargo. At two sigma, the calibrated average of two radiocarbon ages from the complex is cal A.D. 242 (361, 367, 382) 431, and the two-sigma calibrated average of two assays from the Wright Mound is cal A.D. 24 (128) 243 (Richmond and Kerr, this volume; see also Maslowski et al. 1995:31–35). All three ranges are consistent with dates from Ohio Hopewell sites (Greber 2003:97–109).

The strong historic use of the word "Adena" for this area of Kentucky likely was fortunate; in this study the region was not labeled "reluctant Hopewell." Richmond and Kerr very clearly define their manner of dealing with the chronological overlap of "Adena" and "Hopewell." They define a nontraditional Middle Woodland time period from 400 B.C. to A.D. 400

that encompassed both manifestations, rather than allow either to cross "traditional" period boundaries (Richmond and Kerr, this volume). They describe the Wright Mound as "late Adena" and sites such as Amburgey as "Hopewellian influenced." One might question the direction from which the influence came, that is, north, southeast, or both. I concur with their observation that "the Amburgey site provides an example of the pan-regional increase in group ritual that took place between circa 500 B.C. and A.D. 500 in the eastern United States."

A clear difference exists between the archaeological manifestations at the Camargo site complex and at the Hopewell site. This does not mean that the people(s) who built and used Camargo were second-class archaeological citizens. They made choices, consciously or otherwise, within their physical and social environments that followed onto the historical events that happened before their time in the region. A significant question that as yet has no clear answer is, what were the factors that led, in two relatively close geographic areas, to the differences that appear in Middle Woodland times? Accepting a chronological relationship between "Adena" and "Hopewell" as distinguishing two recognizable cultural manifestations in Ross County seems reasonable. Do the differences between chronologically early and late sites in Kentucky and elsewhere suggest that a separate name would be useful for early and "late Adena, Hopewell influenced" sites? I do not know the data to answer this. Does attaching the label "Adena," without specifying a geographic restriction, to sites dated to "Early" and "Middle" Woodland times in the Middle Ohio Valley increase the potential for confusion in comparative studies? Yes.

Some Comments on the Model

We do not have sufficient data to form a detailed chronological account (a.k.a. cultural history) of the archaeological landscape that includes the Adena Mound. A significant range of mound morphologies and ritual features, some of which are not directly associated with human remains (including deposits at the nearby Mound City), have been recorded. During the apparently long-time use of the area for ritual/ceremonial events there was likely a concurrent "embedding of the 'sacred sites' in their wider social context and the awareness that the landscape is not just sacred but also political" (van Dommelen 1999:281). Information for interpretations of possible forms of social interactions, in the wider sense, comes from site architecture. "Because the use of space encoded in architecture is so loaded with cultural information, architecture will signal a variety of messages—about ideas, values, and relationships—either consciously or unconsciously to both residents and visitors" (Cameron 1998:187). Cameron's viewpoint in studying southwestern architecture is useful in considering ritual/ceremonial/civic contexts in the Chillicothe Northwest Group and other regions of southern Ohio.

By historical precedent and in its physical attributes *the* Adena Mound represents an important part of the design and use of ritual/ceremonial/civic precincts in the area. Unfortunately, DNA evidence that might help determine the genetic relationships among the individuals interred is not now available but could still be searched for in future studies (e.g., Mills 2003). I assume it is more likely that a single group used the site for events centered originally on the subfloor tomb and surrounding floor features. That group could have been defined by biological relationships, social customs, ritual duties, or political autonomy.

To me, less ambiguous data on possible group interactions come from sets of conjoined mounds, such as the Worthington Group and from sets of conjoined mounds that were themselves mantled to form one large construction. It is tempting, but on present evidence unwise, to put a chronological order on final mound morphology starting small, medium, conjoined, covered conjoined. For example, mainly on the basis of the absence of obsidian objects, the Seip-Conjoined mounds just northeast of Seip-Pricer Mound are considered to be younger than the conjoined set covered by the final stages of Seip-Pricer. I cannot elaborate here on comparisons of architectural details from the many conjoined sets. They do differ (Greber 1979a, 1991a:15–17). Ritual features lacking directly associated interments were covered by seven conjoined mounds forming a ceremonial center at Turner and by three at the Eagle Mound, Newark. In Ross County, with the assumption of contemporary use of the entire floor, the sizes of groups of burials associated with separate wooden structures at sites such as Hopewell Mound 25 and Seip-Pricer suggest that more than one social group shared the floor. The only available physical anthropological study of one such group is that associated with the eastern structure at Seip-Pricer. It suggests that, demographically, this group likely represents a living social group of men, women, and children (Konigsberg 1988). I consider that this group shared ritual space and responsibilities with two other groups, likely similar in political structure, who used wooden structures that shared the same floor.

A possible solution to the tensions that arise from such sharing is seen among the early conjoined mounds at Hopewell Mound 25. An increase or enhancement in ritual roles and the integration of the duties of such roles builds ties. The regalia associated with three individuals, each from one of the three physically separated areas, suggest that these three shared aspects of some ritual reflecting the life cycle of deer. Images of the three headdresses are superimposed as part of the intricate pattern in a single bone engraving (Moorehead 1922:Plate 82, FMNH 56369). Special headgear has been associated with "Adena" mounds (Dragoo 1963:Figure 16; Webb and Haag 1947), but I do not know of any multiple related designs from the same site.

The Conundrum

> The relationship of Adena to other prehistoric peoples, particularly to the Hopewell of Ohio, has long been a problem of major importance. It is believed that the solution of this problem might have been much farther advanced, long ere this, had Adena been discovered first and thoroughly studied before Hopewell with its great wealth of material culture and its abundant evidence of high artistic development had so impressed the imagination, the language, and the technique of all early investigators. *However, as the results of accident or ill fate, Hopewell was discovered first.*
>
> —William S. Webb and Charles E. Snow, 1945

What to do with history? We build on it. William Webb made significant contributions in the studies he organized of what he called "the Adena Complex of Kentucky." I think that his use of the geographic modifier was and is useful. Unfortunately, in his work, centered on demonstrating that Ohio Hopewell developed from "Adena," not from Wisconsin Trempealeau, he tended to place data from all Kentucky mounds into a single summary data set (e.g., Webb and Snow 1945:247). This was in keeping with the sense of unity that was perhaps an unconscious background thought. He recorded differences but did not dwell on them as we are wont to do today (e.g. Schlarb, this volume). The recognition of the importance of considering relationships in a local area is also not new. In describing the results of his study of the numerous mounds in the Charleston area, McMichael (1971: 94) concluded that "we suggest that they are simply a part of a distinct local tradition which, while influenced by Adena-Hopewell, was generally independent of both."

Literally hundreds of mounds were built in the Middle Ohio Valley. The cultural affiliation of the majority, including ones that have been excavated since 1960, is not known (Greber 1991a:2). Perhaps someday we will have data to demonstrate that mound building in the Middle Ohio Valley began more than five millennia ago in the Archaic time period as it did in the lower Illinois River valley, where such mounds mantled burials (Buikstra and Charles 1999; Charles et al. 1988), and in Louisiana at Watson Brake, where they apparently covered ritual areas (Saunders et al. 1997).

The use of ritual areas is omnipresent through time. The design of such spaces, as noted previously, is "loaded with cultural information" (Cameron 1998:187) and reflects ideas, values, and relationships. The difference in the designs of the ritual spaces at the Adena Mound and at Hopewell Mound 25 is one of the significant distinctions between "Adena" and "Hopewell" in Ross County and in other regions in the Middle Ohio Valley. While rereading Greenman's excellent report on the Coon Mound, I was struck again by the concordance between the architecture of the ritual features mantled by the Coon Mound (e.g., Greenman 1932:Figures 6, 12) and the "rendering of a 'typical' Middle Woodland tumulus" pictured by Buikstra and Charles (1999:Figure 9.6). The less-well-documented central feature of the Adena Mound also bears a resemblance to the Illinois design. This similarity is opposite to the contrast noted by Brown (1979) in his discussion of significant differences in the architectural design of Ohio and Illinois "Hopewell" special spaces. The photograph in Brown's (1979:Figure 27.4) article of the central feature beneath an Illinois mound bears a close resemblance to field photographs in the Coon Mound report (Greenman 1932:Figures 10 and 23).

In the lower Illinois valley, "nearly invisible Early Woodland mortuary activity was followed by the most conspicuous built landscapes in the Midcontinent prior to Euro-American settlement, Middle Woodland, or Hopewellian, peoples again turned to the bluff crest" (Buikstra and Charles 1999:212). The lack of Early Woodland mortuary remains is explained by a population drop in the region, followed by an influx of new peoples from the north during Middle Woodland times. Early Woodland is defined as circa 2550–2100 B.P. This is some 550 years shorter than the 2950–1950 B.P. range given by Seeman (1986:564–566) for the Ohio Valley. His definition of Early Woodland overlaps by a century the definition of Middle Woodland used by Buikstra and Charles (1999:206), 2050–1750 B.P.

As a sidelight conundrum in comparing "Adena" and "Hopewell," could an Illinois "'typical' Middle Woodland tumulus" be contemporary with an Ohio Valley "Adena" mound? What type of relationship, if any, might be reflected in the similarities in ritual design? Early suggested origins of Ohio Hopewell due to influences from Illinois have not been corroborated by the continuing analyses of artifacts and skeletal remains. The disjunction in definitions of time seen in the upper boundary of Illinois Middle Woodland defined by Buikstra and Charles and several estimates from the Middle Ohio Valley (2050–1650 B.P. [Griffin 1978c:260]; 1950–1600 B.P. [Seeman 1996:307]; 2350–1550 B.P. [Richmond and Kerr, this volume]; and 2030–1470 B.P. [Greber 2003:97–98]) does seem to indicate an earlier end to Illinois Hopewell in the Middle Woodland time period.

I do not usually venture far outside Ohio. This tentative foray to the western edge of the Eastern Woodlands in Illinois brings us full circle back to confusions possible in the use of the word "Woodland." Even when it is clearly used in its temporal sense, the boundaries used for breaking up the entire span need to be defined if one wishes to compare contemporary "Adenas" or "Hopewells." Stoltman's (1978:728; emphasis added) comments on the period names he suggested apply equally well to the commonly used divisions of "Woodland": "The period names have been carefully chosen to be terse yet as self-explanatory as possible and to convey the message that they are increments of time (which means that *they cannot be conceived as culturally homogenous*)."

Are the entities "Adena" and "Hopewell" useful in the Middle Ohio Valley? Yes, in Ross County, where we can identify central Scioto Hopewell and central Scioto Adena. We might find useful a new naming system that recognizes both the diversity and the unity of the archaeological cultural remains that overlap in time, space, or both across the Central Ohio Valley, although such a scenario is unlikely. An elegant single word name that combines space *and* time could complicate cross-region comparisons. Because knowledge of space is more readily available, for many purposes longer phrases would at least define a local region: Middle Muskingum Adena, Middle Muskingum Hopewell. The contents of the archaeological remains must still be spelled out. Outside the "Hopewell" areas perhaps a tradition followed by other sciences could be useful. Physicists study *Newtonian* rings, and astronomers use the *Hubble* telescope. After carefully defining the contents and chronological time of the word "complex," those who have identified and studied the sites included in an Adena complex could be honored by using new names, such as the Greenman Adena Complex in the Hocking Valley or the Webb Adena Complex in the Central Bluegrass.

Acknowledgments

I gratefully thank all those who have gathered the information I used in this chapter. I alone am responsible for the interpretations that I hope they or their intellectual heirs will find useful.

Note

The epigraph that appears at the beginning of this chapter is from Robinson (1946:7–8; emphasis added). The epigraph that appears at the beginning of the "Conundrum" section is from Webb and Snow (1945:137; emphasis added).

3

Archaeology at the Edges of Time and Space

Working across and between Woodland Period Taxonomic Units in Central Ohio

Jarrod Burks

Unlike some regions, the Middle Ohio Valley has experienced a dearth in taxonomy construction. Existing taxonomic units (Table 3.1) represent a bewildering array of time periods, phases, foci, traditions, complexes, and cultures, some of which have been so overextended that their usefulness is questionable (Clay 2002). Most chapters in this volume rightly call attention to problems with taxa such as Adena and Hopewell. Many researchers would agree that the concept of Newtown and even our cherished Woodland subperiods (Early, Middle, and Late) have been similarly diluted (Seeman 1980). Yet it is very difficult to talk about the Woodland period without falling back on these taxonomic units.

As a taxonomy user, I do not intend to propose any new taxa here. Rather, I highlight a few things we do know about the Woodland period in central and south-central Ohio (Figure 3.1) and explore how existing taxonomies have hampered investigations of one particular research problem—change in community organization from A.D. 200–600. In part, taxonomic shortcomings have led to an overindulgence in pigeonholing sites into cultural taxa such as Adena and Hopewell or temporal taxa such as Early, Middle, and Late Woodland. Confounding matters is a tendency to use the same terms and attributes as determinants of both cultural and temporal taxa, which works well unless change occurred at different rates across the region. Such is the case in the Middle Ohio Valley. Because of a varied rate of change through time and space, and an out-of-date taxonomy, the origin and process of Middle–Late Woodland period settlement nucleation has fallen through the taxonomic gap.

The Problem of Settlement Nucleation in Central Ohio

Since the 1950s, dozens of early Late Woodland period (A.D. 400–800) contexts throughout the Middle Ohio Valley region have been explored (See-

Table 3.1. Selected Woodland period taxa in use predominantly in southern Ohio

Woodland Period/ Taxon Name	Time Range	Type of Unit	Reference
Early Middle Early Late Woodland	1000 B.C.–200 B.C. 200 B.C.–400 A.D. 300 A.D.–900 A.D.	Time periods	Griffin 1967
Early Middle Late	1500 B.C.–A.D. 100 A.D. 100–500 A.D. 500–1000	Time periods	Murphy 1989
Early Hopewell Middle Hopewell Late Hopewell Latest Hopewell	Relative ordering for select sites based on pottery	Time periods	Prufer 1968
Late Woodland	A.D. 540–1005	Time period	Seeman and Dancey 2000
Red Ochre Early Adena Late Adena Hopewell Phase Newtown Peters Phase Intrusive Mound	1100–500 B.C. 500–150 B.C. 150 B.C.–A.D. 1 A.D. 1–400 A.D. 400–700 A.D. 700–1000 A.D. 700–1000	Cultural complexes	Seeman 1992a
Robbins	Late Adena	Complex	Dragoo 1963
Early Adena Middle Adena Late Adena	500–150 B.C. 150 B.C.–A.D. 1 A.D. 1–250	Cultural developmental stages	Clay 1991b
Peters	Late Woodland	Phase	Prufer and McKenzie 1966
Newtown	Beginning of Late Woodland, between Hopewell and Fort Ancient	Focus, phase, complex	Griffin 1952b
Intrusive Mound	Between Hopewell and Fort Ancient	Culture	Mills 1922
Jack's Reef	Ca. A.D. 700–900	Horizon	Seeman 1992b
Cole	From Late Adena to Fort Ancient	Culture/complex	Baby and Potter 1965; Potter 1966

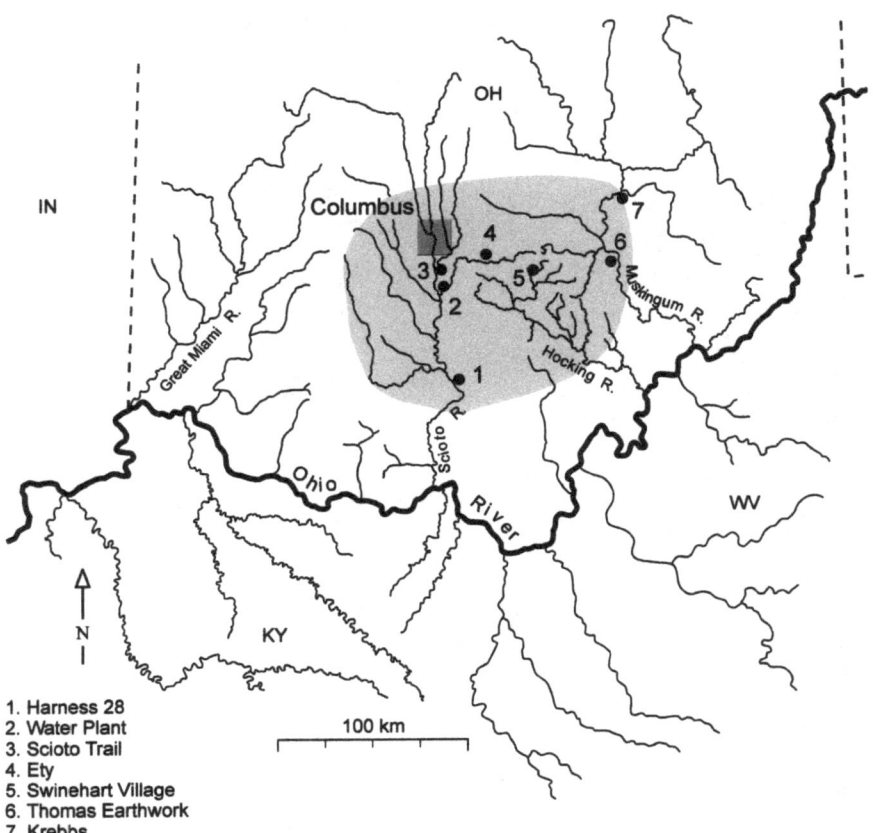

Figure 3.1. Barricaded, nucleated settlements in the central Ohio study area (shown in gray).

man and Dancey 2000). Early Late Woodland settlements clearly reflect a continuity with certain behaviors evidenced in the Middle Woodland period (e.g., projectile weaponry and general subsistence practices). Some researchers (Clay 2002; Clay and Creasman 1999) contend there is little evidence for nucleated village life during the Woodland period, but others argue that most communities from the early Late Woodland period differed markedly from their Middle Woodland predecessors in organization and size. Specifically, the existing data indicate a change from small, dispersed Middle Woodland habitation sites to large, nucleated early Late Woodland villages (Burks 2004; Carskadden and Morton 1996; Dancey 1988, 1992, 1998; Fuller 1981; Maslowski 1985; Railey 1984; Seeman 1980, 1992a; Seeman and Dancey 2000; Shott 1990). This change occurred around

A.D. 300–500 (Middle to Late Woodland period), and in most areas it signaled the decline, end, or lack of the Hopewell phenomenon. Some suggest the impetus for this change in settlement organization came from a heightened need for defense (Dancey 1992, 1998; Seeman 1980; Seeman and Dancey 2000).

One major question that has not received much attention in this discussion of settlement nucleation is, what groups needed to defend themselves and against what or whom and why? Dancey (1992:27) noted that many of the earlier nucleated settlements seem to first occur suddenly in "communities [that] occupied territories outside the networks of Hopewellian interaction systems" at the periphery of core Hopewell areas. He went on to say that nucleation of these peripheral communities was prompted by pressures exerted on limited, stored food resources by non-Hopewellian neighbors. Assuming that this is one viable hypothesis for the origin of Middle–Late Woodland period settlement nucleation, who were these peripheral communities? Problems and inadequacies in existing Woodland period taxonomy complicate our ability to answer this question.

The Use of Woodland Period Taxonomy in Central Ohio

Over the last one hundred years of Woodland period research, discussions of the central Ohio archaeological record have focused on four major themes: mortuary ceremonialism (Dragoo 1963; Greber 1991b), interregional exchange (Brose 1979; Seeman 1979; Struever and Houart 1972), community or settlement organization (Dancey and Pacheco, eds. 1997; Keener and Biehl 1999; Maslowski 1985), and the decline or collapse of major culture groups (Braun 1977, 1986; Dancey 1996). The occurrence of and changes in these four cultural components are commonly used throughout the region for demarcating taxonomic boundaries in two kinds of taxonomic systems—one focused on time, the other on variable-scale cultural phenomena (Table 3.1).

First I consider time. The Woodland period commonly is divided into three subperiods: Early (1000 B.C.–200 B.C.), Middle (200 B.C.–A.D. 400), and Late (A.D. 400–A.D. 1000). The boundaries of these temporal units vary to a significant degree across the region. The development of pottery technology is usually cited as marking the beginning of the Early Woodland period, even though reliable radiocarbon dates place pottery in the area as early as about 1500 B.C., if not earlier (see Table 22.1 in Seeman 1986:566; Keener and Pecora 2003; Pecora and Burks 2004). Another important "first" in the Early Woodland period is mound building, but this behavior does not seem to become common until about 500 B.C. (Seeman 1986).

The end of the Early Woodland period marks a significant change in burial ceremonialism. At about 200 B.C., there was a transition away from the use of mounds as vertical cemeteries, as in the Early Woodland Toephner Mound, located along the Scioto River in central Ohio (Hays 1994; Norris 1985; Piotrowski 1985). In contrast, during Middle Woodland times the dead were processed and finally laid to rest on or near the floors of mortuary ceremonial structures such as those evidenced at Mound City in south-central Ohio (Mills 1922). Many Middle Woodland mounds were constructed over destroyed or dismantled buildings linked to mortuary ceremonies (Brown 1979; Greber 1983). Additional burials were rarely placed in Middle Woodland mounds after initial construction. Along with this change in mortuary ceremonialism, some areas experienced a florescence of earthen enclosure construction on a massive scale during the Middle Woodland (e.g., Ross County, Ohio). Thus, it is plain that mortuary ceremonialism is the primary means for defining our temporal taxonomic units in central Ohio. This, of course, is mostly due to an overemphasis on the excavation of mounds in the last 150 years.

Perhaps no taxonomic boundary in the Midwest has been the subject of as much speculation as the end of the Middle Woodland period, circa A.D. 400. In central Ohio, as in the rest of the Middle Ohio Valley, this boundary is defined by major changes in mortuary ceremonialism, the inflow of nonlocal raw materials, and settlement organization. The construction of large, earthen enclosures and complex mortuary-ceremonial buildings (a.k.a. "Great Houses"), such as those at the Seip (Greber 1976) and Liberty earthworks (Greber 1983) in Ross County, Ohio, ceased almost overnight, from an archaeological perspective. The procurement and use of exotic raw materials such as copper, mica, and obsidian also ended, though some of these objects were still present, perhaps as heirlooms, into the fifth century A.D. (e.g., at Henderson Mound 2 in Muskingum County, Ohio [Carskadden and Morton 1996]). Aggregation of local populations into nucleated settlements (i.e., settlements composed of multiple, contemporaneous households), especially in central and south-central Ohio, is closely linked in time to this apparent downsizing of mortuary ceremonialism and abandonment of earthwork construction (Dancey 1996).

Under the current chronological taxonomy, the same criteria commonly used to subdivide time are also used to define taxa meant to represent archaeological cultures, cultural complexes, or cultural traditions. Thus Adena populations are assigned to the end of the Early Woodland period, Hopewell to the Middle Woodland period, and Newtown, especially in southern Ohio, to the beginning of the Late Woodland period. Using the same set of cultural phenomena to mark boundaries in this chronological framework, as well as in constructing our culture historical taxa, has resulted in two major problems. First, many researchers use the taxonomic terms interchangeably. For example, in many parts of the Middle Ohio Valley, the term "Hopewell" has become synonymous with Middle Woodland period. Some researchers have even temporarily adopted such sociocultural taxonomic terms as Adena and Newtown for use as "temporal subdivisions" (e.g., Railey 1991:60), creating phaselike taxa. Likewise, because no culture group taxa have been proposed in central Ohio for the early Late Woodland period, researchers may be forced to use the term "early Late Woodland" in the sense of a culture group, as they might Adena or Hopewell (Carskadden and Morton 1996). Using time-period terminology instead of other taxonomic units is problematic when all of the cultural baggage that goes along with, for example, Hopewell comes to dominate the way we think about all archaeological deposits from the Middle Woodland period.

A second major problem with using the same criteria to denote chronological and cultural taxa involves time. Many trends seen in Woodland cultural change occurred at different rates with variable starting and ending points across the Middle Ohio Valley. For example, whereas some researchers place the end of both Adena and the Early Woodland period at A.D. 1 (Clay 1992; Seeman 1986), mortuary ceremonialism characteristics of (or, at least, similar to) Adena continue until at least A.D. 200 in parts of the Muskingum (Carskadden and Morton 1996) and Hocking valleys (Abrams 1992a). The need for a more flexible, region-specific taxonomy is plain. In the study of settlement aggregation, inadequate taxa have made research very difficult across large areas (e.g., interdrainage), and they ignore and mask considerable variability.

CASE STUDY: SETTLEMENT NUCLEATION,
ITS ORIGINS, AND THE HOPEWELL-ADENA DIVIDE

The study of Woodland period settlement nucleation is a case in which existing taxonomic units have hindered research in central Ohio. Current interpretations of Woodland period settlement suggest that dispersed Early Woodland Adena populations transitioned into Middle Woodland Hopewell groups who continued to live in communities of dispersed households (e.g., Carskadden and Morton 1997). In these communities, mounds and enclosures acted as burial and meeting places, as well as perhaps territory markers.

For reasons as yet unknown, by A.D. 450, formerly dispersed Hopewell communities became nucleated communities (settlements) of multiple households, and Hopewell enclosures were abandoned. In fact, in central Ohio, nucleated settlements typify the early Late Woodland period as it is known to date (cf. Clay and Creasman 1999). Seeman and Dancey (2000) noted the presence of at least 28 such sites across the Middle Ohio Valley. Some aggregated settlements, especially after A.D. 550, were even surrounded by shallow ditches. Seven known examples of barricaded, nucleated settlements exist in central Ohio (Figure 3.1), four of which have been the foci of major fieldwork (Harness 28 [Seeman and Dancey 2000], Scioto Trail/Zencor [Baby 1971; Baby and Shaffer 1957; Otto 1983], Swinehart [Schweikart 2002], and Water Plant [Dancey 1988; Dancey et al. 1987]) and three that have not (Ety [Jerrel Anderson, personal communication 2002], Thomas Earthwork [Carskadden and Morton 1996], and Krebbs [Carskadden and Morton 1996]). Unfortunately, much of the research that has been conducted on these important sites has yet to be widely published.

Such a profound change in community organization begs the question of origin. Why did populations nucleate, and where did nucleation first begin? Traditionally, archaeologists have attempted to explain nucleation as the result of population growth fueled by maize agriculture, such as Fuller's (1981) work in the panhandle region of West Virginia. But maize was not common in the Middle Ohio Valley until the very end of the Woodland period (Wymer 1992). Some researchers view nucleation and settlement circumscription by ditches and perhaps stockades as representing a growing need for defense (Railey 1991; Seeman and Dancey 2000). Because nucleation seems to be so closely linked to the Late Woodland period, starting about A.D. 400, few researchers look to Adena populations because most associate Adena with the Early Woodland period,[1] which is generally considered to end between 200 B.C. and A.D. 1. Admittedly, A.D. 1 predates any known nucleated settlement by at least 200 to 300 years, but the close association of the taxonomic concepts "Adena" and "Early Woodland" have led researchers to overlook or dismiss some very late dates associated with contexts exhibiting Adena-like characteristics that may be important to understanding the decline of Hopewell groups and the origin of settlement nucleation. To explore this possibility, I will juxtapose a few observations that potentially throw light on the origins of nucleated settlement in central Ohio.

First, although most nucleated Woodland settlements are dated to A.D. 550 or later, a handful from across the region have yielded fairly early dates[2] (Figure 3.2; Table 3.2). South of the Ohio River, the Pyles and Hansen sites have produced calibrated dates as early as A.D. 179 (433) 664 and 235 (421) 636, respectively (Ahler 1988; Railey 1984). Near Dayton, Ohio, the Lichliter site (Allman 1967) was dated to A.D. 132 (430) 664 (Crane and Griffin 1959). At the far eastern reaches of the Scioto Valley, the Strait site has pro-

Archaeology at the Edges of Time and Space / 47

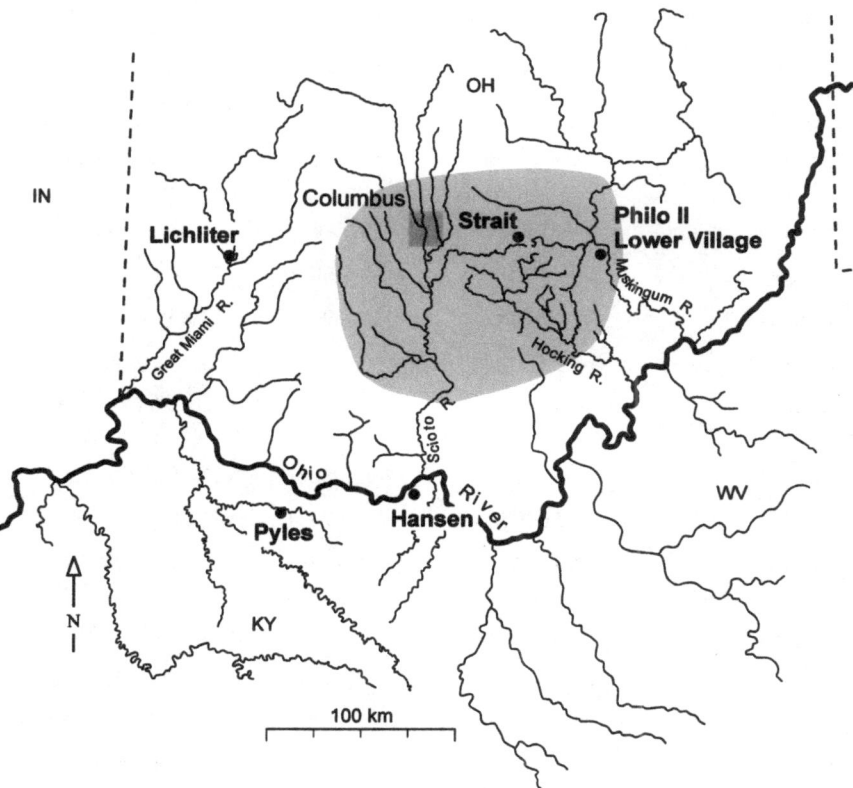

Figure 3.2. Early nucleated Woodland period sites in central Ohio.

duced calibrated dates ranging from A.D. 83 (223) 224 to A.D. 258 (412) 537 (Burks 2001, 2004). Finally, Carskadden and Morton (1996) report finding the remains of the Philo II Lower Village, an early fifth century A.D. nucleated settlement with bladelets and Lowe cluster projectile points, under the remains of a Late Prehistoric village in the Middle Muskingum Valley.[3]

Each of these sites is thought to represent an aggregation of contemporaneous households. At Strait, bladelets and Lowe Cluster projectile points are common, but decorated Hopewell ceramics and other Hopewell exotica are essentially absent (Burks 2004; Burks and Dancey 1999). Interestingly, these early nucleated sites are peripheral to core Hopewell areas and are located away from known Hopewell enclosures. Some sites, including Strait and Lichliter, do not fit comfortably into current concepts of either Hopewell or early Late Woodland because of their radiocarbon dates, large size,

Table 3.2. Radiocarbon assays mentioned in the text

Site	Lab No.	RCYBP		Calibrated Date (2 sigma)
Armitage Mound[a]	Beta 27705	1880	90	50 B.C. (A.D. 128) A.D. 380
Armitage Mound[a]	SMU 2161	1810	45	A.D. 83 (236) 340
Connett Mound 4[b]	DIC 2859B★	1790	50	A.D. 88 (240) 384
Hansen[c]	Beta 15082	1630	90	A.D. 235 (421) 436
Lichliter[d]	M-537	1600	125	A.D. 132 (430) 664
Linn 7[e]	I17126	1850	80	36 B.C. (A.D. 133) A.D. 383
Linn 7[e]	I17127	1780	80	A.D. 68 (243) 426
Locust[f]	ETH 3070	1870	75	A.D. 38 (129) 339
Locust[f]	SMU 1868	1832	146	168 B.C. (A.D. 180, 189, 214) A.D. 538
Osborn Mound[g]	Beta 71531	1870	60	A.D. 4 (129) 321
Pyles[h]	N/A	1590	120	A.D. 179 (433) 664
Strait[i]	Beta 147063	1820	40	A.D. 83 (223) 324
Strait[i]	Beta 147064	1650	50	A.D. 258 (412) 537
Strait[i]	Beta 147065	1750	70	A.D. 132 (258, 283, 287, 300, 320) 415
Strait[i]	Beta-147066	1820	100	A.D. 38 (223) 426

Note: Calibrations performed using CALIB 4.3.
[a]Abrams 1992a; [b]Skinner 1985; [c]Dancey 1988; [d]Crane and Griffin 1959; [e]Carskadden and Morton 1996; [f]Carr and Haas 1996; [g]Carskadden and Morton 1996; [h]Railey 1984; [i]Burks 2001.
★In her original publication Skinner (1985:140) warned that this date "may have been affected by a high root content and should be viewed with caution."

and mix of temporally diagnostic artifact types (e.g., rough slate disks, bladelets, ubiquitous Lowe Cluster projectile points with increasing numbers of the Chesser Notched type [Justice 1987], and undecorated pottery).

My second observation is that in central Ohio (Figure 3.3), away from core Hopewell areas, "Adena"-like behaviors persist until A.D. 200–300 (Greber 1991b), though this "was a time of significant societal adjustment" (Abrams 1992a). A number of mound contexts exhibiting Adena characteristics (e.g., vertical, accretional accumulation of mortuary facilities in

Archaeology at the Edges of Time and Space / 49

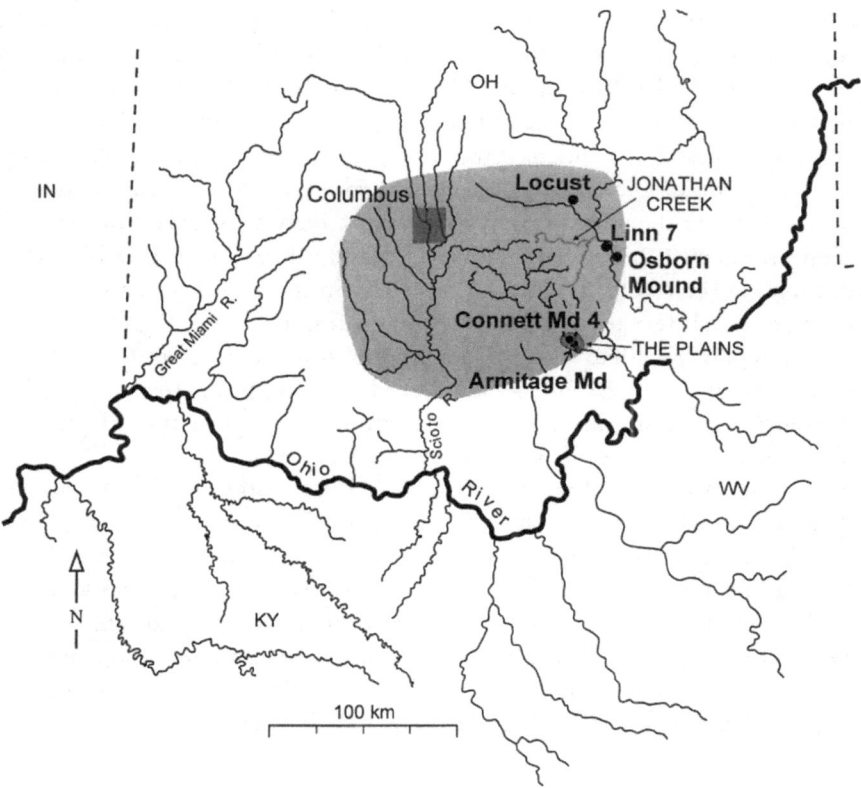

Figure 3.3. Late (post–A.D. 1000) "Adena" sites in central Ohio.

mound fill) in the Hocking and Muskingum valleys have produced calibrated radiocarbon dates that extend into the second and third centuries A.D. These include Osborn Mound at A.D. 4 (129) 321 (Carskadden and Morton 1996:Table 19:1); Connett Mound 4, A.D. 88 (240) 384 (Skinner 1985); and Armitage Mound, 50 B.C. (A.D. 128) A.D. 380 and A.D. 83 (236) 340 (Abrams 1992a). Habitation sites with similarly "late" dates include Locust at A.D. 38 (129) 339 and 168 B.C. (A.D. 180, 189, 214) A.D. 538 (Carr and Haas 1996) and Linn 7 at 36 B.C. (A.D. 133) A.D. 383 and A.D. 68 (243) 426 (Carskadden and Morton 1996:Table 19:1). The few sites with late dates do not at this point suggest any distributional patterns (e.g., whether they cluster near to early nucleated settlements). I am not yet aware of any such late dates, however, for Adena sites in core Hopewell areas, such as Ross County, Ohio.

Third, populations of "Adena" people were actually beginning to occupy settlements that left a footprint larger than typical Hopewell hamlets (ca. 0.45 ha, Dancey and Pacheco 1997:Table 1.1) by as early as A.D. 1 in the Hocking Valley, for example (Abrams 1992b; Black 1979). On the basis of his work in the Plains area of the Hocking Valley (Figure 3.3), Abrams (1992b) suggested that Adena settlement patterns were beginning to change there around A.D. 1, when groups began to leave the hinterlands and take up residence in the river bottoms more intensively. Conversely, in the Muskingum Valley, Carskadden and Morton (1997) have found that hinterland occupation increased after A.D. 1, especially in the areas adjacent to heavily used Hopewell territory, such as the Jonathan Creek area (Figure 3.3). The headwaters of Jonathan Creek are just a few miles away from the early nucleated Strait site. Carskadden and Morton also have found that many Adena sites in the Muskingum Valley river bottoms show great time depth with continued reoccupation from 400 B.C. to A.D. 100.

I mentioned little about the material culture patterns related to settlement change, but there seems to be a gradual transition from traditional late Adena assemblages (Robbins projectile points and plain-surfaced pottery) into traditional Hopewell assemblages (Lowe Cluster projectile points, bladelets, and an increasing percentage of cordmarked pottery). This has created somewhat of a gray area in central Ohio taxonomic units, as many sites are deemed Hopewell or Adena simply on the basis of the presence of a single artifact type, such as bladelets (e.g., Carskadden and Morton 1996).

Conclusion

In this chapter I have attempted to highlight data not normally brought to bear on the question of the origin of settlement nucleation in central Ohio. These data suggest that to understand Woodland period settlement nucleation more fully, researchers need to focus more on the areas traditionally considered as peripheral in existing temporal and geographic taxonomies. This implies conducting more research in the uplands and away from the main river valleys. Such areas may be where the process of settlement nucleation first appears, becoming a trend that eventually sweeps through much of central and south-central Ohio.

Because nucleation has traditionally been regarded as an early Late Woodland phenomenon, we seldom, if ever, look for mechanisms of change in sites placed into the Early Woodland taxa. In some areas of central and south-central Ohio, the three Woodland subperiods and their associated cultural units seem to overlap at about A.D. 200–300—precisely when some of the most elaborate Hopewell mortuary ceremonialism is happening in the Ross County area. This overlap currently is not reflected consistently in existing taxonomic units, and as a consequence, its importance is underemphasized. Similar taxonomic issues attend Woodland period taxonomy in northeastern Kentucky, where researchers have simply dropped the Hopewell taxon in many cases (e.g., Railey 1991).

Once we begin to look more closely at peripheral areas, both in time and space, I think we will find that contemporaneous populations of what we have been calling "Adena" and "Hopewell" were more common than once thought (Otto 1979). Furthermore, in central Ohio many view nucleation as somehow related to, or the result of, the so-called Hopewell decline and look for explanations intrinsic to Hopewell. Yet, some of the earliest nucleated settlements are located near some of the latest so-called Adena areas. If there really are "Adena" populations and "Hopewell" populations living contemporaneously, then settlement nucleation may have been precipitated by changes in the Adena populations and their interactions with the peripheral Hopewell populations, rather than changes intrinsic to the core Hopewell populations. This may support interpretations that suggest an extrinsic factor that eventually led to radical change away from Hopewell mortuary ceremonialism.

Notes

1. Jim Railey is a notable exception. Railey has long recognized a possible link between Woodland period settlement nucleation and so-called Adena populations (e.g., 1991, 1996). For Railey, this linkage came into focus while studying Woodland period settlements in northeastern Kentucky, where little evidence of the Hopewell phenomenon exists.

2. All radiocarbon dates reported in this chapter are calibrated intercepts (in parentheses) with two sigma ranges. All calibrations were calculated using CALIB 4.3 (Stuiver et al. 1998). See Table 3.2 for a list of the radiocarbon dates mentioned in the text.

3. At present, no radiocarbon dates are associated with the Philo II Lower Village. Instead, Carskadden and Morton (1996) rely on absolute dates from two nearby mounds that they associate with the village. Mound B of the Philo Mound group has a calibrated intercept date of A.D. 245 (412) 541 (Morton 1977), and the nearby Henderson Mound 2 dates to A.D. 256 (430) 639 (Carskadden and Edmister 1992).

4

The Bullock Site

A Forgotten Mound in Woodford County, Kentucky

Eric J. Schlarb

The Bluegrass region of Kentucky consists of a slightly karstic, gently rolling plain encircled by physiographic regions of greater relief. The deeply entrenched Kentucky River drains much of the region, flowing through narrow floodplains that are generally poorly suited for human habitation. Nevertheless, the region is well known for an abundance of earthworks representing prehistoric occupations. During the nineteenth century several burial mounds and enclosures were documented in the Kentucky Bluegrass. As early as 1820, Constantine Rafinesque, a naturalist and somewhat colorful professor with Lexington's Transylvania University, surveyed and mapped the large oval structure at Peter Village and documented other Woodland period sites in the Elkhorn Creek drainage (Tune 1985).

A century later, Kentucky archaeologists, most notably William S. Webb and his associates, were thoroughly captivated by the earthworks that conspicuously dotted the landscape surrounding Lexington. During the 1930s and 1940s, under the sponsorship of the Works Progress Administration, Webb directed the excavation of several mounds and enclosures in the Bluegrass region, including the Wright mounds in Montgomery County (Webb 1940); Mount Horeb Earthwork, Drake Mound, and Fischer in Fayette County (Webb 1941a; Webb and Haag 1947); and Riley Mound and Landing Mound in Boone County (Webb 1943). Webb compared the earthen mounds of Kentucky's Bluegrass region to Adena and Hopewell mounds of southern Ohio. On the basis of these comparisons and an Adena diagnostic trait list, Webb concluded that the mounds and enclosures of Kentucky's Bluegrass region were Adena (Webb and Baby 1957; Webb and Snow 1974).

The concepts of "Adena" and "Hopewell" emerged during the first part of the twentieth century based on investigations (Greenman 1932; Mills 1916, 1922) of numerous mortuary mounds in the Middle Ohio Valley (Railey 1991). Archaeologists (Dragoo 1963) initially treated Adena as an Early Woodland period (circa 1000 B.C.–A.D. 1) culture, though today most researchers agree that Adena is a late Early Woodland period (post–500 B.C.) phenomenon. Furthermore, Adena is generally viewed as the precursor of the Middle Woodland period (A.D. 1–500) Hopewell culture. Although a sequential chronological relationship between Adena and Hopewell has been documented in southern Ohio (Greber 1991b), the same association may not exist in Kentucky (Railey 1991, 1996). Adena sites in Kentucky date to the Early *and* Middle Woodland periods (Clay 1980), and the influence of Hopewell in Kentucky is poorly documented

One Bluegrass mound complex that has defied classification as Adena or Hopewell is the Bullock site, which was excavated by Webb and William Haag in 1947. The Bullock site was recorded as a group of three earth mounds—one large mound 18 m (60 ft) in diameter and two smaller mounds (no dimensions given)—on the property of Mr. Harry Bullock, northeast of the community of Pisgah in Woodford County (Haag 1947b). The site is situated on a flat finger-ridge overlooking a small unnamed tributary of the South Fork of Elkhorn Creek, which flows 1 km east of the site (Figure 4.1). In this chapter I summarize the investigations performed at the site; describe the mound, associated mortuary features, and artifact assemblage; and assess the Bullock Mound within the context of Woodland period mortuary practices of Kentucky's Bluegrass region.

Bullock Mound Investigations

According to one of Mr. Bullock's children, the Bullock mounds were visited by William D. Funkhouser and students from the University of Kentucky during the late 1930s or early 1940s (Virginia Scott, personal communication 1998). The largest mound was surveyed systematically in July 1947 by the University of Kentucky. Working under Webb's direction, Haag supervised excavation of the large mound on a day-to-day basis because by 1947 Webb's focus on burial mound investigations had shifted to several enormous reservoir projects in the southeastern United States (William G. Haag, personal communication 1998). During the time of the Bullock Mound excavation, for example, Webb and Haag were also occupied with the Wolf Creek Dam project on the Cumberland River in south-central Kentucky (Haag 1947a).

From July 19 to August 18, 1947, Webb and Haag, utilizing student labor, excavated the largest earthen mound at the Bullock site. Webb initiated investigations of the Bullock Mound, believing it was associated with the Drake Mound, an Adena mound located only 3.3 km to the northeast (Webb 1941a), and the large earthworks located near the confluence of Town Branch and South Elkhorn Creek (Figure 4.1) (Webb and Haag

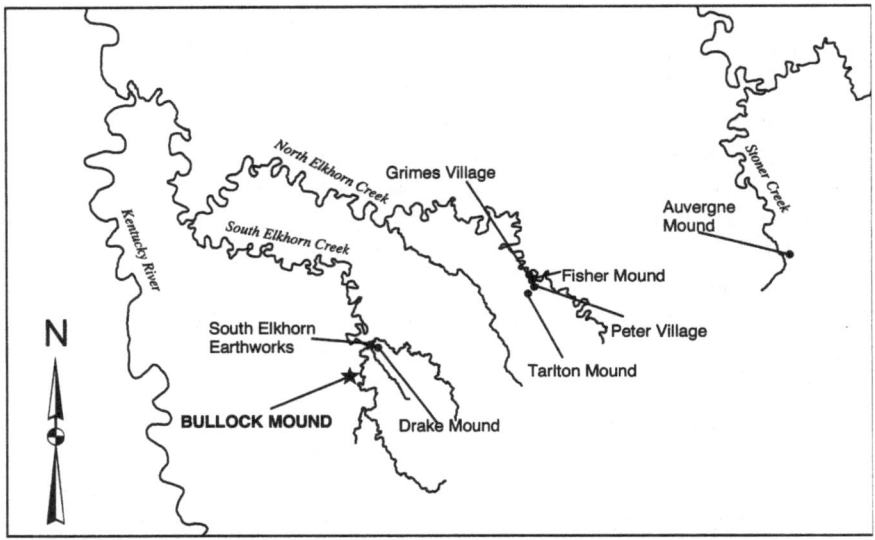

Figure 4.1. Location of Woodland period mound and village sites in the Elkhorn and Stoner Creek drainages.

1947). However, archaeological investigation of the Bullock Mound did not result in the recovery of elaborate Adena burials or associated artifacts.

Webb and Haag never published the findings of the Bullock Mound investigation. Perhaps they were disappointed that this particular mound, lacking a preponderance of diagnostic Adena traits, did not fit nicely into the Adena taxon. Both men were involved with the Wolf Creek Dam project and may have been too busy to deal with it (William Haag, personal communication 1998). In any case, artifacts and field records were curated at the University of Kentucky's William S. Webb Museum of Anthropology, and the Bullock Mound was forgotten.

Bullock Mound Rediscovery

In the spring of 1998, an earthen mound in Woodford County was brought to the attention of University of Kentucky archaeologists by a local amateur. The fields surrounding the mound had been plowed recently, revealing a moderate-to-heavy prehistoric lithic scatter and some prehistoric ceramic sherds. Several flaked stone artifacts and ceramic sherds had been collected by the amateur in the general vicinity of the mound. After examining topographic maps and Kentucky Archaeological Site Survey forms on file at the Office of State Archaeology in Lexington, University of Kentucky archaeologists realized that the Bullock Mound had once again been encountered. A meeting with the owner of the property was arranged, and permission to access the site was granted. The property owner's desire to increase his knowledge regarding prehistoric archaeological sites located on his land was most helpful in expediting another archaeological investigation of the Bullock Mound. The first step in the investigation involved reviewing field records from the 1947 excavations, especially documentation of mound features.

Review of Field Records

The Bullock Mound measured 20 × 10 × 2.6 m (65 × 35 × 7.5 ft) prior to excavation. Webb and Haag took a series of transit readings at 1.5 m (5-ft) intervals and established a grid across the mound surface. Eighty 1.5 × 1.5-m (5 × 5 ft) units were excavated in 6 in levels to the base of the mound, revealing a rectangular submound structure and associated features.

The submound structure was delineated by 80 vertical posthole features that encompassed an area 15 m (45 ft) long and more than 8 m (25 ft) wide (Figure 4.2). Considerable soil burning, designated a burned clay floor, was documented within the rectangular structure. Although the burned area extended to the postholes on all four sides of the structure, the fire seemed to have been most intense in the area between Features 4 and 5. In my opinion the burned clay floor may represent burning of the rectangular structure that once stood there. In addition to the burned clay floor, five features and three additional postholes were recorded within the structure. Artifacts and human skeletal remains were associated with two of the features.

Feature 1 was a pit of soft earth that extended 15 cm (6 in) into the area of the burned clay floor. Similar to Feature 1, Feature 2 was a pit that extended 46 cm beneath the burned clay floor. Feature 3 was an ash bed that contained a 25 cm-thick layer of dark ash mixed with charcoal and what appeared to be the remains of leaves and twigs. Other than the organic material in Feature 3, the three features did not contain artifactual remains.

Feature 4 was described as a central pit, with a concave basin, encircled by a ring of baked clay. I inferred that the basin's subrectangular form may have been intentionally constructed in this shape to mimic the rectangular submound structure. The burned clay ring averaged 61 cm high, 3 m across, and 30 cm thick. Sixteen fragments of calcined and charred human skeletal fragments and seven small pieces of copper were found on the basin floor within the boundaries of the burned clay ring. This location may represent the area in which the cremation actually took place, or the skeletal fragments and copper may have been scooped up from other locations and re-

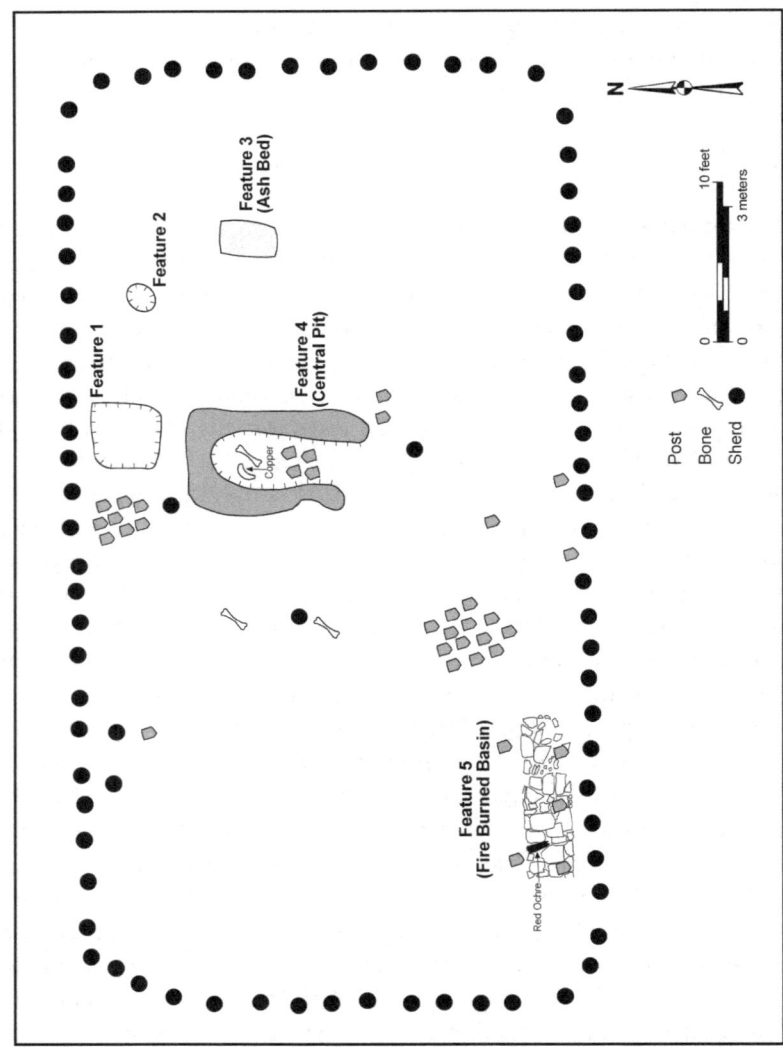

Figure 4.2. Submound post pattern and associated features in the Bullock Mound.

deposited inside the pit. Of note, few artifacts, other than copper, could survive the intense heat produced from a crematory fire (Webb and Snow 1974:68). One should keep this in mind and note that there may have been additional artifacts in the basin that either disintegrated or were not recognized by the excavators. On the original feature form Haag (1947b) stated that the preservation of Feature 4 was excellent, though it showed signs of past disturbance. I suspect that the disturbance was a result of Funkhouser's foray with his students during the late 1930s or early 1940s.

Feature 5 was recorded as a fire-burned basin. This feature, which measured approximately 3.6 m long and 1 m wide, was capped with flat limestone rocks. Some of the rocks outlining the feature were oriented vertically. A small pit considered part of Feature 5 was discovered beneath the limestone cap. A soil sample removed from the pit yielded small fragments of pottery, chert, human bone, red ochre, charcoal, and ash. A very small amount (0.18 g) of charcoal recently extracted from the soil sample yielded an AMS-calibrated radiocarbon date of A.D. 1650 (1670, 1780, 1800) 1950 (190 ± 40 B.P.; Beta-180784). This date is much later than anticipated; the soil sample may have been contaminated during excavation or consisted of modern charcoal that filtered into the feature by means of mechanical plowing or bioturbation.

Artifact Assemblage and Human Remains

Ceramics

Ceramic sherds from the Bullock Mound were compared with the type collection at the William S. Webb Museum of Anthropology. The attributes considered for each sherd were vessel portion, paste color, outside surface color, inside surface color, thickness, temper, and surface treatment. Colors were measured using the Munsell Soil Color Chart.

A total of 90 pottery sherds were recovered from the Bullock Mound in 1947, but due to generally poor preservation and degradation in storage, many of the sherds had crumbled into very small fragments. Consequently, only 48 sherds were suited for analysis.

Paste colors range from red to dark red, outside surface colors vary from light yellowish brown and light brown to dark red and reddish brown, and inside surface colors range from reddish brown to brown and black. All sherds are limestone tempered, though most of the limestone has been leached out, leaving round to semiround voids on the surfaces of the sherds. Exterior surfaces are plain.

Most of the analyzed specimens (n = 34) are body sherds with a mean thickness of 6.2 mm. The mean thickness of the seven base fragments is

8.9 mm. The five rim sherds have a mean thickness of 5.7 mm, and the two shoulder portions average 8.0 mm thick.

Ceramic sherds were recovered from the mound fill, the burned clay floor, below the burned clay floor, and within Feature 4. All of the base fragments were found near Feature 5. The sherds recovered within Feature 4 consist of body sherds, and the ceramics located on the house floor near Feature 1 are body and rim sherds. The six sherds scattered on the house floor are body sherds.

The analyzed ceramics from Bullock Mound are similar regardless of context and are consistent with Haag's (1940) description of Adena Plain, particularly examples of the type from the Middle Woodland period Riley Mound (Webb 1943). The Riley Mound ceramics exhibit the same color range, temper type, and surface treatment as the Bullock Mound ceramics.

LITHICS

The Bullock Mound chipped-stone and ground-stone lithic assemblage includes 28 artifacts: 11 projectile points and point fragments, 6 biface fragments, 4 flakes, 3 hafted scrapers, 1 chert adze, 1 unifacial scraper, 1 edge-modified bladelet, and 1 sandstone abrader.

Six complete projectile points are classified as Kirk Corner Notched (n = 1), Raddatz Side Notched (n = 1), McWhinney Heavy Stemmed (n = 3), and expanding stemmed (n = 1) forms. All of the Late Archaic McWhinney Heavy Stemmed points, which were produced from local Brannon chert, were reworked into hafted scrapers. Five biface fragments, three distal ends and two midsections, were also identified. Reanalysis of one point fragment originally catalogued as a midsection (specimen Wd/10-27) proved that the fragment was the stem of a projectile point or hafted biface. The specimen, produced from Boyle chert, exhibits well-ground excurvate margins, and both faces exhibit fine percussion and pressure flaking. The specimen was broken at the haft-blade juncture, where remnants of a single, thoroughly ground notch were observed. However, because of its fragmentary nature and lack of other diagnostic attributes, this specimen cannot be assigned to a specific temporal or cultural affiliation. Most of the chipped-stone specimens were produced from locally available Brannon or Boyle cherts, but one projectile point is made of a thermally altered quartzlike material, one projectile point is made of nonlocal Wyandotte chert, and the edge-modified bladelet is made of nonlocal Flint Ridge (Ohio) chert.

All points and biface fragments were recovered from mound fill. With the exception of the edge-modified bladelet, likely associated with the mound construction component, the remainder of the formal chipped-stone tools probably were scooped up from older deposits present at the site and mixed into the mound fill during construction.

COPPER

Seven small pieces of copper identified by Webb and Haag (1947) as sheet copper were recovered from the Bullock Mound. Copper is commonly found with Adena burials and cremations (Webb and Snow 1974:68) in the form of bracelets, rings, beads, gorgets, pendants, pins, crescents, and celts (Webb and Snow 1974:99–100). The Bullock Mound copper specimens, found in association with human bone fragments in Feature 4, are only a few millimeters in diameter. The small sizes of the copper fragments preclude functional assessment.

RED OCHRE

Feature 5 contained a small concentration of red ochre. Artifacts covered with red ochre were found at Ricketts Mound in Montgomery County and at Tarlton Mound in Fayette County (Webb and Snow 1974:74). Therefore, the red ochre from the Bullock Mound may be associated with the ceramics found near Feature 5; the sherds may have been painted or covered with the red ochre.

HUMAN REMAINS

Of the 26 highly fragmented, burned human bone elements recovered from the Bullock Mound, 22 fragments were calcined, and four were charred. Five pieces of bone originally classified as human appear to be weathered faunal remains. Transverse and longitudinal checking-warping on many of the human bones (n = 11) indicates the bones were "green" or covered with flesh when burned (Buikstra and Swegle 1989). Fourteen fragments of calcined bone and two fragments of charred bone were found on the basin floor of Feature 4 and designated Burial 1. The other human remains were found in small piles between Features 4 and 5. Although Webb and Haag (1947) reported finding burned human bones in four different "burials," and the remains were bagged as such, the original plan view of the submound structure shows only three unnumbered areas of bone (Figure 4.2).

Burial 1 contained the largest number of human bone fragments (n = 12)— a fragment of irregular bone, possibly a medial fragment of a clavicle; one very small, unidentifiable, unsidable rib fragment; one vertebral body fragment; one distal fragment of a humerus; one left third metacarpal; one fragment of irregular bone, probably os coxa; one right patella fragment; and five unidentifiable long bone shafts. Two tibia shaft fragments are charred; the other bone fragments from Burial 1 are calcined. Burial 2 is represented by three calcined bone elements, all of which are too fragmented for positive identification. Burial 3 consists of seven unidentified, calcined, long bone shaft fragments. Only a charred distal humerus fragment from Burial 4 was available for study.

The three calcined bone fragments from Burial 2 and the one charred bone fragment from Burial 4 were sent to the University of California-Davis for mitochondrial DNA testing on Early and Middle Woodland populations in Kentucky, Illinois, and Ohio (Mary Powell, personal communication 2000). Unfortunately, these samples do not seem to have enough mitochondrial DNA preserved in them for the analyses to be successful (Deborah Bolnick, personal communication 2004).

The burned human remains from Bullock Mound are so few and fragmentary, measuring less than 30 mm, that it is difficult to estimate the minimum number of individuals represented. With the assumption that only one individual is represented, this person was an adult, based on complete fusion of the proximal epiphysis of the left third metacarpal (Buikstra and Ubelaker 1994). The distal epiphysis is missing. The individual was gracile, based on the small size of the relatively well-preserved left third metacarpal, which is much smaller than a study skeleton of a small adult male. Therefore, this individual likely was a female (Zabecki 2001).

Discussion and Conclusion

The artifacts from the Bullock Mound were neither abundant nor elaborate, and no diagnostic Adena chipped-stone artifacts were found. All of the analyzed ceramic sherds, however, represent diagnostic Adena Plain pottery. The sherds are similar to Adena Plain ceramics from the Peter and Grimes villages in Fayette County (Figure 4.1). Clay (1983) argued that the Adena Plain ceramics in the Auvergne Mound, also located in central Kentucky (Figure 4.1), were used in mortuary processing, discarded on the peripheries of the site area, and eventually scooped up with soil and deposited over the central mound area.

The human remains and cultural features at the Bullock Mound indicate that the site served a mortuary function, minimally including the total cremation of at least one adult female, probably on the clay hardpan. Most of the human remains are calcined and highly fragmented. Copper artifacts may have been burned with the individual.

Webb and Snow (1974) asserted that most Adena people were cremated soon after death, the charred bones placed in unmarked graves under thin village middens. In contrast, burials of "high-status" individuals were characterized by extended burial in submound log-lined tombs or in circular, paired-post, submound structures (Webb and Snow 1974:172–173). With the Bullock Mound, however, Webb was faced with cremated remains in a rectangular, single-post, submound structure. Apparently, Webb was challenged with the problem of comparing Adena and Hopewell burial customs.

Using a repeatedly augmented trait list, Webb was content with pigeonholing Adena burial customs, but he could not determine precisely what was emblematic of Hopewell burial customs. At Ohio Hopewell sites such as Mound City and Tremper, cremation was used exclusively (Mills 1916, 1922). Most burials at the Edwin Harness Mound and Seip Mound 1 and Mound 2 were cremations, with only a small percentage extended (Greber 1991b). Ohio Hopewell burials were frequently associated with submound charnel houses, which served as mortuary-processing facilities and provided areas for burial (Brown 1979). The intermingling of Adena and Hopewell burial customs, even in Kentucky, should have signaled to Webb that the trait list approach was inherently flawed.

Clay (1998b) and Greber (1991b) concluded that, although Webb referred to Adena sites excavated in other states, his interpretations of Adena mounds were based exclusively on Kentucky excavations, which precipitated taxonomic problems. Although much of Webb's work was important in providing baseline data on the mounds of the Bluegrass region, it led to biased perceptions of Adena and the Woodland period. Adena populations were considered relatively sedentary, village dwelling, socially stratified, agriculturally based societies that existed during the Early Woodland period (Willey 1966). Consequently, the words "Adena" and "Early Woodland" became inextricably linked within the Middle Ohio Valley, particularly in Kentucky.

Intentionally or not, Webb chose to disregard the most intriguing aspect of the Bullock Mound, namely, the rectangular submound structure. Most Adena submound structures in Kentucky are circular, with posts set in pairs (Webb and Snow 1974:52). In fact, documentation of the paired-post pattern was one of Webb's contributions to Middle Ohio Valley archaeology (Clay 1998b). Though they are rare, rectilinear or rectangular submound patterns have been documented in Kentucky (Webb and Snow 1974:59). For example, the Middle Woodland Riley Mound (Webb 1943) covered a square-to-rectangular submound structure, possibly a charnel house, somewhat similar to the submound structure located below the Bullock Mound.

The Adena burial mounds and enclosures in the Bluegrass region, such as those in the Elkhorn Creek drainage, reflect increased complexity in ceremonial life during the Woodland period. Earthen mound sites, such as Drake and Tarlton mounds, and village sites, such as Fischer and Peter Village, represent Adena occupations (Clay 1987, 1989) dating to the Early or

Middle Woodland periods (Railey 1990, 1996). The Bullock Mound, however, is peculiar.

When Webb and Haag excavated the mound in 1947, they concluded that it was not Adena. The fact that they had uncovered a rectangular, single-post pattern, not a circular, paired-post one, seems to have been significant. Using a trait list approach, Webb and Haag had difficulty assigning a cultural affiliation to the Bullock Mound because the site contained traits that were both Adena (Adena Plain pottery) and Hopewell (rectangular submound structure, bladelet). Confined by the taxonomic trait list, Webb and Haag must have recognized that the Bullock Mound contained some of the ingredients to complete an Adena recipe; however, they may have concluded it was lacking the key ingredients—a circular, paired-post submound structure and vault burials. Perhaps as a consequence, the results of the Bullock Mound investigation went unresolved and unreported.

Dragoo (1963) suggested that resistance of Adena peoples south of the Ohio River explained the relative lack of evidence of Hopewell culture in this area. Analysis of the materials and field records from the Bullock Mound, however, suggests that it is a late Adena site reflecting interaction with Hopewellian groups originating north of the Ohio River. The rectangular structure beneath the mound, which may have served as a charnel house, represents variation in Woodland period mound use and construction. The Bullock Mound may also reflect the presence of more than one social group contemporaneously within the Bluegrass region during this time period. In any case, the Bullock Mound is unique among the earthen mounds of Kentucky's Bluegrass region and challenges our concept of Woodland period mound building cultures in the Middle Ohio Valley. Indeed, the Bullock Mound should be regarded as a physical manifestation of the taxonomic conundrum with which the archaeological community must continue to contend.

Acknowledgments

This chapter is dedicated to Joseph Michalski. Thanks to your enthusiasm and deep interest in the Adena people, the Bullock Mound was rediscovered, and professional archaeology was granted a second chance. Thanks, Joe; I will never forget you. I would also like to thank many individuals who were influential in the writing of this chapter. Without the ardent cooperation of David Thomson of Afalon Farm and Virginia Scott, the Bullock Mound reinvestigation could not have taken place. For generations, Mr. Thomson and his family have been wonderful stewards of the beautiful land on which the Bullock Mound is located. In addition, I would like to thank the new property owner, Rick Trontz of Hopewell Farm, for his sincere efforts to continue protecting the mound. I originally wrote this chapter for Dr. Richard Jefferies's independent study class at the University of Kentucky, and I deeply appreciate his professional guidance and wisdom. William Haag, David Pollack, Sissel Schroeder, Gwynn Henderson, Nancy O'Malley, and George Crothers provided valuable assistance and advice. Melissa Zabecki and Peter Killoran analyzed the skeletal material. Donna Gilbreath and Philip Mink prepared the figures. The Kentucky Organization of Professional Archaeologists and the Kentucky Archaeological Survey provided funding for the AMS radiocarbon analysis. Finally, I would like to thank Melanie Bradshaw for encouraging me to write.

5

Walker-Noe

An Early Middle Woodland Adena Mound in Central Kentucky

David Pollack, Eric J. Schlarb, William E. Sharp, and Teresa W. Tune

Located in Garrard County, Kentucky (Figure 5.1), the Walker-Noe Mound is part of a very large multicomponent site (15Gd56) (Paleoindian through Fort Ancient) that encompasses approximately 49.4 ha and is characterized by a high density of chipped-stone debris. The low ridge on which the mound is located, however, covers approximately 3.5 ha. This small burial mound is situated on the west side of Walker Branch, a small tributary of Paint Lick Creek, which empties into the Kentucky River approximately 23 km north of the site. The mound is located near the interface of the Inner Bluegrass, Outer Bluegrass, and Knobs physiographic regions (McGrain and Currens 1978).

Excavation and subsequent examination of the materials recovered from the mound caused us to question whether the Walker-Noe Mound should be regarded as an Adena site. The artifacts are clearly similar to the ceramics and chipped-stone tools recovered from other Kentucky Adena sites. On the other hand, the internal structure of this mound, consisting of a central burned area and associated cremations, is very different from classic central Kentucky "Adena" mounds, which are characterized by submound structures, extended inhumations, and log crypts. Furthermore, unlike most Kentucky Adena mounds, which tend to be positioned on topographically prominent landforms, the Walker-Noe Mound is located on a low ridge from which the higher elevations of nearby ridge tops and knobs are visible. In attempting to determine the cultural affiliation of the Walker-Noe Mound, we thus found ourselves confronting some of our notions of what is, or is not, Adena. This led us to wonder whether "Adena" is still a viable classificatory term, whether archaeologists working in the Middle Ohio Valley should continue to use it, and, if so, whether the concept should be used somewhat differently than in the past. This chapter summarizes the work conducted at the Walker-Noe Mound, describes the mound and the materials recovered, and assesses the site within the context of Adena mortuary practices in the Bluegrass region of Kentucky. We will note here that

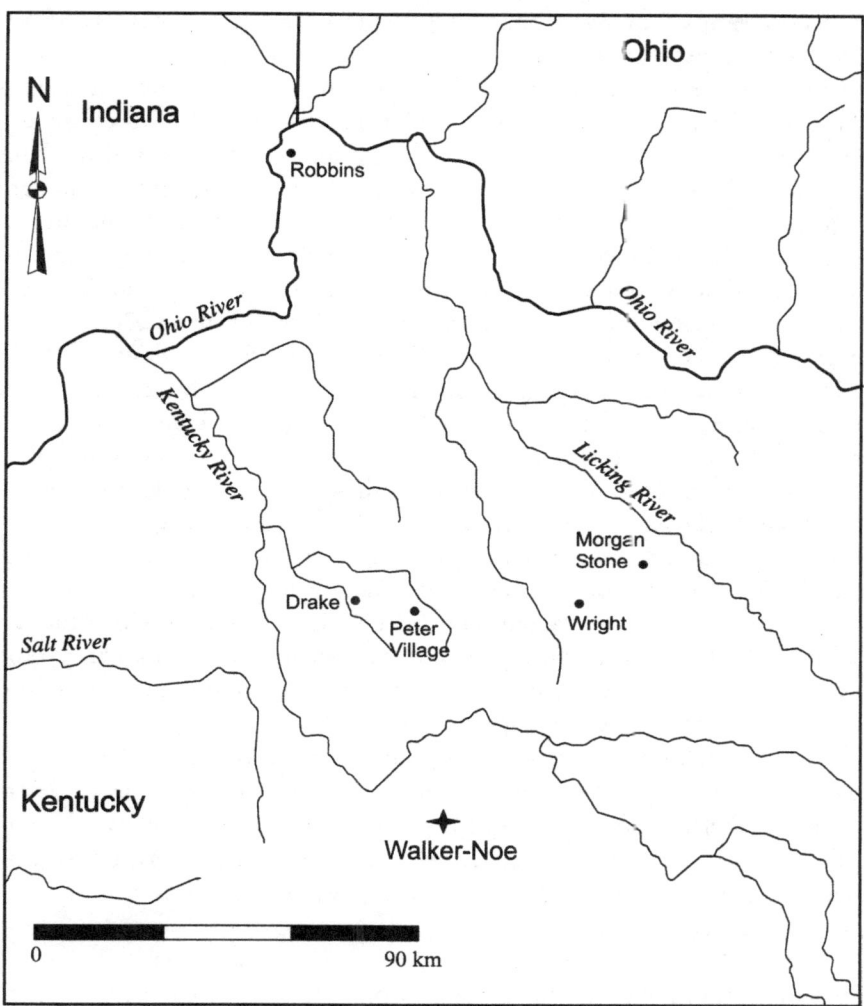

Figure 5.1. Location of Walker-Noe and some related sites.

research on the materials recovered from this site is ongoing and that, as the results of new analyses are incorporated into this study, some of our interpretations of the site may change.

Field Investigations and Site Description

In the fall of 2000, the Kentucky Archaeological Survey conducted excavations at what eventually proved to be a small earthen mound. A landowner plowing a pasture that had not been cultivated in many years uncovered a concentration of calcined bone, prehistoric pottery, and ovate-stemmed projectile points in a very restricted area. Recognizing the significance of this find, he contacted avocational archaeologists, who, after limited investigations on their own, contacted professional archaeologists. This eventually led to the more extensive excavation of the exposed feature. On the basis of this work archaeologists determined that the feature, originally thought to be a small mortuary facility, was actually part of a small, low mound.

During the field investigations, materials were collected in 1 × 1 m units. The plow zone was removed initially in 10-cm arbitrary levels, but later was excavated as one 20 to 25 cm level. Subsequent levels of intact deposits were excavated in 5 or 10 cm increments. The soil, except for the plow zone from select units along the edge of the mound, was screened through 6.35 mm mesh. Flotation and radiocarbon samples were collected from all features and bone concentrations. A plan view of the mound at the base of the plow zone was drawn (Figure 5.2), as were north-south and east-west profiles of the mound. The excavation encompassed 42 m^2 and included about 65 percent of the mound, with only the outer edges of the mound being unexcavated. The diameter of the mound was determined to be approximately 10 m, and the height was about 30 to 40 cm. The degree to which the site stratigraphy (and hence, mound height) was deflated due to plowing could not be determined, but there is no evidence to indicate that the mound had ever been a prominent landscape feature.

In addition to the units placed within the mound, four 1 × 1 m units were excavated 20 m from the mound in the cardinal directions to determine whether the large amount of debitage from the mound plow zone and sub–plow zone deposits was related to processing of the cremations or earlier or later lithic reduction activities. Sub–plow zone deposits were not discovered in any of these units.

Within the mound, removal of the plow zone revealed a centrally located area of burned, red clay loam that encompassed approximately 1.25 m^2 (Figure 5.2). The central burned area, which had an average thickness of 5 cm, contained a large amount of fire-cracked dolostone—a sedimentary rock associated with the Boyle Dolomite Formation, which outcrops near the mound (Anderson 1994; Weir 1969). Surrounding the central burned area was a 5 to 10 cm-thick zone of dark reddish-brown clay loam that encompassed roughly 7.5 m^2. This area also contained a large amount of fire-cracked rock, but somewhat less than was observed in the central burned area. The rest of the mound fill consisted of a 10-cm-thick zone of dark brown silty clay loam. The exposed portion of this zone covered about 27.5 m^2. Smaller amounts of fire-cracked dolostone were associated with this zone compared to the other two zones. In some places, a relict A soil

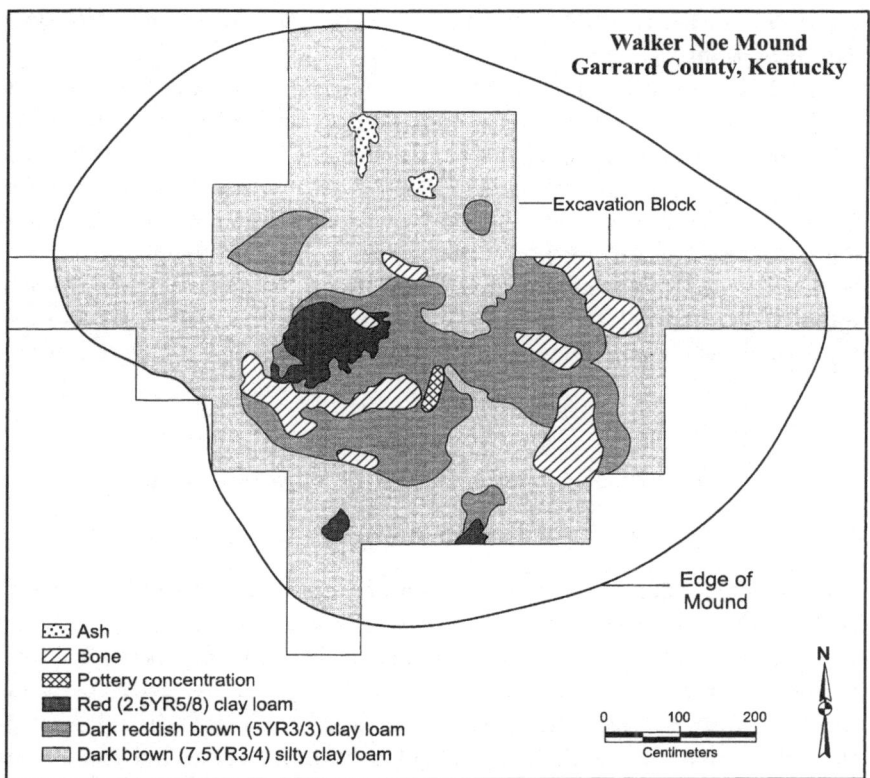

Figure 5.2. Plan view of Walker-Noe Mound.

horizon represented by an olive brown silty clay was documented below the intact sub–plow zone mound deposits; below this zone was a dark yellowish brown subsoil. In other areas the relict A soil horizon was absent, and the mound deposits directly overlaid the subsoil.

A large amount of cremated human bone was recovered from the plow zone directly above the central burned area. Below the plow zone, pockets of ash and bone were observed on the central burned area, and concentrations of calcined bone were documented along the edges of this area and in other parts of the mound (Figure 5.2). Although some charcoal and ash were associated with these bone concentrations, fire-reddened soil that suggests in situ burning, similar to that in the centrally located burned area, was not associated with these deposits. Charcoal from two of the bone concentrations yielded calibrated (CALIB 4.3; Stuiver and Pearson 1993) radiocarbon dates of cal 50 B.C. (cal A.D. 10) A.D. 70 (2000 ± 60 B.P.; Beta-152838) and cal 50 B.C. (cal A.D. 20) A.D. 70 (1990 ± 60 B.P.; Beta-152839) at two standard deviations.

About 15 cm to the east of the central burned area was a large pit containing densely packed burned dolostone. Encountered at the base of the intact mound deposits, the pit had a diameter of 80 cm and extended to a depth of 36 cm below the mound floor into sterile subsoil. Only a few flakes were found in the pit fill, suggesting that the feature was not used to process human remains or for cooking. Its function is problematic.

No other pits were documented within the mound, nor were post holes, submound structures, extended or flexed inhumations or log crypts, all typically associated with Adena mounds in Kentucky.

Artifact Assemblage, Botanical Assemblage, and Human Remains

Ceramics

A total of 2,393 ceramic sherds was recovered from the Walker-Noe Mound (plow zone and intact mound deposits). Of these, body sherds larger than 4 cm^2 and all rim sherds were analyzed (n = 249, 10.4 percent; cross-mended sherds were counted as one sherd). Most (n = 240) are plain-surfaced, limestone-tempered sherds consistent with Haag's (1940) description of Adena Plain, which was based on pottery recovered from three central Kentucky mounds: the Morgan Stone Mound in Bath County and two of the Wright mounds in Montgomery County (Haag 1940:75–79, 1941:266).

The Adena Plain sherds represent a minimum of three vessels. The paste was tempered with finely crushed (1 to 4 mm) particles of limestone temper, much of which has been leached, leaving angular voids. Surfaces are plain or well smoothed. Typical sherd color is reddish to orange-brown. Mean thickness of the body sherds is 7.1 mm, slightly thinner than the published average of 8 to 9 mm reported by Haag (1940).

Consistent with Haag's (1940:75–79) original type description, the Adena Plain vessels from Walker-Noe are best classified as jars with slightly restricted necks and gently outflaring rims. Two of the eight rims thin toward the lip, and the rims have a mean thickness of 9.5 mm. Lips are generally rounded, but some exhibit slight flattening. Orifice diameters range from 14 to 18 cm. One basal sherd suggests a vessel with a slightly rounded bottom. A small node is located 15 mm below the lip of one of the rim sherds. The noded rim is part of a vessel found near the centrally located burned area. This vessel is similar to noded vessels found at the Morgan Stone Mound

(Haag 1941) and the larger of the two Wright mounds (O'Malley 1988:46–62). Thus, the three sites appear to be roughly contemporary.

Of the remaining nine analyzed sherds, one is classified as Wright Check Stamped (Haag 1942b); on the basis of the association of Wright Check Stamped with Adena Plain at sites such as the Wright mounds (Haag 1940), it is probably contemporary with the Adena Plain pottery from Walker-Noe. This sherd was recovered from the plow zone. Another sherd is a limestone-tempered, cordmarked body sherd recovered from the plow zone. It also may be associated with the Adena Plain pottery, but it is somewhat thinner (thickness of 6.0 mm) than the Adena Plain sherds and could postdate the mound. Six specimens are grit-tempered, cordmarked body sherds (mean thickness of 11.8 mm); a grit-tempered, cordmarked rim sherd (thickness of 11.4 mm) has a flat lip and an estimated orifice diameter of 18 cm. These sherds do not resemble Fayette Thick (Griffin 1943a; O'Malley, Tune, and Blustain 1983; Tune 1985), because they are thinner (11.6 vs. 13.5 mm) and differ in temper (grit vs. chert). The thick grit-tempered cordmarked sherds were recovered from similar contexts as the Adena Plain ceramics (plow zone and intact mound deposits), and they may represent a minor Adena ceramic type. However, it is also quite possible that they predate the construction of the Walker-Noe Mound.

Chipped-Stone Tools and Debitage

Adena Stemmed projectile points or point fragments (n = 17) (Cambron and Hulse 1969; Justice 1987; Webb and Baby 1957) account for most of the points recovered from the Walker-Noe Mound. These points range in length from 47.6 to 91.6 mm and were manufactured from Boyle (n = 7), Muldraugh (n = 7), or Crab Orchard (n = 3) cherts. Most were recovered from the plow zone, but a few (n = 3) were associated with the intact mound deposits.

The presence of Adena Stemmed points produced from local Boyle and Crab Orchard chert types, coupled with the large amount of chert debitage (see below), suggests that the points were produced on site. At Peter Village, located north of Walker-Noe in Fayette County, Kentucky (Figure 5.1), Clay (1985, 1987) concluded that Adena Stemmed points of Boyle chert were brought to the site in their finished form, because only a small amount of Boyle debitage was recovered at this site.

Two of the Adena Stemmed points manufactured from Boyle chert are heat damaged, suggesting they were placed with a cremated individual. Six of the seven Adena Stemmed points produced from Boyle chert exhibit no evidence of use-wear and, therefore, may have been produced specifically as burial inclusions. In contrast, the points manufactured from Crab Orchard chert exhibit extensive use through resharpening and probably represent tools used for daily activities.

Adena Stemmed points manufactured from Muldraugh chert, which outcrops about 60 km from the site (Ray 2000), were probably brought to the site as finished products, because no Muldraugh debitage was recovered. Like the points produced from Crab Orchard chert, those of Muldraugh chert were used and resharpened and likely represent tools used for daily activities.

One *affinis* Snyders (Justice 1987:201–203; Winters 1963) point produced from an unidentified gray chert and one bladelet of Boyle chert were recovered from mound fill directly beneath the plow zone. In addition, two bladelets and one bladelike flake also manufactured from Boyle chert were recovered from the plow zone. The recovery of the Snyders point from intact mound deposits suggests that it does not postdate the mound and in all likelihood is contemporary with the Adena Stemmed projectile points recovered from the mound. Because prismatic bladelets are often associated with Middle Woodland components in the Middle Ohio Valley, these artifacts are also considered to be associated with the mound.

Two Late Archaic stemmed projectile points and one Early Archaic Hardin-like point (Justice 1987) were found in the plow zone above the intact mound deposits, and one Early Archaic Kirk Corner Notched point (Justice 1987) was recovered from the relict A soil horizon beneath the mound. These points predate construction of the mound; no Archaic features were identified at Walker-Noe.

Of the more than 61,000 pieces of debitage and other chipped-stone tools, such as early stage bifaces and biface fragments, unifacial tools, and edge-modified flakes recovered from the Walker-Noe Mound, the overwhelming majority was produced from Boyle chert. These materials were recovered from plow zone and intact mound deposits. Off-mound units also produced considerable Boyle chert debitage. Crab Orchard chert is also well represented in the debitage and tool assemblage from all units (plow zone and sub–plow zone deposits). Both Boyle and Crab Orchard outcrop in abundance within the 3.5 ha low ridge the mound is associated with. In addition, Walker Branch, which is situated 60 m from the site's northeast corner, contains a secondary source of Boyle chert, which has eroded from its parent rock (Weir 1969).

The large quantities of debitage and other chipped-stone tools recovered from mound and off-mound contexts at Walker-Noe as well as from several nearby sites are consistent with the reduction of chert cores to produce finished tools or preforms (Schlarb and Lane 1999). The recovery of Archaic points from the site suggests that some of these activities predate construction of the mound. On the basis of the large amount of debitage and other chipped-stone tools recovered from the off-mound units and observed on the surface of the site, the recovery of similar materials from plow zone and sub–plow zone mound deposits suggests that most of these materials were not used in the processing of the Walker-Noe Mound cremations. These materials probably were incorporated into the mound fill during construction of the mound.

Fire-Cracked Rock

Dolostone was the only fire-cracked rock recovered from the mound. A total of 150 kg of dolostone were recovered from the mound, most (122 kg) from the intact sub–plow zone mound deposits. Fire-cracked rock is not abundant on the surface of the mound or in the off-mound units. The association of the fire-cracked rock with the central burned area suggests that the dolostone was used in the processing of the cremations.

Other Artifacts

Other objects associated with the mound are three fragments of groundstone axes or celts manufactured from nonlocal granitic rocks; two hemispheres produced from hematite and limestone; a sandstone abrader; and a polished limestone gorget. All were recovered from the plow zone. A sandstone pipe fragment that has an incised cross-hatch design on the exterior surface was also recovered from the plow zone. It was too fragmentary to assign to a pipe type. Three small copper beads were found with one of the human bone concentrations.

Human Remains

A minimum of 17 individuals were recovered from the Walker-Noe Mound, with infants, adolescents, and adults being present in the burial population. Both fleshed and defleshed individuals were cremated at the site, with most of the individuals being fleshed. Curved transverse cracks on long bone shaft fragments suggest fleshed or incompletely defleshed individuals. Longitudinal fractures characteristic of dry bone burning occur infrequently.

Botanical Remains

Analysis of 25 botanical samples, representing 139 liters of soil, resulted in the recovery of a large amount of carbonized food remains in association with sub–plow zone concentrations of cremated human remains. The samples include a variety of native starchy and oily seed cultigens, including erect knotweed (*Polygonum erectum*, n = 225), chenopod (*Chenopodium berlandieri*, n = 161), maygrass (*Phalaris caroliniana*, n = 84), sunflower (*Helian-

thus sp., n = 15), and marshelder (*Iva annua,* n = 3). Wild plant foods include sumac (*Rhus* sp.), grape (*Vitis* sp.), persimmon (*Diospyros virginiana*), honey locust pod (*Gleditsia triacanthos*), and blackberry (*Rubus* sp.). Small amounts of hickory (*Carya* sp.), black walnut (*Juglans nigra*), butternut (*Juglans cinerea*), pecan (*Carya illinoiensis*), and acorn (*Quercus* sp.) nutshell were also recovered. The presence of cultigens, fleshy fruit and berry seeds, and nutshell points to the consumption of food in conjunction with the mortuary ceremonies that took place at Walker-Noe. A varied wood charcoal assemblage, including 11 species, is dominated by black walnut wood (48.9 percent of wood by frequency). Walnut is usually just a minor tertiary species in central Kentucky collections (Rossen 1991). Its importance at Walker-Noe suggests that walnut was the primary wood type selected for use in cremations.

Discussion

Walker-Noe is a small, low mound that was constructed over a central burned area in which individuals were cremated prior to interment along the mound peripheries. The final cremations seem to have been left on the floor of the centrally located burned area. The mound fill contained a large amount of fire-cracked rock that was used in the processing of the human remains. Some Adena Stemmed points may have been placed with the dead during the cremation process, and Adena Plain pottery vessels may have been used in conjunction with mortuary rituals. The nuts and native and nonnative cultigens found with cremations along the edge of the central burned area suggest that the rituals may have involved the consumption of food. Radiocarbon dates place the mound in the Middle Woodland period, which in Kentucky is dated from 200 B.C. to A.D. 500 (Railey 1990, 1996).

In attempting a cultural classification of the Walker-Noe site, we recognize that archaeologists working in the Middle Ohio Valley have inherited Woodland taxonomic units that were developed before the advent of absolute dating techniques. Cultural classification tended to rely on mound or other earthwork forms, methods of construction, and, to a lesser extent, artifact differences to characterize cultural developments (Greenman 1932; Mills 1901–1902; Thomas 1894; Webb and Snow 1945). With the lack of a well-defined temporal framework, there was a tendency to fit all variation into two "mound-building cultures" that, by the 1950s, had become the archaeology of either Early Woodland Adena or Middle Woodland Hopewell (Willey 1966:268).

Many Kentucky archaeologists now recognize that Adena in Kentucky is primarily a Middle Woodland phenomenon (Railey 1990, 1996) and that it is at least partially contemporary with Hopewellian occupations in Ohio and elsewhere. This contemporaneity has created taxonomic problems when comparing the cultural developments of mound-building cultures in Kentucky and Ohio, because Adena is considered to be a strictly Early Woodland development in Ohio (Seeman 1986). The radiocarbon dates from Walker-Noe contribute to this debate by placing Adena Plain ceramics in the Bluegrass region firmly in the accepted Middle Woodland time period. The association of this ceramic type with an *affinis* Snyders projectile point also suggests contemporaneity with Hopewellian occupations in Ohio.

Research conducted at the Walker-Noe Mound raises other taxonomic questions related to what should be classified as Adena. Although the association of Adena Stemmed points and Adena Plain pottery in the mound suggest it should be classified as an Adena site, the internal structure of the mound differs from the traditional pattern. Walker-Noe lacks a submound structure with circular paired-post patterns, a defining characteristic of Adena mounds (Funkhouser and Webb 1935; Webb 1940; Webb and Snow 1945). Nor does it contain primary extended inhumations in pits or log tombs, and unlike Adena mounds that were often used over an extended period of time and grew quite large through successive burial of additional individuals (Milner and Jefferies 1987), the Walker-Noe Mound seems to have been used for just a short period of time. Support for this suggestion comes from the almost identical radiocarbon dates obtained from different areas within the mound. Finally, unlike most reported Adena mounds, the Walker-Noe Mound is not located on a prominent ridge top, but rather is associated with a low ridge. Even on this low ridge the mound does not occupy a highly visual place on the natural landscape. Thus, solely on the basis of attributes of mound construction and location, the Walker-Noe Mound should not be considered Adena.

Walker-Noe does, however, share with several other Adena mounds one important attribute, namely, the presence of cremated human remains. Cremated remains have been found in several Kentucky Adena mounds, such as the Morgan Stone Mound, the Drake and Fisher mounds in Fayette County, the smaller of the two Wright mounds and the Ricketts Mound in Montgomery County, and the Robbins Mound in Boone County (Webb 1940, 1941a, 1941b; Webb and Elliott 1942; Webb and Haag 1947). At these sites, cremations were primarily restricted to the mound floor or lowest levels of the mound. Almost all of these were interpreted as representing off-mound cremations, with the cremated remains subsequently being interred within a mound (Webb and Snow 1945). An exception to this pattern may be the cremated remains recovered from the Robbins Mound, because Webb and Elliott (1942:489), on the basis of the presence of an area of burned clay in the center of this structure, raised the possibility that some of the remains were cremated within the submound structure associated with this mound. The Robbins example comes closest to matching the cremation pattern at Walker-Noe, where it seems that all of the cremated remains were processed on the mound floor. On the other hand, Robbins differs from Walker-Noe in that most of the individuals buried at Robbins were not cremated. Thus, whereas at Robbins and most Adena mounds cremation was one of several ways the dead were treated, at Walker-Noe it was the *only* burial treatment observed. As such, Walker-Noe can be viewed as a crematorium or charnel facility.

Although the Walker-Noe Mound exhibits attributes that distinguish it from other Adena mounds, on the basis of the presence of the Adena Plain ceramics, Adena Stemmed points, and cremations, we consider the Walker-Noe Mound to be an Adena mortuary facility. We recognize, however, that Adena in the Bluegrass region is characterized by variability in mound use and construction. Clay (1991a, 1998b, this volume) has commented on this variability, leading him to suggest that Adena is no longer a viable or useful archaeological construct. Unlike Clay, we argue that chronological and/or intraregional or interregional spatial variation in how the dead were treated during the Middle Woodland period does not undermine the concept of Adena. Rather, it points to a need to refine what is meant by "Adena" and to account for the variability observed in the archaeological record when interpreting Middle Woodland mortuary practices.

Recognition of this variability also leads us to suggest that researchers focus their efforts at the regional level before looking for commonalities that link all Adena sites over an area as broad as the entire Middle Ohio Valley. Kentucky Adena may best be viewed as consisting of several small-scale tribal societies (Creamer and Haas 1985; Gregg 1991; Sahlins 1968) that were characterized by differences in how the dead were treated. Not only may there have been interregional differences, but within each society individuals may have been treated differently on the basis of their status. Therefore we should not expect that all mortuary sites yielding Adena Plain pottery and Adena Stemmed projectile points were constructed in the same manner and served similar functions. Variability likely characterized Adena burial practices. Sites such as Walker-Noe exemplify this variability and remind us that within Middle Woodland societies not all individuals were treated in the same manner at death.

Conclusions

Walker-Noe is a small burial mound that contains only cremations. It may have been used only once or for a few seasons or years about two thousand years ago. It differs from most Adena mounds in the Kentucky Bluegrass, which were used for extended periods of time and primarily included extended inhumations in pits and log crypts. The lack of accretionary extended inhumations and the reliance on cremation at Walker-Noe reflect variability in Middle Woodland mortuary practices and mound construction in Kentucky. This site also provides us with a caution against relying too heavily on a trait-list approach to defining what is and what is not "Adena." If a strict trait-list approach is applied to the Walker-Noe Mound, we would not classify it as Adena. We believe, however, that such an approach hampers efforts to understand Middle Woodland mortuary practices and ceremonialism.

To gain a better understanding of Middle Woodland mortuary practices, we should consider Adena a dynamic cultural expression, one characterized by variability in mortuary treatment. As we allow for intraregional and interregional variation in Middle Woodland treatment of the dead, we will begin to develop better models of Middle Woodland lifeways and interaction networks. Although Walker-Noe may be an isolated example restricted to the southern Bluegrass region, we suspect that sites such as Walker-Noe were once ubiquitous across the landscape. Because of their low archaeological visibility, they have either gone unnoticed by the archaeological community or have been destroyed by plowing. Although the Walker-Noe Mound does not occupy a prominent visual place on the natural landscape, it undoubtedly constituted an important place on the cultural landscape of Middle Woodland households occupying the southern Bluegrass region of Kentucky.

Acknowledgments

We would like to thank Roy Noe, the owner of the Walker-Noe Mound, for making archaeologists aware of the site and for supporting the archaeological investigations undertaken at this site. We would also like to thank Rick Matchette and Jeff Georgiady for making the materials available to us that they recovered from the site. Rick also was an active participant in the field investigations. The botanical remains were analyzed by Jack Rossen of Ithaca College, and the human skeletal remains were analyzed by Nick Hermann of the University of Tennessee. We would also like to thank A. Gwynn Henderson for her constructive editorial comments, Donna Gilbreath for drafting Figure 5.2, and the many individuals who assisted in the fieldwork and processing of the recovered materials.

6

Middle Woodland Ritualism in the Central Bluegrass

Evidence from the Amburgey Site, Montgomery County, Kentucky

Michael D. Richmond and Jonathan P. Kerr

Archaeological investigations at the Amburgey site (15Mm137) in east-central Kentucky (Figure 6.1) documented a deflated, multicomponent site dating from the Early Archaic through Historic periods. Despite erosion and historic disturbance, the site retained a partially intact Middle Woodland component, the focus of this chapter. The Middle Woodland component was marked by an oval arrangement of post molds associated with at least two features of a ritualistic nature: one ceremonial offering of a Connestee Series tetrapodal vessel and copper ear spools and one thermal pit, possibly used for feasting, a ritual offering, or both, that yielded a copper celt.

The Middle Woodland occupation at Amburgey is important on a number of levels. First, the ear spools represent only the second documented case of these typically Hopewellian artifacts in Kentucky (Katherine Ruhl, personal communication 2001). Second, the site has the markings (e.g., copper artifacts, an imported vessel, an oval arrangement of post molds, thermal features) of a Middle Woodland mortuary facility, yet no inhumations were found. This discrepancy may, however, be attributed to historic disturbance, as will be discussed below. Third, although the site seems to have served a ritual function, it lacks an overlying mound. Finally, the Amburgey site seems to contain elements of the traditional taxonomic unit of Hopewell, not Adena, but is not easily placed within either.

This chapter provides a description of the Middle Woodland component at the Amburgey site, with special consideration given to site structure and function. It is hoped that this discussion will highlight the taxonomic inadequacies of the Middle Woodland period in central and eastern Kentucky and show how these shortcomings contribute to taxonomic inconsistencies in the Middle Ohio Valley as a whole.

Middle Woodland Ritualism / 77

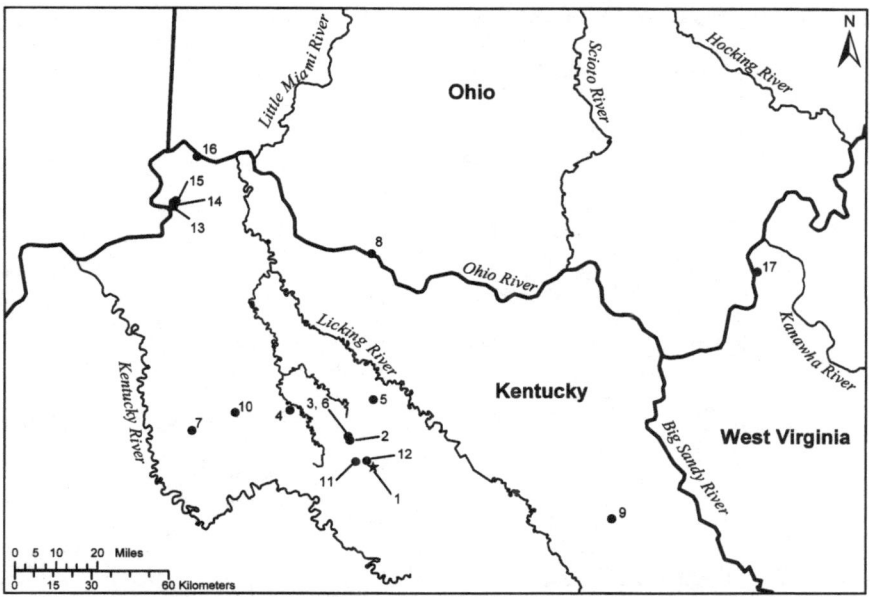

Figure 6.1. Map of the Middle Ohio Valley showing location of the Amburgey site and select Middle Woodland ritual sites. 1, Amburgey; 2, Gaitskill Mound; 3, Green Mound; 4, Auvergne Mound; 5, Morgan Stone Mound; 6, Wright Mound; 7, Bullock Mound; 8, Dover Mound; 9, C & O Mound; 10, Mt. Horeb; 11, Ricketts Mound; 12, Camargo Earthworks; 13, Robbins Mound; 14, Landing Mound; 15, Riley Mound; 16, Crigler Mound; 17, Niebert.

Site Description and Excavation History

The Amburgey site is located on a high ridge in Montgomery County, Kentucky, near the boundary between the Knobs and the Eastern Coalfield physiographic regions. The Knobs are characterized by narrow, rolling-to-hilly ridges that are highly dissected with a dendritic drainage pattern. The Eastern Coalfield region is mountainous and deeply dissected, with steep hillsides, narrow upland ridges, and narrow floodplains (Froedge 1986). The open-air site is situated above Sycamore Creek at an elevation of 274 m above mean sea level. The upland bedrock is Middle and Upper Devonian New Albany shale formations, adjacent slopes are underlain by Devonian-aged Boyle Dolomite, and Sycamore Creek floodplain deposits consist of Quaternary-aged silt, clay, sand, and gravel alluvium (McDowell 1978; Weir 1976).

The Amburgey site was first identified during a cultural resource man-

Table 6.1. Artifacts recovered from features at the Amburgey site

Feature	Unmodified Lithics[a]	Modified Lithics	Ceramics	Floral and Faunal	Other
1	232.5 g	65 flakes	None	7.8 g wood charcoal 23 carbonized seeds	None
2[b]	14.2 g	4 flakes	1 vessel	0.1 g wood charcoal	None
2[c]	17.8 g	3 flakes	None	0.1 g wood charcoal 11 carbonized seeds	2 copper ear spools
4	863.0 g	35 flakes	None	15.6 g wood charcoal 7 carbonized seeds	None
5	13,500.0 g	392 flakes 2 bifaces	None	20.0 g wood charcoal 51 carbonized seeds 24 carbonized nutshell 639 calcined bone fragments	Copper Celt

[a]Quartz gravels and residual chert; [b]vessel fill; [c]below vessel.

agement survey (Stallings and Ross-Stallings 1996). These investigations, which involved pedestrian survey and shovel testing, uncovered a dense scatter of lithic debitage restricted to the shallow plow zone. The estimated site area covered approximately 2,345 m^2 and encompassed the entire ridge top. Although no temporally diagnostic artifacts were recovered, the site was recommended for a National Register of Historic Places evaluation.

This evaluation incorporated additional shovel testing, hand excavation of test units, mechanical removal of plow zone, and feature excavation (Bybee and Richmond 2003; Richmond 2000). Prehistoric cultural materials recovered from shovel tests and test units indicated the site dated from the Early Archaic through Late Prehistoric periods. Most artifacts were restricted to the plow zone and reflected a mixed assemblage. Mechanical stripping revealed four prehistoric features (Table 6.1), an oval arrangement of 11 post molds with 1 to 2 center post molds, and 17 historic graves concentrated in the northeastern portion of the site near the terminus of the linear ridge (Figure 6.2). These features intruded directly into sterile, B-horizon sediments and were partially truncated by historic plowing. The historic graves may have destroyed a significant portion of the Middle Woodland component. Of the four features, Feature 1 was of indeterminate age and cultural affiliation, and Feature 4 was radiocarbon dated to the Late Archaic period. Features 2 and 5 were dated to the Middle Woodland

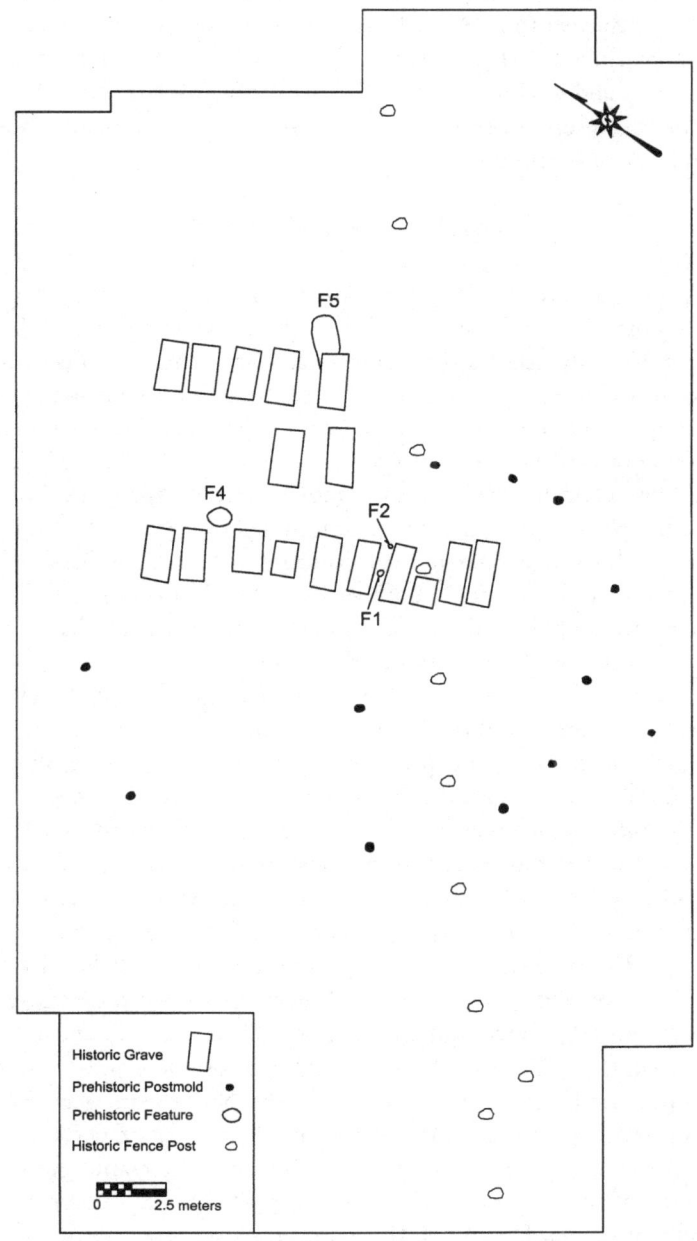

Figure 6.2. Plan view of the Middle Woodland component at the Amburgey site, showing features, post molds, and historic graves.

period on the basis of diagnostic artifacts and radiocarbon dates; the post molds were assumed to be Middle Woodland in age on the basis of association with Features 2 and 5 and their context (associated with Middle Woodland features) and oval arrangement. A soil anomaly was initially classified as Feature 3; closer inspection, however, revealed the anomaly was a root mold and not of cultural origin.

Middle Woodland Features

Eleven post molds formed an oval pattern measuring 17.5 m × 12 m, the northern portion of which was disturbed by the historic burials (Figure 6.2). They may represent a temporary structure or screen. The post molds were delimited as circular soil stains at the Ap/B-horizon interface. They averaged approximately 20 cm in diameter, contained brown silt loam fill, and extended to an average depth of 21.2 cm into the yellow silty clay loam subsoil. The vertically oriented post molds were divided into two classes: those with tapered sides and tapered or rounded bottoms (n = 8, 67 percent) and those with straight sides and flat bottoms (n = 4, 33 percent). A 26-liter sample of fill from four post molds produced carbonized seeds of purslane (*Portulaca oleracea*) and oxalis (*Oxalis stricta*), plants that could have been used as food or medicine (Martin and Barkley 2000).

There was at least one central post mold inside the oval enclosed area (Figure 6.2). It was slightly larger in diameter than the 12 post molds around the periphery. This central post exhibited a tapered profile and extended 39 cm into the subsoil. Although not definitively associated with the Middle Woodland occupation, on the basis of its form and location, Feature 1 may represent another interior post. It was similar in size and shape to the other central post mold. This feature extended 19 cm below the plow zone and was basin shaped, which was dissimilar to the tapered- or straight-sided posts. Feature 1 contained chipped-stone flakes, wood charcoal, and carbonized seeds of dock (*Rumex* sp.), goosefoot (*Chenopodium* sp.), knotweed (*Polygonum* sp.), marsh elder (*Iva* cf. *xanthifolia*), and purslane (*Portulaca oleracea*) (Table 6.1). Marsh elder, goosefoot, and knotweed are well-documented native cultigens in eastern North America (Asch et al. 1972; Smith 1992); however, given the small number of carbonized seeds recovered (n = 8), these remains probably represent plants growing wild near the site. It was not possible to determine whether the remains of goosefoot represented wild or domesticated species because the maximum external diameters between wild and domesticated varieties overlap (Smith 1992). These remains averaged 1.25 × 1.1 × 0.5 mm (L × W × H) (n = 8) and did not seem to have truncated margins, as is typical of domesticated varieties.

Two additional Middle Woodland features, Features 2 and 5, were associated with the oval mold hole pattern. Located within the oval, Feature 2 was identified at the base of the plow zone as a faint circular stain of brown silt loam encircling the partial rim of a ceramic vessel. The feature was 18 cm in diameter and extended from the base of the plow zone to a depth of 8 cm. Feature 2 was located between two historic graves but was not impacted by their construction (Figure 6.2).

Feature 2 contained a fragmented tetrapodal pottery vessel, two copper ear spools, a small number of chipped-stone flakes, and a small amount of wood charcoal (Table 6.1; Figure 6.3). The jar was likely intact when placed in the pit. At the time of recovery, the vessel was broken but retained its original shape. Several upper sherds had broken and slumped into the feature fill. The copper ear spools were found under the base of the vessel. One ear spool was nearly complete, whereas the second was severely corroded by post-depositional processes and was quite fragmentary. Both specimens were completely encrusted with feature fill. A sample of cordage removed from the fragmentary ear spool submitted for radiometric dating yielded an uncalibrated date of 1890 ± 40 B.P. (Beta-158296). The two-sigma calibrated date is cal A.D. 40 (110) 230.

No botanical remains were recovered from feature fill within the pottery vessel. The fill directly below the vessel, however, contained carbonized seeds of squash (*Cucurbita* sp.), goosefoot (*Chenopodium* sp.), bedstraw (*Galium trifidum*), purslane (*Portulaca oleracea*), and sticky catchfly (*Silene antirrhina*) (Table 6.1). Species of the genera *Silene* and *Galium* are recorded ethnographically as having a number of medicinal uses; the latter was also used for incense and fragrance (Moerman 1998).

Because the pit seems to have been excavated solely for the deposition of the artifacts, Feature 2 was classified as an artifact cache, probably associated with ritual activity.

Feature 5 was a large pit uncovered about 4 m northeast of the oval post mold pattern (Figure 6.2). The southern portion was truncated by a historic grave, which was excavated directly into the feature, removing approximately 15 percent of the feature fill. Feature 5 was only 13 cm deep, from approximately 31 to 44 cm below surface; it may have been truncated by historic plowing activities. It was oval in plan view, measuring approximately 2 m × 1 m. The walls tapered inward slightly, and the base was flat. Although historic disturbances partially obscured its morphology, Feature 5 probably was basin shaped in profile.

Figure 6.3. Middle Woodland artifacts recovered from the Amburgey site (clockwise from upper left): Two views of ear spool (top far left); cordage (top center); fragments of ear spool (top far right); Connestee Series vessel (bottom right); both faces of copper celt (bottom left).

Feature fill consisted of black sandy loam with a heavy concentration of charcoal and diffuse mica flecking. The periphery of the feature consisted of an oxidized ring of yellowish brown sandy clay loam mottled 40 percent with black silt loam. This burned lens was approximately 2 to 4 cm thick.

The feature contained approximately 13.5 kg of sandstone and quartz pebbles, many of which were thermally altered. Other artifacts recovered from Feature 5 include a copper celt, a ground-stone celt, a hafted biface resembling the Snyders type (Justice 1987), a broken biface, and chipped-stone flakes (Table 6.1; Figure 6.3). Most of the lithic debitage was thermally altered.

More than 600 calcined bone fragments were recovered from a 60-liter soil sample (Table 6.1). White-tailed deer and a large tooth from the Canidae family are represented, as well as medium bird, large mammal, indeterminate mammal, and indeterminate vertebrate. The Canidae element was a large canine tooth from a coyote or domestic dog. None of the bone was identified as human. The animal bone was so highly calcined and fragmentary that it could not be determined whether the bone was green or dry when burned. In addition, Feature 5 produced a high diversity of plant remains (Table 6.1). Many of these, including walnut (*Juglans* sp.) and hickory (*Carya* sp.) nutshell and goosefoot (*Chenopodium* sp.), pokeweed (*Phytolacca americana*), chokeberry (*Aronia* sp.), eastern redbud (cf. *Cercis canadensis*), and St.-John's-wort (cf. *Hypericum* sp.) seeds, are historically recorded foods. Many of the plant species, as well as recovered bedstraw (*Galium trifidum*), can be used for medicinal treatments, incense, fiber, and basketry (Moerman 1998). A 20-g sample of wood charcoal submitted for radiometric assay yielded an uncalibrated date of 1720 ± 60 B.P. (Beta-174892). The two-sigma calibrated date is cal A.D. 150 (340) 430, which overlaps with the calibrated date for Feature 2.

Feature 5 was classified as a thermal feature. The burned faunal remains suggest that Feature 5 functioned, at least in part, as an animal-processing or refuse pit. The calcined animal bone fragments and edible food remains point to food preparation. Foods may have been prepared for feasting, ritual offerings, or both in conjunction with the ceremonial offering of the tetrapodal vessel and copper ear spools in nearby Feature 2. Bedstraw recovered from both features may have been burned as incense as the respective rituals were performed.

Key Middle Woodland Artifacts

Tetrapodal Pottery Vessel

The globular jar (Figure 6.3) recovered from Feature 2 was made of mica-flecked clay tempered with a moderate amount of sand and rock; a large chunk of coal was observed in one sherd. Petrographic analysis of one sherd by James Stoltman (University of Wisconsin) revealed that paste inclusions consisted of a rock of generally granitic composition including, in descending order, polycrystalline quartz, amphibole, microcline feldspar, and muscovite.

The exterior vessel surface was brushed, save for the neck and rim, which were plain and well smoothed. Portions of the body were also rather plain, probably due to weathering of the exterior surface rather than intentional smoothing. Below the shoulder, the brushed surface treatment is divided into four panels on the body. The brush lines were applied in diagonally oriented strokes, forming a herringbone pattern around the vessel, with the lowest portion of the strokes halfway between the feet and the highest portion of the strokes above the feet.

Total vessel height measures 15.5 cm. The orifice diameter is 15.6 cm, neck diameter is 13.6 cm, shoulder diameter is 13.6 cm, and body diameter is 13.3 cm. The vessel exhibits an excurvate rim and a rounded lip. The lip is thinner than the body, which averages 6.0 mm in thickness. The shoulder has a somewhat angular morphology. Four podal support fragments project from the thin (3.5 mm), slightly rounded base. The cone-shaped feet are severely weathered and can no longer support the vessel.

The pot is classified as Connestee Series, as defined by Keel (1976) for the Appalachian summit of eastern Tennessee and western North Carolina. The Connestee Series includes plain, brushed, fabric-impressed, check-stamped, simple-stamped, and cordmarked surface treatments. The form, size, and other attributes of the vessel recovered from Amburgey conform to the type Connestee Brushed.

Connestee Series ceramics have been identified on numerous sites in northeastern Kentucky, including Hansen (Henderson et al., 1988), Bentley (Henderson and Pollack 1985), and Blanton (Johnson 1982), and in southern Ohio, such as Grimes (Brose 1982; Chapman and Keel 1979). Tetrapodal vessels of probable southern origin also have been recovered from C. and O. Mounds in eastern Kentucky (Haag 1942b; O'Malley 1988), the Main site in southeastern Kentucky (Kerr 1995), the Watkins site in south-central Kentucky (Applegate 2000:125), and Middle Woodland mound sites in Indiana (Adams 1949) and Illinois (Fowler 1957). Numerically, these ceramics are minor components of Middle Woodland ceramic assemblages and do not represent separate occupations. Connestee Series ceramics from Middle Ohio Valley sites were likely imported.

A vessel similar to but smaller than the Amburgey vessel was recovered from the base of one of the mounds (15Mm32) of the nearby Camargo Site Complex in Montgomery County (Fenton and Jefferies 1991). The Camargo vessel has a flaring rim, complete tetrapodal feet, and a flat base. Minor differences aside, the vessels seem to be of the same type. Fenton and Jefferies (1991) classified the Camargo vessel as Connestee Simple Stamped or Connestee Brushed. Two radiocarbon samples from features excavated below Camargo Mound yielded uncalibrated dates of 1780 ± 60 and 1600 ± 60 B.P. The two-sigma calibrated dates of cal A.D. 125 (243) 402 and cal A.D. 337 (430) 601 (Fenton and Jefferies 1991:52), respectively, overlap with the Amburgey dates.

Petrographic analysis of the Camargo vessel by James Stoltman revealed a suite of paste inclusions similar to that seen in the Amburgey pot, but in different proportions. The Amburgey vessel has fewer but coarser inclusions than the Camargo vessel. Stoltman concluded that both vessels originated in the Appalachians, probably North Carolina. They are similar to nonlocal ceramics found in Ohio Hopewell centers, but are unlike typed vessels from the Garden Creek or Icehouse Bottom sites in Tennessee (Chapman and Keel 1979).

Copper Ear Spools

Two copper ear spools (Figure 6.3) were located beneath the tetrapodal pottery vessel at Amburgey. Analysis followed Ruhl (1992), focusing on metric and nonmetric traits (Table 6.2). Ear spool A is nearly complete, though the outer edges of the obverse and reverse discs are slightly fragmented. The specimen is a composite piece, formed from at least three plates and one stem. The stem was wrapped in fiber. No clay was observed between the plates. There are no center holes on the obverse or reverse discs, but there is an obvious dimple in the center of the obverse disc. The center portion of the reverse disc is slightly marred, and a slight dimple is apparent. The profile of the obverse disc shows a continuous cup curvature, and the transition between annulus and cup is abrupt.

Ear spool B was located under ear spool A. It is highly fragmentary due to postdepositional corrosion rather than intentional crushing by human agency (Richmond 2000), which has been documented at several Ohio Hopewell sites (Ruhl 1992). Although most pieces are too fragmentary for analysis, portions of the outer obverse and reverse plates and the stem are recognizable. The profile of the obverse disc is similar to that of ear spool A, although the cup depth is slightly shallower. There is a hole in the center cup of the obverse disc and a dimple in the center cup of the reverse disc. The stem is detached from the remainder of the discs. Although fragmentary, the stem retains an hourglass design.

Fiber cordage was wrapped around the stem of ear spool B. The cordage measures 61 cm in length and 1 to 2 mm in thickness. The cordage was manufactured from bast fibers, which are flexible, elongated strands from the inner bark of plants. Although the species represented by the ear spool B fiber cordage could not be determined, some common bast fibers in the New World are jute (*Abutilon* sp. and *Corchorus* sp.), milkweed (*Asclepias* sp.), Indian hemp (*Apocynum* sp.), and nettles (*Urtica gracilis; Boehmeria* sp., *Laportea* sp.) (Hurley 1979:4).

Copper ear spools are among the most characteristic Hopewellian artifacts (Ruhl and Seeman 1998). They have been found at Middle Woodland sites across much of eastern North America (e.g., Ford 1963, Jefferies 1976), although the artifact form is found most often in the Hopewell heartland of southern Ohio. To date, only one other site in Kentucky, an undocumented

Table 6.2. Quantitative and qualitative attributes[a] of copper ear spools

Attributes (mm)	Spool A[b]	Spool B[c]
Quantitative		
Obverse diameter	34.81	N/A
Obverse cup diameter	17.53	15.14
Obverse center hole diameter	N/A	2.44
Thickness	18.21	N/A
Reverse diameter	32.15	N/A
Obverse/reverse diameter ratio	1.00:0.92	N/A
Center hole diameter	N/A	2.50
Cup depth	3.30	2.70
Outside stem diameter	12.98	N/A
Inside stem diameter	N/A	2.93
Number of plates	3–4	2
Qualitative		
Obverse overlay	Absent	Absent
Obverse center hole	Dimple	Present
Reverse overlay	Absent	Absent
Reverse contour	Concave-convex	Concave-convex
Reverse center hole	Dimple	Dimple
Stem wrap	Fiber	Fiber
Plate joint	Crimped	Crimped
Rivet	N/A	Hourglass
Plate filling	Absent	Absent

[a]Attributes Adapted from Ruhl and Seeman (1998); [b]nearly complete; [c]highly fragmentary.

site in Marion County, has produced copper ear spools (Katherine Ruhl, personal communication 2001); these were curated in 1880 as part of the Raywick Collection at the Smithsonian Institution (Accession No. 12812).

Ruhl (1992) and Ruhl and Seeman (1998) were among the first to conduct detailed studies of bicymbal copper ear ornaments commonly known as copper ear spools. Ruhl's first study (1992) examined 544 ear spools from 20 Middle Woodland (Hopewell) sites in Ohio. Most specimens (n = 207) came from the Hopewell site. Ruhl recorded up to 11 metric and 10 nonmetric attributes for each ear spool. One of the most important stylistic attributes that emerged in her study was the contour profile of the obverse disc, which is the larger of the two "cymbals" designed to be visible in front of the ear when worn. Ruhl (1992:50) produced a chronological seriation of nine types distinguished by the contour profile of the outer plate of the obverse disc; the nine types formed a stylistic progression through time. For example, Type 1 ear spools were recovered from Tremper, considered an early site, whereas Type 8 and Type 9 ear spools were recovered from Marietta and Esch, considered late sites (Ruhl 1992, Seeman 1977).

Ruhl and Seeman (1998) expanded on Ruhl's previous study by increasing the sample size to 632 specimens. Their study employed Carr's (1995) model of material style and utilized many of the attributes recorded previously by Ruhl (1992). Ruhl and Seeman (1998:659) concluded that although there was much variation among specimens, the general style through time remained consistent; changes in manufacturing technique and design through time are indicative of functional changes. They also suggest that past researchers overemphasized the trading of ear spools and that the Hopewell site likely did not function as a central point of ear spool distribution.

The profile of Amburgey ear spool A is reminiscent of the profiles of Styles 6–9 in Ruhl's (1992) seriation or the first of the profiles of Style D in Ruhl and Seeman's (1998) study. This profile type is found near the middle to end of the chronological sequence. Amburgey ear spool A closely resembles specimens from Turner, a site with considerable temporal depth (Katherine Ruhl, personal communication 2001). The fragmentary nature of Amburgey ear spool B prohibited similar analysis and comparison.

Copper Celt

Recovered from Feature 5, the copper celt is nearly complete with only a portion of the proximal end missing from corrosion (Figure 6.3). Several small fragments of mica are embedded on the surfaces of each face. The implement was not wrapped in fabric, as has been noted for similar specimens from other Middle Woodland sites in the region (Webb and Baby 1957; Webb and Snow 1945).

The spatulate-shaped celt is approximately 7.3 cm long and up to 4.2 cm wide, tapering toward the proximal end. The distal end is flared, slightly rounded, and beveled, giving it the appearance of an adze rather than a celt, but the term "celt" is conventionally used to describe such artifacts. The two lateral edges are flat, rather than bladelike. A longitudinal seam is evident along one face of the implement, indicating that it was manufactured by folding raw copper sheets.

Copper celts have been found at various Middle Woodland sites in the Middle Ohio Valley, typically in submound Adena and Hopewell mortuary features (Dragoo 1963; Thomas 1894; Webb and Baby 1957; Webb and Snow 1945). The artifact form is reportedly more common in Hopewell sites (Webb and Snow 1945), although the problems with the early taxonomies on which Adena and Hopewell distinctions were made are well known (Clay 1991a; Griffin 1974). Although no unequivocal evidence for mortuary activity was documented at Amburgey, the copper celt was probably placed with a human burial (Richmond 2000; Richmond and Kerr 2002).

Discussion

The features and artifacts associated with the Middle Woodland component at the Amburgey site present a number of interpretive challenges. The presence of Hopewellian artifacts in a nonmound context and the absence of obvious mortuary ceremonialism (i.e., the absence of human remains) are unusual. Moreover, the post mold pattern at the site does not conform to the expected paired-post circular pattern or rectangular single-post pattern expected at an Adena or Hopewell, respectively, mortuary camp or mound site (Brown 1979; Clay 1986, 1998b; Greber 1979a; Seeman 1986; Webb 1940). Thus, the unique data set associated with the Middle Woodland component at Amburgey necessitates further discussion of cultural affiliation, intersite relationships, and intrasite structure and site function.

The distinctions between Adena and Hopewell as discrete archaeological constructs have received considerable attention (see Seeman 1986:567). Clay (1998b) and Greber (1991b) have pointed out that a distinction may be warranted in the Scioto River valley of Ohio, where Adena precedes Hopewell, but not outside this "heartland." Dealing specifically with central Kentucky, we take the nontraditional approach of placing both Adena and Hopewell within the Middle Woodland period (Railey 1990, 1996). For these purposes, Middle Woodland is defined as the time period from 400 B.C. to A.D. 400 (Clay and Niquette 1992). This approach highlights the continuity between Adena and Hopewell in terms of ritual complexity while acknowledging cultural differences. It also allows for the unencumbered examination of specific sites or regions to see how they are distributed along this continuum.

Adena mortuary mounds are well represented in the central Bluegrass of Kentucky and in Montgomery County in particular. Accretional burial mounds underlain by the remains of paired-post structures characterize these sites. Specific artifact classes found within Kentucky Adena mounds include stone gorgets; tubular pipes; copper bracelets; engraved tablets; galena and barite crystals; mica crescents; Adena and Robbins bifaces; and Adena Plain, Fayette Thick, and Montgomery Incised pottery (Railey 1990; Seeman 1986). Ricketts and Wright Mounds (Figure 6.1), for example, contained a large number of diagnostic Adena artifacts, log-lined mortuary crypts, and covered submound paired-post structural remains (Funkhouser and Webb 1935; Webb 1940).

Although few obvious Hopewellian-influenced sites have been documented in Kentucky, Amburgey is not unique. The Camargo earthworks (Figure 6.1), as mapped by Rafinesque (1824) and later by Squier and Davis (1848), consisted of two conical mounds and three geometric enclosures that were circular, square, and hexagonal in outline. When WPA-sponsored archaeologists investigated the complex in 1941, only the circular (15Mm30) and square (15Mm31) enclosures and one mound (15Mm32) were relocated. Results of the 1941 investigations were not published, however, until Fenton and Jefferies (1991) analyzed the artifacts and field notes from these investigations.

There are several striking similarities and differences between Camargo and Amburgey. The most obvious similarity is the presence of a Connestee Series tetrapodal vessel at both sites, both from similar depositional contexts. The Camargo vessel was located on the submound floor adjacent to two features interpreted as crematory pits (Fenton and Jefferies 1991). The vessel from Amburgey was located in a small pit adjacent to a possible thermal feature or an interior post mold. In both cases the vessels were deposited discretely and were not included with a burial or in a crematory pit.

Post mold features at both Camargo and Amburgey provide evidence of planned constructions. Approximately 32 post molds or small pits were documented at Camargo, but Fenton and Jefferies (1991:50) recognized no patterning indicating a structure outline. They did comment, however, that the post molds indicated that construction associated with ritual activity occurred on a submound activity surface. Considerably fewer post molds were discovered at Amburgey, but the pattern *suggests* an oval structure or screen with two central posts.

The major difference between Camargo and Amburgey is the absence of a mound or mounds, enclosures, and burials at Amburgey. The absence of a mound at Amburgey may be a matter of choice or chance. It is increasingly recognized that the circular or rectangular arrangements of posts beneath Middle Woodland mounds represent ritual structures associated with mortuary rituals rather than domestic activity (Clay 1986, 1998b; Seeman 1986). The structures served to demarcate sacred space within which such rituals as feasting and cremation were performed. In some cases, submound structures were burned as part of the ritual. The structural remains and associated burials were covered with earth, often in accretional stages. Perhaps the artifact cache (Feature 2) and associated feasting pit (Feature 5) at Amburgey represent the beginning stages of such a process. In this scenario, the subsequent stage of mound construction was not completed for unknown reasons. As Clay and Niquette (1992:23; emphasis in original) pointed out for the early Middle Woodland, "In some areas, the dead were processed and life went on *without the benefit of a mound*. Rather, the mound was one track which *might* develop in a community." This generalization does little to clarify the situation at Amburgey, however. No human remains, cremated or otherwise, were disclosed at Amburgey, although the historic burials may have destroyed evidence of Middle Woodland burials. Furthermore, the post molds at Amburgey only hinted at the presence of a structure or screen, perhaps oval shaped. At the very least, there was no evidence of a submound mortuary building similar to the circular structures associated with Adena (Seeman 1986) or rectangular structures seen at some Ohio Hopewell sites (Greber 1979a).

The evidence from Amburgey indicates that Middle Woodland ritual sites are not always directly associated with a mound or earthen enclosure. Another example is the Niebert site in Mason County, West Virginia (Clay and Niquette 1992), at which five circular post mold patterns, four of which had paired posts, were disclosed. The site was interpreted as an early Middle Woodland (Adena) mortuary camp. At least two human cremations were associated with the circular structures. Several thermal features indicated cooking activities, suggesting that feasting was a component of the mortuary rituals at this site (Clay and Niquette 1992).

The functions of the artifact cache, thermal features, and surrounding post molds at Amburgey are unclear. In the absence of human remains, the site cannot be viewed definitively as a mortuary camp, although the artifact assemblage resembles those from Middle Woodland mortuary facilities elsewhere in the Middle Ohio Valley (Clay 1986, 1998b; Seeman 1986). Copper ear spools are typically associated with mortuary or other ceremonial contexts throughout the Eastern Woodlands (Ruhl and Seeman 1998). The presence of copper artifacts, a Connestee Series vessel, and mica further suggest ritual activity. The remaining Middle Woodland artifacts were recovered from ceremonial contexts at the Amburgey site. The presence of nonlocal pottery in a submound context has been associated with ceremonial activity at other sites (Clay 1983; O'Malley 1988). The Connestee Series vessel at Camargo, located adjacent to two crematory pits, is a case in point.

We suggest that feasting in conjunction with ritual offerings constituted the major Middle Woodland activities at Amburgey. The Middle Woodland features, especially Feature 5, yielded burned remains of edible floral (e.g., squash, goosefoot, purslane, walnut, hickory) and faunal (e.g., deer, Canidae, bird) species. It is possible that the remains were burned during preparation for consumption or were burned as an offering for ancestors or the dead. Sticky catchfly and bedstraw, which are recorded historically as having medicinal, incense, and fragrance uses (Moerman 1998), were recovered from both Middle Woodland features and may have played a part in ritual activity at Amburgey. Most of the lithic artifacts from feature contexts were burned. The copper artifacts and tetrapodal vessel were not burned, indicating they were deposited after the burning episode. Thus, the oval post mold pattern at Amburgey likely represents a partition that demarcated areas of sacred space (cf. Clay 1998b; Seeman 1986).

Radiometric dating indicates that Amburgey was roughly contemporary with the nearby Camargo earthworks and Wright mounds, as well as a number of Middle Woodland sites in central Kentucky (Table 6.3). The apparent temporal overlap (Figure 6.4) between the so-called late Adena Wright mounds and the Hopewell-related sites of Amburgey and Camargo reinforces the notion of overlap and continuity between these two archaeological taxa in central Kentucky. Some (Griffin 1958; Seeman 1986; Stoltman 1978) have argued that the comparatively late Adena dates are at odds with the lack of Hopewell artifacts, such as rocker-stamped pottery, platform pipes, and bladelets, at the Adena sites. This position fails to account, however, for the fact that several Adena mounds in Kentucky have produced Hopewellian artifacts, features, or both. For example, a platform pipe, large corner-notched blade, and mica crescents were recovered from the Crigler Mound (Webb and Snow 1943), and the remains of square to rectangular structures were noted beneath the Riley Mound (Webb 1943) and the Bullock Mound (Schlarb, this volume).

Conclusion

The Amburgey site provides an example of the pan-regional increase in group ritual activities that took place between circa 500 B.C. and A.D. 500 in the eastern United States. This period was characterized by ritual activity in nondomestic spaces and long-distance, interregional trade (Clay 1998b; Railey 1990; Seeman 1986). The Amburgey site is unique in that it has characteristics of a Middle Woodland mortuary facility but lacks Middle Woodland burials. Although the absence of human remains could be the result of postdepositional disturbance, a simpler interpretation is that Amburgey is an example of the diversity of Middle Woodland ritual activities. Clay (1986, 1998b) has repeatedly emphasized that Middle Woodland ritual sites served multiple purposes through time, with mortuary ritual often constituting a final use. It seems that the Amburgey site represents ritual activities other than those associated with inhumation.

The Amburgey site is also unusual in that the artifact assemblage includes such elements as the free-standing tetrapodal vessel and copper ear spools commonly associated with Ohio Hopewell, yet the site is located in a geographic area typically associated with Adena and lacking evidence of Hopewellian sites. Amburgey is similar to the nearby Camargo site (Fenton and Jefferies 1991) in this regard. This taxonomic problem is partially due to Webb's (Webb and Snow 1945; see also Clay, this volume) penchant for clas-

Table 6.3. Radiocarbon dates from the Amburgey site and selected late Middle Woodland period sites in central Kentucky

Site	Lab No.	RCYBP	Calibrated Date (2 sigma)	Reference
Amburgey	Beta-158296	1890 ± 40	A.D. 27 (91, 98, 126) 237	Richmond and Kerr 2002
Amburgey	Beta-174892	1720 ± 60	A.D. 134 (263, 275, 388) 432	Richmond and Kerr 2002
Auvergne Mound	Uga-3617	1680 ± 115	A.D. 81 (388) 636	Clay 1983
Camargo Mound	Beta-33159	1780 ± 60	A.D. 84 (243) 410	Fenton and Jefferies 1991
Camargo Mound	Beta-33160	1600 ± 60	A.D. 263 (430) 601	Fenton and Jefferies 1991
Indian Fort Mountain	Beta-2862	1910 ± 60	B.C. 41 (A.D. 82) 240	Moore 1982
Wright Mounds	M-2238	1740 ± 140	B.C. 38 (A.D. 260, 281, 291, 297, 322) 617	Crane and Griffin 1972:159
Wright Mounds	unpublished	1900 ± 50	B.C. 15 (A.D. 86, 102, 122) 237	Crane and Griffin 1972:160

Note: The unpublished date from Wright mounds was run by Nuclear Science and Engineering, Inc., Pittsburgh, Pennsylvania (Crane and Griffin 1972:160). Calibrations performed using CALIB 4.3.

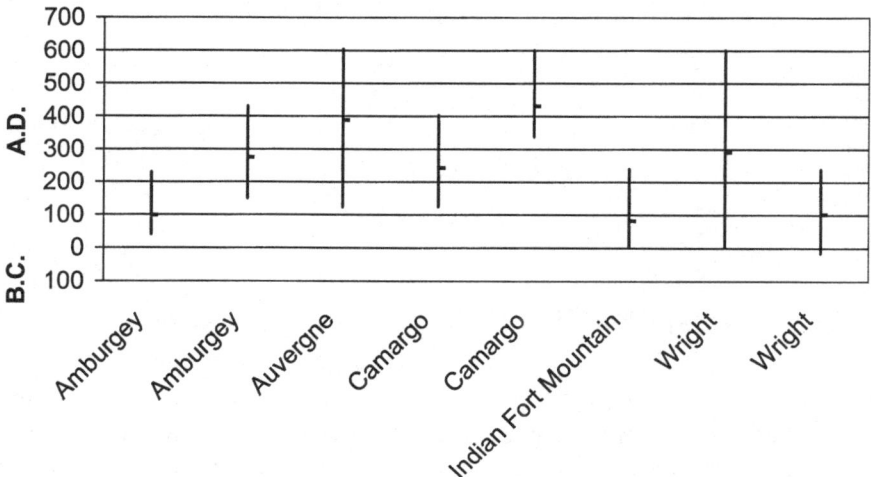

Figure 6.4. Maximum calibrated date ranges from select Middle Woodland sites in central Kentucky.

sifying all excavated burial mounds in the study area as Adena. Amburgey and Camargo demonstrate a degree of temporal overlap and continuity in central Kentucky between the archaeological constructs of Adena and Hopewell. The nature of the relationship between the two is currently unknown, but research at similar sites in Kentucky (e.g., Schlarb, this volume) holds great promise.

Acknowledgments

We would like to acknowledge the Kentucky Transportation Cabinet for allowing us to present these data publicly. Katherine Ruhl provided valuable insight concerning the ear spools and their relative temporal placement. Renee Bonzani analyzed the botanical remains recovered from the site, and Jessica Allgood analyzed the faunal remains. Andy Martin provided valuable assistance with mapping. We thank James Stoltman for performing thin-section analysis of the vessel on a pro bono basis. Comments from Berle Clay, Andrew Bradbury, and Andy Martin improved the quality of the chapter. In addition, the administrative and field staff at Cultural Resource Analysts, Inc., should be commended for their efforts in bringing this project to a successful completion. Finally, we thank the editors for their constructive criticism and for giving us the opportunity to contribute to this volume. Any mistakes or errors of omission rest solely with us.

7
Adena

Rest in Peace?

R. Berle Clay

Nostalgia: Popular Archaeology in the 1930s

Because I have written about Adena (Clay 1983, 1986, 1987, 1998b) and used the concept in an essentialist sense (O'Brien and Lyman 1998:28–29), it might seem an act of ingratitude to turn against it and try to make a case for scrapping it altogether. Indeed, it might be taken as an indication that I have chosen to scrap something called "culture history" for uncharted paths.

This rash move has been stimulated by a train of thought begun by taking down a book that introduced me to archaeology. *The Advance of Science* (Davis 1934) was an impressive volume that stood out on our bookshelves, with its art deco aluminum-colored wrappers and scientific illustrations. The publisher, Science Service, Inc., was housed in Washington in the same building as the National Research Council (NRC) founded by President Wilson, which survived through the 1930s as the nearest thing to the later National Science Foundation. Privately funded by Scripps-Howard, Science Service, Inc., became essentially the publicity branch of the NRC. It continues to be very active on the Web today.

One picture in the volume was my introduction to the Rosetta stone. Imagine my surprise when revisiting it to discover that it was not a photo principally of the Rosetta stone, but rather featured Frank Setzler of the Smithsonian Institution and the NRC holding a small pot from the Marksville site in front of an imitation Rosetta stone in the Smithsonian. The accompanying puffery obviously came from Setzler, by that time *the* specialist on Marksville pottery (Setzler 1933a, 1933b).

Analogous to the Rosetta stone, so said Setzler, this pot had design motifs that were both known and associated with the Hopewell *Mound Builders* and from an unknown group way down the Mississippi River.

> It is Mr. Setzler's opinion that . . . the new "Marksville Variant" of the Hopewell culture might prove to be older in type than the *mound*

builder relics from farther up the valley. The Gulf Coast may have been the original center from which spread the great complex of arts and customs now labeled *"Mound Builder."* At their highest point, the Hopewell type of *mound builders* had great skill at carving in stone, weaving cloth and dyeing patterns in it, hammering copper into many ornamental objects, growing farm crops. . . . So spectacular was the culture of the *Mound Builders* that many people have thought of a *Mound Builder* as some strange, superior race distinct from the Indian. Scientific excavations long since proved this theory unwarranted. *Mound Builders* were Indians. Linking the *Mound Builders* with known historic tribes has been harder to achieve. But with recent discoveries, the cultural events in the Mississippi Valley are beginning to fall into shape. Marksville now appears to show very early *Mound Builders* who seem to merge with the famous Hopewell culture of Ohio. [Davis 1934:327–329; emphasis added]

However, on Mature Reflection . . .

I did not remember any of this Setzler-speak or recall the repetitive invocation of "Mound Builder," but I now realize that later, as a student, I was barraged by a point of view born of these ideas. Furthermore, I now see that Adena, although never mentioned by Setzler, was right in the middle of the "Mound Builder" emphasis. Born of Greenman's (1932) reporting of the Coon Mound, elevating comments made by Mills (1901–1902) to the level of a classificatory tool, Adena had been expanded extensively by Webb using Kentucky materials excavated during the 1930s and early 1940s (e.g., Webb and Snow 1945).

At a tender age Adena was appropriated by influential archaeologists who had only marginal interests in Ohio Valley archaeology, but their explicit developmental implications produced for Adena a historical interpretation with a vengeance. The archaeologists were associated with government programs emanating from Washington during the Depression, and Setzler, as a curator in the National Museum with a voice in NRC policy development, was their bellwether. Setzler's roots were in the Ohio Valley, where he had certainly been exposed to the ideas of his mentor, Shetrone, concerning the southern origin of mound builders. In Washington, however, his interests expanded considerably, together with the impacts he would have on U.S. archaeology. The specific cultural historical reconstructions archaeologists developed, stimulated by Setzler, would ultimately prove wanting, but aspects of their interpretation linger, attached to Adena with shifted meanings. Now it may be best to move ahead, minus Adena as an integrating concept, although it may have local applications. Perhaps started with the best of intentions to order local archaeological matters in conceptual space, it has been hopelessly confused by conflicting interests.

Bringing Midwestern Archaeology to Kroeber's Attention

Perhaps the two most important archaeologists in this process besides Setzler were James Ford and Gordon Willey, neither associated with the Adena concept. Ford surveyed in Louisiana in 1933 with research funds from the NRC, followed by excavation with Setzler at Marksville in the fall of that year, the first cycle of Depression-funded archaeological excavation. Willey, somewhat his junior, also had his archaeological beginnings in the southeast, but in the slightly later work relief programs of the Roosevelt New Deal.

In hooking up with Setzler during his (Ford's) formative years as an archaeologist, Ford made contact with perhaps the most active inheritor at that time of a long tradition of official Washington interest in Indian mounds (e.g., Squier and Davis 1848). Raised in the Ohio Valley and educated in Ohio with archaeological fieldwork there and in Indiana, Setzler was steeped in the mound excavations of Moorehead and Shetrone. As a curator at the National Museum, Setzler continued work at Marksville where Fowke left off in 1926 (O'Brien and Lyman 1998:54). Aware of Hopewell in Ohio and the Marksville pottery, which he labeled as Hopewell, in the early 1930s Setzler was in the process of fashioning a historical relationship between the two. Using age-area reasoning, he became convinced that the cultural influences had gone up the Mississippi River from southern beginnings and, furthermore, that those beginnings might have Middle American ramifications, a position taken by his mentor, Shetrone (1930b:405). Marksville, however, was the spoor in the Mississippi Valley that had eluded earlier workers, at least following Setzler's interpretation of its ceramics.

Although his National Museum duties led him to range widely (Setzler 1935), Setzler returned from time to time to the Ohio Valley, including serving as supervisor of the Chicago field school at the Kincaid site in 1940 (Cole 1951:vi). He rose in the profession of Washington anthropology and in the National Museum, the American Anthropological Association, and the Anthropological Society of Washington (O'Brien and Lyman 1998:53). Much later, Setzler excavated the Welcome Mound in West Virginia, which he considered "Adena," for the National Museum, with indifferent and poorly published results (Setzler 1960).

It seems that through time Setzler moved sharply away from his interests in chronology and culture history, so important to his 1930s interpretation of Marksville. This is especially evident in his coauthorship with Julian Steward (Steward and Setzler 1938) of a short theoretical article that Walter W. Taylor (1948:7), generally critical of his contemporaries, pronounced a "fine" paper. James Ford and Setzler apparently became estranged in later years, and perhaps this was related to Setzler's intellectual movement away from culture history toward configuration in the late 1930s, in contrast to Ford's lifelong immersion in what Taylor (1948:42–43) termed "chronicle."

After his experiences with Setzler, Ford worked widely in the southeast and published a series of papers on his Louisiana work that established him regionally. He met Willey through relief archaeology in Louisiana in the later 1930s. Willey moved around through Depression-era archaeology in the southeast (e.g., Ford and Willey 1940; Willey 1949c) and elsewhere, then to his mature interests in Middle and South America, sometimes with Ford in tow. Furthermore, Willey was intellectually close to Ford, and by his own admission (Willey 1999:ix–x), it was Willey who revamped Ford's (1936) cumbersome ceramic classification system with a breath of fresh air from the American southwest—binomial nomenclature. Single-minded as Ford apparently was as a young man, he listened to the more urbane Willey, perhaps to counter his deficient background in archaeology.

Their joint *American Anthropologist* article (Ford and Willey 1941), beyond somewhat "legitimizing" archaeology in the practice of anthropology, was extremely important in setting the interpretation of Adena, that fledgling Ohio Valley creation of the Midwestern Taxonomic System (MTS). Decades later, Albert Spaulding (1985:301) stuffily suggested that "Kroeber clearly judged that Ford and Willey had rescued archaeology of the eastern United States from a group of [unnamed!] backward intellects." Acceptance by Kroeber, a preeminent academically trained and based anthropologist, clearly made their synthesis an instant classic, casting Adena in stone before it had ever been adequately digested by the archaeological community that had proposed it and certainly before the classificatory implications of the MTS had really been thought out. As Spaulding (1983:23) pointed out in a telling comment on 1930s archaeology and the confusion of the MTS in particular, "Analytical sophistication is a hard-bought thing, and the first steps are the hardest."

The article was very much a product of an official Washington obsession with Mound Builders, a focus that was fueled by the Smithsonian mound survey. Indeed, Cyrus Thomas (1894), far from solving the Mound Builder question, had merely whetted official interest in the *origins* of Mound Builders, if not in their Native American descendants, and Ford and Willey rose to the occasion. They must have been highly influenced by Ford's association with Setzler, and they were certainly egged on in their publishing venture by official Washington in the person of Henry B. Collins (Baca 2002:153–154), Ford's mentor, who had Mississippi origins as an archaeologist and was an established, published professional working at the Smithsonian. As Willey (1999:xiii) noted, "It was our basic thesis that most of the ideas about mound and earthwork construction, pottery and general cultural elaboration originated in the south, essentially in the Lower Mississippi Valley. We felt that even earlier beginnings of these ideas might be traced further southward to Mesoamerica, though we made no attempt to elaborate on that point." This statement harkened back to earlier comments made by Shetrone (1930b:405).

Ironically, the "backward intellects" noted by Spaulding tended to be any archaeologists, with the possible exception of Setzler, who had the hands-on experience with Adena that Ford and Willey lacked. Yet these same archaeologists (Shetrone?) developed the ideas that motivated Ford and Willey. Perhaps Spaulding was referring more precisely to adherents of the MTS, for it was Ford's genius, as Willey put it, to introduce a sense of history into the eastern United States that had been lacking in archaeological interpretation. Indeed, in reviewing examples of Webb's prodigious output from Kentucky, Willey (1949a:69; 1949b:70) linked the shortcomings (as he saw them) in Webb's interpretations to Webb's adherence to the MTS as it had developed into a general division of prehistoric time into the Archaic, Woodland, and Mississippian.

Ford was obsessed with deriving the eastern "Mound Builders" from a Mesoamerican hearth, following Setzler's representation of Washington officialdom. With Willey in 1941, Ford divided post-Archaic Mississippi Valley prehistory into four stages: Burial Mound I, Burial Mound II, Temple Mound I, and Temple Mound II. Adena was virtually synonymous with Burial Mound I, and it derived from Mesoamerican cultural influences that had entered the lower Mississippi Valley through Tchefuncte, later in Marksville, and so on. Although, as Willey later pointed out, they did not stress the Mesoamerican origins in 1941, such beginnings were definitely on their minds, emerging explicitly in print within four years (Ford and Quimby 1945:95).

The idea that mound builder culture had its beginnings in the lower Mississippi Valley was a product of strained age-area reasoning stemming principally from Ford's pioneering ceramic analyses of Louisiana collections. Ford and Willey (1940:141) suggested that only in the lower Mississippi Valley (in contrast to Illinois and Ohio) was Marksville period (read "Hopewell") pottery found *both* in burial mounds and on village sites. Because a "tendency toward the ceremonial survival of old traits" is to be expected in "the peripheral areas of a culture distribution," the restriction of Hopewell

Adena: Rest in Peace? / 99

pottery to burial mounds in Ohio and Illinois indicated that the culture had its origins in the south (Ford and Willey 1940:141). This conclusion was clearly a product of Ford's (1936) typological analysis and an embellishment of the sort of age-area explanation Setzler had been crafting during the previous decade (published in an abbreviated form by Science Service). It dovetailed nicely with the fact that the Ohio Valley archaeologists of the day had not figured out where the Hopewell villages might be, a problem that still concerns them today.

Later, Willey (1969:67) was somewhat apologetic, suggesting that "the essay, though in many ways crude and naive, was the first broad perspective of the archaeology of the East which imparted a sense of history; some of it has since been corrected, but much of it stands." Continuing, "It bore the heavy stamp of Ford's thinking, which tended to be single minded, focused, and 'romantic'" (1969:68).

In an example of their naiveté, the authors made a remarkable confession, perhaps primarily a product of Ford's parochial single-mindedness, for Willey (1999:xiii) would judge that perhaps 75 percent of the article was Ford's contribution. They (Ford and Willey 1941:326) commented that "it is rather unfortunate that the excellent work which has been done in certain peripheral areas and the remarkable finds which are occasionally made should have resulted in focusing attention on other parts of the East to the exclusion of the Mississippi Valley." This unwitting comment, seemingly slighting the archaeology of much of the eastern United States that did not fit their vision, highlights a singular weakness in their 1941 thinking. They were blinded by Ford's obsession with the Mississippi Valley and a strong teleological presumption that cultural evolution in Kroeber's Eastern Maize Area was directed toward, and could be historically explained by, the development of maize agriculture deriving from Mexico. In their synthesis, Adena, linked by diffusion with the lower Mississippi Valley hearth, joined ranks with other cultural manifestations in this march toward corn agriculture and higher civilization.

The pair saw their contribution as giving a historical perspective to eastern United States prehistory, and they continued to hone it throughout their professional lives. Ford's (1969) thinking finally emerged at the end of his life with his paper on his conception of the North American Formative (taking the lead from his old coworker Willey) and its trait-by-trait link from the Southeast backward to Mesoamerica, South America, Japanese Jomon Culture, thence to somewhere in the hinterlands of Central Asia, regarded by his admirers (O'Brien and Lyman 1998:6) as the worst piece he ever wrote. Ford's fantastical ideas died shortly thereafter with him, although they were lavishly published in a Smithsonian volume (Ford 1969).

Unlike Ford, Willey went on to become a major contributor to culture historical thinking in Americanist archaeology. His thoughts went through two stages—crystallizing first in his 1958 publication with Phillips and later in a text on North American archaeology in 1966. In 1958 he advanced his idea of five "stages" of cultural development: Lithic, Archaic, Formative, Classic and Post-Classic. His essential argument about the Formative as it occurred in the eastern United States seems to have been built on the belief that "on the basis of sheer size of the mounds and earthworks, we have to infer a concentration of population, or at least a concentration of control over a large population, backed up by a stable food supply" (Willey and Phillips 1958:156). Of course, the agriculture and the earthworks were Mesoamerican innovations in his view. Adena became the "earliest reorientation of eastern Archaic culture along lines that we can designate as Formative" (with agriculture, high population densities, and mechanisms for social control) (Willey and Phillips 1958:157–158). Still, as a maturing culture historian, his position always remained flexible enough to entertain purely local contributions to the development of Adena. Thus, he could make a flowery tribute to Webb (and his old supporter Kroeber!) when he reviewed (1949b:70) his Fischer Mound report written with William Haag (Webb and Haag 1947; emphasis added) to the effect that Webb's "appraisal of the copper 'boatstone,' the copper antler headdress, and the modified tubular pipes, showing their significant position in the developmental chain of Archaic-Adena-Hopewell, is *as skillful as Kroeber's perceptive infection of a time-sense into the Uhle collections of Peru.*" Still, as he explains in a footnote to this tribute (1949b:70), he recognizes that their demonstration of antecedents to Adena copper headdresses in the Eastern Archaic, coupled with Willey's own recognition of their much later occurrence in "Florida Glades culture," was a good indication that, whatever the Mesoamerican inspiration for Adena, it was indeed a culture historical "thing of shreds and patches" with roots in the local scene as well. Here, in a book review(!), Willey reveals himself as a sophisticated participant in the culture historical dialogue, unlike Ford, one able to meld new, discordant ideas into his own views without missing a beat.

Willey's notion of a New World Formative, stemming from his collaboration with Phillips, as well as from Ford's work, came across in his 1966 summary of North American archaeology, which was staple fare in college programs for the next 20 years. Interestingly, the subject dimmed in importance for him only in the 1980s, to be replaced with the problem of "what happened to Hopewell in the transition to Mississippian," a question that in a sense had been solved for one generation of government-financed archaeologists by the late-nineteenth-century Smithsonian mound survey

(Thomas 1894), although obviously not to Willey's (1985:353) satisfaction. Willey's position on mounds was picked up and reinterpreted by others (e.g., Jennings 1974).

Griffin, the preeminent archaeologist with local knowledge, never bought either the local interpretation of Adena or Willey's stage version of culture change, and in a review (1959:415) of Caldwell's (1958) *Trend and Tradition in the Prehistory of the Eastern United States,* he declared that "one of the conclusions offered by Caldwell is of the inadequacy and inapplicability of the stage classification of Willey and Phillips to the prehistory of the Eastern United States. With this I am in complete agreement." Other than Caldwell (1962), who repeated the point in an article on the Eastern Woodlands in Willey and Braidwood's (1962) grandiosely titled *Courses towards Urban Life,* few eastern United States archaeologists disputed Willey's views.

Moving Adena Firmly Inside the Beltway

I stress how much this view of things—especially that Adena was an essential developmental part of a southern mound-building tradition with Mexican origins—represented an insider consensus linked with government archaeology. Although it has perhaps not been recognized as such, it was more than, as Spaulding (1985:301) labeled it at a later date, "the faint persistence of nineteenth-century Mound Builder fantasies." Simply, it was an official government dogma that was linked with the distribution of federal funds for archaeology in the 1930s and certainly supported by the superb record that Webb and his associates established in excavating and publishing Adena sites in Kentucky. By the 1930s Setzler apparently controlled the distribution of funds through the Council on State Archaeological Surveys at the NRC, spoke for the Smithsonian, and was central in the disposition of federal emergency relief funds for excavation. He maintained "a low profile throughout these years but undoubtedly wield[ed] a big stick" (Haag 1985:275) and was very much Webb's patron, as he was both Ford's and Willey's.

After World War II, Setzler, with Julian Steward and other archaeologists in Washington (Wendorf and Thompson 2002:319), was instrumental in forming the Committee for the Recovery of Archaeological Remains, which shaped postwar government archaeology. Webb, its first head, fielded postwar river basin survey projects in the Wolf Creek Reservoir of Kentucky. Although Webb was known as an archaeologist who was deliberate in his thinking and stubborn in defending his own decisions (Griffin 1974:vi), he can hardly have been unaware of the importance of government support to his own work.

Ultimately, Webb (Webb and Snow 1945), too, would tentatively derive Adena from Mexico, perhaps stung by Willey's (1941) criticism of the Wright Mound report (Webb 1940) that Webb had not gone far enough in pointing out the connections between Kentucky Adena and Middle America. Webb's argument would be dressed up with inferences from skull shape and comparisons with the bogus "Tepexapan Man" from the Valley of Mexico, producing a historical narrative that, Griffin (1974:v) grumped, "would be immediately discarded by modern researchers." Perhaps Webb was merely falling in line with official dogma. After all, he was a military man known as "Major." He knew the source of his archaeological prestige and research funds. In Gilbert and Sullivan terms, he was a perfect "modern Major General."

Another Washington insider, Albert Spaulding (1952, 1955), also embraced the idea of Adena from Mexico. Going beyond Ford and Willey, Spaulding (1955:19–20) elevated Adena to the level of a *major cultural type*. In a formula that was often repeated, he (1955:19–20) suggested that the "sheer size of the mounds . . . and the complexity of the mortuary practices" indicated a "complex social organization and an efficient economic base." He added (1955:20), "Most archaeologists infer that the Adena people cultivated corn, tobacco, gourds, and presumably other plants."

Of note, it was Spaulding who would emerge as director of the Archaeology Division of the National Science Foundation from 1959 through 1963, replacing the NRC and carrying on Setzler's mantle. Willey and Braidwood would be the first archaeological recipients of NSF largesse in 1954 (Yellen and Greene 1985:332). Ford followed with a grant for research in Middle America, and it would be Spaulding (O'Brien and Lyman 1998:301) who would permit Ford to shift research funds to a more general search for the New World Formative. Note that in his own mythologizing, Binford (1972:3–8) has dealt glowingly with Spaulding while disparaging Griffin. In the early 1960s Spaulding's continued control of the NSF purse strings, coupled with a significant expansion of graduate training in archaeology after Sputnik, was a major economic factor involved in the emergence of the "New Archaeology" through its support of academy-based, peer-reviewed archaeological research, by then viewed as qualitatively more significant than "salvage" archaeology.

Meanwhile . . . Back in the Trenches

Most archaeologists in the Ohio Valley disagreed with the Washington-based interpretation, at least in its culture historical entirety. A strong tradition of local archaeology always maintained that Adena was a local product.

Adena: Rest in Peace? / 103

Richard Morgan (1952) forcefully placed Adena in a developing local tradition and never thought otherwise. His detailed and informed review (Morgan 1946) of *The Adena People* (Webb and Snow 1945) suggests that he would have been a potent force in redefining the concept to make it work more reasonably on a local level had he not made a precipitate exodus from the profession.

Griffin never seriously derived Adena/Hopewell from Mexico. Equally important, he (1952a:356) was also a major force in articulating local origins in the Archaic, shaping the culture history consensus that Dragoo (1963, 1964) would elaborate in the 1960s. A comparison of Ford and Willey (1941) with Griffin's (1946) "Change and Continuity in Eastern United States Archaeology," also prepared in 1941, is instructive. It indicates that Griffin, although interested in ceramics, had more broad-gauged interests in culture than Ford or Willey. Whereas that pair often used ceramics to make a culture historical point, Griffin, coming from a region of the eastern United States where Ford's ceramic sequence for the lower Mississippi Valley was not relevant, was always cautious about using hypothetical stages to describe prehistoric sequences. Griffin's (1958:11–16) discussion of Middle Woodland ceramics, at this point tightly tied to archaeological contexts, placed him far beyond Ford's attempts, which seem stricken with an obsession with the flow of time in which the archaeological context of ceramics seemed at times superfluous.

In his summary of Adena ceramics, Griffin (1945:245; emphasis added) commented:

> I am at a loss to understand the statements of Ford and Willey that the "Burial Mound I complex provided the basis for the well-known Adena culture," on the assumption that Tchefuncte is the fountain of the early Woodland period in the Mississippi Valley. It might be better said that Adena provided the basis for "Burial Mound I." On the matter of priority of one area over the other as far as concrete data is concerned there is absolutely no evidence. *It is simply a matter of assuming the source of burial mounds and rationalizing from that point.*

How right he was!

Griffin (1952b) emerged in the postwar period as a champion of the new radiocarbon dating method, and he used the dates, although he (Griffin 1958:22–24) was at times perplexed by them, to hammer migrationist interpretations. Summarizing those for Adena and Hopewell, Griffin (1958:2) declared that the emerging sense of the antiquity of Hopewell had "made all the migration theories obsolete" and added that "this is not to deny that culture spreads or develops through the behavior of people: I recognize that cultural elements are not spread overland by crows or carried downstream by logs." Griffin's interpretation of the Hopewell sequences in Ohio, Illinois, and the lower Mississippi Valley knocked the wind out of any idea that any sort of mound- or enclosure-building complex moved up the Mississippi. Setzler's 1934 interpretation, from which had developed the romance with Mesoamerican origins, could be laid to rest—but not completely, however, because versions of southern origins would still reemerge (e.g., Webb 1968). If Griffin saw the principal problems of eastern U.S. archaeology as related to chronology, then in radiocarbon dating he saw the solution. Here he believed that his inability to deal more decisively with Adena was due to the "the lack of adequately documented radiocarbon dates that could aid in developing a sense of the gradual growth of this culture from relatively simple, low burial mounds . . . to large multistage structures . . . which come into the period of Hopewell dominance" (Griffin 1964:236).

But in his own work Griffin was singularly unable to advance beyond chronology. Thus Griffin became one of Taylor's (1948:82–90) examples of the faults in Americanist archaeology. As an illustration, consider when Griffin (1958:1), speaking of Hopewell, wrote, "I shall not define the Hopewellian complex, but will depend upon my readers to have, or obtain, a general idea of its major characteristics" and spoke variously in that paper of a Hopewellian "culture" and a Hopewellian "complex." Griffin's failure to define Hopewell reflects a general failure of archaeologists of the time to explain reasonably just what it was they were studying, and this has dogged Hopewellian studies.

Exactly the same problems have beset the Adena concept. In his discussion of Adena, Griffin (1958:2–5) shifted between "complex" and "culture" and never dealt directly with a significant problem that radiometric dating revealed, namely, that there was considerable temporal overlap between Adena and Hopewell. How one sorted out and ascribed the expanding "trait" list that seemed to clump into Adena or Hopewell, and explained it all in human terms, was simply a task that could not be adequately addressed at the time. But by the early 1960s, Griffin (1964:237) could pronounce the end of the view of Adena as some sort of direct cultural descendant of Middle America. There would, however, remain the question of whether agriculture was somehow responsible for the earthmoving and cultural elaboration of Adena and Hopewell, as Willey and Phillips (1958) maintained with their positioning of Adena in the Formative Stage. It would take a generation of archaeobotanists to demonstrate that this was probably not the case however much the Ohio Valley may have been involved in non-maize plant domestication.

Adena: Rest in Peace? / 105

One of the more comprehensive publications in the history of Adena as a concept is Dragoo's *Mounds for the Dead* (1963), which represented an intense period of museum study in a major attempt to periodize Adena. Coming at a time when the use of radiocarbon dating was expanding, but really at the end of a period in which culture sequences were a regional focus, Dragoo was interested in placing Ohio Valley Adena in an explicit time sequence. This he did through the vehicle of his Cresap Mound excavation. The careful reader will find in the Cresap report, however, a wealth of curious problems and statements resulting from the interaction of "typology" and "traits" with new radiocarbon dates, suggesting that the report was hardly an adequate guide to Adena, despite its pretensions. Actually, Dragoo had a chowder of Adena "traits" up in the air, together with an equally disparate bunch of concepts. They came down in taxonomic slots very ambiguously dated by C-14.

A parallel product of Dragoo's involvement with the Cresap Mound was his attempt with Ritchie to define the eastern limits of Adena (Ritchie and Dragoo 1960). In his review, Griffin (1961) argued that there was no good evidence for an eastward migration of Adena and that any trait similarities could be explained by contact and exchange, a position that seems to be borne out by other fieldwork (see Black 1979). For all Dragoo's careful "typologizing," built on the efforts of earlier workers, Adena has proved to be an impossible classificatory term. It was not helped by publication of the McGraw site excavations, in which the authors cast Adena as a "phase" in the "Scioto Tradition," which played a game of hide-and-seek with a parallel "Hopewell Tradition" during the Central Ohio Valley Woodland Period (Prufer and McKenzie 1965:130) partly because that scenario held to a Middle American "model" (although not historical origin) for Hopewell, stressing an agricultural base for Hopewell.

The Adena symposium at Ball State (Swartz 1971) featured all sides of the Adena issue, but the article by Fitting and Brose (1971) about says it all, backed up by the comments by Orrin Shane, Edward McMichael, and Griffin himself. As Fitting and Brose pointed out, Adena was never even good MTS in that it never dealt with archaeological sites; it was a classification of traits, with the assumption that the traits were Adena. Adena grew into a taxonomic Boy Scout list of merit badges grounded in no archaeological contexts. Applied in the real world, *any* small burial mound in the Middle Ohio Valley tends to get called "Adena," excavated or not. By extension, *any* potsherd anywhere near said mound tends to get called "Adena" regardless of *any* excavated information from the mound or even the physical characteristics of the sherd. Expanding this type of reasoning throughout the 222-trait list (as of 1957), Adena rapidly lost any precise meaning.

The symposium participants all had rather similar comments to make on the state of Adena archaeology. As it was being used, the Adena concept was unworkable because regional differences were not being adequately considered. As McMichael (1971:95) stated: "The concept of Adena would be of more utility if its definition and inclusiveness were considerably curtailed." He was quite willing to write out of Adena altogether the mounds and enclosures of the Kanawha Valley in West Virginia that had been included by Greenman (1932) and Webb and Snow (1945), archaeological sites McMichael knew from his own work (see Trader, this volume).

What is impressive to me is that the comments in that volume (Swartz 1971) bore so little fruit in later years (mea culpa). This may have been due to the format in which the proceedings of the symposium were presented and the somewhat obscure publishing venue. Then again, the participants were quickly dispersed through death and old age and to other regions and interests.

Griffin actually contributed little to sharpening up the taxonomy of Adena, making it more useful as a culture historical concept, although thoroughly condemning it in the Ball State symposium and elsewhere. His detachment may reflect a view that Adena was, if not Webb's "baby," the focus of his contemporary, Richard Morgan; this view may have deflected Griffin's interests to Ohio Hopewell instead. In his role with *the* Ceramic Repository, Griffin was very influential in defining ceramic types and, through their attributes, giving them culture historical meaning. Yet this sort of typologizing, divorced from archaeological context, became increasingly suspect as a source of knowledge about cultural relationships (Taylor 1948: 141), however much the lower Mississippi Valley would continue to carry the torch for it, most importantly in the work of Harvard University (Phillips 1970). Griffin was rarely interested, for example, in the frequencies of individual types in given sites or in speculations on the composition of complexes comprising several types, as is especially evident in his (Griffin 1945) article on Adena ceramics, even though he did include sherd counts from early collections in his survey and made inferences from them. It was as if he picked up sherds one at a time, noted their characteristics, and mentally filed away his interpretation of their culture historical significance. It was exactly this type of reasoning, extended to other artifact categories, including the whole Adena trait list, that created and maintained the classificatory problem, perhaps to his chagrin. Griffin might have focused on typology and the classifications that it implied, but he seems to have been unwilling to tackle a more complex level of culture interpretation. As Fitting and Brose (1971:30–31) pointed out, the Adena concept classified artifacts and not archaeological sites.

Adena: Rest in Peace? / 107

But the problem was compounded by the twist Ford and Willey gave to Adena, perpetuated by textbooks such as Willey's (1966). Grounded in simplistic notions of general evolution, these archaeologists raised Adena almost to the level of an evolutionary stage in the onward progress of eastern U.S. civilization with strong developmental implications. Perhaps if Ohio Valley Adena had not been followed by Ohio Hopewell, the pressure would not have remained to use the Adena concept to serve in some way as a necessary developmental step on the road to greater cultural complexity. Given this pressure, who cared about the individual site contexts, for Ohio Hopewell demanded the existence of earlier and more primitive Adena. Adena lived on with a life of its own.

What Next?

I think all researchers are aware of what has to be done because the solution was outlined in 1970 at Ball State, although in a rambling fashion. That is, we must return to the field and develop local sequences of archaeological sites (not simply artifact types) that express space/time variation in human behavior. I can only touch on the solution, which represents nothing more than the sort of good culture historical integration Taylor (1948:40–44) called for in 1948, although he confusingly called this level of interpretation "historiography," using an archaic glossing of the term that, in the hands of historians, means something quite different. I call this "deconstructing" Adena (Clay 2002), a concept created during an era that saw the classificatory terms *themselves* as the end product of archaeological research, not intermediate analytical tools. Others (Seeman 1996) have expressed exactly the same need for Hopewell and for the same reasons.

Like many early classificatory constructs, Adena was wretchedly drawn, its shortcomings accentuated as new data became available. Others have come to much the same conclusion as I have. Julian Thomas (1991:xiii), in "rethinking" the southern English Neolithic, put it with style: "The search for change through time is itself seen as a means of disrupting the presumed continuities which underlie conventional wisdom."

An excellent example of this "return to the region" is McConaughy's (1990) recasting of the Adena/Hopewell Upper Ohio sequence in the West Virginia panhandle into two phases, drawing on local sites as typical examples. He suggested these may be followed by a "third Early Woodland phase corresponding to the final period of use of the Cresap site, perhaps related to the Robbins phase of Northern Kentucky" (McConaughy 1990:1), employing a construct not, to my knowledge, actually used in Kentucky. Finally, this sequence is followed by a Middle Woodland, Fairchance phase defined on the Fairchance site in his area (see Trader, this volume). The importance of this regional view lies in the fact that it sets the stage for a comparative study of this portion of the Ohio Valley, where local culture may have been following a certain trajectory of sociopolitical development, differing significantly from other areas, such as north-central Kentucky (infra Clay 1998b).

At least into the 1970s, this process of local sequence building was generally seen as hampered by a database that consisted mainly of mound excavations, many of them from a period in which contexts were not adequately recorded. Still, McConaughy's (1990) work, reordering principally the mound evidence, indicates that these data can be rethought without the straightjacket of the Adena concept, even without the benefit of nonmound data. Indeed, the plea that it would take new, nonmound data to move Adena studies (or Hopewell) off dead center can be construed largely as entrapment in orthodox interpretations of the significance of mounds. To Webb's credit, he and his supervisors provided the first adequately excavated and recorded mound contexts as grist for the Adena mill, but he never really explored nonmound contexts. Still, because the mounds were well excavated, I continue to find them important sources for new ideas about the ritual they represent, but I am less and less willing to view them as products of a unitary phenomenon (contra Clay 1998a). Regardless of what I have said, read my lips: Adena does not exist!

Even a lack of data is no longer the case, although the quality of data varies from region to region. In certain areas, such as the Muskingum Valley, thanks to Jeff Carskadden and Jim Morton (1996), and the Hocking Valley, thanks to Elliot Abrams (1989, 1992a, 1992b) and others, we are beginning to assemble information on adequately dated settlement systems apart from mound contexts. These data will add meat to viable and useful local sequences. In southeastern Indiana, Don Cochran's (1996:342–352) careful analysis of ritual contexts has demonstrated changes through time that have been obscured in the past by assuming that sites were or were not Adena. I mention these workers only as examples of changes in approach in the practice of Ohio Valley archaeology that have taken place since 1970. But, as Greber (1991b:21–22) reminded us with force, these local sequences are probably quite variable, to the extent that I think it obscures the issue to lump them all in an Adena culture, cult, or what have you.

This importance of local sequences has been brought across to me by my involvement in reporting the Woodland culture sequence for the mouth of the Great Miami River. I am now prepared to divide what would once have been called Adena in that limited area into no less than three sequential culture phases on the strength of ceramics (Clay 2002). This process of

Adena: Rest in Peace? / 109

classification will not be simply an exercise in suspect ceramic history. But, having defined local sequences, having "done" Taylor's (1948) chronicle, I am ready now to move on to his level of reconstruction (historiography), on the way, I hope, to the comparative study of culture (at least that is how he termed it in 1948). I do not feel inclined to move in the directions of the kind of culture history that got Ford and Willey in trouble and, in fact, plagues any archaeologist who has the temerity to believe he or she can really reconstruct culture history.

I stress, however, that in this process we are better off not to rely on the term "Adena," simply because it has far too many implications and assumes far too much similarity between cultural entities, even within the central Ohio Valley. The cultural sequence in the Muskingum drainage is not the same as that in the Kentucky Bluegrass or along the Ohio River main stem below Cincinnati, and in the variation between them we will—I hope—finally understand the dynamics of culture that produced in certain places those mounds and enclosures that continue to fascinate us.

I long ago realized that any attempt to define or criticize the term "Adena" led to ever-widening negotiations with other archaeologists because the term has been central, however ill defined, in Ohio Valley archaeology. Most researchers tend to take an entrenched view of Adena, reflecting their parochial uses of the all-embracing classificatory term. In her discussion of the Adena-Hopewell sequence in the central Scioto valley, N'omi Greber brought this out with tact. Her leadoff is essentially a peroration to the whole problem (Greber 1991b:21; emphasis added): "As one studies the culture contrasts and continuities across the various tributaries of the Central Ohio River, *there is no reason to assume that all the culture histories within each valley were the same and many reasons to assume that they were not.*" Yet she suggested that when Webb organized his significant Kentucky contributions under "Adena," he may not have made the best choice in terms (a point with which I totally agree!), especially when the point was to compare Adena with Hopewell. In fact I suggest Greenman (1932) made the same ill-considered choice in reporting on the Coon Mound in the Hocking Valley and calling it Adena, because the problem of the Adena-to-Hopewell transition there is just as acute as it remains in Kentucky (Greber 1991b:20–21; Waldron and Abrams 1999:101–103).

However, these comments follow Greber's reconstruction of the culture change from Adena to Hopewell as chronicled in those two local sites, "the" Adena Mound and "the" Hopewell site. In short, she took the position that, whatever archaeologists outside the central Scioto may believe, there *is* a culture historical sequence from Adena to Hopewell at Chillicothe. She has the considerable authority of the two "type" sites in her intellectual backyard. This is a somewhat more elegant restatement of Griffin's point about Adena in 1970 (Swartz 1971:158) when he said: "Certainly one place where no one can argue that there is Adena is on Governor Worthington's mound." Greber made a strong case, set against her general view of the problems of Adena as a classificatory term, for the validity of Adena as a term in a local Scioto valley sequence. But essentially the same position also tends to be taken by workers approaching the same question elsewhere in the obvious absence of either of the type sites and, at times, by taking considerable license with typology. In so doing Adena still tends to rise to the level of a developmental stage, if only as a heuristic device (cf. Waldron and Abrams 1999:101). This, to my mind, is a treacherous conceptual formulation.

8
Reflections on Taxonomic Practice
James A. Brown

Taxonomy and Its Discontents

Archaeological taxonomy in the midcontinent has remained remarkably conservative despite a history of persistent critique. Why has the taxonomy of archaeological units remained so stable? It would be facile to make this conservatism out to be an overly cautious reaction to the various critiques. Rather, a better case can be made for stability as an outcome of unit taxonomy as a common language for descriptive communication—what we can call an index function. In other words, taxonomy has a conventional aspect to it that necessitates attention to detail lest miscommunication emerge through careless or inconsistent usage. Although there was a period in American archaeology when the epistemological basis of taxonomy was a subject of debate, formal empiricism has given way to an acknowledgment that systematics is constructed to facilitate its indexical function. The formal, spatial, and temporal coordinates of archaeological data are a means for recovering these units (Wylie 2002). The space-time indexical function would suffice as argument on its own if it were not for an increasing use of artifacts as sources for information that is more important than their formal taxon-defining characteristics. As a consequence, debates about the goals of archaeological reasoning largely bypass formal considerations, shifting attention to contexts, nonartifactual properties of that context, and properties of the artifacts. It is in the spirit of the communicational aspect of systematics that I offer the following remarks.

Two issues are going to concern me in this chapter. Each of these exemplifies a specific long-standing abuse of taxonomic usage that needs to be dealt with far more explicitly and directly than it has been up to now. The first of these is the way in which trait-based intercomponent formal similarities have been converted into temporal or quasitemporal taxons. The "Late Woodland Period" is an obvious instance in which a category of formal similarities has been translated into a temporal one without qualification within the Midwest. The second issue has to do with the unproblematic way in which traits have been employed to identify "cultures." A prime example explored herein is that of "Adena Culture."

Contradictory masters have distorted taxonomic practice. Distinctions of form have wrestled with both historical continuities and evolutionary stage thinking. Each of these has had its persuasive advocates (Dunnell 1982; Krieger 1944, 1960). But debates about the proper objective of archaeological theory have led to greater attention on the quality of arguments that archaeologists have articulated. More often than not, those arguments depend on nonartifactual evidence left out of formal taxonomies. As a consequence, the formal artifactual content incorporated into taxons assumes the role of proxy for underlying practice or behavior. The utility of this content lies increasingly with the attributes and properties that reside in artifacts. These properties are frequently more informative about society, political economy, and other nonmaterial aspects than formal attributes themselves. Residue analysis, geological sourcing, and even radiometric dating come under the umbrella of "properties."

The first of these has been to assert the authority of objective measures to distinguish groups of similar archaeological components. From its inception the primary burden of the Midwestern Taxonomic Method has been to express degree of similarity (or difference) between taxons (Lyman and O'Brien 2003). At the same time, users of the method have had to face a number of problems. Among them are the following: How are these degrees going to be measured? How are determinative traits to be determined? How are differing levels of similarity going to be arranged conceptually? McKern's (1936) solution to the last-named problem was to adopt overtly a hierarchical arrangement in a conscious reference to then-accepted virtues of biological taxonomy (Lyman and O'Brien 2003).

The shortcomings resulting from subordination along a single dimension led to the jettisoning of the MTS (or at least its formal methodology and taxonomic hierarchy) for a multidimensional space-time systematics promulgated by Willey and Phillips (1958). Formal resemblances were made to share taxonomic rank with a temporal dimension. Together the two were considered to provide the essentials necessary for a demonstration of historical connections. For instance, contemporaneous connections become successful horizon styles in the manner of the Hopewell Interaction Sphere. Cross-temporal connections are more problematic, but nonetheless they have the utility of calling attention to the theoretical orientations of the proponents. At this level of proposed connections, the interjection of theory becomes very obvious. But these modifications are nothing compared to more burdensome complications.

Taxonomic principles embraced for sound reasons at that time remain ones that are important to this day. They were conceived of as a methodical, rule-based solution to the undisciplined naming of "cultures." Although scattershot naming is less of a problem now, a disciplined approach to taxon definition—or the process of "delimitation"—will always remain important. Although McKern was aware of the problem of boundary definition, he did little to address it theoretically. In his showcase demonstration of the utility of the MTM to discriminate the Rock River focus Middle Mississippian (a.k.a. Aztalan) from three Upper Mississippian foci, McKern (1945:161) recognized the closeness of the two categories but argued off the table for their "clear-cut cultural divergence." So much of this divergence was based on ceramic attributes that accounted for about *half* the traits; it would not surprise me to find that a different choice of trait groupings would produce a different outcome than his. Although the taxons endure, albeit with refinements within the Upper Mississippian ones, the cultural relationships between all of them are even more controversial today than when McKern wrote.

These debates respecting cultural connections involve new data sets and an increasing concern with the history of societies, a subject that McKern (1943) regarded—in concert with most contemporary thinking—as unsuited to archaeology. In line with contemporary thought, he regarded the material record as having to do with material culture. The study of societies and political units was beyond the capacity of the material record to inform. Obviously, many more sites make up our inventory of relevant components, now more finely divided than ever into temporal units. There hardly exists a single named "focus" that has not been divided into temporal units with content that allows for their ready recognition. But the method continues to work because archaeologists today have a detailed sense of what constitute "linked traits"—those observables that belong to stylistic progressions and vocabularies having a common origin. More than 60 years of practice have shown that the core utility of taxonomy has to be its tie to particular archaeological assemblages. Its function in a very real sense is to allow taxonomic names to substitute for lists of traits or physical objects found in a set of archaeological components.

Despite much inveighing on taxonomy for its blindness, let me state that the problem does not reside with its disciplined approach, but with the secondary, often unstated, theoretically driven texts that are expected to be borne on the backs of taxonomy (Kehoe 1990). From the outset, taxonomy held out the hope as an essential step toward the uncovering of ancient culture's "real" history. We should have gone well beyond this early faith in objects in and of themselves as a means for answering all of the historical and anthropological objectives that archaeologists have sought from material collections. Contemporary approaches are now much more sophisticated about our use of artifacts. It is clear that ecofacts, as well as artifacts, are equally valid starting places for analysis. Like artifacts, ecofacts are not the objects of explanation. Although the material world stands apart from explanation and narrative, the two mutually interrogate each other. Any doubts about this statement can be dispelled by considering that this material record was created by the actions and practices of bygone peoples. The types of pots that populate taxonomies do not replicate each other; only the people who made, used, and disposed of them do.

The big problem before us is the unexamined imposition of cultural-historical or cultural evolutionary narratives on taxonomy. The material record does not dictate narratives. Rarely can a unique narrative be found to fit this record empirically (Terrell 1990). More common is that we can come to some agreement over what a particular material record signifies through a triangulation of distinct arguments as Alison Wylie (2002) has instructed us. That means taxonomy and narrative stand on their own ground. Taxons become the named terms contained in a narrative, but they do not direct that narrative. In other words, we recognize more explicitly that we see the material record through two eyes, one having to do with formal similarities between assemblages and the other having to do with their imagined history.

Taxonomic Reflections

My operating perspective is that taxons occupy what Dunnell (1971) terms a class-property space. In the simplest case such spaces are generated by the cells in a two-by-two table. The headers of the rows and columns are composed of traits and artifacts deemed relevant. Expand this simple case to an N-dimensional table, and it is possible to visualize taxons as being defined by specific sets or blocks of cells. Subdivisions of that space become recognized by distinctions, as Albert Spaulding (1977) noted many years ago, not by shared traits. My major difference with Al is that I do not think that types or taxons possess "natural" breaks. Nor would I argue that the task of typologists/taxonomists is to discover culturally determined breaks. Quite the contrary, taxonomy belongs at the level of the tangible world of countables and feelables. In this view, the proper task of taxonomy is organizing the world that is directly observable. Interpretation, or, to be more honest, the creation of narratives about the past, uses the physical remains, but not in its taxonomic format. Some of the best interpretive work makes use of artifacts as sources of information that have the desirable feature of being controlled by specific archaeological context. Their precise context thereby articulates with a host of dates, contexts, artifacts, and artifact assemblages. Taxonomy merely becomes a way of placing that context in some sort of culturally labeled property space.

In this perspective taxonomy should strive toward effectiveness in conveying precision to the extent that the material record allows. The cultural properties needed to label unambiguously an archaeological context or collection should determine the property space within which taxons are created. I hear talk of "too many phases," as if some a priori taxonomic principle was being violated. The response to phase construction should be—can any trained observer identify these taxons consistently? If yes, then it should stand; if not, it should be merged into one that can. Taxons such as the "phase" create problems when they are gerrymandered to fulfill certain culture-historical expectations.

The Late Woodland Period

By way of example let us turn our attention to the confusing taxon "Late Woodland Period." It is a peculiar kind of period—one that is defined by cultural content, a configuration of sorts, and "Late Woodland" obviously means something different depending on where one is situated on the continent. "Periods" of such a kind are tricky and work only when there is broad assent about the significance of their content. They operate in particular kinds of contexts. A good example is that of the "Victorian period." Its continued utility is in its ability to capture cultural features of the Western world belonging to the second—steel and railroad—phase of Industrial Revolution prior to the First World War. But there is ambiguity aplenty in its use, depending on whether one is American or British. For the latter it is coincident with the long reign of a particular head of state. In the United States the term really is a period that captures the cultural character of post–Civil War industrialization without the name of a British monarch interfering with its utility.

The Late Woodland period does not have even the advantages afforded by the concept of the Victorian period. It is not tied to any kind of technological transformation. It is merely a holdover from a high-level taxon of the Midwestern Taxonomic Method that had little recognizable utility in past practice. In a recent review by McElrath et al. (2000) of what made up "Late Woodland," the authors found little unity in the concept. Only its core traits, well known from the MTS, have recognized utility throughout the Midwest. Within its time span, which varied by region, three "transformations" could be recognized: increasing balkanization of social groups, the adoption of the bow and arrow, and the rise of maize agriculture in importance. The term "Late Woodland" recognizes the utility of time, but concedes to preexisting conceptions on the basis of formal resemblances. Chronology is conceived of as relying on the taxon "Woodland" that occupies the highest and most abstract level of the MTM. The relatively clearly defined Middle Woodland delimits the early end. I emphasize the conditional here because the increasing reliance on Hopewellian stylistic elements to define the Middle Woodland is not unproblematic (Stoltman and Christiansen 2000:497). So we have here the increasing use of "horizon-type" taxonomic operations to delimit the archaeological content of the first centuries of the Common Era. No such horizon exists at the late end. Even the presence of European contact is of limited help because this material appears progressively later as one moves west from the Atlantic Coast. Of course the major exception is the intervention of another kind of cultural content, called Mississippian Culture. Finally, the trait-centered heritage of the "Woodland" taxon prevents some archaeologists from even considering Late Woodland in the Southeast at all (but see Anderson and Mainfort. 2002a: 14–19).

Even the less temporally bounded evolutionary concept of a "Late Woodland Stage" does not deal with its evolutionarily significant divisions in subsistence and settlement organization. As the aforementioned review article made clear, these transformations are embedded within the stage in specific regions only, not throughout (McElrath et al. 2000). The problem here resides with the configuration of the traits approach. It is suitable for the organization of museum collections of artifacts, but it is poorly applicable as an analytical construct. It might work as a taxon of sorts if—to use the jargon introduced above—the class property space was compact. But the very generality of traits and their individual distributions broadly elsewhere makes the concept of Late Woodland problematic. McElrath et al. (2000:23) explicitly recognize this in their avowedly configurational statement that:

> although maize agriculture and the bow and arrow were adapted elsewhere in North America at approximately the same time, it is systemic historical interaction that forged the Midwest into a recognizable culture area and established the underpinnings for the late prehistoric cultural landscape. . . . Although virtually none of these traits are universally shared, their nonlocalized distribution and overlapping geographic appearance suggest their importance as ingredients in the

recipe of an evolving Late Woodland ideological brew. The origin of many of these elements is extraregional. . . . But all are reformulated by Native peoples of the Midwest within the dynamic framework of a Late Woodland conceptual matrix.

The exceptions here and elsewhere represent a bad compromise between the dimension of time and the hierarchy of trait similarities used by the MTM. Neither is served by this muddled solution. It has the unfortunate effect of inflating the importance of shell-tempered ceramics above other criteria and of ignoring other unifying attributes, such as the transformative appearance of maize agriculture.

Why is the MTM such a poor foundation? It is because this systematics indexes assemblages in terms of shared traits. They are not restricted solely to objects, although such complete units of material culture were more conducive to the "catalogue-of-cultural-life" perspective that imbued the MTM. None other than Will C. McKern freely employed attributes of objects. The rationale behind this step is easy to grasp. If traits are regarded as culturally realized objects, then attributes distributed among these objects are likewise conditioned by routines of production—in the conception of culture of that day, all learned behavior. But this attribute-taking step had an unfortunate consequence. It allowed for building differences by magnifying selectively certain traits. For McKern it meant that he could demonstrate a high degree of dissimilarity between the Upper Mississippian and Middle Mississippian when a lion's share of the traits contributing to the difference were multiple nuances in shell temper. It is fair to say that McKern achieved the results that he needed to fulfill the theoretically driven conception of hierarchical separation of trait-centered cultures.

The hierarchical structure of the MTM leads to additional problems. For one, shared trait levels suggest phylogenies. Glottochronology is an excellent analogue. Each is an example of a directed graph. The MTM shares all of the problems that these models have. Culture is not a phylogeny. That notion should have gone the way of the Linton-Kroeber model of culture as a banyan tree whose branches interlaced (Linton 1955). Culture is not composed of gemmules moving through roots and branches, even if Clarke (1968) tried to resurrect it in his famous study. Culture is dissolvable, divisible, reformable, and capable of reconstitution. Sometimes cultures are bounded sufficiently to regard them as essentially closed systems. This perspective is implied by the bounded branches of the banyan tree. Just as often, material culture is found in unbounded fields in which the bounded branch conception would not apply. Social units are masked in the open-field case.

Equally problematic are the cases where objects are reserved for highly designated interment, most specifically with elite dead. The distribution of objects belonging to the Southeastern Ceremonial Complex exemplifies this situation well. Most studies of Mississippian period archaeology have a difficult time placing this miniculture in a specific context. The pigeonhole problem is solved by treating the complex as a characteristic of the period or a part of the period. That solution does little to account for the highly exclusive location of cult objects and for the equally limited number of distinct styles. Yet common features are present, suggesting unifying principles that link regionally segregated taxons in an alternative taxon. To round out this critique, I will add that the differential effects of power relations likewise have a distinctly contra-taxon effect on local cultural expressions. In complex environments intergroup power relations condition the content of components. Obviously, there comes a point when undirected trait counting blinds one to fruitful intersocietal connections.

Archaeologists no longer need to depend on traits to measure the passage of time. We now have a toolkit of absolute dating techniques. Chronology is best indexed by an absolute time as supplied by radiocarbon. Hence, the Late Woodland period should be redefined on the basis of important, chronologically sensitive features of cultures in the Eastern Woodlands. For starters I would advocate the upper limit at the circa A.D. 1000 timeline when maize agriculture makes a strong representation in much of the Eastern Woodlands, and the remainder is transformed to one extent or another indirectly.

Adena Culture

Let us consider another case. The Adena taxon is atypical but nevertheless serves to make an important point. Adena remains a pre-MTM taxon that has been incompletely organized even into the MTM, to say nothing of the Willey-Phillips (1958) space-time systematics (Webb and Snow 1945). It is not a taxon that makes any sense when judged by applications in other areas, even by contemporaneous standards. The history is telling. Greenman (1932) saw in Mills's (1901–1902) Adena Culture trait list an opportunity to generalize more broadly. He modeled his Adena according to Spier's (1921) age-area thesis that informed so many pre–World War II historical reconstructions. Hence, where Mills's Adena culture was richest was the place to center his age-area application. Core or typical mound sites provided the reservoir of artifacts from which connections could be constructed. Greenman's expectations were that the number of traits would diminish with distance from the southern Ohio center and that this drop-off was natural and a result of the diffusionary process. He selected the Adena

Mound itself as the type specimen in a "process [that used] the zoological method of identifying a species . . . as far as it is possible to do so" (Greenman 1932). The number of shared objects dropped to the point of trivial similarity was beside the issue. Griffin (1974:vii) stated with little trace of irony that:

> Greenman very clearly demonstrated by his trait list and analyses that all the mounds classified as Adena shared only one major cultural feature—the building of mounds into which burials were placed. They held in common very little in the way of burial practices or grave goods. Furthermore, only the Adena Mound had as many as 33 of the 59 generalized Adena traits; Beech Bottom Mound in West Virginia evidenced 29; one mound had 18; two mounds each had 17. In fact, 57 of the 70 mounds that Greenman called Adena had 10 or fewer traits identified by him as Adena.

One might envision a ray of redemption to this scheme if age-sensitive attributes were enlisted. But any notion of discrimination between these and other kinds of attributes was beyond the capabilities of 1930s archaeology. The age-area model fit the expectations of the age. It only assumed that the center lay where the number of shared traits was greatest and that this central accumulation of traits was the result of commensurately great time depth. Yet despite this blemished history of taxonomic abuse, Adena Culture endures. I can only cite the glaring differences in mortuary treatment that present from drainage system to drainage system to support the conclusion that the time is ripe to redefine Adena components in ways that are comparable to other Woodland taxons.

Conclusion

It was Junius Brew (1946) who famously wrote that archaeologists needed more classifications, not fewer. That is, there need to be more different kinds of classification rather than refinements to an existing one. In the spirit of this dictum, we should separate chronological relationships from formal similarities in assemblages. Historical connections are not to be identified with formal similarities.

9
Learning from the Past
The History of Ohio Hopewell Taxonomy and Its Implications for Archaeological Practice

Lauren E. Sieg and R. Eric Hollinger

The term Hopewell has been rather loosely assigned.
—Will C. McKern, 1936

All efforts to communicate about a subject, including taxonomic approaches, are cumulative, building on and refining previous research. To determine where taxonomy can or should go in the future, we must review how a particular taxonomic system has emerged. Here, we review the history of Hopewell taxonomy and discuss the implications of this history. We utilize the lessons learned from recent taxonomic reevaluations by Great Lakes, Midwestern, and Plains archaeologists to reconsider Hopewell taxonomy and propose that the convergence of temporal, spatial, and formal dimensions that is "Hopewell" most closely corresponds to the integrative taxon "horizon" as defined in Willey and Phillips (1958:33).

History of Hopewell Taxonomy

Hopewell classification efforts can be divided into two groups: classificatory schemas that were developed prior to the emergence of systematics and those that were developed afterward. The first group corresponds to research during the nineteenth and early twentieth centuries, the latter to archaeological work dating from the mid-twentieth century to the present. These schemas have produced enduring contributions that remain significant to the practice of Middle Woodland archaeology. At the same time, they have also generated problems that continue to plague Hopewell taxonomy.

Caleb Atwater (1820) was the first antiquarian to compile descriptions of numerous sites in the Ohio Valley. Atwater's conclusions about these sites remain relevant today. Atwater divided sites into two types: earthworks and mounds. He recognized that "our antiquities belong not only to different eras, in point of time, but to several nations" (Atwater 1833:10). The distinc-

Learning from the Past / 121

tion between different types of earthen architecture by time and form was an important conceptual development. Atwater also differentiated sites on the basis of function, inferring purposes such as defense, religious practice, and "diversion." The first two functional interpretations have persisted (e.g., Greber 1996; Prufer 1997). Ceremonial interpretations have been further developed (e.g., Hall 1997; Seeman 1995), but the defensive role of enclosures has been questioned (e.g., Riordan 1995).

In 1848, Squier and Davis provided a more comprehensive examination of Hopewell sites and an informal classification system for them, although they did not identify Hopewell as a distinct archaeological manifestation. Squier and Davis organized the sites described in their publication *Ancient Monuments of the Mississippi Valley* (Squier and Davis 1998 [1848]) into geographically broad regions that we now identify as the Ohio Valley, the Southeast, and the Upper Midwest. Rather than organizing sites according to space or time, Squier and Davis focused on form, i.e., earthen architecture. They classified sites according to presumed function, dividing them into enclosures for defense, sacred and miscellaneous enclosures, mounds of sacrifice, sepulchral mounds, temple mounds, mounds of observation, anomalous mounds, and stone heaps. Although these categories are not employed today, divisions based on form are still utilized. Enclosures are frequently divided into the categories of hilltop (irregular) and geometric, with the latter further subdivided by shape (e.g., Byers 1987; Greber 1997).

In the late nineteenth and early twentieth centuries, Ohio Valley archaeology fluoresced, with large excavations at major enclosures and mounds throughout Ohio. Fowke (1902), Moorehead (1890, 1892, 1897–1898), Mills (1901–1902, 1906, 1907, 1909, 1916, 1917, 1922), Putnam (1885, 1886), and Shetrone (1920, 1926; Shetrone and Greenman 1931) were among those who initiated the era of professional archaeology at Ohio Hopewell sites. By the late 1800s, archaeologists recognized that at least two distinct groups had been present in the Ohio Valley prehistorically (Moorehead 1892; Putnam 1884). Moorehead (1892) based his differentiation on cranial morphology, whereas Putnam (1884) distinguished the two groups on the basis of material culture. For both men, one archaeological group, the "mound builders," was associated with the mounds and enclosures, and the other, unspecified group was associated with large village sites. This distinction remains in use today; large village sites are typically associated with one group or "culture" (Fort Ancient), and enclosures and mounds are generally associated with another (Woodland). Putnam (1884) further theorized that the mound builders were not one large group, but were instead composed of many entities. Fowke (1902:148) also recognized that archaeological remains in Ohio represented several groups of unrelated peoples, probably of different time periods. He considered the different forms of earthen architecture—mounds, large hilltop enclosures, small hilltop enclosures, and geometric enclosures—to be the products of different groups of people (Fowke 1902:102). Archaeologists are still grappling with the question of how many cultural entities were associated with mounds and earthworks, as the taxonomic focus of this volume demonstrates.

Mills (1906:95) introduced the terms "Hopewell" and "Fort Ancient" for the archaeological groups recognized by archaeologists such as Moorehead and Putnam. Mills (1906:95) argued that Fort Ancient preceded Hopewell, due to what he believed were the more advanced architectural and artistic achievements of Hopewell. He later modified his view to place both Fort Ancient and Hopewell within the same time period (Mills 1916:204). Mills also introduced an evolutionary schema containing three stages within the Hopewell culture: an Adena stage, represented by the Adena and Westenhaver mounds, followed by a stage of intermediate complexity, represented by the Seip and Harness mounds, and then the most complex stage, represented by the Hopewell and Tremper sites (Mills 1916:284). Shetrone, however, argued that Adena and Hopewell were distinctive culture "types," alike only in their use of nonlocal raw materials (Shetrone 1920:159–160). He agreed that Fort Ancient and Hopewell were contemporaneous (Shetrone 1920:170–171). The terms "Hopewell" and "Fort Ancient" remain part of our taxonomic parlance, although their chronological ordering is now better understood. Likewise, the term "Adena" endured, as did interpretations of the chronological and typological relation between "Adena" and "Hopewell," although these interpretations were not universally accepted (e.g., Greber 1991b; Brown, Clay, and Sieg, this volume).

Shetrone (1920:159) was the first to delineate the spatial distribution of "Hopewell culture" sites, noting their occurrence "in the Scioto valley, from Columbus southward, with important isolated seats" at Newark, Marietta, Cincinnati, and along the lower Little Miami River, "with some evidence of occupation across the Ohio river to the south; and along the belt extending northwestward from Ohio, across Indiana and Iowa." Shetrone (1930a:187) later expanded the geographical extent of Hopewell sites to include similar earthworks further to the north and west, in Michigan and Wisconsin, although he believed that the Hopewell culture was "centered in south-central Ohio" (Shetrone 1930a:165). In his writings, Shetrone (1920:144) used "culture" as abbreviation for "culture group" or "culture variety," and he used "Hopewell" to refer to "peoples" and "band or tribe" (Shetrone 1930a:191). Shetrone's distribution of "Hopewell" sites is similar to later "Hopewell Interaction Sphere" distribution maps (e.g., Seeman

1979:260), although it did not extend into the Southeast. Today, the region of south-central Ohio is still referred to as the "core" (e.g., Pacheco, ed. 1996).

SYSTEMATICS-INFLUENCED RESEARCH

With the increasing number of archaeological collections, many of which were surface collections or from poorly provenienced excavations, it became necessary to develop a systematic method for organizing archaeological materials (Willey and Sabloff 1980:106). Two taxonomic systems have been proposed for Midwestern archaeology: the Midwestern Taxonomic Method (McKern 1939) and the Willey-Phillips system (Willey and Phillips 1958).

In 1932, Will McKern circulated a draft method for organizing archaeological information. The manuscript was titled *Culture Type Classification for Midwestern North American Archaeology*. In December 1932, a group of Midwestern archaeologists met at the University of Chicago to discuss this approach and its application (McKern 1939:301). The manuscript was revised by committee and recirculated by McKern for critique. After more revision, McKern presented the manuscript in 1934 at the Annual Meeting of the American Anthropological Association in Indianapolis (McKern 1934). The taxonomic system was again modified at the 1935 Conference on Midwestern Archaeology held in Indianapolis and sponsored by the National Research Council Committee on State Archaeological Surveys. At this conference, the precise taxonomic position of Hopewell was considered by various participants, including Frank Setzler, Thorne Deuel, McKern, and James Griffin (O'Brien and Lyman 2001). It is interesting that participants at the 1935 meeting noted that "the chief difficulty seemed to be the determination of the relations of the manifestations to which the term Hopewell has been rather loosely assigned" (McKern 1936:330). The system was presented in its final form as the Midwestern Taxonomic Method in 1939 (McKern 1939).[1] In practice, however, the MTM already was being applied to archaeological phenomena in the Midwest (Cole and Deuel 1937; Deuel 1935, 1937), Northeast (Ritchie 1937), Southeast (Greenman 1938), and Central Plains (Strong 1935), and similar schemes were being developed in the Southwest (Gladwin 1936; Gladwin and Gladwin 1934) prior to McKern's 1939 article.

The MTM emphasized the organization of the formal attributes of archaeological data and explicitly disregarded their spatial and temporal dimensions (McKern 1939:302–303). The MTM classified material culture through the use of trait lists. Complexes of shared traits ranged from the most localized unit, the *focus,* to the most generalized unit, the *base.* Between these, in decreasing order of traits in common, were the *aspect, phase,* and *pattern*. Thus, shared traits grouped components together as a focus, foci were linked through common traits within an aspect, and so on. The MTM recognized some traits as *diagnostics,* or representative of a particular manifestation, and others as *linked* traits, traits shared between manifestations (McKern 1939:305). Diagnostic traits that differed between the manifestations or units were *determinants* (McKern 1939:305).

When McKern first began to apply the MTM to what he termed "a Wisconsin Variant of the Hopewell Culture," he recognized a "Basic Hopewell," of which he considered "Ohio Hopewell" to be the "most complex expression" (McKern 1931:239). McKern found that "Hopewell pottery shows a basic similarity to a Woodland Area type" (McKern 1931:239). He later recognized Woodland as a *pattern* and grouped the Mississippi and Woodland patterns together in the same generalized *base* (McKern 1937), such as his hypothetical "Horticultural-Pottery Base" (McKern 1939:310). Deuel (1935) also defined a "Woodland Basic Culture" and a "Mississippi Basic Culture" as the two main pottery-bearing taxa in the Midwest. According to notes on the 1935 meeting, attendees suggested a "Woodland Pattern" distinct from an "Unnamed Pattern" that contained two phases, an unnamed phase containing the "Adena Aspect" and the "Hopewellian Phase" containing three unlisted aspects (McKern 1936:330). When Cole and Deuel applied the MTM to Hopewell, they defined it as the "Hopewellian culture phase of the Woodland pattern" (Cole and Deuel 1937:16).

Although the MTM did not attempt to integrate temporal or spatial dimensions of the material culture, McKern noted that historical or developmental relationships may be readily identifiable in some cases, but organization of formal attributes would be a necessary prerequisite to efforts to identify such relationships (Fisher 1997:119; McKern 1939). Paralleling the genesis of the MTM were efforts to develop an approach that gave priority to historical and ethnic relationships among archaeological manifestations. Interest in the connections among historic, ethnographic, and archaeological data was evident at the Birmingham Conference on Southern Pre-History sponsored by the National Research Council Committee on State Archaeological Surveys in 1932 (Guthe 1952:9–10). The potential of this "temporal approach" (Guthe 1952:10) was first demonstrated by Strong (1935) in *An Introduction to Nebraska Archaeology,* where he merged the units of the MTM into a chronological organizational scheme. The temporal approach, formally designated the direct-historical approach (Wedel 1938), remains an important analytical tool, although it has been criticized when inappropriately applied. Although the MTM was used to organize the formal dimensions of material culture, mounting frustrations with the fact that it was ill equipped to accommodate chronological and spatial concerns led to a synthesis of these approaches (Guthe 1952:10).

In the 1940s and 1950s, some tools developed by the MTM were combined with spatial and temporal information. In their synthesis of eastern United States prehistory, Ford and Willey (1941) organized archaeological "cultures" in time, space, and form. They ordered the archaeological manifestations of southern Ohio into temporal "stages" such as "Burial Mound I" and "Burial Mound II." Without absolute dates for archaeological materials and sites, their proposed chronology suffered (Ford and Willey 1941:331). The Burial Mound I stage was thought to begin around A.D. 900 in the Middle Ohio Valley, and the Burial Mound II stage ranged from A.D. 1100–1600. Ford and Willey positioned the "Adena culture" in the Burial Mound I stage and included "Hopewell culture" in the early portion of the Burial Mound II stage. Archaeological units in other regions that were contemporaneous with the Ohio Hopewell culture and shared its characteristics were identified as "Hopewellian" or "Elemental Hopewellian" (Ford and Willey 1941:328–330). Beyond these "cultures," Ford and Willey made only passing reference to a "Woodland Cultural Pattern," which included all other manifestations that might be considered "Woodland" (Ford and Willey 1941:341).

The Midwestern Taxonomic Method was rarely used in its most purely conceived form. It was being modified and integrated with temporal and spatial concerns for two decades prior to the first publication of the Willey-Phillips system (Phillips and Willey 1953). This system was further developed in subsequent articles (Phillips 1955; Willey and Phillips 1955), before publication in its final form in 1958 (Willey and Phillips 1958). Willey and Phillips (1958) borrowed from and built on concepts in use by archaeologists all over the world, assembling a series of specific taxonomic units. Their volume, now in its sixth printing (Willey and Phillips 2001), has served as a benchmark for Americanist archaeology and established the dominant taxonomy used today (Ramenofsky and Steffen 1998).

According to Willey and Phillips (1958:40), archaeological analysis should be divided into two types of analytical units—those that capture "formal and static" characteristics of the archaeological record (essentially building on the MTM) and those that represent the "fluid and historical" patterns of the record. The former consists of components and phases, the latter of horizons and traditions. They argued that, in their scheme, "there is no built-in taxonomic relationship" between the two types of analytical units (Willey and Phillips 1958:42). The system allows, however, for the "interplay" of time/space and the archaeological record; it is conceived in terms of integration, rather than rigid distinctions. For instance, Willey and Phillips

(1958:42) faulted Adena and Hopewell typologies for their lack of sensitivity to spatial and temporal detail, due to their focus on variable, overly broad traits.

In the Willey-Phillips system (1958), the spatial units most often employed are *area, region,* and *locality.* The only purely temporal unit is the *period.* Formal or archaeological units include the *component* and the *phase.* The taxonomic units *tradition* and *horizon* are considered integrative units because they unite or crosscut multiple phases. See Willey and Phillips (1958, 2001) for definitions and discussion of these units and explanations of the rationales for their selection.

Once the Willey-Phillips system was introduced, it was applied in different ways to "Hopewell." Caldwell (1964), for example, considered Hopewell a tradition. Similarly, Hall (1979) described Hopewell as a culture climax and a tradition. After initially identifying Hopewell as a horizon (Seeman 1979), Seeman later identified Hopewell as a phase (Seeman 1992b). Griffin argued that "the term Hopewell should be restricted to those Indian remains in southern Ohio of about A.D. 1–350. The large number of contemporary societies in the United States and south-central Canada can be recognized as regional expressions that indicate relationships to Ohio Hopewell in varying degrees but that had their own developmental histories" (Griffin 1997:413). Hall (1997:156) described Hopewell as a phase in regionally based "small traditions." Other researchers have sidestepped the problem of taxonomy by using the term "Hopewell" without taxonomic qualifiers. In some instances, researchers have used such terms as the Hopewell "phenomenon" (e.g., Hawkins 1996) or "Ohio Hopewell" to avoid taxonomic issues (e.g., Dancey and Pacheco 1997; Pacheco 1996).

Concerned about the lack of clarity in Hopewell taxonomy, Caldwell (1964) proposed the concept of "the Hopewell Interaction Sphere" to explain the widespread distribution of similar mortuary activities, exotic mortuary goods, and distinctive styles in the Middle Woodland period. Caldwell (1964:135).characterized interaction spheres as "the interactions among separate societies . . . resulting in what appears to be a distinctive set of phenomena." These separate societies were regional traditions, such as those recognized today as the Havana, Crab Orchard, and Scioto traditions (Seeman 1979). Caldwell (1964:138) suggested that "exact similarities in funerary usages and mortuary artifacts over great distances" demonstrated a pan-regional interrelation among Hopewell societies. The geographical area with evidence of such interaction was subsequently labeled the "Hopewell Interaction Sphere." The Hopewell Interaction Sphere was recognized by the presence of stylistically similar mortuary artifacts, features, or both.

According to Seeman (1979) and Struever and Houart (1972), raw materials that circulated in the Hopewell Interaction Sphere included copper, mica, obsidian, quartz, meteoric iron, silver, galena, cannel coal, pipestone, hematite, pyrite, and high-quality flint. Organic materials such as pearl, conch shell, shark teeth, and bear canines and claws were also distributed throughout the area encompassed by the Interaction Sphere. Finished goods consisted of copper ear spools, breastplates, headdresses, rings, bracelets, cut-outs of mica and copper, stone gorgets, pipes, celts, beads, plummets, pendants, tinklers, Hopewell ware, and finely made projectile points and prismatic blades. This list of exotic materials and goods (i.e., nonlocal raw materials and finely crafted objects) has provided the basis for continued "trait list" approaches to identifying Hopewell sites and objects.

The Hopewell Interaction Sphere model provided a means for researching Hopewell as an economic, ceremonial, and social system without addressing its taxonomic position. Other economic models focused on the exchange networks and their organizational or subsistence implications (e.g., Braun 1986; Seeman 1979; Struever and Houart 1972). Ceremonial and social models focused on the ideological forces at work in the Hopewell Interaction Sphere. Caldwell (1964:142) attributed "religion-based interaction spheres as the organizing principle" behind the formation of Hopewell. Similarly, Seeman (1995:122–123) has argued that "minimally, Hopewell also must be seen as an ideological system. . . . Hopewell is really the conjunction of two types of cultural systems—one, social structural and the other, symbolic." Cowan (1996) recently interpreted Hopewell Interaction Sphere goods as the means for transmission of social and ideological information about their owners. Research on the social dimension of Hopewell that does not explicitly define Hopewell as a social-ceremonial system can be found in Greber (1976, 1979, 1996), and additional analysis of Hopewell ritual has been provided by Greber (1996) and Hall (1997). Although these approaches to Hopewell research were not designed to resolve taxonomic questions, they recognized spatial, temporal, and formal qualities of the archaeological record. The fact that space, time, and form were a part of these studies despite inadequate taxonomic units underscores the need for an explicit and well-defined taxonomy that can be widely used.

The Legacy of Taxonomic Use and Misuse

Historically, Hopewell research has been plagued by four interrelated problems. First, Hopewell as an archaeological unit was defined before the advent of formal taxonomic systems. Second, without formal taxonomic units, Hopewell was defined by an expanding set of exotic goods skewed toward mortuary and ceremonial objects, obscuring other cultural patterns demonstrated by habitation and subsistence data. Third, the ever-increasing number of "Hopewellian" goods led to the identification of Hopewell sites throughout eastern North America, implying a widespread cultural similarity and creating a problem of scale for research. Finally, inconsistent, imprecise, or incomplete use of taxonomic systems has prevented the consistent application of clearly defined Hopewell units.

Defining Hopewell in the absence of a well-developed classification system has led to conflicting interpretations. For example, early researchers were unable to distinguish between the mounds and enclosures of different time periods and people. Only one cultural category, "mound builder," was applied to the earthworks. As a result, an understanding of the spatial and temporal differences between sites was obscured, even if it was hypothesized that different cultures were responsible for different sites (e.g., Atwater 1833). Moreover, because it was focused on "mound builder" sites, early research did not address habitation-related sites, components, or material culture. For example, Atwater's typology lacks information on habitation sites, although he considered information on habitations relevant in determining who built the earthworks (Atwater 1833:105). Squier and Davis (1998 [1848]) also omitted habitation sites from their functional categories. Thus, in addition to confusion over the spatial, temporal, and formal differences among "mound builder" sites, these early efforts at classification established a trajectory in which domestic or habitation data were omitted from consideration.

The continued reliance on trait lists has also been a drawback for Hopewell taxonomy. Traits considered representative of Hopewell range from broad patterns, such as the construction of mounds for mortuary purposes (Hall 1997), to specific activities, such as the horizontal use of demarcated space for a range of ceremonial activities (Greber 1991b). Hopewell is most frequently identified, however, by the presence of particular raw materials and finished goods enumerated by Struever and Houart (1972) and Seeman (1979). Categorization of sites as "Hopewell" on the basis of one or a few Hopewell traits (see Greber 1991b) has resulted in a higher archaeological visibility than may be justified. If the distribution of putative Hopewell sites were mapped using this standard, the area covered would include more than half of the continental United States, plus a considerable portion of south-central Canada. Cultural variation cannot be recognized or appreciated with this approach (e.g., Baerreis 1994 [1949]). Moreover, distribution studies based strictly on the presence or absence of Hopewell material do not accurately portray the *extent* to which populations in an area were part of Hopewell. More Hopewell material is found in some areas, especially southern Ohio, than in others (e.g., Greber 1991; Stothers et al. 1979; Vickery 1979), implying that participation in Hopewell activities was uneven across space. Participation was likely not uniform in the temporal dimension, either; it waxed and waned within and between generations (Greber

2003). It is also important to note again that the traits considered "Hopewellian" do not include habitation sites or habitation materials.

The final problem with Hopewell taxonomy discussed here is the confusion created by the misuse of terms or the complete absence of taxonomic units. Caldwell summarized the former problem in his statement that Hopewell has been identified as "a civilization, a culture, a complex, a phase, a regional expression of a phase, a period, a style, a cultural climax, migrations of a ruling class, a technological revolution, a social revolution [and] an in-place development out of previous antecedents" (Caldwell 1964:136). Taxonomic units have been applied in conflicting ways, for instance, Hopewell cannot be both a phase and a period as these units are defined by Willey and Phillips (1958). Spatial, temporal, and cultural categories have also been conflated and misused. For example, "Middle Woodland" is used to refer to a temporal period, and "Hopewell" is used to refer to a culture that dates to the Middle Woodland period. Unfortunately, the terms are sometimes used interchangeably. In addition to the problems with inconsistently or incorrectly applied terminology, there are many examples of cases in which no taxonomic term has been used, sometimes deliberately and sometimes unconsciously. The absence of taxonomic terms makes it difficult to understand the units involved and impossible to compare them. Unless an explicit definition of terms is given, the use of such terms as "Hopewell" is ambiguous at best. For example, "Hopewell" may refer to a group of people or an archaeological unit (of space, time, form, or some combination). A consistently applied and consistently used taxonomy is necessary for comparability between studies.

Early archaeological work made tremendous contributions to the understanding of Midwestern prehistory, both in the collection of data and in the dispelling of notions such as the mound builder myth. It provided a rough outline of temporal, spatial, and formal divisions. Early archaeological interpretations were refined with the introduction of systematics. Nevertheless, a heavy reliance on broad trait lists, seriation made in the absence of absolute dating, and misapplication of taxonomic units have resulted in a legacy of confused terminology and interpretations. Archaeologists now have the opportunity to incorporate new information, reassess earlier data, and build on previous work to refine the taxonomy in use for the Middle Woodland period in Ohio.

Recent Taxonomic Reviews

Out of necessity, archaeologists continue to grapple with taxonomy. As the volume of recovered archaeological material continues to increase, so does our need to organize and communicate about that material. The last decade has seen a renewed effort on the part of Midwestern archaeologists to reevaluate their taxonomies in light of recent discoveries, such as the 1996 symposium on Oneota taxonomy (Hollinger and Benn 1998) and the 1997 symposium on Great Lakes taxonomy (Williamson and Watts 1999). To varying degrees, participants in these sessions reviewed taxonomic problems for their respective regions of interest, refined the application of traditional taxonomies to their data, and suggested future directions for the use or, in some cases, abandonment of traditional taxonomic approaches.

The sessions also revealed difficulties and frustrations with the application of taxonomic systems, the most serious of which are identical to those that have been raised since the introduction of systematics in archaeology. These include the general lack of an understanding of the intended role of taxonomy; the misapplication of taxonomic terms and concepts; the potential for overuse of or overdependency on taxonomy; the proliferation of new taxonomic units; and, perhaps most often voiced, the disjuncture between taxonomic systems and cultural systems and processes. Nonetheless, these sessions demonstrated that taxonomic systems, particularly the Willey-Phillips system, continue to provide useful schemes for the organization of archaeological information.

A Reconsideration of Hopewell Taxonomy

We agree that the Willey-Phillips (1958) system remains the most useful taxonomic system for organization and communication of archaeological information, including "Hopewell." In this system, the taxonomic units *tradition, phase, subphase, culture, civilization,* and *period* are inappropriate units for "Hopewell." The integrative unit *horizon,* however, is well suited for the "Hopewell" phenomenon.

The horizon is "a primarily spatial continuity represented by cultural traits and assemblages whose nature and mode of occurrence permit the assumption of a broad and rapid spread" (Willey and Phillips 1958:33). A horizon links roughly contemporaneous phases and is usually marked by *horizon styles,* distinctive artifact designs or styles, and *horizon markers,* distinctive artifact or feature types existing over extensive geographic space. Willey and Phillips's (1958:37) definition of horizon includes the phrase "a primarily spatial continuity," which has been interpreted as the basis for emphasizing the spatial dimension of the horizon over the formal and temporal elements. It is revealing that Willey and Phillips (1958:37) were more careful to couch the word "primarily" in parentheses in their definition of *tradition* as "a (primarily) temporal continuity." Gordon Willey (personal communication 2001) later expressed regret for the confusion regarding the wording of the definition for horizon and explained that the broad spatial extent should be a hallmark of a horizon, but not any more significant than the dimensions of time or form. The lesson that time, space, and form are *equally important* dimensions should be remembered when considering the other taxa in this system.

We also need to guard against the misinterpretation of the *horizon* as somehow equivalent to the *period*. Willey and Phillips (1958:28) warned that as soon as such units are ranked "in order of time, they become 'periods.' As periods, of course, they are theoretically not spatially limited; they may be extended indefinitely." A horizon is spatially broad, whereas a period has no spatial attributes. A horizon is brief, whereas a period can be as long as the archaeologist desires, bracketing it with arbitrary dates, or with what Willey and Phillips (1958:32) called "extracultural dating criteria."

Unlike an arbitrary period, the beginning and ending dates of horizons may exhibit some degree of variation by locality or region. As Willey and Phillips (1958:33; emphasis in original) emphasized, "The archaeological units linked by a horizon are thus assumed to be *approximately* contemporaneous." They (Willey and Phillips 1958:33–34) stressed that "the assumed correlation is not necessarily horizontal but may, and probably does, have a 'slope' depending on the amount of time required for spread of the elements used as horizon markers." Therefore, in addition to the continuous need for regional refinement of dating on the basis of emerging data and interpretations, it should be expected that horizons will have "slopes" or clines and that the "broad and rapid spread" of cultural traits may have occurred on a sliding scale. As our control of the formal, temporal, and spatial dimensions continues to increase, we should be able to use these horizon slopes to trace the finite timing and directions of exchange and cultural diffusion. The period concept does not permit such temporal flexibility, and because periods do not have inherent cultural dimensions, they lack such potential for contributing to discussions of cultural dynamics.

The identification of "Hopewell" as a horizon is not new. Seeman (1979: 237) considered Hopewell to be a horizon and proposed a Hopewell Phase of the Scioto Tradition centered in southern Ohio and linked to other regional traditions by a "Hopewell Horizon." Willey and Phillips (1958:39) implied that Hopewell was a horizon when they noted that "Hopewellian zoned rocker-stamped pottery, when looked at from the standpoint of its geographic extension in the eastern United States, may be quite legitimately thought of as a horizon phenomenon." Willey and Sabloff (1980: 175) also noted that the Interaction Sphere concept shared many of the characteristics of the horizon style. Without using the word "horizon," many researchers have conceptualized the broad spread of "Hopewell" in terms comparable to that of the horizon. For Ford and Willey (1941), a horizon was implicit in their use of the term "Hopewellian" to identify the cultural traits shared with the "Hopewell Culture" of Ohio. Numerous other descriptions of "Hopewell" conform closely to the concept of the "horizon" (e.g., Griffin 1997:413; Hall 1997:156). The "reliability" of this unit, as measured by its repeated use, suggests that the horizon concept is the most appropriate for Hopewell.

We see a Middle Woodland period that temporally brackets multiple regional and local phases throughout eastern North America. Many of these approximately contemporaneous phases appear as spatially contiguous units because they share similar cultural traits and assemblages. These traits include such horizon styles as the spoonbill design, zoned rocker-stamped pottery, and cross-hatch–filled zones engraved on stone and bone, as well as such horizon markers as copper breastplates, bicymbal ear spools, panpipes, platform pipes, mica cutouts, Ross type bifaces, conjoined geometric earthworks, shark teeth, and objects made of obsidian and Knife River flint. Not all Middle Woodland period phases possess traits that would cause them to be included within the Hopewell horizon. The spatial extent of the Hopewell horizon is very broadly distributed, but discontinuous, extending from Ontario to the Gulf of Mexico and from the Atlantic to the Plains (Brose and Greber 1979). The temporal limits of the Hopewell horizon are more finite than those of the Middle Woodland period within which it is identified. Its duration varied by region, producing the variations in the beginning and ending dates across the horizon. This is why, for example, the radiometric dates for the Hopewell horizon in the lower Illinois River Valley differ from those for the horizon in southern Ohio.

Caveat Taxonomist: Let the Taxonomist Beware

Use of the term *horizon* requires caution, because the concept does not match sociocultural phenomena. Phases, traditions, complexes, and variants—and any similar taxonomic units—are not equivalent to cultures, tribes, religions, or ethnicities. Likewise, a horizon is not the equivalent of an interaction sphere, an exchange network, or a social structural and symbolic system. Horizons, like other taxonomic units, are the archaeological interpretations of formal, spatial, and temporal residues of such cultural phenomena; this is why we are careful here to use the Hopewell horizon in the present tense. Taxonomies are simply the tools used to order spatial, temporal, and formal data and should be used with care. Expecting a taxonomic system to model past cultural phenomena accurately and satisfactorily is asking it to do something that it cannot. Taxonomies that seek to assign ethnological equivalents to taxonomic units will always fall short of their mark. Applying a tool to a task for which it was not intended rarely works and often damages the tool, the material being manipulated, or even the wielder of the tool.

The need to organize and communicate information will continue, and as long as this need exists, so too will the need for taxonomic systems. As a technique for ordering data, taxonomies should be designed to match the research goals at hand (Rouse 1960; Sanger 2002). At the same time, they must also be designed with reliability, validity, and researcher comparability in mind (Ramenofsky and Steffen 1998; Sanger 2002) because they organize information and provide the basis for further archaeological interpretations. It is through comparisons of the temporal, formal, and spatial attributes of these units that archaeologists then make inferences about the cultural and historical processes that produced them. Only when taxonomic concepts are shared may we have the most meaningful and productive discussions about past cultures (Sanger 2002).

Acknowledgments

This manuscript is an expanded version of the conference paper "The Problem of Hopewell Taxonomy: A Review" presented at the 48th Annual Meeting of the Midwestern Archaeological Conference. We thank the discussants, Darlene Applegate and Robert Mainfort, and fellow presenters at the conference for their helpful comments. We also benefited from discussions of taxonomy with N'omi Greber, William Green, and Dale Henning. We are especially grateful to the late Gordon Willey for his time and help in clarifying our questions about the Willey-Phillips system and other taxonomic issues. Finally, we acknowledge the editors of this volume for their assistance in refining the manuscript. Any errors and omissions remain our own.

Note

The epigraph for this chapter is from Will C. McKern (1936).

1. Although this method is sometimes referred to as the "McKern Method," McKern explicitly stated that its creation was a collaborative effort that could not be attributed to one particular author. McKern (1939:301) wrote that "although the present writer's name has been repeatedly associated with this method, it should be made clear that no single individual can be accurately held responsible for the final product."

10

Rethinking the Cole Complex, a Post-Hopewellian Archaeological Unit in Central Ohio

William S. Dancey and Mark F. Seeman

In a volume dedicated to "the use and abuse of taxonomy," it seems appropriate to begin with a definition, an identification of what taxonomy is supposed to do. In brief, taxonomy is a tool that organizes phenomena for explanation (Dunnell 1971). Seldom are taxonomies seen as ends unto themselves. Universally, they are measurement instruments constructed of attributes thought to be culturally significant. They become the language of explanation if they help increase our understanding of the data. Conversely, if our taxa do not provide useful insights, either because they were poorly conceived in the first place or, more typically, because new data have introduced qualitatively different relationships, they should be changed or discarded. The case examined here, the "Cole Complex (Horizon)" of central Ohio (Baby and Potter 1965), principally in the upper Scioto and the upper Muskingum river drainages, may represent the latter case.

Taxonomies are constructed in conjunction with problem solving—unraveling a puzzle. In the case of the Cole Complex, which was proposed in the mid-1960s, the puzzle seems to have been as follows: How can we account for Late Woodland period archaeological remains in southern Ohio? Were Late Woodland period people descended from Middle Woodland period populations? Did the Fort Ancient tradition develop out of the local Late Woodland period populations, or was it intrusive? If intrusive, what happened to the indigenous people? If not intrusive, why was maize agriculture not adopted fully, if at all, by communities above the latitude of Columbus? This is an interesting set of related questions, none of which have been completely answered (see also Potter 1968:62). Whether or not the Cole Complex survives as a taxonomic unit, the questions stimulating its origin remain significant ones.

Over the years little has been published on Cole sites, and many Ohio Valley archaeologists have abandoned the concept. Those who do cite it often do so with hesitation. Shott (1989:33), for example, wrote that the

Cole Complex is the "most important—yet problematic—unit in central Ohio Late Woodland systematics." Other researchers (e.g., Carskadden and Morton 2000) have embraced the concept wholeheartedly. However, even those who still use the concept voice concerns about its meaning and scale. Does it apply to an ethnic group, to a pottery type, or to a horizon style? Is it located only in the central and eastern parts of the state in the upper Scioto and Muskingum drainages, or does it have a pan-regional distribution? More commonly, the concept is not used simply because many of the sites originally identified as "Cole Complex" are now known to fit more comfortably in some other taxonomic unit.

Definition and Distribution

Baby and Potter (1965:5–6) originally defined the Cole Complex as "a post-Hopewellian manifestation of a basic Woodland or Scioto tradition present in the Ohio Valley from Late Adena to Fort Ancient times." According to their analysis, Cole Complex sites were identified by the presence of Cole Cordmarked and Cole Plain pottery, a functional ware that was present among Middle Woodland populations and persisted into the Late Woodland period. Cole Complex communities did not engage in elaborate Hopewell ceremonialism and, by comparison, lived a simple life. Burial mounds were few, grave goods plain, enclosures small, and settlements dispersed. Baby and Potter also postulated trade and exchange between Cole and contemporary Fort Ancient societies to the south.

The Baby and Potter (1965) description of Cole ceramics came from four sites located in the Scioto and Miami river valleys: W. S. Cole, Zencor, O. C. Voss Mound, and Lichliter (Figure 10.1). Subsequently, at least 20 more sites were found to contain similar materials. In her master's thesis, Potter (1966) added Erp, Hudson Mound, Voss Village, Shipley, Henderson Road, Olen Corporation, Highbank Park, Fishinger Road, Blacklick Park, St. Joseph Cemetery, and Wolf Rockshelter, among others. Nearly all Cole sites are located in the Till Plain of central and west-central Ohio, although several lie in the Glaciated Plateau in east-central Ohio.

Historical Review of the Literature

The Cole concept was formulated after excavation of the O. C. Voss Mound site in 1963 (Baby et al. 1966), when a comparison was made of the artifacts from this site with those from the W. S. Cole site, excavated in 1947, the Highbank Park site (a.k.a. Orange Township Works), excavated in 1952 (McCollough 1972), and the Zencor site, excavated in 1957 and 1958 (Baby

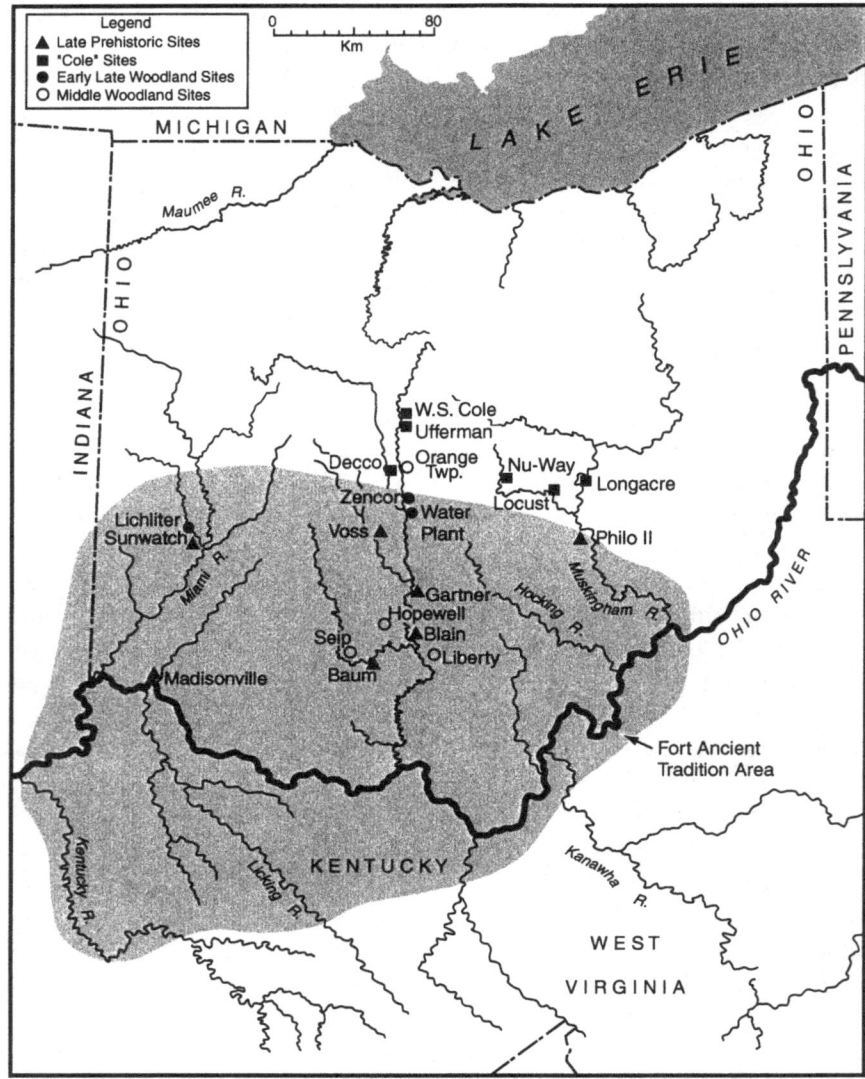

Figure 10.1. Locations of select sites referred to in the text.

and Shaffer 1957). Potter (1966) gave descriptions of the sites containing Cole pottery and commented on the cultural complex as a whole, although, as in the original paper, ceramic analysis predominated. In the same year, a report was published on the O. C. Voss Mound site (Baby et al. 1966), a ceramic sample from which figured prominently in the earlier 1965 paper.

The O. C. Voss Mound report contained a brief elaboration of the Cole Complex as a cultural unit, and an unpublished report on 1966 excavations at the O. C. Voss Village site (Baby et al. 1967) employed the concept, as did a file report on 1967 excavations at the Enos Holmes site (Baby et al. 1968). The Holmes site is located in southern Ohio in the middle Paint Creek drainage. Subsequently, a more extensive treatment of Cole assemblages and sites appeared in Potter's (1968) book on Ohio prehistory.

By 1968, it is possible to see the evolving concept of Cole as connoting a Late Woodland "lifestyle," one that continued through time until well after the advent of a Mississippian gestalt farther south. In this sense, Cole was conceptually more similar to the definition of the Late Woodland stage that had developed to the north in Michigan and New York, especially by Ritchie (1965:xvii, 300), than to ongoing taxonomic developments in the Ohio Valley and south. Cole-as-lifestyle was thus more akin to a "stage" concept (sensu Krieger 1953) rather than a strict division of time or space, although nowhere do Baby and Potter employ this systematics explicitly.

In the 1960s Prufer and McKenzie were also working in central Ohio, with notable excavations at Peters Cave (Prufer and McKenzie 1966) and Chesser Cave (Prufer 1967). Prufer and McKenzie's taxonomic efforts were much more squarely in the tradition/horizon/phase language of Willey and Phillips (1958), and not surprisingly there was a sharp dialogue at the time regarding the relationships of Prufer and McKenzie's Peters and Chesser phases to the Cole Complex. The only indicator in print of these discussions is Prufer and McKenzie's (1966:250; emphasis added) statement that

> after the completion of this manuscript, the authors had an opportunity to acquaint themselves with Late Woodland material from Ohio recently analyzed by Raymond S. Baby and Martha Potter of the Ohio State Museum. Clearly these materials are closely related to the finds from *Peters Cave B*. Spatially they were found in two discrete areas, Franklin County and the Miami drainage. Baby and Potter have defined these units and synthesized them into a *Cole Horizon* (Baby and Potter, 1965). Inasmuch as *Peters Cave B* is closely related to these materials, though probably somewhat earlier, and clearly in a different region, *the Peters Phase should be conceived of as a unit of the Cole Horizon.*

Interestingly, in 1965 Baby and Potter nowhere referred to Cole as an archaeological horizon; however, by 1966 they did (Baby et al. 1966:17).

In their 1970 taxonomic reorganization of Fort Ancient materials, Prufer and Shane (1970) were the first to nip at the Cole construct. Here they suggested that the O. C. Voss Mound site, a key site of the Cole Complex, seemed more likely to have been a Fort Ancient rather than a Cole site, and they proposed the notion of a Fort Ancient "Voss phase" for the central Scioto valley (Prufer and Shane 1970:257; see also Griffin 1978b:554). In 1971 Baby used the Cole concept in a paper on house types in prehistoric Ohio, but he also began to refer to Cole as the "Cole Culture" (Baby 1971:196). Working in an area slightly to the south and east of the central Scioto, Murphy (1975:13; emphasis in original) spatially extended Cole as a horizon concept to include sites in his own area, the Hocking Valley and to what he referred to as the "*Newtown phase* of the Cincinnati area." Murphy (1975:234, 246) was sympathetic to Baby's position of including the Baldwin site near Lancaster, Ohio, in the Cole Complex, in contrast to Prufer and Shane's view. Also in the mid-1970s, Phagan (1977) excavated several sites along the Olentangy River and dug several test pits at the Cole type site. He did not use the term "Cole Complex" in describing these sites, although he recognized that the sites contained Late Woodland deposits.

In the late 1970s Seeman studied artifacts from southern Ohio Late Woodland sites and evaluated the utility of Newtown, Cole, Peters, Intrusive Mound, and other taxonomic units in an often-cited unpublished paper (Seeman 1980). On the basis of examination of museum specimens from sites identified previously as Cole, he suggested that Zencor, Lichliter, and Swinehart conform more to the Newtown definition and chronologically should fit in the early portion of the Late Woodland period; that O. C. Voss Mound, Erp, Olen Corporation, and Henderson Road are more at home in Fort Ancient; and that only W. S. Cole, Ufferman, Green Camp, and Fryman qualify as legitimate Cole Complex sites. Concerning the chronological position of Cole, he advanced two possible interpretations: "These sites could immediately precede Fort Ancient, or they could constitute a separate, less complex adaptation contemporaneous with Fort Ancient" (Seeman 1980:10). He favored the second.

In 1980 Dancey (1988) investigated the Water Plant site on Big Walnut Creek and found evidence of a nucleated community similar to the Newtown settlements of northern Kentucky and southwestern Ohio. Similarities were also noted with artifacts from the nearby Zencor site, one of the key Cole Complex type sites. The following year Otto (1983) returned to Zencor and began excavating units along the southern end of the settlement where it extended onto land owned by the Columbus Public Schools (Scioto Trails School). In neither case was Cole considered the applicable taxonomic unit, and the sites were referred to simply as "early Late Woodland" in publications, reports, and popular material.

In 1982 Barkes (1983) examined ceramics from W. S. Cole, O. C. Voss

Mound and Village, DECCO, and Ufferman. She found differences among these materials and the defined Newtown, Baum, and Peters ceramics, concluding that the Cole Cordmarked type should be restricted to a subset of the original definition. For her, the type is distinguished by collared rims; exterior cordmarking up to the lip; flat, undecorated lips; grit tempering; and nodes, lugs, flanges, and castellations. Vessel shoulders are rounded, necks constricted, and rims slightly everted. Radiocarbon dates from samples obtained during Phagan's (1977) excavations at the W. S. Cole site, in which Barkes took part, point to the twelfth and thirteenth centuries A.D. as the period of the type's greatest popularity. From this Barkes (1983:21) concluded that Cole Complex sites are "Late Woodland sites culturally, but temporally contemporaneous with the Late Prehistoric Fort Ancient Tradition."

In 1984 Morton constructed the first effective cultural chronology for the central Muskingum drainage. He reserved Cole for the post-A.D. 1000 period, and he has continued to identify Cole components in east-central Ohio (Carskadden and Morton 2000; Morton 1984a, 1984b, 1989). In the following year, Seeman's (1985) monograph on the Locust site, a small multicomponent site in the Licking Valley, was published. Pottery similar to that from DECCO, Ufferman, and W. S. Cole was present, and, on the basis of the available data and associated radiocarbon dates, Seeman interpreted the site as a non-Fort Ancient seasonal camp of a small-site-oriented community of the thirteenth century A.D. The ceramics were typed as Cole Cordmarked on the basis of Barkes's (1983) redefinition (Seeman 1985:57).

Recent references to the Cole concept have come from Shott (1989, 1990), whose reviews of much of the literature cited above led him to conclude that the Cole concept covered too long a time span (1,000 years), aggregated highly dissimilar assemblages, contained deposits with conflicting radiocarbon dates and historically significant ceramic types, and included artifact types that are more at home in northern areas than in the Middle Ohio Valley (Shott 1989:32–34).

Current Potential Cole Complex Sites

As noted above, many sites on the original Cole list have been dated and now are known to fit better taxonomically into other established units. Notably, Zencor and Lichliter are characterized by ceramic assemblages of Newtown style and thus can be dated confidently to the early portion of the Late Woodland period, between A.D. 500 and 600 (Seeman and Dancey 2000). O. C. Voss Village and Enos Holmes fall in the Late Prehistoric period and contain Fort Ancient style ceramics (Seeman 1980).

One particularly intriguing site on the Cole Complex list is the Highbank Park site located on a 30-m-high bluff overlooking the Olentangy River in Franklin County. In this chapter we refer to the site as the Orange Township Works to acknowledge Squier and Davis's (1848:36) description and map and to avoid confusion with a similarly named Middle Woodland period site in Ross County (the High Bank Works; Squier and Davis 1848:50). The Orange Township Works consists of a 1-m-high earthen embankment that is bordered along its entire length (ca 460 m) by an exterior ditch and is broken in three places by entryways. The enclosed area, estimated at ca 35 ha, slopes to the west at an 8-degree angle and is cut in three places by deep ravines, one of which extends to the valley floor. Field notes (Baby 1952) of the 1952 trench that cross-sectioned the embankment east of the northern entrance way and extended ca 100 m into the interior reveal that few artifacts were encountered and that assignment of the site to the Cole Complex may rest on the presence of a single flared base projectile point.

Two properties of the site suggest that a Middle Woodland placement might be considered for the Orange Township Works. The first is that the discontinuous embankment is a common architectural design among Middle Woodland earthworks (Squier and Davis 1848). Second, the Ohio State Museum trench revealed two strata, red in the center and yellow on the exterior. Similar evidence of periodic enlargement of the enclosure walls is common in the Middle Woodland period (Prufer 1997). At the very least, we urge a reevaluation of the Orange Township Works/Highbank Park site to determine accurately when the embankment was built. Because of our own belief that the case for Middle Woodland period placement is persuasive, we are not including this site in our discussion of the validity of the Cole concept.

Making up for the loss of many reputed Cole Complex sites, archaeological research in central Ohio subsequent to the 1960s has yielded new materials that are strongly similar to those recovered from the W. S. Cole type site. These include DECCO (Dancey 1998; Phagan 1977) and Ufferman (Barkes 1983) in the Olentangy River valley, located not far downstream from W. S. Cole, as well as Nu-Way (Hooge 1986–1987) and Locust (Seeman 1985) in the Licking Valley and Longacre I, Longacre II, Copeland Island, and Philo II in the central Muskingum Valley (Carskadden and Morton 2000), among others. As a result, components identified as "Cole," ironically, enjoy more ceramic homogeneity today than when the concept was originally proposed in the 1960s. Because of limitations on space, we have chosen to examine only the W. S. Cole site and its downstream neighbors, Ufferman and DECCO, in greater detail. Like the Cole concept itself, two of these sites may not be what they seem, as the brief descriptions and evaluations below reveal.

W. S. Cole Site (33DL11)

The W. S. Cole site is located on the southeastern slope of a low glacial feature such as a kame or esker. It was visited in 1947 by Richard Morgan, curator of archaeology at the Ohio State Museum, after he had been contacted by Genevieve Cole, who had found the skeletons of a woman and infant and a broken pottery vessel on the edge of a shallow depression excavated into the side of the gravely ridge. Morgan reportedly recognized the pottery style as Late Woodland and arranged to have the site investigated by a crew from the Ohio State Museum. Work took place in July 1947 under the direction of Raymond Baby (1947). The investigation included a transit survey over a .2-ha area surrounding Mrs. Cole's discovery, test pitting (11 3 × 5 ft units) over a .04-ha area, and excavation of a trench through the depression where the skeleton and vessel were found.

The W. S. Cole archaeological deposit is usually interpreted as a residential settlement consisting of a shallow, elongated basin with pit features in the center and a burial at one end (Potter 1966). A reexamination of the files and collections curated at the Ohio Historical Society Collections Center, however, suggests that a strong argument can be made that the W. S. Cole site functioned exclusively as a cemetery. The evidence for this alternate explanation comes from the original trench excavation and accompanying test pitting, along with test pitting done in the 1970s, as described later.

With regard first to the trench, as reported in the field notes (Baby 1947), the W. S. Cole deposit consists fundamentally of two strata. The lower one (Stratum I) is made up of gravel interspersed with pockets or lenses of sand and gravel or compact clay and sand indicative of a glacial deposit. The four features excavated by the Ohio State Museum crew were dug into this stratum. Above this is a layer (Stratum II) of mixed sand, gravel, and clay containing small amounts of unevenly distributed sherds, human bone, shell, and animal bone. The surface of this stratum had been exposed long enough for a "sod" to develop. On the west end of the trench, a sharply defined, downward cut can be observed in the stratigraphic profile, and on the eastern end a lens of dark humus was recorded. The cultural features are buried under this stratum.

Originally this evidence was explained as a midden deposit (Stratum II) that formed in the ruins of an abandoned structure, which in turn had at least one burial dug into its floor along with a number of storage pits (Baby

1947). Alternatively, the same information can be explained as the historic period disturbance of a prehistoric cemetery. From this perspective, the cut on the west of the profile is seen as being produced by a metal tool. Whether dug for gravel or to loot burials, according to this explanation all but one of the burials within the 1947 archaeological trench were removed by this activity. The one that was missed, of course, was the one found by Mrs. Cole.

Additional support for this alternative explanation comes from artifact distributions within the trench and from the results of the 1947 test pits. With regard to the trench, mapping the distribution of human bone fragments and pottery sherds revealed clustering around the edges of the pit features, such as could occur if a pit was being cleaned out. Because human bone is a significant proportion of the artifacts ringing the Stratum I cultural features, and because Mrs. Cole's discovery included a skeleton and a pottery vessel, we argue that the pits are the bottoms of burial pits, not storage pits covered by midden.

Nearly all of the 11 test pits dug in 1947 were barren of artifacts, establishing that the cultural remains at the W. S. Cole site were concentrated in the area of the trench. If there was a settlement at this location in prehistory, it was short lived and special purpose.

The W. S. Cole site was tested again in 1977 by Carl Phagan (1977). His crew dug 7 1 × 1 m sq test pits over the same area as tested in 1947. As in the testing 30 years earlier, Phagan's test pits came up with few artifacts, except for Test Pit 2. This test pit exposed what appeared to be midden soil because of its blackness. Also, there were clear strata in the side walls and sherds in the upper layer. Given that this area is downslope from the trench and only several meters away from it, it is possible that Test Pit 2 penetrated through the back dirt from the trenching.

Three radiocarbon dates have been acquired for the W. S. Cole site, as shown in Table 10.1. The first two (Carr and Haas 1996) are on bone from the margins of two features in the bottom of the depression and may be associated with the archaeological burial event. However, if our hypothesis is correct, they may have been dislocated by quarrying or looting. The third comes from the potential looter's back dirt and may not be trustworthy. Thus, all three may be in disturbed contexts. With the removal of the potentially most seriously disturbed sample, the one from Phagan's Test Pit 2, the calibrated dates from the other two put the occupation sometime in the early thirteenth century A.D.

If this alternative explanation is true, the W. S. Cole site becomes even more enigmatic. This is a unique type of burial for this region and occurs without precedence in the known local occupational history. Ironically, what might have been an early case of Late Woodland settlement archaeology in

Table 10.1. Radiocarbon dates from central Ohio Cole Complex sites

Provenience	Lab. No.	Material dated	RCYBP	Calibrated date (2 sigma)
W. S. Cole				
Feature 1	SMU-2083	Bone	656 ± 113	A.D. 1163 (1300, 1374, 1377) 1445
Feature 3	ETH3926	Bone	715 ± 75	A.D. 1189 (1285) 1402
Test pit 2	DIC-2284	Wood charcoal	680 ± 55	A.D. 1258 (1296) 1401
Ufferman				
Unit N14W1	DIC-2843	Wood charcoal	700 ± 50	A.D. 1243 (1290) 1394
DECCO				
Feature PR01	DIC-1079	Wood charcoal	820 ± 45	A.D. 1069 (1221) 1283
Feature PB01	DIC-1076	Wood charcoal	790 ± 55	A.D. 1159 (1259) 1296

Note: From Maslowski et al 1995; calibrations calculated using CALIB 1.3.

central Ohio may actually present the same dilemma as encountered in the mound-rich regions—little knowledge of residential sites.

Ufferman Site (33DL12)

Only 0.6 km south of the W. S. Cole site and also on the east side of the Olentangy River is the Ufferman site. The site was surveyed, recorded, and excavated by Carl Phagan in 1976. A report was written by Barkes (1978), and Ward (1980) submitted a report on the site as his senior thesis at Ohio Wesleyan.

Like the W. S. Cole site, Ufferman consists of human burials (at least five) interred in the side of an esker; it also was badly damaged by recent disturbance, a sugar camp in this instance. The ceramics from Ufferman are identical to those from the W. S. Cole site (Barkes 1983). Two charcoal samples obtained during excavations conducted in 1976 (Ward 1980) produced radiocarbon dates, one in the early ninth century A.D. and the other in the early thirteenth century A.D. (see Table 10.1). In his senior thesis, Ward (1980) argued that the site represented a settlement with attached burials, yet we think a case can be made that Ufferman is mostly a cemetery, as we suggest for W. S. Cole.

DECCO Site (33DL28)

Quite different from the W. S. Cole and Ufferman sites is the DECCO site, which is located 23 km south of Ufferman on the valley floor of the Olentangy River across from the Orange Township Works. The DECCO site was stripped by Phagan (1977) in 1977 after discovery of potential cultural features and artifact clustering on and in the plow zone. Troweling and shovel scrapping revealed a sharply defined circular post mold pattern with associated pit features along with two burials and a small sheet midden (Dancey 1998).

The site apparently contains the remains of at least two occupations, one in the late Middle Woodland period and the other in the Late Prehistoric period. The Middle Woodland period occupation includes the structure and several scattered pits from inside and outside of it. Four radiocarbon dates, one from a post mold in the structure wall and the other from an internal pit feature, were obtained (see Table 10.1) (Maslowski et al. 1995). There are no published explanations of the DECCO data, but this occupation seems to represent the remains of a short-lived household. If this is true, and if the Orange Township Works is Middle Woodland, the two together might be pointing to the existence here of a Hopewellian community such as the ones more common in southern Ohio (Dancey and Pacheco 1997). With

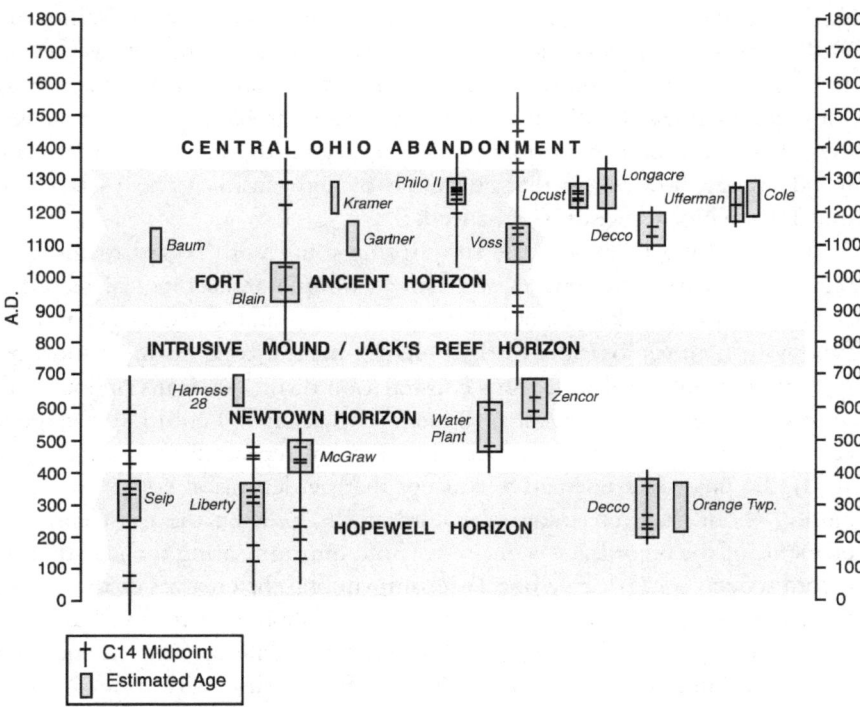

Figure 10.2. Time-space chart of significant Woodland and Late Prehistoric period sites in central and eastern Ohio.

regard to the Late Prehistoric period occupation, researchers found two burials and associated pit features along with a shallow midden that date to the Late Prehistoric period, in the early twelfth century A.D. (Maslowski et al. 1995). This date was obtained from charcoal from a burial containing a jar nearly identical to the Cole Cordmarked type definition: fully cord-marked, rounded shoulder, inverted and collared rim, and four castellations evenly spaced around the rim.

Discussion

Figure 10.2 is a time-space chart of the sites discussed in this chapter along with other well-known sites dated between A.D. 1 to A.D. 1500. From this typical distributional display of data we have a choice about where to go with the analysis. One choice is to group similar assemblages on the assumption that the groupings represent distinctive archaeological cultures. This is the familiar approach taken by the Midwest Taxonomic System

(McKern 1939; Griffin 1946) and the phase-based systematics of Willey and Phillips (1958). The other, less familiar choice is to leave the data as they are and map the distribution of cultural traits directly on the time-space array. This approach has the disadvantage of increased problems of data management because it does not employ the simplifying mechanism of the phase. Its advantage, however, is that awareness of and sensitivity to variation in the archaeological record is enhanced.

It is tempting to choose the simplifying route with regard to the Cole Complex. All the ingredients are there: a unique archaeological record of cemetery burial in kames, floodplain settlement, and a distinctive pottery type within an ecologically distinct environmental zone during a short period of archaeological time. This constellation of unique traits undoubtedly points to a significant variant of human adaptation and cultural heritage in central Ohio. However, as has been pointed out repeatedly (especially Plog 1974), the phase is a normative concept that by definition comes to a conclusion about the archaeological record and focuses on the most common elements of the record. As a concise way of communicating the idea that the record reflects some degree of relationship among the creators of the record, the phase is immensely useful. Perhaps its role should be reserved as a tool of synthesis after detailed study of the record comes to some conclusion about past human organization in the region over time. Given our interests in tracking the processes of human cultural stability and change on as small a scale as the record will permit, we have chosen to avoid the temptation to create a Cole phase and judge that the data do not justify the continued use of the various other Cole taxa—complex, horizon, culture, and, worst of all, Cole Indians—in the literature.

By way of approaching an end to our evaluation of Cole, it is useful to summarize what we know. First, the pottery type Cole Cordmarked is, or could be, a useful construct. We have shown that the initial definition of 40 years ago is much too broad to be employed today. According to our conception, Cole Cordmarked should be reserved for those ceramics in central Ohio that have cordmarked surfaces, appliquéd or folded rim strips, castellations, and grit tempering (Figure 10.3). In terms of overall construction, examples of this type are similar to early and middle Fort Ancient pottery found immediately to the south, as might be expected, but Cole Cordmarked vessels lack strap handles, standardized fields of surface decoration on the vessel shoulder, and shell tempering. Historically, the shell-tempering state was often seen as the most significant character in building a Woodland/Mississippi divide in the heyday of the Midwestern Taxonomic System. Cole Cordmarked pottery occurs in the central Scioto and adjacent Licking and Muskingum valleys of interior Ohio. On the basis of radiocar-

— 1 cm

A

— 1 cm

B

Figure 10.3. Typical Cole Cordmarked rims. A. Munroe Basin site, Muskingum County, Ohio (courtesy of James Morton and Jeff Carskadden), castellation prominent; B. Nu-Way site in Licking County, Ohio (courtesy of the Licking County Archaeology and Landmarks Society), castellation weakly expressed.

bon dates from Philo II, Copeland Island, Longacre I, Locust, DECCO, Ufferman, and W. S. Cole, one can say that the Cole Cordmarked pottery type was manufactured and used mainly in the twelfth and thirteenth centuries A.D. Ironically, the largest ceramic assemblages that Baby and Potter worked with in the 1960s—those from Zencor, Lichliter, and O. C. Voss Mound—do not have ceramics meeting the above criteria. Cole Cordmarked pottery thus pertains entirely to the Late Prehistoric period; the notion of "Woodland" or even "Late Woodland" affiliation should be erased as a modifier for this material.

Second, sites producing Cole Cordmarked pottery are uniformly small but are so poorly sampled that higher-level taxonomic units constructed to group assemblages are tentative at best. Third, the only sites that have identified flotation samples, Locust, Longacre I and II, and Philo II, suggest that maize agriculture probably was not as important as it was in the Fort Ancient alluvial farmlands to the south or in the maize- and fish-based settlements of Lake Erie and its tributaries to the north (Seeman 1985:99). This is ironic because the Till Plains of central Ohio are today the breadbasket of the state. All that can be said at this point is that this was not the case in the thirteenth century A.D. and that here there were probably other kinds of adaptations for which other kinds of archaeological taxa may be appropriate.

How should we categorize those sites in central Ohio that have produced Cole Cordmarked pottery if the phase concept is inappropriate and the associated nonpottery material underdefined? Most elegantly, such sites can be categorized according to a period scheme; that is, radiocarbon dates and ceramic attributes permit assignment to the Late Prehistoric period, generally taken as postdating 1000 A.D. in the Ohio Valley. Second, we are comfortable in placing such sites within the evolving tradition of indigenous ceramic manufacture and decoration through the Woodland and Late Prehistoric periods in the region. Beyond that, we do not believe the data warrant additional compartmentalization at this point or, to be more precise, that any such attempts would go beyond what the available data allow. By maintaining a "loose" approach to taxonomy in this case, we believe we are less likely to mask the processes pertaining to the major questions we are likely to ask of these materials in the future.

Acknowledgments

Thanks to Darlene Applegate and Bob Mainfort for their invitation to join this bold venture and for their helpful editing and criticism. Thanks also to Jim Morton and Paul Pacheco for their response to our queries. We profited greatly from their advice and that of the reviewers, yet we must assure them that we take full responsibility for the accuracy of the data in this paper, the construction of the argument, and the conclusions. We also gratefully acknowledge the Ohio Historical Society for granting access to the museum collections and records bearing on some of the sites discussed here.

11

The Many Messages of Death

Mortuary Practices in the Ohio Valley and Northeast

Sean M. Rafferty

American archaeology is now in a critical period. This situation can be viewed in two ways: critical in that current theoretical and methodological developments are of great importance to the future of the science or critical in that we, as scientists, are forced to look back critically on work that has formed foundations to our interpretations. Where these foundations are found to be flawed, misapplied, misunderstood, or simply wrong, the critical reevaluation of previous concepts and interpretations can not only right past errors or erroneous assumptions but also lead to new and innovative ways of investigating old problems. Nowhere, perhaps, is this more salient than in reexaminations of temporal and spatial taxonomies that have formed the structural frame on which decades of archaeological interpretations have been hung.

Taxonomy is simply the arbitrary categorization of data. This applies to any taxonomic science, be it archaeology or biology. Just as there is a basal reality to biologic taxonomy in the form of reproductively isolated species, there is a similarly real foundation in archaeology in the form of artifacts. In both sciences, however, successive taxonomic hierarchies, such as genera and families for biology, or phases and periods for archaeology, are arbitrary constructs of the scientists. As such, they ideally should be formed with an eye toward the types of problems and questions with which archaeologists (and biologists) are presented. A taxonomy is a tool for a specific interpretive task, rather than a real "thing" in any absolute sense.

This does not mean that individual researchers should develop their own scheme of organizing empirical data for their own purposes; that would lead to chaos and an inability to compare results. It does mean, though, that taxonomic structures are open to reevaluation, modification, or even rejection in light of new data.

This is precisely the situation we now face with respect to the taxonomy of archaeological material culture of later prehistory in the Ohio Valley.

Taxonomic sequences of "cultures," "phases," or "foci," originally formulated prior to the development of radiocarbon dating, have formed the backbone of archaeological interpretations since their inception in the early twentieth century. Increasingly, new data conflict with these older taxonomic structures, and what were initially simple, orderly sequences of "cultures" are found to be far more complex. This trend is not limited to the archaeology of the Ohio Valley region; similar reassessments are under way in other study areas (e.g., Miroff and Knapp 2004). One common theme to many of these critical approaches is a renewed attention by archaeologists to the spatial and temporal scales of our analyses.

Scales of Analysis in Early and Middle Woodland Ohio Valley Taxonomy

Despite more than a century of archaeological research in the Ohio Valley, there are sizable differences in the quality of data for many prehistoric periods. Perhaps no period of prehistory better exemplifies this than the period from approximately 3000 to 1000 B.P., a time range commonly designated the Early and Middle Woodland periods. Particularly vexing within the Early and Middle Woodland periods is the issue of elaborate mortuary mound sites, still known by their original designations, "Adena" and "Hopewell." Early interpretations of the Early and Middle Woodland periods sought to explain variation in the archaeological record in terms of the migration of populations into and out of the Ohio Valley. Specifically, Adena populations seen as native to the Ohio Valley were thought to have been pushed out of that region into peripheral areas to the east and northeast by an incursion of Hopewellian populations (Ritchie and Dragoo 1960) from the south or west (Ford and Willey 1941).

Although such constructions were compatible with then-current knowledge and explanatory frameworks (Lyman et al. 1997), they were ultimately replaced by more sophisticated models emphasizing local continuity and in situ development. Connections between archaeological cultures of the Ohio Valley and other regions were "explained" by trade and the diffusion of cultural practices (e.g., Struever and Houart 1972) rather than population movements. These developments mirrored trends in Americanist archaeology as a whole, as the culture history approach was gradually replaced by the processual paradigm. Studies of Adena and Hopewell complexes of the Early and Middle Woodland periods were still largely based on comparisons of mortuary complexes, as that type of archaeological data is overrepresented for these periods.

The focus on mortuary complexes during the Early and Middle Woodland periods has skewed attention toward highly elaborate expressions at the expense of simpler mortuary practices north and east of the Ohio Valley. These regions also have Early and Middle Woodland mortuary complexes, but their material culture is less elaborate, especially with regard to earthen architecture, which is largely absent. The situation has changed in past years, however, with increasing attention to the importance of the use of multiple scales of analysis (Cobb and Garrow 1996; Marquardt 1992; Marquardt and Crumley 1987).

Scales of analysis refer to the size and inclusiveness of the units of data that are employed in archaeological investigations. Most research has taken place either at the local scale of a single site, or relatively small sample thereof, or at the regional scale in the form of syntheses that cover broad geographic expanses. There are pragmatic reasons for focusing research at these scales. Analyzing a single site is a comparatively easy problem to tackle, and broad regional synthetic characterizations are possible by comparing numerous sites from written sources. There are equally real problems with this distinction between local and regional scales. First, it conditions archaeologists to view the past in terms of a false dichotomy of local versus regional patterns, ignoring the fact that small and large scales exist in a dialectic relationship, with patterns at either scale influencing the other. Also, it emphasizes essentialist views, with broad, regional similarities in archaeological cultures being assigned taxonomic designations that imply normative uniformity and mask variability and distinctiveness. Finally, these essentialist constructs often take on the connotation of evolutionary stages, with cultural developments over time being assumed to arise due to functional adaptations rather than historical contingencies.

Archaeological research that incorporates multiple scales of analysis characteristically places local patterns in a regional context. Two scales, local and regional, form the structure of the research (Rafferty 2001). Scales of analysis are arbitrary units developed by the archaeologist that can be manipulated as needed to meet the goals of any research project. I argue that more attention must be paid to intermediate scales of analysis, which focus on ecologically bounded territories likely to have constrained social interaction at the regional scale and formed natural settings where populations probably shared a cultural identity.

When a multiscalar perspective is applied to the archaeology of the Ohio Valley through the Early to Middle Woodland periods, data from local-scale analyses of specific sites, particularly large mortuary sites excavated during the early twentieth century (e.g., Mills 1922; Shetrone 1926, 1937; Webb 1940; Webb and Funkhouser 1940), have been used to formulate regional syntheses of Adena or Hopewell "culture" (e.g., Dragoo 1963; Seeman 1979; Webb and Baby 1957; Webb and Snow 1974). This was exemplified by the trait-list approach, which sought to lump a bewildering degree of archaeological variability into essentialist taxonomic categories (e.g., Greenman 1932).

Although archaeologists recognize the need for the categorization of archaeological data in terms of regional regularities, there is the tendency not to see the trees for the forest. Our attention to regional-scale patterns in archaeological data (e.g., Nassaney and Sassaman 1995; Rafferty 1995, 2004) must coexist with intermediate-scale, ecologically bounded units that were probably much more real to the agents of prehistory—prehistoric cultures in the specific anthropological sense of populations sharing a common worldview and ideology. Archaeological analyses that deal at this intermediate scale, such as Hays's (1994) analysis of the lower Scioto or Greber's (this volume) study of the central Scioto River valley, present a picture of numerous related but distinct "Adenas" and "Hopewells" on the basis of the archaeological data. In all likelihood, such populations viewed themselves as quite different from their neighbors, whom archaeologists have included within the same taxonomic designation. "Adena" and "Hopewell" are potentially misleading terms, as is the case with other taxonomic constructs such as "Mississippian," "Iroquoian," or even "Woodland" in that they imply greater uniformity in prehistory than the data show to have been the case. These terms are entrenched, however, and do serve the purpose of providing some organizing principle to the data; after all, there are still regional patterns, and we have to call them something. That said, it is vital that we bear in mind that within these regional taxa we are really dealing with numerous distinct cultures, probably situated in ecologically bounded territories. I turn now to an example to illustrate my point.

Adena Burial Rituals

Burial mound sites of the sort associated with Adena and Hopewell cultures were the loci of prehistoric rituals. Although we must tread carefully when making cross-cultural generalizations, few anthropologists would dispute that the process of dealing with the dead is always a ritualized practice. Before proceeding, I need to define what ritual is and what it does. Anthropological treatments of this topic are far too voluminous to summarize here, so I will provide the operational definition that has informed my own research. Rituals are programmatic, goal-oriented, repetitive social practices. Although rituals always have an emic goal, such as facilitating a rite of passage, when viewed from an etic perspective, they serve the function of communicating ideological messages that are both shaped by, and themselves influence, social structure. Ritual, then, is one way in which society reproduces itself.

There are some regional-scale similarities in the archaeological remains of Adena and Hopewell mortuary rituals. Adena mounds, for instance, represent the end of a characteristic cycle of ritual events (Clay 1998b). This may, or may not, begin with the construction of a charnel house, possibly with subfloor burials. This structure may then be covered in an earthen mound, possibly with burials in its fill or surface. There is then often, but not always, a series of mound-building episodes, each including the interment of additional burials. At some point, this sequence seems to end, generally with a final capping episode, and the mound's use as a burial site ceases.

Note the prevalence of ambivalent modifiers in the preceding paragraph: "may," "possible," "often," and "generally." This goes beyond the typical reluctance to make absolute statements on the basis of a fragmentary archaeological record. Such imprecise language is required, instead, because there is a huge amount of variation in the burial practices represented at sites considered to be Adena. Although many Adena mounds are accretional, built in numerous episodes, some were built in only one. Some include numerous burials in the fill or on the surface of the mound, whereas others were built around a single interment. Some burials include numerous artifacts, whereas others lack accompanying artifacts. When viewed at intermediate analytical scales, however, some patterns do emerge, as illustrated by analysis of Adena sites in the Middle Ohio Valley.

Ohio Valley Adena Sites and Ritual Patterns

SITES

I have examined site structures and burial assemblages of a sample of Adena mounds from three regions: the Ohio River in northern West Virginia, the Licking River of northern Kentucky, and the Scioto River in central Ohio. The sample includes six Adena mound sites: the Cresap and Natrium mounds in West Virginia (Dragoo 1963; Solecki 1953); the Wright and Ricketts mounds in Kentucky (Funkhouser and Webb 1935; Webb 1940; Webb and Funkhouser 1940); and the Davis and Toephner mounds in Ohio (Baby and Mays 1959; Hays 1994; Norris 1985) (Figure 11.1).

Cresap Mound might be considered a typical Adena burial mound. Located on a wide terrace of the Ohio River, the site was not an isolated example of Adena in the area; two smaller, disturbed mounds were located nearby, and the Moundsville area is a major locus of Adena sites, including the Natrium Mound (see below) and the Grave Creek Mound (Townsend

Many Messages of Death / 155

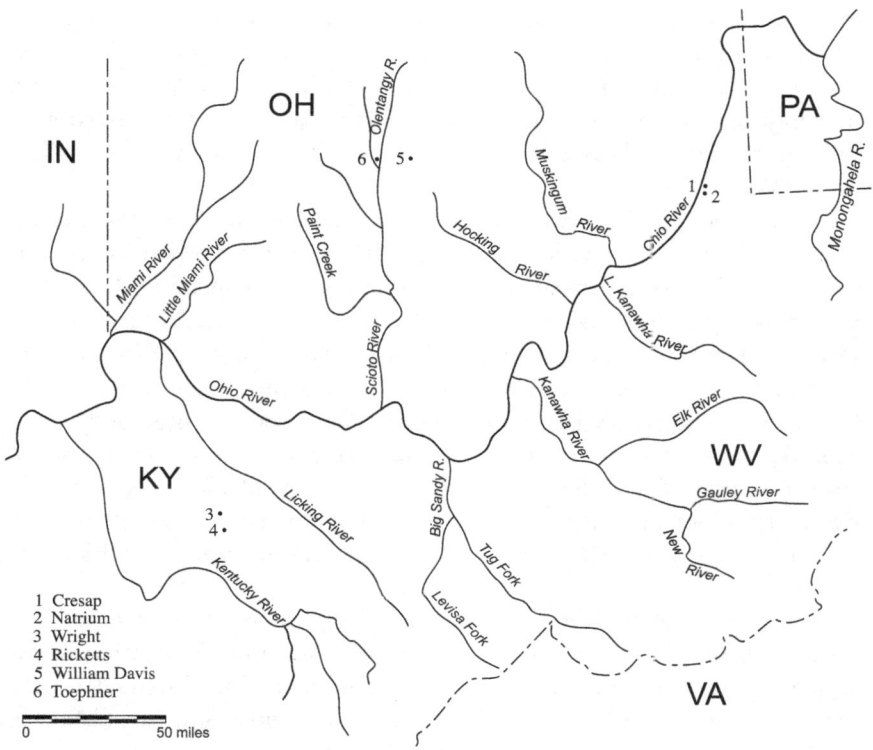

Figure 11.1. Adena mound sites used in analysis.

and Norona 1962). Cresap was excavated by Dragoo in 1958 (Dragoo 1963). The excavations are most notable in that they were the first to find intact and stratified early, middle, and late Adena artifacts in one context, thus providing a key to the interpretation of all other Adena sites. Five radiocarbon assays were obtained from separate contexts in the mound (Dragoo 1963:294) and are presented here as two-sigma calibrated dates using CALIB 4.3. Note that the older University of Michigan dates were routinely reported with the standard deviation doubled; the actual figure is used here. One date of cal B.C. 2463 (2115, 2099, 2038) 1740 is clearly too early and should be discounted. The remaining four dates are more internally consistent: cal B.C. 1004 (761, 679, 670, 609, 597) 180; cal B.C. 406 (360, 273, 260) 93, cal B.C. 406 (347, 321, 227, 223, 204) cal A.D. 21; and cal B.C. 201 (38, 30, 21, 11, 1) cal A.D. 130.

The latter four dates generally agree with the artifact assemblage, specifically the projectile point seriation, which includes ovate-base Adena points in the lower, primary mound, and rectangular-base Cresap points (similar to Robbins points from Kentucky) in the upper mound contexts. We can say with reasonable assurance that the submound structure and primary mound probably date between ca. 600 and 300 B.C., and the upper portions of the mound date to between ca. 300 B.C. and the end of the first millennium B.C.

Cresap Mound, like many Adena burial mounds, did not start out as a mound. Mound construction at the Cresap site was preceded by the construction of a large, circular, wooden building. Such submound structures were initially interpreted as residential structures indicating the remains of villages (Dragoo 1963; Fetzer and Mayer-Oakes 1951; Webb and Snow 1945), but they are now viewed as mortuary-processing structures and the loci of Adena mortuary rituals, with ephemeral residential sites located away from the mounds (Clay 1998b). This perspective places mortuary houses and associated mounds on the margins or intersections of loosely knit territories of neighboring Adena groups. In addition to the submound structure, Cresap Mound contained numerous internal features, many of which were burials.

In total, 53 burials were identified at Cresap in two concentrations, one near the base of the mound and the other in the middle, relating to two separate periods of mound construction. Burials included extended inhumations, individual skulls, bundle burials, and cremations. Age data were available for 40 (75 percent) of the burials and sex data for 18 (34 percent). Most (90 percent) were mature individuals, including 2 young adults, 33 adults and 1 mature adult. Subadults were absent, as were infants, and children accounted for only four individuals (10 percent). The sex sample was heavily skewed toward males (15 as opposed to only 3 females), though this might reflect the researcher's bias, which could have overestimated the number of male versus female skeletons (Dragoo 1963).

The Cresap artifact assemblage represents a broad spectrum of Adena tools/weapons and adornment artifacts. Of the 53 burials, only 16 (30 percent) lacked preserved artifacts; 9 of these were skulls, bundles, or cremations. The artifact assemblage for all the burials is dominated by large numbers of tools/weapons category artifacts, especially chipped-stone points, blades, or other stone tools. These were found with approximately half of the burials. Although the majority of the 15 identifiable male burials had at least some tools/weapons category artifacts, none of the individuals identified as females had any tools/weapons in association, and only 1 out of 4 of the children had any. It would seem that these artifacts were associated with males at death, which does not preclude females from having used such artifacts in life. Adornment artifacts are less common; only seven individuals

(13 percent) were found in association with copper, bone or shell beads, or textiles (Dragoo 1963).

The Natrium Mound is located in Natrium, West Virginia, 20 km south of Moundsville on a terrace of the Ohio River (Solecki 1953). Several other mounds are nearby. The mound was excavated prior to the advent of radiocarbon technology (1948 and 1949), and no subsequent assays were taken on any soil or charcoal samples that may have been collected during the original excavations. Solecki (1953:317) considered the site to be late Adena. However, the presence of both ovate-stemmed Adena points and rectangular-stemmed points similar to Robbins points, as well as the round profile of the blocked-end tubular pipes, indicates that the mound was begun in earlier times than late Adena. Because these traits were placed by Dragoo (1963) in the early to middle Adena range, the Natrium Mound probably brackets the middle to late Adena time periods, ranging between 300 B.C. and 1 A.D.

At the time of excavation, Natrium Mound was 3 m in height and 16.5 m in maximum diameter—roughly two-thirds the size of Cresap. The mound was also constructed in several phases, spanning the early Adena and late Adena "Robbins" phases. There was evidence of an external ditch around the mound. This could indicate that the site was originally a "ceremonial circle," or a ditched, low-mounded enclosure with a gap or gaps aligned at cardinal points (Clay 1998b:9–10). Some ceremonial circles were devoid of any cultural material, others contained mortuary camp structures, and some (as might be the case at Natrium) were eventually converted into mounds. Clay (1998b:18) argued that the two different ritual spaces—postconstructed buildings and ceremonial circles—could have represented "alternate definitions of similar ritual space" and that both served as mortuary camps. Although a total of 48 burials were identified in Natrium, demographic information was reported for only 23 individuals. Of these, 16 were fleshed burials with probably extended orientation, 3 were cremations, and 3 were bundle burials (including 1 skull). Mound burial was preferentially given to adults, because only 1 possible child was identified in the burial population; the remaining individuals included 18 adults (15 burials, 2 bundles and 1 skull), 1 mature adult, and 3 cremations (Solecki 1953). Sex data are limited, with two individuals (one burial, one bundle) being identified as male and the rest as indeterminate.

The artifact assemblage from Natrium is generally similar to that from Cresap. The most numerous category is tools/weapons, with 23 out of 48 individuals (48 percent) having at least one such artifact. Adornment artifacts, including copper and bone and shell beads, are present in 11 out of 48 inhumations (23 percent). One of the largest quantities of adornment artifacts (including 233 copper beads and 38 shell beads) was from the possible child burial, with only one adult burial having more and most having much less (Solecki 1953). This could indicate that adornment artifacts were not associated with achieved status and were appropriate for immature individuals as well as adults. The other possibility, that adornment artifacts were in some way indicative of a system of ascribed status, is less likely given the wide distribution of adornment artifacts within Adena burials in general and the lack of other indications of significant ranking among Adena sites.

To the west of the Cresap and Natrium mounds, many of the reported Kentucky Adena sites were excavated by William S. Webb in the 1930s and 1940s. The results of those excavations led to the earliest conceptions of Adena settlement pattern and social structure (Webb and Baby 1957; Webb and Snow 1974). The Kentucky sites often yielded many artifacts, tended to feature log tomb burials rather than pit burials, and were constructed after 300 B.C. The log tombs have been interpreted as multiple-use crypts that were periodically reopened and cleaned out to accommodate new burials (Clay 1998b; Mainfort 1989). Reuse left the later Kentucky sites with fewer but more elaborate burials, and it is impossible to say how many individual burials a given crypt accommodated over time; the artifacts placed in the burials are collective, rather than individual, representations, because they can not be associated with any single, specific interment (Mainfort 1989). It is possible that some grave goods were removed when a new body was interred, but it is still impossible to know with any specificity what objects were associated with which individual due to the secondary burial practices central to these log tombs. These distinctions have been argued as representing real social differences among Adena populations. Clay (1998b:16) proposed that "there were broad Adena 'breeding populations,' for example north and south of the Ohio River. This is an indication that Adena is hardly the monolithic 'culture' and 'peoples' it was once supposed to be."

One of the best-known Kentucky Adena sites is the Wright Mounds site, which is located on a bluff above a small creek near the town of Mount Sterling in north-central Kentucky. Two radiocarbon determinations were obtained in the early 1970s on charcoal from the Wright Mound (Mainfort 1989:165). At two sigma, the calibrated dates are cal B.C. 38 (A.D. 260, 281, 291, 297, 322) cal A.D. 617 and cal B.C. 15 (A.D. 86, 102, 122) cal A.D. 239. The dates are consistent with the material culture from the site, which suggests a late Adena age. Wright probably is roughly coeval with the later stages of both the Natrium Mound and the Cresap Mound sites.

There are three mounds at the site, numbered Mm 6, 7, and 8; two of these, 7 and 8, are very small, and 8 was not excavated. Mound 6 was one of the largest recorded Adena mounds at the time of its excavation, measuring more than 9 m in height (and had originally been higher and steeper before erosion) and up to 57 m in basal diameter. Excavation revealed that Wright Mound 6 was constructed in a similar accretional sequence as other Adena mounds, but at a greater scale in terms of its absolute size. As was the case for the Cresap Mound, the Mound 6 locality was originally used as a mortuary camp, with evidence of at least six overlapping structures (Webb 1940).

Of the total 21 burials identified at Wright Mound 6, 5 (24 percent) contained mature females, the highest proportion of females in any Adena burial population in the sample. One mature adult was, in fact, a skull buried with an adult female (Burial 6); this could represent a "trophy skull" (although there is no evidence that these were trophies of combat; rather, they probably represent animistic offerings). One male child was identified from a tomb in the primary mound. Fifteen individuals (including the skull burial with Burial 6) were recovered from log crypts, two isolated skulls were deposited in mound fill contexts, and the remaining individuals were recovered from unelaborated burial pits (Webb 1940). All of the fleshed burials were extended and laid on their backs. There were no cremations, and only three out of the entire burial population were disarticulated skulls (one male and two indeterminate). Fourteen burials were of young adult age or older, with one subadult, one child, and the rest indeterminate. Males accounted for nine burials and females for five, and the rest were of indeterminate sex.

The picture presented by the artifact associations for the Wright Mound is that of a highly formulaic mortuary program, in contrast to the burials from sites in West Virginia or Ohio. With few exceptions, individuals at Wright were interred with adornment artifacts as the main grave goods, and almost without exception these consist of shell disk bead necklaces and one or two copper bracelets. Only 7 of the 21 burials were not buried with adornment artifacts; 1 of these was the skull associated with Burial 6, 2 others were isolated skull burials, and 1 was buried decapitated. None of these would have been recognizable as specific individuals at the times of their interments; such recognition apparently was a requisite for the inclusion of horizontal status markers. Tools/weapons category artifacts are rare as grave goods, although substantial amounts of such artifacts, including chipped-stone points, blades, and debitage and ground-stone tools were recovered from the mortuary camp beneath the mound and from within the mound fill.

Also located in Montgomery County near the town of Mount Sterling, the Ricketts Mound site was excavated by Webb with the assistance of William D. Funkhouser in 1934 and 1939 (Funkhouser and Webb 1935;

Webb and Funkhouser 1940). There are no radiocarbon dates available for the Ricketts Mound site. The Ricketts artifact assemblage is very similar to the range of types present in the Wright Mound assemblage. These include the presence of rectangular-stemmed points, beveled-end blocked-end tubular pipes made of limestone, sandstone elbow pipes, and log tombs. Given the generally similar nature of the artifact assemblages of Wright Mound 6 and Ricketts, we can reliably put Ricketts between approximately 200 B.C. and A.D. 1.

When recorded, the mound was approximately 3.5 m tall and 30 m in diameter. The upper portions of the mound had been disturbed by unprofessional excavations. These early excavations encountered an unknown number of burials, as well as burial offerings, including copper, bone, and lithic artifacts, including a sandstone elbow pipe. Due to this disturbance of the outer mound, Webb and Funkhouser made little attempt at delimiting stratigraphy, making current interpretations of the site difficult and subject to inference on the basis of the structure of other sites. There is no mention in either of the two site reports of any submound features, such as the mortuary camp structures beneath Cresap and Wright or the possible ceremonial circle beneath Natrium. The excavation reports make no attempt at determining whether there was a sequence of construction events, but on the basis of the size of the mound and the presence of rock pile features within the mound body, it is probable that there were at least two construction episodes.

Ricketts, although smaller than Wright, had a burial population of 40 individuals, nearly twice that of Wright. This seems to be due mostly to a higher incidence of pit burials; 25 individuals were interred in unadorned burial pits, occasionally with some bark shrouding. Seven log tombs contained the remains of at least 15 bodies. The range of individuals buried at Ricketts is consistent with the Adena demographic pattern evidenced at the other sites. The majority category is adults, with a maximum of 24 identified. Mature adults seem to be absent, but some could be concealed in the nine indeterminate individuals who were assigned to the adult category on the basis of skeletal size and grave feature dimensions. Eight individuals were identified as male adults and young adults, and six were identified as female adults and young adults; as was the case for Wright, there were proportionally more female burials at Ricketts than in the West Virginia samples. Also, one child and one infant were interred in single-pit features within the lower mound, and a second infant was placed in a log tomb with the extended remains of one adult female and one cremated individual of indeterminate age and sex (Funkhouser and Webb 1935; Webb and Funkhouser 1940). Fleshed burials in extended orientations account for at least 21 and as many as 30 individuals, and 5 were cremations. Bundles seem to be absent at Ricketts.

The Ricketts artifact assemblage is also similar to that recovered from Wright Mound 6. Compared to tools/weapons category artifacts, adornment artifacts are again more widely distributed in the burial population, occurring as grave goods in burials of all demographic groups. However, tools/weapons were present in greater quantities at Ricketts than at Wright, and they were dominated by bone tools and debitage. Only three burial features (two log tombs and a burial pit from the lower mound level) contained chipped-stone points or blades, and the number of these objects associated with burials (five) is minuscule in comparison to the West Virginia sites. All individuals with tools/weapons category artifacts were adults or cremated individuals of indeterminate age (Funkhouser and Webb 1935; Webb and Funkhouser 1940).

North of that area, the central Ohio region has long been recognized as one of the primary areas of Adena occupation. The Adena concept itself was first conceived on the basis of excavations in Ohio (Greenman 1932), and the entire cultural complex is named for the Adena site located in Chillicothe (Mills 1901–1902). Some of the most impressive Adena sites (in terms of size and burial populations) were located within the Scioto River valley (see Hays 1994). Radiocarbon evidence suggests that Ohio Adena sites are generally younger than those in Kentucky. Most Ohio sites also yielded fewer grave goods.

Located in central Ohio, east of Columbus, on top of a gravel ridge near a minor stream, the William H. Davis Mound site was excavated by Baby and Mays (1959). At the time of excavation the mound measured 6 m tall and 24 m in diameter. The mound was constructed directly on top of a Terminal Archaic cemetery, which is not dealt with here. Construction information is only available for the very bottom of the mound because the top of the mound was removed by bulldozers prior to archaeological investigations. What little information that survived indicates that the mound followed a similar accretion pattern of construction as the other sites I have discussed so far.

No radiocarbon assays were ever taken for the Davis Mound site. Artifact evidence indicates that after the Terminal Archaic, the site was used up through the early stage of Adena, probably from approximately 500 to 300 B.C. This is based on the presence of Adena type points, with ovate stems and weak shoulders, and an absence of later Adena period points with their characteristic stronger shoulders and straight, rectangular stems. There are points intermediately between Adena points and later types, but a general absence of classic late rectangular-stemmed points. Ceramic sherds (all from nonfeature fill contexts) were of the Dominion-Thick type, which has elsewhere been associated with earlier Adena contexts, prior to 300 B.C. (Hays 1994:263–266). All burials from the Davis Mound were interred in unadorned pits, with no multiple-use tombs, another trait of early Adena sites.

In total, 29 individuals were buried in the Davis Mound. One of the individuals was represented by a "trophy" skull associated with another burial; it might more appropriately be considered a grave inclusion than an interment. Only two individuals, both of whom were adults, could be aged definitively. Of the remainder, 17 were interpreted as possible adults, for a maximum adult population of 19; 1 was a possible young adult; 1 was a possible subadult; and 1 was a child. All these fleshed interments were extended on their backs. There were three cremations, and bundles are absent. Seven interments, including three burials, the three cremations, and the one skull, contained the remains of individuals who could not be aged. Sex could not be determined for any of the 29 individuals (Hays 1994).

The artifact assemblage for Davis was very sparse, and Hays (1994:276) noted that 80 percent of the total artifacts from the site were not found in burial contexts but rather were placed on the mound floor or in mound fill. Artifacts in definite association with burials were few in number, with less than 40 percent (11 burials) of the burial population buried with anything, and in most of those cases they had only a few items. Five burials had associated chipped-stone points or blades, including both identified adults. Adornment artifacts accompanied only two burials, with copper beads present in one burial and two bone beads found in the other (Hays 1994:276).

The Toephner Mound is one of the largest and most complex mounds in the Scioto River valley. The site was excavated by Baby in 1953 (Hays 1994; Norris 1985) under salvage conditions. Baby submitted radiocarbon samples from log tombs at Toephner, although the embryonic state of radiocarbon technology at the time limits the utility of the resultant dates. One date was discredited, and the remaining dates range from 427 to 250 B.C., all with a regrettably large standard error of ± 200 years (Hays 1994:317; Norris 1985:131). The most likely interpretation of these dates is that the Toephner Mound site was constructed over a relatively short period of time during the transition from early to middle Adena (ca. 500–200 B.C.). This time range agrees with the material culture from the site, which shows a combination of earlier and later artifacts (early Adena points and later Robbins points) and features (earlier pit burials overlaid by later log tombs).

Toephner Mound seems to have been constructed in six stages. The first stage involved the excavation of three large burial pits in proximity, which were then surrounded by a large earthen ring. The largest pit, located in the center of the mound, contained 11 burials, including 2 young adult females (both bundles), 2 adult males (1 bundle, 1 extended), 4 adults of indeterminate gender (2 extended, 1 bundle, and 1 cremation), 1 mature adult (flexed), and 2 indeterminate burials (1 bundle, 1 extended). A second, shallower pit included seven burials, with one adult male (extended), two adults (one extended, one cremation), and four indeterminate (two bundles and two cremations). The third pit contained three burials, including two adults (one extended, one cremation) and an extended young adult. These three pits were covered with soil to a height of 0.75 meters and 3 meters in diameter to form a primary mound. The pits were lined with bark, and multiple burials were then placed inside. Hays (1994:304) reported that the soil covering the burials contained what Baby noted as "midden" remains, which is probably detritus from graveside ritual feasting, as noted by Clay (1986, 1998b). During Stage 2 of the mound's use, the majority of the burials (21 in all) within the mound were interred. There was a shift in burial practices at Stage 3 and Stage 4, when seven out of eight of the mound's log tombs were constructed. The final two stages saw the construction of one last log tomb and the capping of the mound to its final height.

Most of the 85 individuals interred in Toephner Mound were adults and mature adults (n = 53, or 62 percent). Eleven children and infants (13 percent) are represented, roughly twice the proportion of immature individuals of any other site in the sample. Females account for nearly half the burials where sex could be determined, a proportion that is conspicuously greater than that for any other site considered here. For nearly one-quarter of the population the age and sex could not be determined, although the remaining individuals were very well preserved.

Despite the large number of burials at Toephner, grave goods are present in only small numbers, in much the same pattern as was found at the William Davis Mound. Sixty-one burials (more than 70 percent) contained no artifacts beyond possible clothing remains. Tools/weapons category artifacts are present in 12 burials, primarily adults or mature adults. Adornment artifacts are rare, present in only two adult burials, both from subfloor mass burial pits in the form of copper and shell beads (Hays 1994:317; Norris 1985:131). Ritual artifacts are similarly rare, found in only eight burials (including one burial with evidence of red ocher, the only such burial in the mound). Two graves, both containing adults (one with a child as well) contained ground stone cones, and two to four burials were associated with gorgets, the imprecision coming from the fact that one gorget is in proximity to two burials, making it difficult to say whether it was associated with both, either, or neither of them. Also in this category were two smoking pipes. The artifact assemblage for Toephner presents a picture of uniformity in death. The paucity of artifacts presents the same unified face present at Davis. Within that uniformity, however, we still see evidence of certain individuals or categories of individuals being identified with certain artifacts categories, including tools and weapons.

RITUAL PATTERNS

On the basis of the preceding information, the six Adena sites were analyzed for three categories of data: the physical nature of each mound and the reconstructed sequence of events that created it, the nature of the burials within and beneath each mound, and artifacts associated with the burials. The physical nature of the mound includes such criteria as the presence or absence of premound architecture and the intensity of mound-building episodes. The nature of mound burials primarily refers to the use of burial pits for single interments, as opposed to the construction of more energy-intensive log tombs or mass burial pits for multiple or sequential interments. Finally, there is the nature of burial populations themselves, focusing on the demographic profile of each site and how the presence or absence of different types of artifacts, such as tools or adornment artifacts, correlates with age and sex. I identified similarities within all three data categories within each region, and sites within each region are distinct from sites in other regions.

Both West Virginia sites are near the Ohio River and are of similar size and volume. Cresap and Natrium mounds began as loci of premound ritual activities, evidenced by submound burial and ceremonial features and structures. Both sites were constructed in several phases, each phase including the interment of dozens of individuals in pit burials, bundle burials, and cremations. At both Cresap and Natrium, the burial populations are dominated by adult males, and the few females and subadults had few associated artifacts. Burials at each site contained a variety of artifacts, including tools, weapons, and adornment artifacts.

With regard to the Licking River sample from Kentucky, the first distinction is one of chronology: both sites are probably late manifestations, dating after 300 B.C. These mounds were formed in an accretional sequence of construction episodes, with more soil being added in each episode; however, there were fewer construction episodes than was the case for the West Virginia sample. Prior to mound construction, the site of Wright Mound 6 was the location of a sequence of structures built and rebuilt. There is no mention in the site reports of any submound features at Ricketts, such as the mortuary camp structures beneath Cresap and Wright or the possible ceremonial circle beneath Natrium; given that the Kentucky sites were excavated in a less hurried and generally more professional manner than the Ohio sites, it is likely that submound features would have been uncovered had they been present at Ricketts. Both Kentucky sites feature a different mode of burial, with some individuals being interred in reusable, log-covered crypts through which numerous individuals were cycled over time (Mainfort 1989). Although grave goods are as numerous as in the West Virginia mounds, the character of the assemblages is different, with most artifacts being adornment objects. Mound demography is again skewed toward adults, but there is a rough parity in sex.

The two Ohio sites in the sample were excavated under salvage conditions. There are no records of submound mortuary structures at either site; use of each site began with the interment of individuals in unenclosed burial pits. Both mounds were formed accretionally but with a more complex sequence of construction episodes than was the case for either the Kentucky or West Virginia samples. Adults dominated the burial population, but there was a significant minority of children at Toephner. Both sites are distinctive in their lack of burial goods; most individuals at both sites lacked associated artifacts. These Ohio sites probably date early in the Adena sequence, and Davis also has a Late Archaic burial component.

The three samples can be clearly distinguished from each other using the three categories of data discussed above (Table 11.1). The West Virginia mounds began with premound structures and were built accretionally. Burials were placed in pits. Adult males are predominant and were interred with a variety of grave goods. The Kentucky mounds may or may not cover several structures and were built in fewer but more intensive stages. Many individuals were placed in log-covered crypts. Both males and females are represented in the mounds, and grave inclusions emphasize bodily adornments. The Ohio sites apparently were not constructed over buildings and were built in complex sequences. Most interred individuals were adults who were placed in pits, and there were few grave inclusions.

Although this sample of mound sites shares a structural grammar, the regional subsamples are composed of distinctive traditions or dialects. I have made the case that the general structure of the Adena ritual practices as a whole presents an ideological statement of an egalitarian ideology, punctuated with statements of achieved status (Rafferty 2001, 2004). I would now add to this assessment that there are regional traditions within this ideological structure. The Ohio sites seem to be most egalitarian in their message, whereas the West Virginia sites seem more accented with the statements of achieved status, with their numerous wealthy adult male burials.

Conclusion

Clearly, much diversity exists within the Early Woodland period, both at the regional scale of the Ohio Valley Adena and at the pan-regional scale of the Eastern Woodlands. Distinct regional patterns for Adena sites have been

Table 11.1 Regional Adena traditions

Region	Mound Structure	Burial Form	Assemblage
West Virginia (Ohio River)	Complex accretional with subfloor structures	Pit burials, adult male focus	Numerous artifacts, individual representation
Kentucky (Licking River)	Simple accretional, possibly with multiple subfloor structures	Adult male and female ossuaries	Adornment artifacts, collective representation
Ohio (Scioto River)	Complex accretional, no subfloor structures	Adult pit burials	Few artifacts, individual representation

identified in terms of mound structure; the mode of individual burials; and the nature, frequency, and variety of burial artifact offerings. These differing patterns are indicative of significant differences in the ritual practices associated with death among the areas discussed in this chapter. Such differences in death rituals are probably indicative of broad cultural differences between regions, because these are practices that are characteristically deeply entrenched in a culture's identity (Beck 1995). Although previous researchers have often treated Adena as a monolithic category with a characteristic "burial cult," these patterns indicate a far more nuanced cultural landscape.

"Woodland" is not an all-or-nothing affair, but rather a complex milieu of societies that interacted to varying degrees, with groups in some broadly separated regions incorporating similar ritual burial practices, groups in other regions seeming to resist the "Woodland" in favor of social relations arrayed around "Archaic" technologies, and societies in yet other regions exhibiting seeming indifference to either pattern, focusing internally but still adopting a "Woodland" lifestyle. More work is needed at regional scales within ecologically bounded territories, such as major river drainages, to shed light on the range of variability within and between cultural traditions during this period. I am hardly the first to call for this, but the truth is that regional-scale surveys are difficult and costly to implement. If, however, we are ever to understand "the many messages of death" and cultural traditions in general, a middle ground in our analytical scales must be emphasized.

12

Taxonomic Homogeneity and Cultural Divergence in the Midcontinent

David S. Brose

Give us the tools and we will finish the job!
—Winston Churchill, 1940

You Can't Tell the Players Without a Program

In a recent electronic symposium (Wandsnider 2003) reviewing the philosophical reality of time as expressed in archaeological study, two quotations from Philip Arnold (2003) epitomize the bases of a major taxonomic issue. First, Arnold (2003:9) said, "The ethnographic record exhibits cause and effect, dynamic relationships, while the archaeological record comprises static relationships." Arnold agreed with this in a meta-language way, and that is the only way in which it is anything but a linguistic paradox: the successive record of the ethnographic present can be equally well shown to be merely a series of static relationships linked only by our psychological predisposition to interpret the world in terms of cause and effect (Hume 1779). Indeed, deriving hypotheses about the past from observations about present processes has long been recognized as a fallacy (Aristotle 1955 [325 B.C.E.]), but valid or not, no historical discipline has yet escaped this impasse.

Arnold (2003:9) also turned Binford (1968, 1983) on his head when he stated, "If the past and the present are no different with respect to anthropological issues [then] the anthropologists learn nothing by conducting archaeological research." Now, Arnold disagreed with this statement because he does not think that the object of archaeology is the reconstruction of past ethnography. I also disagree with this statement, but for very different reasons. We may remain interested in the details of specific past societies and still recognize that a method that relies on oversimplified analogy is flawed. Indeed, a rigorous demonstration that the past and the present are no different in regard to anthropological issues would be a monumentally important discovery if it were true in any but the most trivial way. So the objectives of archaeological study should not be so narrowly construed, from either the systematic perspective of Arnold (2003) or from our taxonomic perspective (O'Brien and Lyman 2001), that we could never expect to recognize such a demonstration were one to occur. But that constricted vision is all we could ever expect if we adopt the unfortunate view of archaeology as fit only to tell the grand story of human cultural evolution.

We should applaud Wandsnider's symposium, both because it calls for more critical thinking about disjunctions in our concepts of time in archaeology and because it reveals as a major concern the problems arising from disjunctions between the scale of the questions being asked and the scale of the data being collected. Of course, I shall argue that the study of the human past can succeed not only to the degree that the scales of data and questions are similar but also to the extent that our descriptions of past and present scales are critically rethought, for we cannot know whether the scales of the problems are comparable if we have no comparability between the tools with which to measure the scales. And archaeology's taxonomic constructs (Gardin and Peebles 1992) are the only mental tools that can measure comparability between the data being collected and the way we conceive of and organize and talk about the data.

The Measure of Older Taxonomies

As is clear, the previous discussions were never really questions about understanding the absolute or relative nature of time in archaeological discussion. Since the mid-nineteenth-century work of Darwin and Dana, geologists and biologists have understood that studying differing natural processes called for differing temporal perspectives (Brose 1992, 2002). Even earlier, in the late eighteenth century, casual archaeologists such as Jefferson (1984: 218–233) could see that different parts of the data they studied had accumulated in different ways and that often the cultural factors responsible for those processes had stretched over differing temporal durations. Of course, since Thucydides (1923 [431 B.C.E.]) historians have known this was an inescapable aspect of the documentary record (Fisher 1970). Taphonomy, microstratigraphy, critical historical scholarship, and cladistics are only some of the corrective techniques historical disciplines have developed to deal with these vexing phenomena (Brose 2002; Sherratt 1982).

Now, despite much recent excitement over again recognizing these aspects of historical data (e.g., Wandsnider 2003), what does seem to be new is that archaeology is again being forced to recognize that our very basic ways of conceptually organizing the archaeological record have not caught up with our field and laboratory work. We need corrective techniques for the anthropological taxonomy we use in archaeology, as Caldwell (1958) and

Griffin (1967) noted and as Stoltman (1978) and Kehoe (1998) have continued to urge.

We know that no set of collective terms captures all the variability of their referents (Feyerabend 1999). And as anthropologists we know that each ethnic unit, material-culture set, or ecological adaptation-sharing group, and all of their materials and the methods by which they have come to possess these, as well as their personal and expressed meanings for any participant in the group and every nonparticipant, all change at different rates. That is why even the most accurate cultural classifications can only be ephemeral in their application (and the interminable arguments about the "reality" of types survive only to the extent this precept is ignored). Small wonder that broader cultural taxa have proved difficult to apply to the seemingly fixed archaeological record of the midcontinent (e.g., Fitting and Brose 1971). And small wonder there are those who derogate the need for regional taxonomic critique, invoking some poetic *gestalt* in its place.

Sour Taxonomic Grapes

In one of Aesop's fables, the fox that could not reach the grapes hanging above him muttered that they were probably sour. It is not an appealing paradigm for archaeology, but it may be apt. In every part of the Ohio Valley climate, flora, fauna, human genetics, demography and physiology, and human politics, economics and ideology all changed at variable rates over the past millennia and will do so over the coming millennia. Certainly a synergistic and diachronic analysis of these changing systems would be of intellectual value—perhaps even of practical value (see Anderson 1981; Ford 1977; Griffin 1961). But each morning the sun rose on functioning planetary, biological, and cultural systems that interacted with each other in unique ways.

A vector analysis of those complex permutations, not merely a stochastic study of their final trajectory, must be of equal, if not greater, intellectual validity in an era when even the most simple systems seem to respond to chaotic complexity in rather unpredictable ways (cf. Brose 1992). And the exposition of each permutation is certainly of great public interest. In fact, since Harlan I. Smith's innovative 1911 report on a prehistoric site near Maysville, a major objective of Ohio Valley archaeology has been to look at prehistory as if it were the material remains of activities performed by people who might have been studied by anthropologists (cf. Brose 1972).

But that is just what Dunnell (1971) told archaeologists to avoid when he accused them of borrowing sociocultural models to do ethnographies of dead people, thus losing the ability to study change, which he called archaeology's one real virtue. Certainly grand evolutionary studies are wonderful tales—perhaps even true tales, although experimental proof will be difficult to arrange. But as with any other good theory, they must be capable of providing explanatory links and unexpected revelations in data collected for purposes other than the evolutionary study itself. And like Dunnell's, most such studies are capable only of segregating sets of objects in time and space to illuminate their trend while explicitly denying these operations could help us discover how or why these sets were reflective of their makers' intentions. How could the study of Ohio Valley prehistory end up this way? The explanation lies in the history of the region's discovery, its colonial exploration, and its prehistoric revelation.

Unlike other parts of the continent, the Ohio Valley held no aboriginal descendants of its long-time prehistoric occupants when the wonders of its archaeological record burst on Western historical consciousness at the end of the eighteenth century (Brose 1972). And whatever their sociopolitical legacy (Brose 2001), the Federal period's exotic conceptions of the Ohio Valley's cultural beginnings had little resonance in the literature of professional archaeology. Indeed, the real direction given to Americanist archaeology in the Eastern Woodlands was set in the period after the Civil War, when its unknown temporal dimensions were thought to occupy less than one thousand years. With the presumption that ethnolinguistic affiliations were permanent, migration, conquest, and other social dynamics recorded for relatively recent historic groups were assumed to be operative, if not determinate, explanations for the archaeological phenomena then rapidly accumulating (Clay, this volume; O'Brien and Lyman 2001).

The 1929 Conference on Midwestern Archaeology systematically tried to use a hierarchical study of functional patterns of material culture in order to derive ethnic identities and relationships of the cultures behind the archaeological data. And in the United States after the Works Progress Administration years, Midwestern archaeology tried to use hierarchical patterns of material culture and deliberately adopted the explanatory paradigms of (museum-oriented) population biology (Brose 2001). McKern's 1929–30 Midwest Taxonomic Method explicitly sought morphologically based classification systems for the prehistoric cultures (of Wisconsin) in which temporal, developmental, and evolutionary considerations could not be known a priori, but which might well be elucidated from properly organized data.[1] This taxonomic system had a distinct Linnaean heritage and an explicit deferral of what would come to be called the direct historic approach. With such a derivation, it is no surprise that the generation trained in that system found it well suited to organizing long-term anthropological phenomena (archaeological cultures or artifact assemblages) in the terms of biological evolution.

Because their roots lay in the explication of local historical traditions from the stories of aboriginal tribes, some of which were still occupying traditional grounds, the taxonomic terms and systems used by southeastern or Iroquoian archaeologists were better suited to look at particular and relatively short-term phenomena. In that very different mode, the 1932 Conference on Southern Pre-History tried to bring anthropological life to archaeology through the study of the geographic distributions of specific material and linguistic patterns in the late prehistoric and early historic record. No conjunction of these positions was attained in the 1935 Indianapolis Archaeological Conference, as John Swanton clearly noted, and at that conference New England and eastern Canadian woodland archaeology became footnotes on Iroquoian studies (O'Brien and Lyman 2001).

Although there were places in the midcontinent where these approaches abutted one another, through most of the twentieth century remarkably few archaeologists worked in more than a single arena, and those who did showed a facility for local modes of representation and largely ignored syntheses. Dealing with pan-regional phenomena of interest to both southern and northern archaeologists, such as Hopewell, with differing perspectives focused on the same phenomenon, led to no little confusion—confusion that was not lessened by the oft-quoted line, "American archaeology is anthropology or it is nothing," an injunction of little use (see also Arnold 2003:6).

On one level, archaeology is a craft: a series of quasi-geological, pseudo-forensic techniques. In that case, what matters is the theory linking the practice of these techniques to particular objectives. Beyond that, to claim archaeology is or should be anthropology (i.e., to accept as its own the methods and goals of anthropology) is ambiguous. Such ambiguity is not because anthropology is not a laudable discipline through which to study humanity, but because it is several such disciplines. To the extent that we are concerned with the past, we might wonder why we have not chosen the term *paleoanthropology*.

As it turns out, paleoanthropology has been restricted to the record of evolutionary biophysical changes in hominid genera and species. This is so because any historical discipline with so few samples and such great lacunae is restricted to studying the differences between its data—that is, to studying change itself (and evolution is not the only explanatory paradigm available or offered for change [cf. Hume 1963 (1779)]. In no such study is there a really convincing explanation of the vectors of change as they might have been caused by or applied to any one of the samples on the continuum. That is, we may argue that over several million years the descendants of one or another form of *Homo erectus* had become *Homo sapiens,* but we have little ability to study the effect of the long-term evolutionary process we hypothesize on any single specimen of ancient hominid.

If archaeology can reconstruct the behavior of some past human society or societies in an appropriately broad environmental and social context, then *paleoethnology* would be an integrated study of societies tied together by physical interaction over some specified time and space. We might have an excellent *paleoethnography* of the middle Scioto River valley (Ohio) second- to sixth-century site occupants or of the coeval occupants of the middle Tennessee River, but we certainly have nothing like an acceptable *paleoethnology* of Hopewell, and the only *paleoanthropological* studies that so treat it (e.g., Bender 1985a, 1985b; Braun and Plog 1982) render it so nearly indistinguishable from Early Bronze Age Britain as to be inapplicable to any but the few sites on which the study focused—the certain sign of inadequate scientific theory.

Because we want both kinds of archaeology, we need taxonomic units designed as tools to help us do both kinds of archaeology. But although all agree that taxonomic units should help us identify and solve significant archaeological problems, there is no consensus on what constitute significant archaeological problems, and that is because there is no consensus as to the proper objectives of archaeological research: whether they are to present to our understanding a number of past human societies or whether they are to provide data from which we might explain how past human society (rather than any particular society) changes.

Like medieval metaphysicians, this debate seems to divide archaeologists into realists and idealists. Some hold that our taxonomic units should help us understand and discuss any second- to sixth-century Ohio Valley site as a particular limited example of a partially studied and imperfectly known Ohio Valley Middle Woodland. Others hold that the very concept Ohio Valley Middle Woodland is a convenient construct we have built up using more focused taxonomic units to identify and interpret some number of presumed second- to sixth-century sites. We do consider these to be significant questions, and we look for changes in taxonomy for a solution. But the solution is to be more critical about the kind of taxonomic *structures* we apply, rather than to continue to argue about the *terms,* for the more we talk to one another about cultural angels dancing on taxonomic pins, the fewer we may discover are listening.

So if we distinguish paleoethnography from paleoanthropology as human evolution, we may conclude that the latter approach is oversold as a method for understanding culture. With too little attention to the limits of every archaeological record, even of short periods in restricted areas, paleoanthropology is the focus on regional sequences spanning millennia. Ignoring the fact that our society has been unable to foresee the environmental or social consequences of even its simple decisions, paleoanthropology uses the same computational models to describe the probable course of human society as a whole. I think we are guilty of having been told so often what evolutionary archaeology should do that we have come to believe we are doing it.

Our profession's mentors taught us to bring together time and place and cultural content into archaeological constructs, such as the Black Sand tradition, or the Hopewellian episode, or the Early Late Woodland period. At the same time, we are exhorted by a broader audience to breathe life into these constructions, and so we have the Adena People or the Hopewell Cult or the Shawnee. Little wonder we generate confusion in the minds of the general public (including undergraduates), and little wonder at the continual tension at meetings of those who should know our historical limitations: archaeological structures designed to study evolution spanned generations, whereas the ethnographic and historic glimpses of relevant social groups seldom lasted a season.

Perhaps we should have taken our taxonomic lessons from the paleontologists from whom we have adapted many other tricks of our trade. For instance, in the White River (Indiana) or the Wheeling Creek valley (West Virginia) we could have late first-century or mid-fifth-century deposits and either upland and/or floodplain or rockshelter facies. Any one of these units also could be some form of intentional depositional environmental, such as mound structure or cache, or natural accidental depositional environment, such as a midden or collapsed shelter. These would be the archaeological equivalent of rock stratigraphic units for one part of southern Indiana or northern West Virginia.

We, too, could create a taxonomy for the cultural content of any of these units regardless of geographic or depositional or chronological status. Some cultural content could be directly discoverable (exotic material, fire pit, arthritic mature male with significant adolescent nutritional stress). Some contents could be inferred from ethnographic analogy or historical observation (temple, Lower Shawnee Town, men's house), and some contents could be stylistically determined with variable specificity (Snyders point, Adena tablet, Mississippian bottle).

From conjunctions of specific cultural contents within specified stratigraphic units, we could identify the archaeological type sections, each of which would be specified to characterize that particular permutation as exemplary for a number of other archaeological situations explicitly determined to be similar enough for the purposes of the problem being investigated. That is, a type unit could be created by describing all of the relevant characteristics of the Hopewell Site Mound 25 or the Fort Ancient site or the Owl Hollow village and letting that type unit serve as reference for the larger class of similar phenomena we wish to discuss and study. I might also add that because the Hopewell site is without parallel in its region and era, it is a poor choice as a type section.

Now, some might argue that these are the kind of taxonomic units we already deal with as Ohio Valley archaeologists. We have Hopewell and Middle Woodland and an Ohio River valley, and these are just such units. But although these may look as if they were such carefully constructed taxonomic units, they are not. And they are not because we have never determined the kind of phenomena to which they are to be applied.

Paleontological taxonomy works because its application is controlled by a body of critical paleontologists who establish the locations, the depositional context, the contents, and the limits of applicability of each taxonomic unit *before* deciding to which taxonomic unit any given piece of rock is to be assigned. Here let me say that the issue is not how we identify any one of such archaeological characteristics (difficult but, strictly speaking, technical problems). The real issue is how we should use the permutations of these characteristics for analytical discourse. It seems to be an idea whose adoption is needed.

Considering prehistoric Midwestern exchange systems (Brose 1994a), I urged that the limiting conditions of the region be considered and that the phenomena under investigation be operationally defined in ways that distinguished between our ability to identify the phenomena of interest and our interest in learning by what mechanisms those phenomena had changed in the past. I also called attention to the need to identify carefully the applicability of unproven generalizations that some wanted to use to organize the changes we identified in the sequenced archaeological record, while at the same time we used those generalized cultural explanations to reflect the social significance of the mechanisms underlying those changes for the sometime participants in some ethnographic moment now long past. I believe the use of such critical limits must underlie our new taxonomy designed to address one or another (but not unwittingly both) aspects of our discipline. In rethinking these issues, I recognized that the entire argument about the reality of ceramic types, still current in the Ohio Valley, could be traced to the difference in perceiving the type of anthropology that archaeology should do. It seemed to go back to those very unlike Midwestern and Southeastern/Iroquoian approaches to archaeology, intersecting in the endless discussions of whether ceramic attributes or ceramic types are appropriate units of archaeological analysis.

For various reasons, statistical methods seldom result in persuasive types for many ceramic traditions. Nonetheless, replicative studies can illuminate sequences of actions whose analyses reveal long-term regional social interaction and temporal change, and combinations of attributes associated on vessels can reveal significant local and temporally bounded social interactions (e.g., Brose 1994b). The point here is that, with explicit boundaries and an explicit statement of the scale of the problem to which it is being applied, ceramic taxa can be created to serve either paleoanthropology or paleoethnography. But, emblematic of the discipline, no single ceramic taxon is likely to serve both aspects of archaeology well. And as the history of our discipline too often documents, controversy continues to result when we operate in a laissez faire manner with regard to which kind of objective is chosen for which taxon.

Thus, archaeological taxonomy in the Ohio Valley, too, illustrates that those who do not remember the past are condemned to repeat it (Santayana 1968:408 [1905]). And it can also illustrate why the solution to every particular local issue must be consistent with a broader view of what kind of taxonomic units local and regional and interregional archaeology can use. These considerations must, in turn, relate to a clear understanding of the realistic goals we set for archaeology as a whole.

Let us then take a critical view of what it is that we can do and why we wish to do it. Our study of the past in the Ohio Valley, as throughout much of the continent, can give to the present much of antiquarian interest. If we were willing to think critically and speak clearly, we might provide the present a perspective on cultural and environmental change that could be of great, if not critical, value for the future.

When the only tool you have is a hammer, everything looks like a nail.
—8th U.S. Army V-MAG, 1964

Note

1. "Do you know who made you, Topsy?"
   "Nobody, as I knows on," said the child, with a short laugh. The idea appeared to amuse her considerably; for her eyes twinkled, and she added,
   "I spect I grow'd. Don't think nobody never made me."
   —Harriet Beecher Stowe, *Uncle Tom's Cabin*

When it comes to understanding the importance of the classificatory systems within which they contextualize their data, many American archaeologists resemble Topsy. But few interpretive systems just "grow'd," and understanding their historical differences often leads to more appropriate choices among them.

I suggested earlier that the Midwestern Taxonomic Method sought morphologically based classification systems for prehistoric cultures because McKern and his colleagues fully recognized that a useful classification system had to study the actual and highly varying forms of archaeological objects, locations, or cultures, or the times and spaces over which they could be identified archaeologically, before they could design the parameters of their classification systems. In their metaphysics, the adherents of the Midwestern Taxonomic System were idealists, or nominalists, who would build the system to fit the data and who expected that accumulations of data that were new, or of differing form, would lead to changes in the classification system.

Most of the earlier interpretive archaeological systems (whether of artifacts, of sites, or of cultural complexes) were derived by induction from imperfectly articulated ethnographic or ancient history models by archaeological theorists who sought unvarying types of things, places, or societies in order to illustrate relationships in time and space. As a result, in those classificatory systems the static ethnographic or historical terminology of tribes and villages, and the linked chronology of dynasties and architectural orders, came to be imposed on still-incomplete archaeological data. That is, these systems were predicated on Neoplatonic realist metaphysics that looked at the data as some marred version of what the system said it should have been and for whom new or different data were aberrations to be marginalized as merely of particular antiquarian interest.

For those with more historical interest, I note that following the philosophical traditions of Late Antiquity, European culture has been dominated by these two very different approaches to organizing phenomena. Plato and his followers considered any physical phenomenon merely an imperfect and ephemeral representation of the perfect, eternal reality. For example, every dog we could ever see will be different in some way because each can be only a poor, limited example of the ideal, unchanging form, "dog." With such a metaphysical position, the general class "dog" is real, and every individual could determine which imperfectly realized physical objects or phenomena should be called a "dog" by comparing each to our idea of the "real" dog. Plato and his followers believed our inclusive ideas of "real" phenomena were absolute and innate; they were not learned; and they never changed. Many religions and socioeconomic systems hold realist metaphysical views.

Following an overreliance on Aristotle, Arabic and late-medieval scholars proposed that the general concept of an ideal "dog" was merely the name for a collective idea. Such an ideal "dog" could only be conceived of by ignoring some morphological differences and agreeing on the significance of some morphological similarities among physical phenomena, in this case a set of animals. A shift from Platonic "realism" to Aristotelian "idealism" underlay the early Renaissance/late thirteenth-century rekindling of science in Europe. For idealists (or later, nominalists), inclusive ideas of phenomena are conventions that can and often do change on the basis of new agreements about the phenomena (or its forms) the ideal group is agreed to represent.

13
Valley View
Hopewell Taxonomy in the Middle Ohio Region
Lauren E. Sieg

To paraphrase Walt Whitman, the prehistoric Midwest was large, and contained multitudes. This rich variability can be obscured by areal syntheses that focus on the broad distribution of certain traits (e.g., Caldwell 1958; Fitting and Brose 1971; Griffin 1967, 1978c), leading to interpretations of widespread cultural similarity. "Hopewell" is one archaeological manifestation that has been studied with such syntheses (e.g., Seeman 1979). Although the extent of the Hopewell horizon can be appreciated through such top-down approaches, other taxonomic units associated with the Hopewell horizon may be more apparent using a smaller-scale, bottom-up analysis. Here, I utilize a bottom-up approach to define regions, localities, and phases during the Middle Woodland period. Using the definitions established by Willey and Phillips (1958), I identify these units through examination of the artifact assemblages and architecture of sites within spatially restricted areas. Regions through which the Hopewell horizon extended are briefly mentioned; because space is limited and the focus of this volume is on Middle Ohio Valley taxonomy, not interregional taxonomy, they cannot be fully developed. Proposed localities within Ohio, especially the Little Miami Valley, are discussed. Data from several Middle Woodland period sites in the Little Miami locality are reviewed to determine what, if any, phase units may be defined for this locality.

The Problem of Hopewell Taxonomy

The ability to differentiate archaeological units crosscut by the Hopewell horizon has been hampered by several factors. First, a horizon is a unit that emphasizes similarities, rather than differences, across regions. Thus, studies of the Hopewell horizon have emphasized the shared distribution of nonlocal raw materials and similarly styled objects, rather than local developmental sequences in which these items were only one part of a larger material culture. As Struever and Houart (1972:78) observed, "The concept of a unitary Hopewell Culture appears to be both the result of archaeological sampling error, stemming from the proclivity of investigators for excavating Middle Woodland period mortuary sites, and the result of attempting to define prehistoric cultures in terms of an undifferentiated trait list." The importance of regional study has become even more apparent when detailed analyses of burial (e.g., Greber 1976) and exchange (e.g., Seeman 1979) patterns suggest a high degree of intersite variability.

Another problem (but also a surmountable one) in the differentiation of taxonomic units within the Hopewell horizon is the bias introduced by the material culture used to define them. Hopewell horizon markers and styles are generally features, objects, and types found in mortuary and ceremonial contexts, thus omitting the large portions of the archaeological record obtained from other contexts. Traits considered diagnostic of Hopewell sites include mounds (with or without burials), earthen enclosures, and particular artifact types, including distinctively zoned and/or stamped pottery, bicymbal ear spools, platform pipes, panpipes, and items made from nonlocal raw materials, such as mica and copper. Also present on Hopewell horizon sites, but not equated with the horizon, are less distinctive but ubiquitous objects such as undecorated ceramics, lithics, and faunal debris. Not all Middle Woodland period sites in Ohio show evidence of the Hopewell horizon, although they do contain Middle Woodland period assemblages (e.g., Stothers et al. 1979). Assessments of cultural similarity and difference, therefore, must incorporate domestic assemblages, which include grit- or limestone-tempered ceramics, small lamellar blades, Snyders points, faunal material, and botanical remains.

Furthermore, studies that rely on trait lists generally use the presence/absence of traits across an entire site, rather than the frequency of a trait in a particular context. The result is a composite picture of perhaps several hundred years of activity at a site that reduces the visibility of phase-specific markers. Careful attention to context and the use of relative frequencies may provide a better means for differentiating units in space, time, and form (Baerreis 1994 [1949]).

Ohio Hopewell Taxonomy: Regions, Localities, and Phases

I have approached this study using the taxonomy developed by Willey and Phillips (1958). I consider Hopewell to be a horizon within the Middle Woodland period (200 B.C.–A.D. 400) (Sieg and Hollinger, this volume). The Hopewell horizon is distinguished by horizon markers and horizon styles, including features and objects frequently associated with what has been labeled the Hopewell Interaction Sphere (Caldwell 1964; Seeman 1979; Struever and Houart 1972). This horizon links phases across Ohio, the Midwest, and the eastern United States.

REGIONS

The broad area crosscut by the Hopewell horizon has been divided into regional traditions, such as Scioto, Crab Orchard, Havana, and Point Peninsula (e.g., Caldwell 1964; Hall 1997; Seeman 1992). Seeman (1992) uses the term "tradition" in the Willey-Phillips sense (Willey and Phillips 1958:37) to span the entire Woodland period. Caldwell (1964) and Hall (1997) restrict their analysis of regional traditions to the Middle Woodland period and model their conceptualization of these units on Redfield (1955). Green (1999:34) suggested that such regional traditions may be conceptualized as regional variants, which he defined as "network[s] of related though not necessarily precisely coeval phases or local sequences." In Green's taxonomic scheme, multiple regional variants make up a tradition. Either as regional traditions or variants, these units have been defined by form and by space, and they differ from one another in both of these dimensions. Some aspects of the settlement and subsistence systems are different between regions, such as the large, well-made pots found on habitation sites in the Havana region and the smaller, less-well-made vessels common to habitation sites in the Scioto region, which imply differences in food production and perhaps household size. Regions also differ in items considered diagnostic of the Hopewell horizon, such as the copper cutouts in Scioto region sites and complicated stamped pottery from Swift Creek region sites. Because traditions emphasize continuity in form over time whereas horizons involve new forms that appear to have rapidly spread, Hopewell horizon markers should not be associated with traditions. I propose that, for now, differences in form should be reserved for the definition of phases and that differences in space should be emphasized to define regions and localities. Traditions, variants, and other appropriate units then can be established by grouping smaller taxonomic units. The use of the unit "phase" permits a more precise analysis of local and regional developments.

The geographic locations of the above regional traditions or variants can be used as the basis for defining regions. Willey and Phillips (1958:20) regarded a region as "a geographical space in which, at a given time, a high degree of cultural homogeneity may be expected but not counted on." Implied in this definition is a similarity in form (the indicator of cultural homogeneity), but Willey and Phillips left open the possibility of cultural diversity within a region by noting that multiple phases may be present within a region. They (Willey and Phillips 1958:19) observed that "archaeological regions are likely to coincide with minor physiographic subdivisions" such as a river valley. Willey and Phillips (1958:19) noted that a region is "roughly equivalent to the space that might be occupied by a social unit larger than the community." Although "a social unit larger than the community" may correspond to the social organization of a particular region, this description is not used in defining regions here. Instead, the elements of space, time, and form are used. These elements—not cultural entities—are the building blocks of taxonomy in the Willey-Phillips system (1958).

A region is a midlevel spatial taxonomic unit, larger than a locality, such as the Little Miami locality, but smaller than an area, such as the Midwest. The regions in Ohio that were crosscut by the Hopewell horizon include the Middle Ohio Valley and portions of the Upper Ohio Valley (Figure 13.1). According to Willey and Phillips's guidelines, these regions correspond to a particular geographical setting in the Midwest. Taxonomic confusion is avoided by using geographic names for regions in the Ohio Valley rather than names that have already been associated with a phase or other taxonomic unit. Other regions crosscut by the Hopewell horizon include the Western Basin, lower Illinois Valley, Kansas City, central Missouri, Straits of Mackinac, Driftless Region of the upper Mississippi Valley, lower Wabash, Kanawha River, Middle Tennessee, Little Tennessee River, lower Mississippi Valley, Tombigbee drainage, Crystal River, St. Johns River, and Santa Rosa–Swift Creek (see Brose and Greber 1979). This list is not comprehensive; it can (and should) be refined by regional experts (see Anderson and Mainfort, eds. 2002).

Localities Within the Middle Ohio Valley Region

The largest number of earthworks, the highest concentration of objects made from exotic raw materials, and the greatest variety of exotic raw materials found within the Hopewell horizon are from sites in the Middle Ohio Valley region (e.g., Greber 1991b:1, 1998:601). In recent publications, formal variation across the Middle Woodland period Middle Ohio Valley has been recognized (e.g., Greber 1991b, 2003; Pacheco 1996:32). Using the Willey-Phillips system, we can identify smaller spatial taxonomic units—localities—within this region. Willey and Phillips (1958:18; emphasis added) defined a locality as a "*spatial unit,* varying in size from a single site to a district of uncertain dimensions; it is generally not larger than the space that might be occupied by a single community or local group . . .

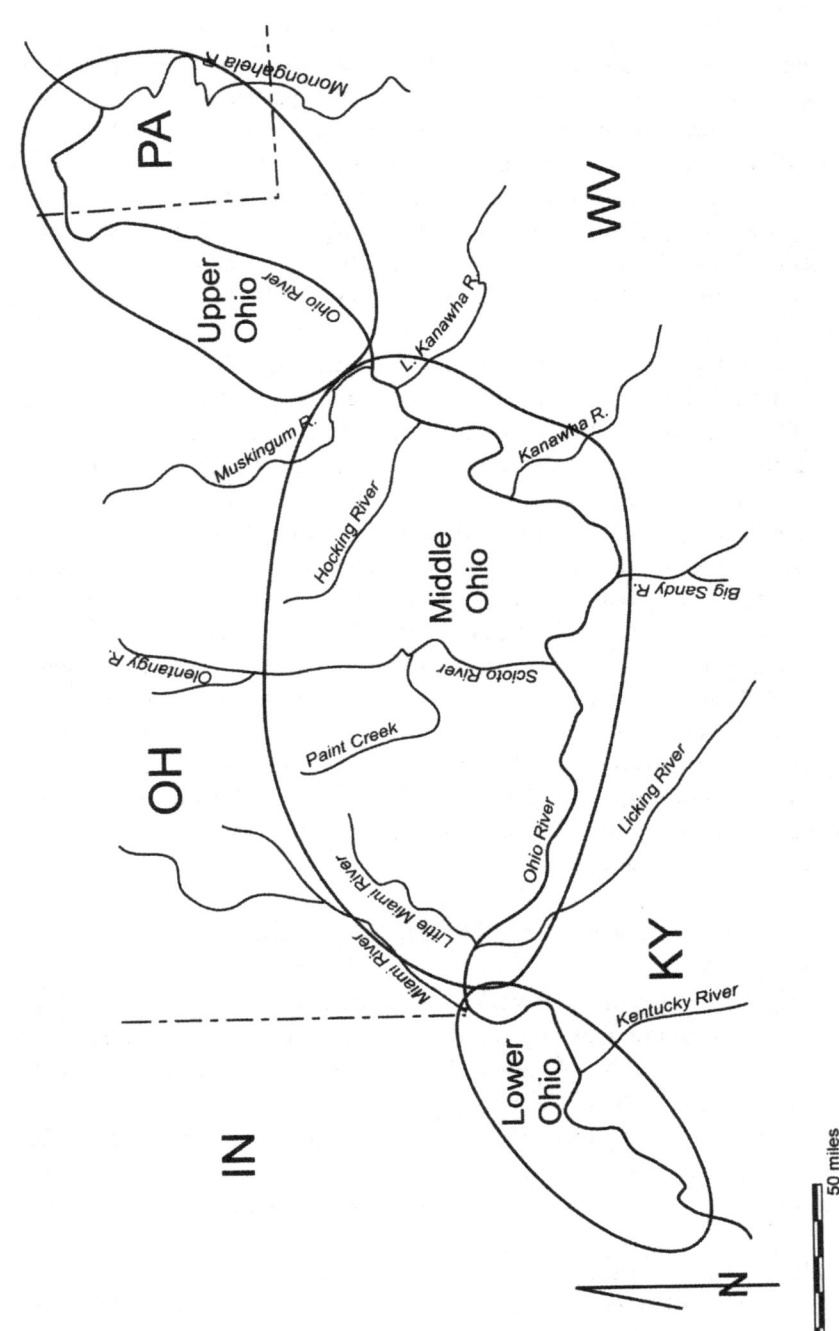

Figure 13.1. Regions along the Ohio River.

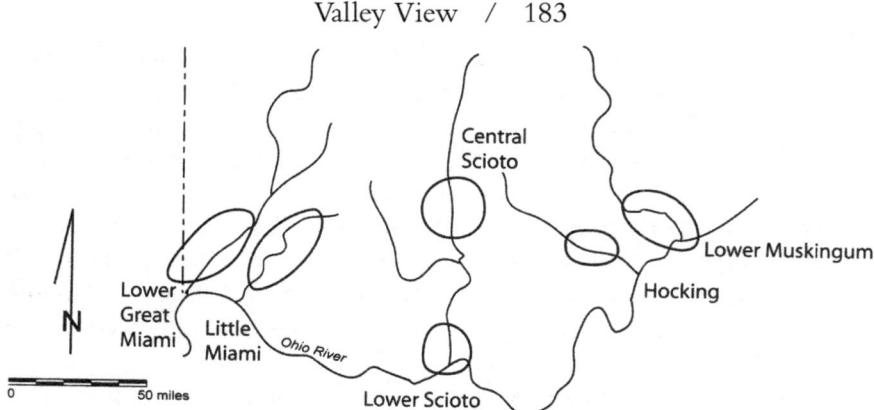

Figure 13.2. Localities in the middle Ohio region.

a geographical space small enough to permit the working assumption of complete cultural homogeneity at any given time." A locality is smaller than a region; thus localities are encompassed by a region.

Within the Middle Ohio Valley region, several localities can be distinguished. These localities roughly correspond to specific river drainages, such as the central Scioto (Greber 1991b), lower Scioto, Licking, Hocking, lower Muskingum, central Muskingum, Great Miami, and Little Miami (Figure 13.2). Although these localities are defined on the basis of geography, archaeological data from sites within them may display formal and temporal differences that can be used to define phases; phases for the Little Miami locality will be explored below. It is interesting to note that some of these localities contain both "Adena" and "Hopewell" sites (see Greber, this volume). This juncture of "Adena" and the Hopewell horizon offers an opportunity to study further the relation among "Adena," the Hopewell horizon, and the Middle Woodland period in the Middle Ohio region.

The central Scioto locality encompasses sites on the Scioto River, Paint Creek, the north fork of the Paint Creek, and their tributaries. Sites in this locality are concentrated around the Chillicothe area of Ross County and include such well-known sites as Hopewell, Hopeton, Liberty, High Bank, Cedar Banks, Mound City, and Adena Mound. The lower Scioto locality is located in Scioto County, at the southern end of the Scioto River, and includes sites on the Scioto and its tributaries; Portsmouth and Tremper are two sites found in this locality. The Licking locality is based in the Licking River drainage in Licking County; the Newark Earthworks, an unusually extensive and complex set of geometric enclosures, embankments, and mounds, is the most prominent site in this locality.

The Hocking locality includes the Hocking River and its tributaries; sites within this locality are clustered in the Wolf Plains archaeological district and include the Connett mounds and Armitage Mound (Murphy 1975; Norris and Skinner 1985; Skinner and Norris 1984b). The southern Muskingum River and its tributaries in Washington County make up the lower Muskingum locality; Marietta is the best-known site located here. Additional clusters of sites occur farther north, in the northern half of Muskingum County and in the southern half of Coshocton County (Carskadden and Morton 1997); perhaps these should be considered part of a central Muskingum locality.

Within the Great Miami locality, sites occur along the lower portion of the Great Miami River and its tributaries in Hamilton and Butler counties, Ohio, and southeast Dearborn County, Indiana. Miami Fort is one of the larger sites in this locality. Finally, the Little Miami locality includes areas around the Little Miami River and its tributaries; sites in this locality include the Fort Ancient, Turner, and Stubbs earthworks.

The Little Miami Locality

Data from six major sites—Turner, Milford, Camden Works, Stubbs, Fort Ancient, and Fosters—are reviewed here to characterize the Little Miami locality. Site layout, construction materials, artifacts, settlement data, and mortuary programs are summarized. Distinctive aspects of sites in the Little Miami locality are briefly described, and the Hopewell horizon markers and horizon styles present in the locality are noted.

The six sites in this study consist of enclosures (hilltop or geometric), mounds, and sometimes settlements. There are a limited number of basic shapes: irregularly shaped hilltop enclosures and geometric enclosures located on terraces (Table 13.1). It is interesting to note that the geometric enclosures (Turner, Milford, Camden Works, and Stubbs) are located in the southern portion of the locality, whereas the hilltop enclosures (Fort Ancient and Fosters) are located in the northern portion (Figure P.1), although there is no reason inherent in the topography for the earthworks to be distributed in this way. Stubbs, Milford, and Camden Works most closely resemble the earthworks from the central Scioto locality by virtue of their circle-and-square designs. Turner and Milford are unusual geometric enclosures in that they are partially located on a hilltop and partially located on a lower terrace. Turner is also unique in having no conjoined square or rectangular forms, despite being a geometric enclosure. Of the two hilltop enclosures, the complexity of the architecture at Fort Ancient makes it unusual; it consists of several conjoined enclosures, as well as some geometric features, such as the parallel walls. At sites or portions of sites positioned on

Table 13.1. Site location and architectural forms in the Little Miami locality

Site	Turner	Milford	Camden Works	Stubbs	Fort Ancient	Fosters
Landform	Second terrace; hilltop	Third terrace; hilltop	Terrace	Second terrace	Hilltop	Hilltop
Overall form	Geometric	Geometric	Geometric	Geometric	Irregular and geometric	Irregular
Geometric shapes	Circles, ovals	Circle, square, parallel walls	Circle, square	Circle, square	Parallel walls	N/A
Relation of parts	Connected	Conjoined and connected	Connected	Conjoined	Conjoined and connected	Conjoined?
Ditch	Around hilltop circle	Unknown	Unknown	Unknown	Follows contour of embankment walls	Follows contour of embankment walls
"Graded way"	Circle to oval	Circle to Circle	None	Circle to river	South Fort to river	Unknown

a hilltop, the embankment walls are accompanied by a ditch, and a graded way connects higher and lower elevations.

At these sites from the Little Miami locality are features related to the Hopewell horizon. Like other sites with evidence of the Hopewell horizon, Turner, Milford, Camden Works, Stubbs, Fort Ancient, and Fosters are distinguished by the presence of earthen enclosures and mounds. All these sites were most likely constructed over substantial periods of time. Radiocarbon dates suggest that construction of these sites continued throughout the Middle Woodland period (Table 13.2). At least two construction episodes are generally apparent in the stratigraphy of the embankment walls (Table 13.3). For sites at which stratigraphic data are available, contrasting soil colors were used in the embankment and mound fill. The available evidence suggests that these sites not only contain burials but also served many other functions besides mortuary activity. Burial forms include cremations and extended burials, with and without burial goods.

Sites in the Little Miami locality contain a variety of characteristic Hopewell horizon exotica, such as copper ear spools, as well as some unusual items. Most of the horizon markers and horizon styles found in the Little Miami locality were excavated at Turner and Fort Ancient. Copper plates, copper cutouts, bicymbal ear spools, mica cutouts, platform pipes, a panpipe, conch shell cups, Hopewell ware, clay figurines, meteoric iron, ornaments of fossil, and bone incised in a Hopewell horizon style were found at Turner (Willoughby and Hooton 1922). Copper plates, bicymbal ear spools, a platform pipe fragment, Hopewell ware, mica fragments, and obsidian objects have been recovered from Fort Ancient. There are fewer objects that are horizon markers from Stubbs, but obsidian, Knife River flint, and mica fragments have been found in surface collections at the site (Genheimer 1997). Excavations at the Smith site, an occupation site on the bluff overlooking Stubbs that is contemporaneous to the earthworks, yielded obsidian fragments, cut mica fragments, and Hopewell ware (Sunderhaus et al. 2001). Due to the limited data from Camden Works, Milford, and Fosters, evidence of Hopewell horizon styles or markers is not readily available.

The Little Miami locality sites also exhibit architectural and feature forms unique to the locality (Table 13.4). At all excavated enclosures, limestone was used extensively in the construction of enclosure walls. Limestone was used in the inner cores of walls, as facing for the walls and mounds, and as pavements in open areas. At Turner, it was also used to line graves. Besides the unusual degree to which limestone was used, enclosure sites in this locality are distinguished by the large amount of wooden architecture present. For example, approximately 17 structures were documented outside the embankment walls at Stubbs (Cowan and Sunderhaus 2002), and one was

Table 13.2. Radiocarbon dates from sites in the Little Miami locality

RCYBP	Calibrated Date (2 sd)	Site	Reference
2340 ± 130	B.C. 798 (398) 60	Fort Ancient	Connolly 1995:296
2340 ± 60	B.C. 756 (398) 212	Pollock	Riordan 1995:96
2270 ± 65	B.C. 408 (380) 172	Pollock	Riordan 1995:96
2220 ± 70	B.C. 402 (354, 291, 256, 251, 232, 217, 213) 60	Pollock	Riordan 1995:96
2040 ± 160	B.C. 401 (43, 6, 4) A.D. 339	Fort Ancient	Sieg and Connolly 1997:168
2025 ± 105	B.C. 359 (39, 28, 23, 9, 2) A.D. 234	Pollock	Riordan 1995:96
2000 ± 70	B.C. 195 (A.D. 2, 14, 16) A.D. 131	Pollock	Riordan 1995:96
1990 ± 90	B.C. 201 (A.D. 4, 8, 21) A.D. 236	Fort Ancient	Connolly 1995:296
1970 ± 100	B.C. 201 (A.D. 28, 41, 50) A.D. 316	Fort Ancient	Connolly 1995:296
1970 ± 80	B.C. 170 (A.D. 28, 41, 50) A.D. 236	Fort Ancient	Connolly 1995:296
1960 ± 80	B.C. 168 (A.D. 31, 38, 53) A.D. 238	Fort Ancient	Connolly 1995:296
1960 ± 70	B.C. 152 (A.D. 31, 38, 53) A.D. 227	Pollock	Riordan 1995:96
1950 ± 60	B.C. 88 (A.D. 34, 36, 61) A.D. 219	Pollock	Riordan 1995:96
1930 ± 130	B.C. 347 (A.D. 75) A.D. 400	Fort Ancient	Connolly 1995:296
1920 ± 170	B.C. 377 (A.D. 78) A.D. 527	Fort Ancient	Sieg and Connolly 1997:168
1920 ± 60	B.C. 43 (A.D. 78) A.D. 239	Stubbs	Cowan and Sunderhaus 2002:13
1890 ± 70	B.C. 41 (A.D. 91, 98, 126) A.D. 321	Fort Ancient	Connolly and Sieg 1996:154
1890 ± 70	B.C. 41 (A.D. 91, 98, 126) A.D. 321	Stubbs	Cowan and Sunderhaus 2002:13
1890 ± 60	B.C. 36 (A.D. 91, 98, 126) A.D. 316	Stubbs	Cowan and Sunderhaus 2002:13
1870 ± 50	A.D. 27 (129) 317	Pollock	Riordan 1995:96
1865 ± 65	A.D. 3 (130) 335	Pollock	Riordan 1995:96
1850 ± 70	A.D. 4 (133) 376	Stubbs	Cowan and Sunderhaus 2002:13
1850 ± 50	A.D. 33 (133) 321	Turner	Greber 2003:102–103
1840 ± 60	A.D. 30 (134, 159, 170, 196, 209) 340	Pollock	Riordan 1995:96
1830 ± 90	B.C. 36 (A.D. 182, 188, 215) A.D. 414	Fort Ancient	Connolly and Sieg 1996:164
1830 ± 50	A.D. 73 (182, 188, 215) 337	Pollock	Riordan 1995:96

Continued on the next page

Table 13.2. Continued

RCYBP	Calibrated Date (2 sd)	Site	Reference
1820 ± 70	A.D. 30 (223) 390	Stubbs	Cowan and Sunderhaus 2002:13
1810 ± 70	A.D. 33 (236) 402	Stubbs	Cowan and Sunderhaus 2002:13
1800 ± 80	A.D. 31 (238) 409	Fort Ancient	Connolly 1995:296
1800 ± 70	A.D. 68 (238) 409	Pollock	Riordan 1995:96
1800 ± 60	A.D. 77 (238) 391	Stubbs	Cowan and Sunderhaus 2002:13
1790 ± 70	A.D. 73 (240) 415	Stubbs	Cowan and Sunderhaus 2002:13
1790 ± 60	A.D. 81 (240) 402	Pollock	Riordan 1995:96
1790 ± 50	A.D. 88 (240) 384	Turner	Greber 2003:102–103
1780 ± 120	B.C. 38 (A.D. 243) A.D. 538	Fort Ancient	Sieg and Connolly 1997:168
1780 ± 50	A.D. 95 (243) 391	Turner	Greber 2003:102–103
1770 ± 70	A.D. 81 (245, 310, 315) 423	Stubbs	Cowan and Sunderhaus 2002:13
1770 ± 60	A.D. 89 (245, 310, 315) 415	Stubbs	Cowan and Sunderhaus 2002:13
1750 ± 60	A.D. 129 (258, 283, 287, 300, 320) 423	Fort Ancient	Connolly 1995:296
1750 ± 60	A.D. 129 (258, 283, 287, 300, 320) 423	Stubbs	Cowan and Sunderhaus 2002:13
1740 ± 50	A.D. 134 (260, 281, 291, 297, 322) 419	Turner	Greber 2003:102–103
1730 ± 60	A.D. 132 (261, 278, 324, 331, 335) 429	Stubbs	Cowan and Sunderhaus 2002:13
1710 ± 50	A.D. 229 (265, 267, 341, 375) 429	Turner	Greber 2003:102–103
1690 ± 120	A.D. 74 (362, 366, 383) 636	Pollock	Riordan 1995:96
1650 ± 50	A.D. 258 (412) 537	Turner	Greber 2003:102–103
1640 ± 60	A.D. 256 (417) 557	Stubbs	Cowan and Sunderhaus 2002:13
1620 ± 70	A.D. 256 (425) 601	Fort Ancient	Connolly 1995:296
1620 ± 60	A.D. 259 (425) 597	Pollock	Riordan 1995:96
1570 ± 250	B.C. 87 (A.D. 442, 448, 468, 482, 530) A.D. 984	Fort Ancient	Connolly 1995:296
1550 ± 50	A.D. 394 (536) 641	Stubbs	Cowan and Sunderhaus 2002:13

Table 13.3. Embankment wall fill, mound fill, and burial types in the Little Miami locality

Site	Turner	Milford	Camden Works	Stubbs	Fort Ancient	Fosters
Types of earthen fill	Light and dark clay	Unknown	Unknown	Light and dark clay	Yellow and gray clay	Red (burned) and gray clays
Presence of sod blocks	Unknown	Unknown	Unknown	Unknown	Yes	Unknown
Burial types	Cremations, extended burials in mounds or stone graves	Unknown	Unknown	Unknown	Cremations, extended burials in mounds	Unknown

Table 13.4. Use of stone, other architectural elements, and evidence for habitation at sites in the Little Miami locality

Site	Turner	Milford	Camden Works	Stubbs	Fort Ancient	Fosters
Use of stone	In walls, as pavements, in graves	Unknown	Unknown	On one side of wall	In walls, as pavements, in mounds	In walls
Interior architecture	Limestone pavements, wooden structures	Unknown	Unknown	Wooden structures	Limestone pavements, wooden structures, plaza?	Unknown
Exterior architecture	Limestone pavements, wooden structures	Unknown	Unknown	Wooden structures	Limestone pavements, wooden structures, plaza?	Unknown
Evidence of habitation	Debris in walls	Unknown	Unknown	Structures outside enclosure; on hilltop	Structures inside and outside enclosure	Unknown

found at the Smith site (Sunderhaus et al. 2001). These structures ranged from C-shaped to rectangular in form. Most were interpreted as "houselike" (Cowan et al. 1999:13), but one very large C-shaped structure was found at the base of the circular mound outside the enclosure. Among the houselike structures was one circular, double-post structure, a form that has traditionally been considered Adena (Cowan et al. 1999). At least 11 structures have been excavated from contexts within and outside the embankment walls at Fort Ancient (Connolly and Sieg 1996; Lazzazera 1997). Most of these have been interpreted as houses, but the series of overlapping structures on the exterior is abnormally large and may have served other purposes. The presence of a similar number of structures was suggested in the Turner report (Willoughby and Hooton 1922), which documented numerous posts as well as submound structures. The submound structures at Turner likely related to ceremonial or ritual uses, but a large number of posts were also documented at the base of the walls and in the open space of the "Great Enclosure." The function of these structures is unknown. Although many structures are documented in the Little Miami locality, none represent a "great house" with the range and intensity of activity of the submound structures under mounds in the central Scioto locality, such as Harness Mound at Liberty (Greber 1983) or Mound 25 at the Hopewell site (Greber and Ruhl 2000). Most of the documented wooden architecture from earthwork sites in the Little Miami locality was not covered by a mound, in contrast to that documented in the central Scioto locality.

A frequent criticism of many Hopewell studies is that they lack information on domestic habitation areas. Two recent volumes (Dancey and Pacheco, eds. 1997; Pacheco, ed. 1996) have attempted to redress this shortcoming, but evidence for habitation remains scant in comparison to data on the mounds and enclosures. Assuming that the lack of domestic structures within or immediately adjacent to the earthworks in other parts of the Middle Ohio Valley is not a matter of excavation or sampling error, this is a fundamental difference among localities. Although settlements may also be present near enclosures in other localities (e.g., Coughlin and Seeman 1997; Lepper and Yerkes 1997), these settlements generally seem to be short-term occupations at some distance from the enclosures. In contrast, evidence from recent excavations in the Miami locality suggests that settlements occurred within and/or abutting the enclosures (Connolly and Sieg 1996; Cowan and Sunderhaus 2002; Lazzazera 1997). At Fort Ancient, the structures within the North Fort are of comparable radiocarbon age and seem to be related to a small nucleated settlement (Connolly and Sieg 1996). The presence of artifacts from these structures suggests concentrated, if not extensive, use (Sieg and Sunderhaus 2004). At Stubbs, the structures may not have been created for long-term or intensive occupation, but their sheer number and similar radiocarbon age demonstrate that a large group of people congregated in the area at least on a periodic basis.

In addition to the Hopewell horizon markers already noted, there are some unusual objects from the Little Miami locality that may warrant further attention. In the Turner collection are several unusual artifacts: two large redstone boatstone effigies of mythological creatures; hammered and cut sheets of gold; the mica serpent and bears; and two plates of copper with a series of holes cut into them in which objects were probably suspended. The presence of these artifacts underscores one of the major intrigues and complexities of Hopewell taxonomy—each site is unique. This uniqueness complicates the work of taxonomy, but it is a powerful testament to the creativity of the prehistoric inhabitants of the Middle Ohio region.

For redundancy we must turn to the more mundane assemblages of the Middle Woodland period. Artifacts from this time period include grit-, limestone-, grog-, or sand-tempered pottery with plain rims; lamellar blades; and Snyders or Snyders-like points. Subsistence remains include deer, turkey, aquatic resources, nuts, domesticated goosefoot, maygrass, little barley, and sumpweed. The data on nonhorizon materials are unfortunately quite limited. Early archaeologists did not collect domestic-related material as thoroughly as modern archaeologists do. In addition, surface collections rarely include ceramics, faunal material, and botanical remains.

In the Little Miami locality, subsistence data presently are limited to the Fort Ancient site; deer, fowl, and fish are present (Yokell 1997), and botanical analysis is ongoing. On the other hand, each of the sites in this analysis produced typical Middle Woodland period bladelets, point types, and pottery types, especially McGraw Plain. Information on the lithic assemblages from these sites is most abundant. When compared to sites in the central Scioto locality, a smaller number of lithic raw material types is present at sites in the Little Miami locality (Vickery 1996). Prufer (1968:149) suggested that poorer quality McGraw Plain ceramics were more abundant in the Turner assemblage than in assemblages from sites in the Scioto Valley. McGraw Plain from Fort Ancient also is crumbly, fragile, and apparently poorly made (Sieg and Sankalia 1997; Sieg and Sunderhaus 2004). Compared to the central Scioto locality, two trends emerge from these scant data: limited types of lithic raw materials and less-well-constructed McGraw Plain pots in the Little Miami locality.

I will summarize by saying that the artifacts and features from sites within the Little Miami locality show evidence of the Hopewell horizon and similarities to sites in other localities within the Middle Ohio Valley region. Hopewell horizon styles and horizon markers are present in the as-

Valley View / 193

semblages, as are features and materials typical of Middle Woodland period throughout the region. At the same time, sites in this locality also possess some unique traits, both in their architecture and in their artifacts.

Phases in the Little Miami Locality

Even within a locality, there is a high degree of variability among sites, suggesting that it may be possible to delineate additional taxonomic units. For instance, Greber (1997) noted considerable variation among Hopewell horizon sites within the central Scioto locality. With the basic spatial units outlined in the delineation of localities, attention can turn to the temporal and formal dimensions of the archaeological record for the definition and evaluation of phase units.

According to Willey and Phillips (1958:22), a phase is "an archaeological unit possessing traits sufficiently characteristic to distinguish it from all other units similarly conceived[,] . . . spatially limited to the order of magnitude of a locality or region and limited to a relatively short time span." Variation is an expected part of any archaeological assemblage and should be incorporated into phase definitions. At the same time, caution must be exercised in the definition of phases. An overabundance of phases that are based on minor variation in artifact types, time, or locality may obscure rather than clarify our understanding.

Phase definition has been attempted previously in the Middle Ohio Valley (e.g., Prufer 1975, Seeman 1992b). For example, Seeman (1992b) defined two phases for the Middle Woodland period in south-central Ohio, particularly sites in the Scioto River valley. The first, the Late Adena Phase, dates from 150 B.C. to A.D. 1. According to Seeman (1992b:26), artifacts diagnostic of this phase include Robbins points, Adena Plain pottery, and incised and stamped pottery. During the Late Adena Phase, exchange of nonlocal materials expanded. The mortuary program increased in complexity and included the use of crypts, log tombs, charnel houses, and mounds, often in groups. Circular embankments and ditches also were constructed. Habitation sites were apparently small, impermanent, and repeatedly occupied (Seeman 1992b:27).

Seeman's Hopewell Phase dates from A.D. 1 to 400 and is distinguished by a marked increased frequency in nonlocal materials and finely crafted objects. Assemblages include corner-notched points, lamellar blades, and McGraw Plain pottery. Evidence for ceremonialism suggests that ritual activity increased in cost and scale from the previous phase and involved other activities in addition to mortuary ritual. Mounds and enclosures were larger during this phase; earthwork centers were concentrated in specific locales. Small, dispersed settlements were present in the main valleys (Seeman 1992b:27–28).

As defined by Seeman (1992b), both Adena and Hopewell phases can be documented in most of the localities identified above. However, it may be more appropriate to begin with locality-specific phases because there are differences in form (construction materials, exotica present, settlement patterns, earthwork forms, and so on) exhibited from one locality to the next. If no significant differences between locality-specific phases are found after these phases are defined, then they should be merged into region-specific phases. In the Little Miami locality, radiocarbon assays and differences in ceramics can be used to distinguish phases. The phases proposed here are a tentative start toward taxonomic clarification of one locality in the Middle Ohio Valley during the Middle Woodland period; it should be possible to refine them with future research.

Radiocarbon assays offer insight into possible temporal differences for sites in the Little Miami locality (Table 13.2). A series of early dates from preembankment wall features at Fort Ancient suggest that construction began early at this site, but the preembankment dates from Turner are slightly later. An earlier initial date for the hilltop enclosures is supported by the Adena Plain ceramics in the Fosters assemblage. This may reflect a generally earlier time frame for hilltop enclosures and a generally later time frame for geometric enclosures. A similar temporal difference in initial construction of hilltop and geometric enclosures is evident on a regional scale, as suggested by the suites of slightly more recent radiocarbon dates from the geometric enclosures in the central Scioto locality when compared to dates from the hilltop enclosures in the Little Miami locality (Greber 2003). Due to the limited number of radiocarbon dates and the complex construction histories of sites in these localities (Greber 2003:111), it is difficult to determine whether this difference corresponds to larger regional differences in the temporal depth of earthwork construction. Despite a difference in initial construction dates, radiocarbon assays from features associated with the mounds, earthen walls, and occupations at these sites indicate that construction continued throughout the Middle Woodland period in the Little Miami locality for both geometric and hilltop enclosures.

Ceramic data provide another avenue for discerning formal and temporal differences within the Little Miami locality. Riggs (1998) distinguished two temporally distinct groups of McGraw series ceramics from Turner. Grit temper predominated in the earlier assemblage, limestone in the later assemblage. The most common surface treatments in the earlier assemblage were undecorated smoothed surfaces, followed in frequency by smoothed-over cordmarked surfaces; in the later assemblage, almost all surfaces were smoothed cordmarked. Lip treatments in the early assemblage were predominantly plain smoothed, whereas in the later assemblage they were roughly divided between plain smoothed and smoothed-over cordmarked. These data support Prufer's seriation of ceramics from Middle Woodland period sites in southern Ohio, which showed a higher frequency of plain pottery at earlier sites and a higher frequency of cordmarked pottery at later sites (Prufer 1968).

From the limited data discussed above, at least two phases can be proposed for the Little Miami locality. Given the current paucity of data, the dates for these phases are somewhat tentative. The earlier phase dates from circa 200 B.C. to circa A.D. 50. During this phase, ceramics were predominantly plain, grit-tempered jars. Some "Adena" artifact types, such as Adena Plain ceramics, were present. Hopewell horizon markers appeared during this phase, and construction of hilltop enclosures began. In the later phase, from approximately A.D. 50–400, Hopewell horizon markers were present in greater frequencies. Construction of geometric enclosures began, and construction of the hilltop enclosures continued. Wooden architectural forms proliferated. Radiocarbon and artifact evidence from Fort Ancient indicates that limestone pavements were built during this period. Ceramic types were predominantly smoothed-over cordmarked, limestone-tempered jars.

The general time frame and some of the artifacts from the phase division proposed by Seeman (1992b) correlate to these phases. Phases in the Little Miami locality are distinguished from phases for other localities, however, on the basis of differences in architecture and domestic assemblages between these localities. Sites in the Little Miami locality contain much more stone and wooden architecture than other regions. Most of the wooden architecture at these sites seems to be domestic in function. The domestic assemblages are marked by a reduced variety of lithic raw materials and a reduced quality of pottery when compared to sites farther to the north. Finally, some unique artifact forms are present in the Little Miami locality. Because of these differences between the localities, I consider phases from the Little Miami locality to be distinct from the phases proposed by Seeman (1992b) for the Scioto River valley.

As suggested by Greber (this volume), the naming of taxonomic units provides an opportunity to honor pioneering archaeologists in the Middle Ohio region. In this spirit, I propose calling the earlier phase in the Little Miami locality the Essenpreis Phase, in recognition of Dr. Patricia Essenpreis's work to define construction sequences at Fort Ancient (Essenpreis and Moseley 1984). I propose that the later phase be named the Metz Phase in recognition of Charles Metz's work at Turner and other Little Miami locality sites (Metz 1878, 1881). Additional research may show that these phases are essentially equivalent to those outlined by Seeman (1992b) and should be merged with them. When they defined the phase unit, Willey and Phillips (1958) recognized that additional archaeological research could result in a consolidation of separate phases or a partitioning into more phases. The phases that ultimately emerge from taxonomic studies in the Middle Ohio region should avoid existing names such as "Adena" or "Hopewell" to reduce taxonomic confusion.

A Phase Is Just the Beginning

This analysis, admittedly based on limited data, represents an initial attempt to explicitly define phases for the Little Miami locality of the Middle Ohio Valley region using the Willey-Phillips (1958) system. By formally defining the patterns noted in taxonomic terms, I hope that this study can become the basis for further analysis that will either confirm or reject the recognition of distinct phases for this locality and other parts of the Middle Ohio Valley. By defining such units, researchers will be better able to explore the web of relationships implied by similarities and differences in time, space, and form, using them to contextualize both site-specific and broad interregional data.

Attempts to create a more refined taxonomic system are only the beginning; they establish the units used to study the social, economic, political, ritual, or other processes that played a role in the lives of people living in southern Ohio during the Middle Woodland period. Taxa do not answer the question of "what is or was Hopewell?" but they do provide a common and, we hope, unambiguous vocabulary with which we can discuss this problem.

Acknowledgments

The comments and suggestions of several individuals have greatly improved this chapter. The discussants at the Midwest and SAA conferences—Darlene Applegate, N'omi Greber, Barry Lewis, Robert Mainfort, and James Stoltman—provided valuable comments about refining terminology and proceeding cautiously. Discussions with Eric Hollinger about the correct use of Willey-Phillips terminology were also helpful. Finally, I would like to thank Darlene Applegate for organizing these sessions and motivating us to reconsider Ohio Middle Woodland period taxonomy.

14
Building Woodland Archaeological Units in the Kanawha River Basin, West Virginia

Patrick D. Trader

The Kanawha River drainage of central and western West Virginia (Figure 14.1) has been subject to archaeological scrutiny for well over one hundred years. Early mound studies by Smithsonian Institution archaeologists in the 1880s (Thomas 1894) helped to resolve the dilemma of the mound builder myth but did little to address issues of archaeological classification. Following the Smithsonian-sponsored investigations, the Kanawha River basin was largely ignored until the mid-twentieth century, when Edward V. McMichael and the West Virginia Archeological Society conducted archaeological investigations at Woodland period sites. In this chapter, I briefly review attempts by McMichael and Mairs (1969), Wilkins (1979), and Hemmings (1985) to construct archaeological units in the Kanawha River drainage. I summarize recent Woodland research in West Virginia and present an alternative scheme of Woodland phases for the Kanawha River basin.

Previous Woodland Period Studies

A Brief Historical Narrative

During the 1960s, Edward V. McMichael, West Virginia State Archaeologist, was responsible for surveying, documenting, and excavating archaeological sites throughout West Virginia, but the focus of much of his early work was centered in the Kanawha River basin (Figure 14.1). On the basis of these investigations, McMichael formulated a chronological framework for the Woodland period—one that has changed little over the past 40 years. Pivotal to the development of the framework was McMichael's 1960 survey of Nicholas County and his excavations at Mount Carbon Village in Fayette County. Also important were a series of salvage operations at Leslie Mound in Putnam County; Golf Course Mound in Boone County; and Brown Heirs Mound, Murad Mound, and Young Mound in Kanawha County (McMichael and Mairs 1963, 1965, 1969; Youse 1969). During these investi-

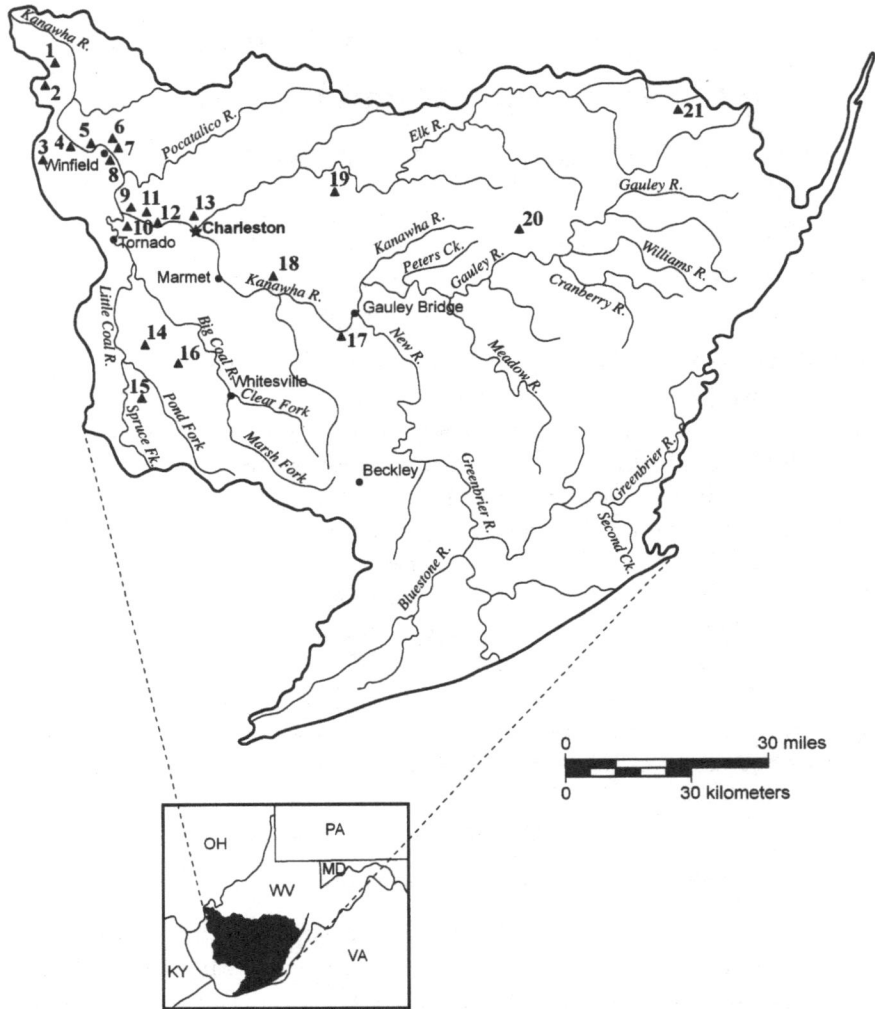

Figure 14.1. Map of the Kanawha River basin showing locations of important sites. 1, Woods and Childers; 2, Kirk/Newman Mounds–Niebert; 3, Jenkins House site; 4, Harris site; 5, CDC site; 6, Winfield Locks; 7, Parkline site; 8, Leslie Mound; 9, Brown Heirs Mound; 10, Murad Mound; 11, Ennis Mound; 12, Young Mound; 13, Charleston Mound group; 14, Gore Mound; 15, Golf Course Mound; 16, Mountain View site; 17, Mount Carbon Village; 18, Burning Springs; 19, Coco Station; 20, Buck Garden Run Shelter; 21, OSB 2 site (after Sheets and Kozar 2000; Courtesy United States Geological Survey).

gations, McMichael began to formulate ideas for a Woodland classification scheme in the Kanawha River basin. The framework was completely solidified by the end of the decade (McMichael and Mairs 1969), culminating in designation of the Kanawha Tradition, prior to McMichael's untimely death in 1972.

The Kanawha Tradition provided the first formal classificatory framework for the archaeological record in the Kanawha River basin in West Virginia. Dated from 1000 B.C. to A.D. 1200, the Kanawha Tradition was characterized by preagricultural pottery-bearing assemblages. McMichael and Mairs (1969) divided the Kanawha Tradition into five phases on the basis of ceramic styles, lithic assemblages, subsistence remains, settlement patterning, mortuary traits, and radiocarbon dates (Figure 14.2). They incorporated the previously formulated constructs of "Adena" and "Hopewell" into the classification. With respect to systematics, McMichael and Mairs offered no explanation of the conceptual framework that they used to develop the classification, and they failed to clearly define the "phase" unit, often using it interchangeably with "complex." It seems, however, that their work was rooted in Willey and Phillips's (1958) classificatory approach and the diffusionist culture history paradigm. In McMichael and Mairs's (1969:37) words, the Kanawha Tradition was a "heuristic device, and mainly of value only for the understanding of other archaeologists." Nonetheless, the Kanawha Tradition had a far more lasting impact than that of a simple "heuristic device."

Ten years after McMichael and Mairs (1969) published their Woodland units for the Kanawha River basin, Wilkins (1979) presented a critical reevaluation of the Kanawha Tradition phase framework on the basis of his investigations at the Gore Mound in Boone County (Wilkins 1977) and other mounds in West Virginia (Fowler et al. 1976) (Figure 14.1). Basically, Wilkins (1979) found the Kanawha Tradition inadequate in its descriptions of Adena and Hopewell. According to Wilkins (1979:74), the elaborate mortuary and ceremonial activity found in the Charleston area should be considered an in situ development rather than a product of Hopewellian invasion as McMichael suggested. Furthermore, Wilkins believed that the Charleston area mounds could be placed within an Adena context. Although Wilkins (1979) retained the Kanawha Tradition construct and followed the five-phase division proposed by McMichael and Mairs (1969), he revised temporal boundaries of phases, renamed phases, and rejected migrationist views of culture change (Figure 14.2).

In 1985, Hemmings suggested a revised Woodland classification for the Kanawha Valley (Figure 14.2) on the basis of the latest archaeological research, especially investigations of mounds within the Kanawha River ba-

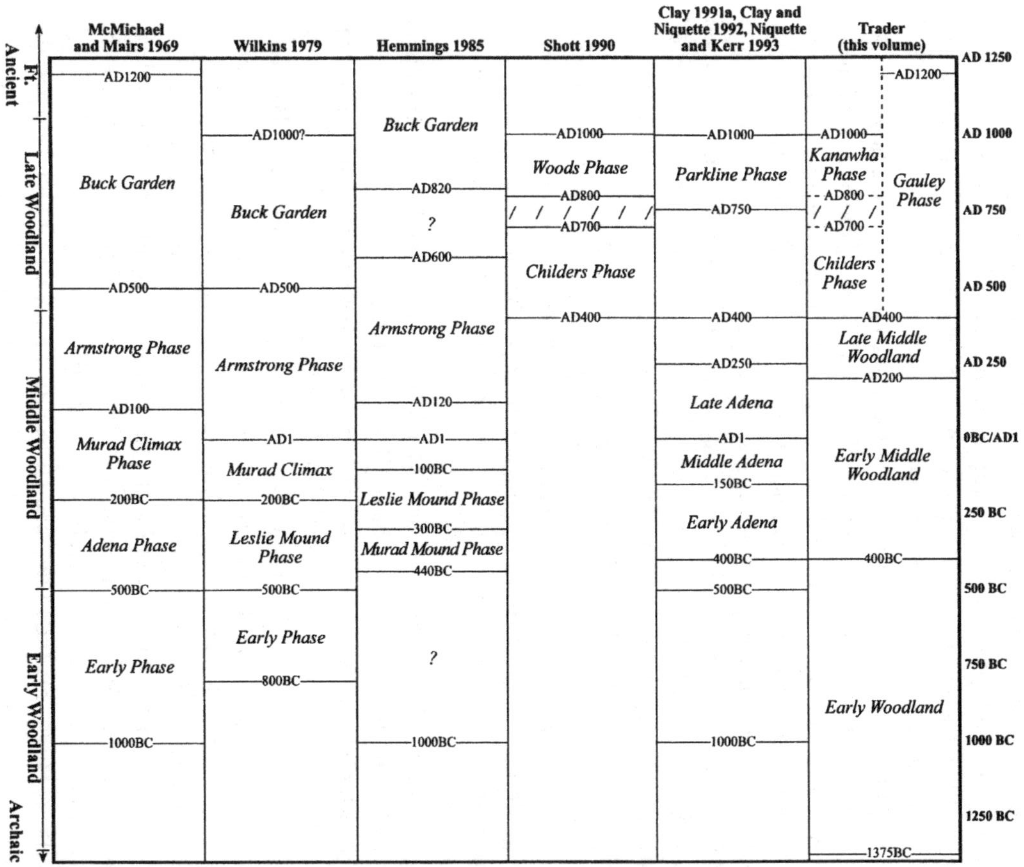

Figure 14.2. Comparison of Woodland period phases in the Kanawha River basin.

sin and elsewhere in light of new radiocarbon assays. Hemmings offered a reworked interpretation of Kanawha Tradition phases, revising temporal boundaries of phases and combining previously defined phases into a new phase.

Discussion

The development of Woodland units for the Kanawha basin has followed a short but tortuous path. As the first archaeologist to study closely the prehistoric record in the drainage, McMichael essentially was presented with a blank slate that he filled as best he could. By the 1960s there had been a century-long history of unit construction in other parts of the Ohio Valley, but this was not the case in West Virginia. It is important to remember that McMichael and Mairs developed the Kanawha Tradition within a period of only seven years and formulated two Kanawha Tradition phases (Armstrong and Buck Garden) over a span of only two years. When the Kanawha Tradition and phases were presented, they were badly needed. Despite Hemmings's and Wilkins's attempts to improve the classification, there are several reasons why we should question the reliability and validity of this scheme.

Elements of McMichael and Mairs's classification were based on inadequate contextual data and misinterpreted radiocarbon dates. McMichael and Mairs's classification lacked clear data regarding settlement patterns, site organization, and subsistence. They insisted on pulling Hopewell into the mix to describe the Murad Climax and Armstrong phases, though few classic Hopewell traits were documented at such sites. This can be likened to putting a square peg into a round hole; it just does not fit. From a historical perspective, McMichael and Mairs were not alone in placing local Woodland manifestations within a pan-regional concept of Hopewell. Because the Hopewell Interaction Sphere stretched from Kansas City to Georgia (e.g., Johnson 1979; Smith 1979; Struever 1964), it made perfect sense to include West Virginia within the construct. This common practice made the units the explanation and narrative, instead of using the units in describing the explanation and narrative (see Brown, this volume).

Wilkins's (1979) and Hemmings's (1985) revisions to McMichael's classification did little to improve it. In fact, their revisions did little to change it, other than to redefine temporal boundaries, reuse poorly defined phases, and shuffle the interval of mound construction back and forth between Early and Middle Woodland period phases. Little contextual data were added to either the Early Woodland or Late Woodland phases, primarily because the most contested issue was the chronological placement of the mounds, and few archaeologists were conducting research at Early or Late Woodland period sites.

In sum, though progress was made over the last several decades, archaeologists still lack a reliable Woodland classification for the Kanawha River basin. Before offering my own classification, I present an overview of recent Woodland period research, focusing on radiocarbon dates, ceramic typology, subsistence practices, settlement patterns, and mortuary behavior at 14 Woodland habitation and mound sites.

Recent Archaeological Investigations

After McMichael left West Virginia in 1967, archaeologists at the Archeology Section of the West Virginia Geological and Economic Survey turned their attention away from the Kanawha River basin to mound sites in the upper Ohio River valley and the northern panhandle of West Virginia. Although the West Virginia Archeological Society continued to conduct salvage excavations at Kanawha Valley mounds, such as Ennis Mound (Youse 1980), their investigations did not occur at the frantic pace of the 1960s. In large part, recent archaeological investigations in the Kanawha River drainage have been conducted by cultural resource management archaeologists, and their efforts have led to significant developments and discoveries concerning Woodland period chronological units, chronometric dates, site types, and subsistence strategies.

One important recent development was Clay and Niquette's (1992) redefinition of Woodland period chronological units in the Kanawha River basin (Figure 14.2). The Early Woodland period (1000–400 B.C.) corresponds to the interval postdating the introduction of pottery and predating mound construction. Mound construction marks the lower boundary of the Middle Woodland period (400 B.C.–A.D. 400), which subsumes both Adena and Hopewell mortuary ritual systems. According to Clay and Niquette (1992), the majority of mound construction is considered Adena in origin but Middle Woodland in time.[1] The end of mound construction marks the lower boundary of the Late Woodland period (A.D. 400–1000), and agriculturally based, nucleated villages (Fort Ancient period) mark the upper boundary.

Equally important was the formulation of three new phases dated to the Late Woodland period in the Kanawha River basin (Figure 14.2). Although these three phases are associated with the Late Woodland period occupations in valley bottom settings along the Kanawha River basin, the Buck Garden Phase (McMichael 1965) continues to be used to delineate Late Woodland period assemblages within the interior and mountainous portions of West Virginia (Figure 14.2).

The Childers Phase (A.D. 400–700 or –750) was defined on the basis of excavations at the Childers site in Mason County and subsumes the early Late Woodland period in the Kanawha River basin (Shott 1989). The phase is characterized by Childers Series ceramics consisting of both cordmarked and plain varieties tempered with siltstone, limestone, or sandstone. Cordage impressions of Childers ceramics are predominately S-twist. Vessel forms include high- and low-shouldered jars with conical or rounded bases. Although angled shoulders are not common, they do occur (Shott et al. 1993:8–9). Diagnostic projectile points include Chesser Notched and Lowe Flared types (Shott et al. 1993).

The Woods Phase (A.D. 800–1000) was defined on the basis of excavations at the Woods site, also in Mason County, and subsumes the late Late Woodland period in the Kanawha River basin (Shott 1989). The phase is characterized by Woods Series ceramics, which are similar to Childers Series ceramics except for the absence of angular shoulders and the predominance of Z-twist cordage (Hughes et al. 1992:165). Woods Phase ceramics include siltstone-tempered plain and cordmarked varieties.

The Parkline Phase (A.D. 750–1000) is contemporary with the Woods Phase and was defined on the basis of excavations at the Parkline site in Putnam County (Niquette and Kerr 1993). Diagnostic pottery is Parkline Series ceramics, which consists of plain and cordmarked varieties tempered with siltstone, sandstone, chert, and limestone. Decorations include punctations, notching, and incising along the vessel body and lip. Vessel shapes are small and large globular forms with constricted, slightly flaring orifices and collared rims. As with Woods Series ceramics, Z-twist cordage dominates on cordmarked vessels (Niquette and Kerr 1993:53).

Site Descriptions

Coco Station Site

Recent investigations at the Coco Station site, an open habitation located adjacent to Blue Creek in northeastern Kanawha County (Figure 14.1), provides evidence for the introduction of ceramics into the Kanawha River basin and new insights into Early Woodland subsistence and settlement strategies (Voigt et al. 1998). Voigt et al. (1998) identified four varieties of Fayette Thick pottery on the basis of minor temper inclusions, average thickness, surface color, and association with distinctive rectangular-based bifaces. Radiocarbon evidence suggests that the three Early Woodland occupations at Coco Station date between about 1500 and 200 cal B.C., but one date (Beta-94346) is an obvious outlier (Table 14.1) Calibrated radiocarbon assays associated with features containing Fayette Thick ceramics provide some of the earliest dates for the introduction of ceramics in the Kanawha River basin, between about 1375 and 900 cal B.C. (Voigt et al.

Table 14.1. Radiocarbon assays mentioned in the text

Site	Lab #	RCYBP	Calibrated Date (2 sigma)*
Coco Station[a]	Beta-94348	3110 ± 60	B.C. 1517 (1401) 1135
Coco Station[a]	Beta-94346	2290 ± 60	B.C. 475 (387) 200
Coco Station[a]	Beta-94351	3000 ± 70	B.C. 1413 (1259, 1230, 1220) 1004
Coco Station[a]	Beta-95183	2600 ± 60	B.C. 889 (797) 543
Coco Station[a]	Beta-94352	2950 ± 60	B.C. 1375 (1207, 1202, 1189, 1179, 1156, 1142, 1130) 945
Coco Station[a]	Beta-81582	2880 ± 60	B.C. 1260 (1039, 1030, 1023) 901
Winfield Locks[b]	Beta-48609	2780 ± 120	B.C. 1290 (917) 776
Winfield Locks[b]	Beta-48093	1460 ± 50	A.D. 445 (605, 610, 616) 663
Winfield Locks[b]	Beta-48095	1510 ± 50	A.D. 427 (544, 549, 558) 649
Winfield Locks[b]	Beta-48096	1480 ± 50	A.D. 434 (600) 659
Winfield Locks[b]	Beta-48097	1480 ± 60	A.D. 429 (600) 663
Niebert[c]	Pitt-0180	2820 ± 40	B.C. 1109 (973, 956, 941) 841
Niebert[c]	Pitt-0179	2020 ± 60	B.C. 196 (38, 30, 21, 11, 1) A.D. 124
Niebert[c]	SMU-2273	2230 ± 60	B.C. 400 (357, 286, 258, 243, 234) 118
Niebert[c]	Pitt-0313	2270 ± 40	B.C. 400 (380) 203
Niebert[c]	Beta-20928	2140 ± 80	B.C. 391 (195, 195, 173) A.D. 47
Kirk Mound[c]	Beta-21017	1820 ± 60	A.D. 67 (223) 380
Kirk Mound[c]	Pitt-0111	2135 ± 50	B.C. 359 (171) 3
Kirk Mound[c]	DIC-2845	1340 ± 40	A.D. 642 (666) 773
Newman Mound[c]	Beta-22023	2360 ± 80	B.C. 764 (401) 206
Newman Mound[c]	Pitt-0296	2180 ± 45	B.C. 382 (342, 324, 202) 93
Harris[d]	Beta-120807	2150 ± 60	B.C. 382 (197, 190, 176) 2
Harris[d]	Beta-120808	1880 ± 60	B.C. 15 (A.D. 128) A.D. 319
Harris[d]	Beta-120809	2190 ± 60	B.C. 394 (347, 321, 227, 223, 204) 53
Harris[d]	Beta-120810	1200 ± 50	A.D. 687 (782, 790, 815, 842, 859) 977
OSB Two[e]	Beta-80479	2250 ± 130	B.C. 762 (363, 269, 262) A.D. 21

Table 14.1. *Continued*

OSB Two[e]	Beta-80467	650 ± 60	A.D. 1266 (1301, 1372, 1378) 1413
OSB Two[e]	Beta-75410	2150 ± 80	B.C. 393 (197, 190, 176) A.D. 22
OSB Two[e]	Beta-80475	1970 ± 70	B.C. 164 (A.D. 28, 41, 50) A.D. 219
OSB Two[e]	Beta-80468	1330 ± 120	A.D. 441 (674) 979
OSB Two[e]	Beta-80470	1080 ± 130	A.D. 665 (981) 1221
Mountain View[f]	Beta-143153	1680 ± 40	A.D. 256 (388) 432
Mount Carbon Village[g]	M-1835	1130 ± 120	A.D. 659 (897, 922, 942) 1162

Note: Calibrations performed using CALIB 4.3.
[a]Voigt et al. 1998; [b]Hughes et al. 1992; [c]Clay and Niquette 1992; [d]East et al. 1998; [e]Stathakis et al. 1997; [f]Espenshade et al. 2001; [g]McMichael 1968.

1998:29, 103). Subsistence remains from Coco Station include carbonized acorn nutshell, hazelnut, and grape and sunflower seeds recovered from feature contexts dated to 1375–980 cal B.C. (Voigt et al. 1998:210) (Table 14.1). The sunflower achene was too fragmented to determine whether it was a wild or domesticated variety. No identifiable faunal remains were recovered (Voigt et al. 1998:209). Settlement data suggest that Coco Station is relatively small (0.4 ha). Primary feature types were shallow basin-shaped hearths and deep cylindrical storage pits (Voigt et al. 1998). Voigt et al. (1998:268) suggested that Coco Station was reoccupied by successive Early Woodland groups and used in different ways, expressed as activity loci reflected in artifacts clustering around feature groupings. The most common activity was the manufacture of biface preforms.

Winfield Locks Site

Situated on a terrace adjacent to the Kanawha River in Putnam County (Figure 14.1), the Winfield Locks site is multicomponent, with Early Archaic, Late Archaic, Early Woodland, and Late Woodland occupations. Investigations at the Winfield Locks site yielded diagnostic Early Woodland ceramics from dated contexts. A local variety of Half-Moon Cordmarked, *var. Winfield,* characterized by siltstone-tempered plain or cordmarked vessels, was recovered from a feature with an associated calibrated date of cal B.C. 1290 (917) 776 at two sigma. Also at two sigma, the calibrated average of radiocarbon dates from other features at the site is cal A.D. 536 (599) 643 (see Hughes et al. 1992:199, Table 10.1). Lithics associated with the Early Woodland occupation include Orient Fishtail and Cogswell projectile points. The few botanical remains from the Early Woodland occupation at Winfield Locks include black walnut, acorn, and hazelnut nutshell fragments. No evidence of domesticated plant species was identified (Crites 1992:188). The Early Woodland faunal assemblage is also small, consisting of a few fragments of box turtle and white-tailed deer (Yerkes 1992:196). According to Hughes et al. (1992:210), the Early Woodland occupation at Winfield Locks was probably short term and seasonal, reflecting a continuation of Late Archaic lifeways.

Childers Series ceramics from the Winfield Locks site are thin walled, siltstone tempered, and plain or smoothed cordmarked with S-twist impressions. Rims are flat, and some sherds have distinctive angular shoulders (Hughes et al. 1992). Diagnostic projectile points associated with the Childers Phase occupation include Lowe Flared and Chesser Notched. Animal species associated with the Childers Phase include white-tailed deer, eastern cottontail, turkey, and box turtle (Yerkes 1992). Wild plant species recovered include hickory, walnut, acorn, sumac, maygrass, sumpweed, and honey lo-

Building Units in the Kanawha Basin / 207

cust; sumpweed and maygrass achenes fall within the range of nondomesticated populations (Crites 1992). The Childers Phase occupation at Winfield Locks was relatively small (0.2 ha), oval, and compact. Hearth features dominate the habitation site, although post molds possibly representative of structures, windbreaks, or drying racks were also identified. The faunal, botanical, and lithic assemblages of the Childers Phase occupation suggest that the site was used repeatedly for brief periods of time over several years by small groups of people (Hughes et. al. 1992:210).

Evidence of Woods Phase occupations at the Winfield Locks site is rather limited and is represented by siltstone-tempered ceramics with nonangular shoulders and plain and smoothed cordmarked Z-twist surface treatments (Hughes et al. 1992:167–168). Diagnostic projectile points are Chesser Notched. There are no radiometric assays from Woods Phase features at the Winfield Locks site. Subsistence data are nonexistent because the only botanical remains consist of a small amount of maple wood charcoal (Crites 1992). Settlement during the Woods Phase at Winfield Locks was described as "expedient" (Hughes et al. 1992:212).

CDC #1 Site

The CDC #1 site is located on an alluvial terrace of the Kanawha River in Putnam County (Figure 14.1). The site is multicomponent, with Late Archaic through Late Prehistoric components. Early Woodland ceramics recovered from the CDC #1 site are similar to Half-Moon Cordmarked as defined for the Ohio River valley and are cordmarked and grit-tempered with crushed sandstone and limestone (Davis and Anderson 1997). Diagnostic Woodland projectile points recovered from the site include Adena, Snyders, and Jack's Reef (Davis and Anderson 1997:45). No faunal or botanical remains were recovered from the CDC #1 site, so there are no radiometric determinations for this site. The site is relatively small several small trash pits were excavated. The occupation at CDC #1 site was interpreted as a series of short-term camps (Davis and Anderson 1997).

Niebert Site

At the Niebert site, an open habitation located on the first terrace of the Ohio River (Figure 14.1), the remains of five circular paired-post structures were identified. Four calibrated radiocarbon assays associated with Feature 151 (within Structure 3) span more than 1,000 years (Clay and Niquette 1992) (Table 14.1). As Clay and Niquette (1992:8) noted, these widely ranging dates are problematical and make dating the feature and structure difficult. However, as they indicated, if the earlier and later dates are ignored, the other two dates are considered acceptable and yield a corrected average of around 375 B.C. (Clay and Niquette 1992). Investigations at Niebert also identified a local variety of Adena Plain ceramics, classified as variety *Flatfoot,* associated with a radiocarbon date of cal B.C. 391 (195, 173) cal A.D. 47. This and other assays are listed in Table 14.1 (Clay and Niquette 1989:121). Adena lithic artifacts were limited to four contracting stemmed Adena-like dart points (Clay and Niquette 1992:8). Botanical remains recovered from feature contexts include carbonized pine, hickory, oak, red mulberry, tulip tree, redbud, and black locust wood charcoal; carbonized hickory, black walnut, butternut, and acorn nutshell; and carbonized goosefoot, maygrass, and squash rind. A single achene of sumpweed and sunflower was also recovered from feature contexts. The goosefoot seeds seem to represent a wild species (Wymer 1989:141).

Clay and Niquette (1992:3–8, 19) concluded that, collectively, the five structures at Niebert served as mortuary camps used for postmortem treatment of the dead prior to burial at other locations, such as the nearby Kirk and Newman mounds. Radiocarbon dates from Niebert are comparable to those reported for both Leslie and Murad mounds by McMichael and Mairs (1963, 1969) and fall well within the period of major mound construction reported elsewhere for the Kanawha basin (Hemmings 1985; Wilkins 1979). Recent work at Kirk and Newman mounds has documented other facets of Middle Woodland period mortuary ritual.

Kirk Mound

The Kirk Mound, located on an Ohio River terrace (Figure 14.1), is situated within the limits of a larger multicomponent site containing Paleoindian through Late Prehistoric period artifacts. Of the seven excavated submound features, only three were specifically related to mortuary activities; the functions of other features with mound activities could not be determined (Clay and Niquette 1992:10). Artifacts include Robbins projectile points, leaf-shaped cache blades, and mica fragments. The small ceramic assemblage consists of siltstone- and grit-tempered sherds with plain, cordmarked, and smoothed-over cordmarked surfaces. Late Woodland Woods Series ceramics were recovered from feature contexts that likely postdate mound construction and use (Clay and Niquette 1992:11).

Botanical remains recovered from feature contexts include carbonized hickory and black walnut nutshell; carbonized hickory, oak, and pine wood charcoal; carbonized goosefoot, maygrass, bedstraw, sumac, vetch, huckleberry, and rush seeds; and a single corn kernel. There was no indication whether the goosefoot or maygrass remains were wild or domesticated species. Botanical remains associated with the Woods Phase feature include hickory and butternut nutshell, red oak charcoal, and a single corn cupule

Building Units in the Kanawha Basin / 209

(Clay and Niquette 1992:10–11). Three calibrated radiocarbon assays from charcoal yielded dates of cal B.C. 359 (171) 3, cal A.D. 67 (223) 380, and cal A.D. 642 (666) 773 at two sigma (Clay and Niquette 1992:12) (Table 14.1). The context of the charcoal for the last date cited is questionable. At the Kirk Mound, evidence for mortuary activities on a submound prepared surface suggests this location was used prior to mound construction as an alternative mortuary camp for preburial treatment of individuals subsequently interred at the Newman Mound (Clay and Niquette 1992:10–19).

Newman Mound

Like the Kirk Mound, the Newman Mound is part of a larger multicomponent site located on an Ohio River terrace (Figure 14.1). Five shallow basins at Newman Mound yielded artifacts, calcined bone, and botanical remains (Clay and Niquette 1992:14). Feature 3 contained small amounts of calcined bone and probably represents a redeposited cremation. Feature 6 contained the cremated remains of one child. Artifacts from feature contexts include chert debitage, plain siltstone-tempered sherds, and fire-cracked rock. Botanical remains recovered from feature contexts are charred hickory and walnut nutshells, one carbonized sunflower seed, and fragments of hickory, red oak, and pine wood charcoal. Evidence of cultigens is limited to a very small sample of squash rind. There was no indication whether the sunflower seed was representative of a wild or domesticated species (Clay and Niquette 1992:15). Artifacts recovered from the Newman Mound include Robbins points, a large ceremonial blade, celts, gorgets, and a pipe. At two sigma, a charcoal sample taken beneath Newman Mound yielded a calibrated radiocarbon date of cal B.C. 764 (401) 206, and a sample associated with a burial within the mound yielded a calibrated date of cal B.C. 382 (342, 324, 202) 93 at two sigma (Clay and Niquette 1992) (Table 14.1).

Harris Site

The Harris Site is an open habitation located on a ridge crest overlooking the Kanawha River in Putnam County and it covers an area of 0.3 ha (Figure 14.1). The site is multicomponent, with Archaic, Middle Woodland, and Late Woodland components (East et al. 1998). Excavated features include roasting pits and post molds or small pits. The ceramics from Middle Woodland features could not be typed, and no diagnostic lithics were recovered from dated feature contexts. Hickory nutshell dominates the botanical assemblage, with smaller amounts of walnut, hazelnut, and butternut. Evidence of possible cultigens is limited to maygrass seeds and squash rind, but these materials were collected from undated features (East et al. 1998). Three calibrated radiocarbon dates from Middle Woodland feature contexts suggest an age between about 200 B.C. and A.D. 200 (Table 14.1).

The Parkline Phase occupation identified at the Harris site is defined by the presence of Parkline Cordmarked ceramics, which are siltstone-tempered, smoothed exterior cordmarked ceramics with Z-twist cordage (East et al. 1998:84–85). The Parkline Phase is represented by a single feature containing Parkline Cordmarked and Parkline Plain ceramics, but no diagnostic lithic artifacts. Botanical remains from feature contexts include oak, ash, hickory, sycamore, willow, maple, and elm wood charcoal as well as carbonized hickory, walnut, acorn, and hazelnut nutshell fragments. No native cultigens were recovered. The faunal assemblage includes small mammal bone fragments and four large mammal bone fragments tentatively identified as white-tailed deer (East et al. 1998:93). Wood charcoal from the Parkline Phase feature yielded a calibrated radiocarbon date of cal A.D. 687 (782, 790, 815, 842, 859) 977 at two sigma (East et al. 1998:94) (Table 14.1). The late Late Woodland component at the Harris site is interpreted as a short-term occupation that may represent a small camp or specialized processing area (East et al. 1998:94).

OSB Two Site

OSB Two is a habitation site located on an elevated floodplain of an unnamed tributary of Right Fork in Braxton County (Figure 14.1). The site is multicomponent, with diagnostic artifacts representing Early Archaic through Late Prehistoric occupations (Stathakis et al. 1997). A series of calibrated radiocarbon dates ranging from between about 3900 B.C. and A.D. 1400 confirms a succession of occupations dating from the Middle Archaic through Late Prehistoric (Table 14.1). Little data were collected concerning the Early Woodland occupation of the site. A single post-mold feature with a two-sigma calibrated date of cal B.C. 762 (363, 269, 262) cal A.D. 21 contained only lithic debitage. Diagnostic artifacts associated with the Early Woodland occupation were scattered and included Susquehanna Broad and Merom Cluster point types.

According to Stathakis et al. (1997), the Middle Woodland occupation at the OSB Two site is represented by Watson Ware ceramics and a single Snyder/*affinis* Snyder projectile point. Because Watson Ware ceramics are associated with the upper Ohio River valley and the OSB Two site is found near the northern periphery of the Kanawha River basin, the identification of Watson Ware at this locality seems problematic. The Middle Woodland component at OSB Two is clustered near a possible structure. Features include hearths, pits, and a post mold. Limestone- and grog-tempered ceramics were recovered from a pit feature with calibrated radiocarbon dates of cal

B.C. 393 (197, 190, 176) cal A.D. 219 and cal B.C. 164 (cal A.D. 28, 41, 50) cal A.D. 219, both at two sigma (Stathakis et al. 1997:Table 32) (Table 14.1). Middle Woodland contexts yielded mast and seed crops as well as fleshy fruits and berries; identified cultigens include squash, gourd, and possibly corn (Rossen 1997:4). As at the Harris site, there is a dearth of Eastern Agricultural Complex cultigens, with only a single maygrass seed recovered from the OSB Two site (Rossen 1997).

The Late Woodland period at the OSB Two site is represented by hearth and post-hole features with calibrated dates of cal A.D. 441 (674) 979 and cal A.D. 665 (981) 1221 at two sigma (Stathakis et al 1997:94, Table 32) (Table 14.1). The Late Woodland artifact assemblage includes debitage and Jack's Reef and Madison point specimens. Few Late Woodland subsistence remains were recovered; botanical remains are limited to wood charcoal, black walnut nutshell, and a sumac seed. The Late Woodland component was not associated with any particular phase.

Mountain View Site

The Mountain View site is one of the few excavated late Middle Woodland habitation sites in the Kanawha River basin. Located along a tributary of the Big Coal River (Figure 14.1), excavations disclosed two roasting pits and a scatter of fire-cracked rock in association with siltstone-tempered ceramics and a Chesser/Lowe biface. Botanical remains recovered from feature contexts included wood charcoal, hickory nutshell, acorn shell, and walnut shell, but no evidence of cultigens was found. Charcoal from a feature containing ceramics and the Chesser/Lowe biface yielded a two-sigma date of cal A.D. 256 (388) 432 (Espenshade et al. 2001:Table 9) (Table 14.1).

Burning Springs Branch Site

The multicomponent Burning Springs Branch site is located on a terrace at the confluence of Burning Springs Branch Creek and the Kanawha River in Kanawha County (Figure 14.1). Ongoing investigations by Cultural Resource Analysts, Inc., have yielded thick (10–12 mm), sandstone-tempered cordmarked Early Woodland ceramics in association with narrow and highly pointed "spike-like" projectile points and other stemmed point varieties. Found in association with Early Woodland artifacts are Terminal Late Archaic materials, including sandstone and steatite bowls. Other Woodland occupations at the site include a Late Woodland component represented by Levanna and Jack's Reef points. There are two to three post-mold structural patterns stratigraphically below Late Prehistoric structure features (Michael Anslinger, personal communication 2003).

Jenkins House Site

The Jenkins House site is an open habitation located on a terrace overlooking the Ohio River in Cabell County (Figure 14.1). Recent investigations by Cultural Resource Analysts, Inc., uncovered a Woodland occupation defined by sandstone-tempered, limestone-tempered, and crushed/prepared-rock-tempered pottery with cordmarked and plain surfaces. Although some Middle Woodland materials may be present, preliminary observations suggest that much of the Woodland assemblage is of Late Woodland affiliation. The Late Woodland occupation may include both Childers Phase and Parkline Phase materials (Michael Anslinger, personal communication 2003).

Childers Site

Childers, the type site for the Childers Phase, is a habitation site on a high terrace overlooking the Ohio River near the western edge of the Kanawha River basin (Figure 14.1). Excavations and plow-zone removal exposed a concentration of features and one structure enclosed by a trench. Other feature types are basin-shaped and bell-shaped pits as well as primary inhumation burials. Radiocarbon dates suggest that Childers was occupied for a relatively short time around A.D. 655 (Shott et al. 1993). Botanical analysis identified charcoal from 28 tree taxa and seeds from 60 plant species. Cultigens recovered from the site include squash, tobacco, corn, and plants of the Eastern Agricultural Complex, particularly goosefoot, maygrass, and erect knotweed. Oily seeds include sumpweed and sunflower. The remains of mast species and fleshy fruits were abundant (Shott et al. 1993:20–21). Exploitation of animal species focused on white-tailed deer, turkey, and box turtle (Shott et al. 1993:18).

Woods Site

Woods, an open habitation located on a relict levee along the Ohio River (Figure 14.1), is the type site for the late Late Woodland Woods Phase. Radiocarbon dates suggest that Woods was occupied between A.D. 800 and 1000 (Shott 1989). Feature and artifact densities at the Woods site are less than those documented at the Childers site. Features are distributed in five distinct clusters, suggesting households. Identified feature types include hearths, storage or cooking pits, earth ovens, and burial pits. The botanical assemblage includes seed crops and maize. Considered together, evidence suggests some permanency to the occupation at Woods (Shott and Jefferies 1992).

Parkline Site

The type site for the Parkline Phase, Parkline is a habitation site located on the first terrace of the Kanawha River in Putnam County (Figure 14.1). Early and late Late Woodland occupations are present. The earlier Childers Phase occupation is represented by Childers Plain and Childers Cordmarked ceramic varieties and dates between A.D. 400–750 (Niquette and Hughes 1991:115–116; Niquette and Kerr 1993). Projectile points from Childers Phase features are Chesser Expanding Stemmed type (Niquette and Kerr 1993:49). Childers Phase features are spatially separated from Parkline Phase features and include shallow basin-, bell-, and cylindrical-shaped pits. Botanical remains from the Childers Phase occupation include charred acorn, black walnut, and hickory nutshell, as well as red oak, pine, and hickory wood charcoal (Crites and Kerr 1991). Goosefoot, maygrass, and erect knotweed seeds were recovered, as were rind fragments from a domesticated species of squash (Crites and Kerr 1991:169). According to Niquette and Kerr (1993:49), subsistence during the Childers Phase at Parkline is similar to that at the Childers site with one major distinction—occupants at Parkline procured their resources rather than producing them. As noted above, botanical remains recovered at the Childers site were extensive and included corn and all members of the Eastern Agricultural Complex. Niquette and Kerr (1993:50) suggest that the Childers Phase occupation at Parkline was short term and may represent an extractive camp.

The Parkline Phase occupation at the Parkline site, radiocarbon dated to circa A.D. 900, is characterized by two distinct feature clusters (Niquette and Kerr 1993), suggesting striking similarities with the Woods site (Shott et al. 1993). As noted above, feature clusters were also identified at the Woods site. Similar cluster features at the Parkline site suggest the presence of households. Cultural features include hearths and earth ovens, possibly used for processing mussels (Niquette and Kerr 1993). Botanical remains indicate a preference for hickory and acorns. Charred seeds include maygrass and domesticated goosefoot and erect knotweed; maize kernel fragments were recovered from a feature (Niquette and Kerr 1993). Niquette and Kerr (1993) suggested that during this later phase the Parkline site was occupied by small, highly mobile groups and represented a small camp.

Discussion

How do these new data fit with old ideas of the Woodland period in West Virginia? First, more data are available concerning the Early Woodland period. We now have some of the earliest dates for the introduction of ceramics into the region before 1000 B.C. This date has long served as the transition between the Late Archaic and Early Woodland periods, though actual evidence was lacking; now there are pottery assemblages from dated contexts to support this chronological division in the Kanawha Valley. Second, new data concerning Middle Woodland period mortuary behavior bolster long-held suspicions that mounds were a product of Adena ritualism; however, this behavior has been placed firmly within a Middle Woodland chronological context. Third, the continued lack of evidence for a significant Hopewell presence in the Kanawha River basin disproves McMichael's theories of Hopewell-influenced mound construction. Fourth, Middle Woodland habitation sites, which have been overlooked in the past, have now been identified in the region. Finally, with respect to the Late Woodland period, investigations at the Childers, Woods, and Parkline sites have effectively eliminated the idea of a Buck Garden presence along the main stem of the Ohio and Kanawha rivers. Unfortunately, little work has been conducted in the interior and mountainous portions of the Kanawha River basin, where Buck Garden is still recognized.

Recent investigations in the Kanawha River basin have resulted in several improvements in Woodland archaeological units, particularly those related to the Late Woodland period. Shott (1990:88) recognized that "McMichael's (1968) chronological scheme for West Virginia . . . is symptomatic of the underdeveloped state of Late Woodland systematics in the region; McMichael's scheme in effect does not recognize a Late Woodland period, instead distinguishing Middle Woodland from Late Prehistoric at A.D. 1000." In essence, McMichael's Buck Garden Phase was a "shotgun" approach to defining the Late Woodland occupation for the region. As noted by Wilkins (1979), the Buck Garden Phase was a catch-all term for the Late Woodland. The region was ready for an overhaul of Late Woodland phases, so the delineation of three new phases along the main stem of the Kanawha River was a much-needed development.

A Proposed Classification

Over the past 40 years, significant advances in Woodland period archaeology have been made in the Kanawha River basin. Early research, especially at mound sites, resulted in the formulation of the Kanawha Tradition and several phases (McMichael and Mairs 1969). McMichael's archaeological units for the Kanawha River basin were only slightly revised by subsequent archaeologists, because critical reviews of McMichael's work focused instead on whether the numerous mounds in the region were the result of Adena or Hopewell ingenuity (Hemmings 1985; Wilkins 1979). Although period units have been clarified (Clay and Niquette 1992), and several

Building Units in the Kanawha Basin / 215

new phases have been formulated in the last 15 years (Shott 1989; Hughes et al. 1992; Niquette and Kerr 1993), more can be done in delineating Woodland archaeological units—especially those dealing with the Early and Middle Woodland periods—in the Kanawha River basin. For instance, in their descriptions of mound construction and mortuary behavior, Clay and Niquette (1992) have placed these phenomena within the Middle Woodland period, a scenario that is reminiscent of Wilkins (1979) and Hemmings (1985) but fails to recognize variation in mound construction within the Middle Woodland period (Figure 14.2). In addition, a reassessment of the Buck Garden Phase in the interior and mountainous portions of the Kanawha River basin remains necessary.

In light of recent investigations and the accumulation of radiocarbon dates, updated chronological and formal units are needed. The scheme presented here reconsiders temporal boundaries between Woodland periods and describes new phases for the Middle and Late Woodland periods, incorporating recent data on mortuary behavior, settlement patterns, and subsistence practices (Figure 14.2). In essence, I suggest that the Kanawha Tradition is no longer a viable classification scheme for the Woodland archaeological record of the Kanawha River basin.

EARLY WOODLAND PERIOD

Recent excavations at Early Woodland sites have offered intriguing data about this poorly documented period. Although I support Clay and Niquette's (1992) description of the Early Woodland period as the interval between 1000 and 400 B.C., recent investigations at Coco Station suggest that the beginning point for Early Woodland could be as early as 1375 B.C. (Table 14.1). The lower- and upper-boundary criteria for the period are the introduction of pottery and the advent of mound construction, respectively. Although recent studies have provided significant data about this period, the database remains rather limited, and additional information is needed before formal units (e.g., phases) can be defined for this period in the Kanawha River basin. Therefore, I reject McMichael and Mairs's (1969) and Wilkins's (1979) "Early Phase," which was used to describe assemblages marking the transition from Archaic to Woodland lifestyles in the Kanawha River basin, due to insufficient evidence.

Investigations at Coco Station, Winfield Locks, CDC #1, and Burning Springs Branch sites have provided information about the Early Woodland period. Early Woodland assemblages are characterized by Fayette Thick and Half-Moon Cordmarked pottery; rectangular-based and contracting stem bifaces; collected plant (acorn, hazelnut, black walnut, grape, sunflower) and animal (box turtle, deer) resources; and small, seasonally reoccupied sites. To date, little evidence of Early Woodland mortuary practices has been reported.

MIDDLE WOODLAND PERIOD

Evidence from both mound and habitation sites is considered in delineating Middle Woodland units. Although I support Clay and Niquette's (1992) time range (400 B.C.–A.D. 400) for the Middle Woodland period and their identification of mound construction as the lower-boundary criterion, I argue that the Middle Woodland period should be divided into two subperiods on the basis of mortuary variability (Figure 14.2). I have also moved away from traditional labels such as "Adena" to lessen confusion concerning this period.

The Early Middle Woodland subperiod (400 B.C.–A.D. 200) is characterized by mound construction. On the basis of chronometric data from Kirk, Newman, Leslie, Murad, and Young mounds, we can date most mound construction in the Kanawha River basin as occurring between 400 B.C. and A.D. 200. Characteristic mortuary behavior consisted of accretional burial mounds with associated tombs, circular paired-post structures, and cremations. Ceramics recovered from mound contexts include Armstrong Series, local varieties of Adena Plain, and Montgomery Incised. Evidence for habitation sites in this subperiod is limited, but the OSB Two, Harris, and Mount Carbon Village sites have provided some data. Ceramics at OSB Two and Harris sites were problematical; therefore, Early Middle Woodland habitation sites are identified by Armstrong Series ceramic and Adena Stemmed point types. This subperiod subsumes McMichael's (1962) Armstrong Complex, which originally was defined as *the* Hopewell presence in the Kanawha River basin.

The lower-boundary criteria for the Late Middle Woodland subperiod (A.D. 200–400) are the decline in mortuary elaboration and the end of mound construction. All Middle Woodland sites postdating the period of mound construction and containing Snyder point types are assigned to the Late Middle Woodland subperiod. Evidence for Late Middle Woodland habitation in the Kanawha River basin is meager, being limited to scattered occurrences of Snyders and *affinis* Snyder point types at sites such as Mountain View. Admittedly, the evidence for this subperiod is sparse and based on a single radiocarbon date from a single site. Additional research in the Kanawha River basin is needed to fill data gaps for this subperiod.

LATE WOODLAND PERIOD

On the basis of investigations at Childers, Woods, Parkline, Mount Carbon Village, and various Nicholas County sites, we can date the Late Wood-

Building Units in the Kanawha Basin / 217

land period between A.D. 400 and A.D. 1000 (Figure 14.2). The lower-boundary criteria for the Late Woodland period are Childers siltstone-tempered plain and cordmarked ceramic varieties, Lowe/Chesser projectile points, semicircular villages, and small, extractive camps. Deer and turkey are the dominant animal species utilized, and all members of the Eastern Agricultural Complex are well represented. Corn occurs in small amounts. Upper-boundary criteria are shell-tempered ceramics, small triangular points, fortified nucleated villages, and an agriculturally based economy—all hallmarks of Fort Ancient.

Two distinct Late Woodland site types and site assemblages are documented in different portions of the Kanawha River basin. First, along the main stem of the Kanawha River, villages are located on river terraces, and ceramic assemblages are characterized by siltstone-tempered, cordmarked vessels. The Childers Phase, defined by Shott (1989, 1990), applies to the early Late Woodland period in this portion of the drainage basin (Figure 14.2). The later portion of the Late Woodland period has previously been associated with the Woods and Parkline phases (Niquette and Kerr 1993; Shott 1989, 1990). Closer inspection indicates little variation in ceramics, lithics, settlement patterns, and subsistence practices between Woods and Parkline Phase assemblages. Therefore, I propose a new phase—the Kanawha Phase—that subsumes the Woods and Parkline phases. The Kanawha Phase (A.D. 800–1000) is characterized by Woods and Parkline Series ceramics, Lowe Cluster and small arrow points, clustered features representing households, and a horticultural economy. Important plant species included both wild and domesticated species, such as acorns and maize. Corn plays a larger role in Kanawha Phase diet than during the Childers Phase.

In more mountainous regions of the Kanawha River basin, such as along the Gauley River, Late Woodland occupations are confined to rockshelter contexts, and ceramic assemblages are dominated by grit-tempered cordmarked Buck Garden Series. Lithic assemblages consist of expanded stemmed and triangular projectile points, chipped-flint celts, bone gorgets, and cannel coal pendants. The Buck Garden Phase, on the basis of data from the Buck Garden Run Shelter, was delineated for this portion of the drainage basin by McMichael (1965). Because little evidence for Buck Garden Phase sites is found outside the Gauley River drainage, I propose assigning the Late Woodland period occupations within the interior mountainous regions to the Gauley Phase (Figure 14.2).

The Gauley Phase is characterized by Buck Garden series ceramics and expanded stemmed and triangular projectile points. Most known occupations are in rockshelters, but Buck Garden Series ceramics were recovered at Mount Carbon Village, an open habitation site in Fayette County. A feature containing Buck Garden Series ceramics at Mount Carbon Village has an associated calibrated radiocarbon assay of cal A.D. 659 (897, 922, 942) 1162 at two sigma (Table 14.1). The presence of Buck Garden Series ceramics at Mount Carbon Village, located just downstream of the confluence of the New and Gauley rivers, suggests that the site is located in a zone where characteristics of the Kanawha and Gauley phases overlap. Gauley Phase subsistence practices remain unknown.

Discussion

The classification scheme proposed here for the Kanawha River basin offers several advantages over earlier classification systems proposed by McMichael and Mairs (1969), Wilkins (1979), and Hemmings (1985), as well as more recent schemes suggested by Clay and Niquette (1992), Niquette and Kerr (1993), and Shott (1990). First, my definition of the Early Woodland clarifies a previously little-understood period and pushes the beginning date to 1375 B.C. Second, by replacing such terms as "Adena" and "Hopewell" with Early and Late subdivisions of the Middle Woodland period, I avoid burdening this period with all the baggage associated with those terms. Third, I accept the Childers Phase as apt for defining the early Late Woodland period in the Kanawha River basin. Fourth, by subsuming the Woods and Parkline phases into the Kanawha Phase to define the late Late Woodland period, I avoid potentially confusing problems in assigning sites to one of two similar, if not identical, phases. Finally, subsuming the Buck Garden Phase into the Gauley Phase allows the placement of sites located within the interior mountainous regions of the Kanawha River basin without the ambiguity long-associated with the Buck Garden Phase.

Conclusions

McMichael's Kanawha Tradition and phase framework—the first formal classification for the Woodland period in the Kanawha River basin of West Virginia—provided the foundation for Woodland period archaeology in West Virginia for 40 years. However, recent investigations suggest that this framework is no longer viable. New evidence places the Early Woodland period between 1375 to 400 B.C. The Middle Woodland has been subdivided into the early Middle Woodland (400 B.C.–A.D. 200) and the late Middle Woodland (A.D. 200–A.D. 400) on the basis of mortuary variability. The lower boundary of the Late Woodland period in the Kanawha basin is defined by the Childers Phase (A.D. 400–700/750), and the upper boundaries are defined by the Kanawha Phase (A.D. 800–1000) along the Kanawha and

Ohio River valleys and by the Gauley Phase (A.D. 400–1200) in the mountainous interior regions.

Despite recent investigations, gaps remain in our knowledge concerning Woodland occupations in the Kanawha River basin. In general, research themes should be developed for the Woodland period, exploring settlement patterns, subsistence practices, mortuary behavior, and technology. We also need larger comparative data sets, including ceramics, lithics, faunal, and botanical specimens to assist in exploring these research themes. Recent advances in Early Woodland period research have expanded our knowledge of this period, but additional information is needed. The Early Woodland represents a major transition in lifeways between the Archaic and Woodland periods; however, a limited database prohibits the development of phases for this period. The Middle Woodland period represents a significant change in mortuary behavior in the Kanawha River basin, and much research has been conducted at mortuary sites; however, there is little information concerning habitation sites during the early Middle Woodland period. Research should be directed toward understanding settlement patterns and subsistence practices at habitation sites. Similar information is needed for late Middle Woodland habitation sites as well. Despite extensive investigations along the main stems of the Kanawha and Ohio rivers, more data are needed concerning the transition between the late Middle Woodland and early Late Woodland periods. The identification of additional Childers Phase sites is necessary to understand this transition. Likewise, additional research is needed at Kanawha Phase sites to define site types, settlement patterns, and subsistence practices better.

Future research certainly will result in and require revisions to our existing classificatory frameworks as well as prompt development of new frameworks. Although classificatory work is important, it is not the end product of our research. The ultimate goal of the archaeological unit should be to develop archaeological narratives and explanations of past lifeways. However, our explanation of the past is only as good as the units that were developed to explain them. The development of rock-solid units can only improve our ability to formulate good research questions and develop means by which to answer those questions.

Acknowledgments

I would like to thank the editors of this volume for inviting me to share my ideas concerning Woodland taxonomy in West Virginia. I also thank them for their insightful suggestions, comments, and critiques. I thank Dr. Donald Linebaugh at the University of Kentucky for his support. Other colleagues at the University of Kentucky, including Dr. George Crothers, offered helpful comments. Mr. Michael Anslinger of Cultural Resource Analysts, Inc., kindly provided information concerning current research at the Burning Springs Branch and Jenkins House sites. I especially thank Dr. Gwynn Henderson for her rigorous comments and the long hours we have spent discussing Edward V. McMichael and the Woodland period of West Virginia. Finally, I thank Donna Gilbreath for drafting figures for this chapter.

Note

1. In describing the mounds as Adena and Middle Woodland, Clay and Niquette (1992) supported the previous positions of both McMichael, who chronologically placed the mounds in Middle Woodland period, and Wilkins (1979) and Hemmings (1985), who argued the mounds were Adena.

15

Some Comments on Woodland Taxonomy in the Middle Ohio Valley

Robert C. Mainfort Jr.

The Woodland-era (circa 1000 B.C. to A.D. 900) archaeological record of the Ohio River valley is an appropriate focus for confronting issues in archaeological taxonomy for several reasons. First, the archaeological record of this region is extraordinarily rich and complex, as exemplified by the many earthen enclosure and burial mound sites. Second, this region gave rise to some of the earliest broadly inclusive archaeological taxons in eastern North America, namely, Adena and Hopewell, both of which were conceived prior to the development of the Midwest Taxonomic Method. The subsequent inclusion of numerous, complex sites within poorly conceived taxonomic units, Adena and Hopewell in particular, created a taxonomic morass that continues to bedevil researchers to this day. The chapters included in this volume represent important steps toward moving beyond this legacy. My purpose in this concluding chapter is not to provide synopses of the preceding chapters but rather to draw on them in a more general discussion of some taxonomic issues.

More than a half-century ago, Phillips et al. (1951:61–62) astutely noted that:

> there is magic in names. Once let a hatful of miserable fragments of fourth-rate pottery be dignified by a "Name," and there will follow inevitably the tendency for the name to become an entity, particularly in the mind of him who gives it. Go a step further and publish a description and the type embarks on an independent existence of its own. At that point the classification ceases to be a "tool," and the archaeologist becomes one.

This statement makes clear that Phillips, Ford, and Griffin, always on the cutting edge of the discipline, also must be credited with being the first Americanist archaeologists to employ a postmodernist perspective in their writings! Although Phillips et al. (1951) did not mention "culture," "focus," or "phase" in their admonition—the focus of their landmark study was chronology, not regional taxonomic unit formulation—their point is equally, if not more strongly, applicable to these archaeological units.

Creation of culture-historical units was central, however, to Phillips's (1970) modestly titled *Archaeological Survey in the Lower Yazoo Basin, Mississippi, 1949–1955*, which is far more expansive than the title suggests. Seemingly unmindful of the cautions he, Ford, and Griffin expressed 20 years earlier, Phillips formulated roughly 80 archaeological phases spanning the entire lower Mississippi River valley and encompassing approximately 2,500 years. Phillips (1970:3) wanted "to apply some of the precepts set forth" by Willey and Phillips (1958), specifically "to see whether 'historical integration'" [i.e., the creation of archaeological phases] was "a practicable approach to archaeological understanding." That said, one might expect the monograph to include some explicit guidance for constructing phases, but it does not, and Phillips (1970:523) admitted that his procedures were "regrettably non-objective."

His approach ranged from defining a phase on the basis of a single site, "hoping that more components will be reported" (Phillips 1970:871), to postulating the existence of a phase on the basis of the lack "of the more specific Cairo Lowland markers" (Phillips 1970:929), to defining phases on the basis of minor variations in the frequencies of various ceramic types (Phillips 1970:930–939), to saying, "In a good many cases sites are plotted as Nodena [phase] solely because [Stephen] Williams says that is what they are" (Phillips 1970:934). The last construct refers to one of four late Mississippi period phases "of special importance" that Phillips (1970:930) considered to be "valid culture-historical units"! Although Phillips (1970:868) repeatedly stressed that his phases were "tentative formulations" and that a number of phases were "shaky propositions" (1970:912), the mere existence of these taxonomic units (as published entities, certainly not as archaeological realities) continues to structure archaeological research in the lower Mississippi valley to this day, even as Griffin (1973:379) feared, and proves the veracity of the observation by Phillips et al. (1951) cited above.

The ensuing decades have seen a proliferation of phases throughout eastern North America, mostly without the degree of self-reflection so evident in Phillips's writings. Thus, these largely intuitive constructs are now fundamental to the structure of research throughout a vast area. Not only are most phases poorly defined and poorly justified but also the assignment of sites to phases and the creation of phases seem to have become, in themselves, major research goals. Often lost sight of is the fact that phases, like other taxonomic constructs in archaeology, are simply tools to be used for exploring research questions.

A major problem with the systematics of Willey and Phillips (1958), held in common with McKern's earlier approach to cultural classification, is that the degree of similarity or dissimilarity among archaeological units—particularly archaeological components used in creating phases—is overwhelmingly dependent on the choice of traits used for comparison and the relative weighting accorded each trait. Traits can vary in scale from earthen architecture to artifact types to attributes of objects. Thus, assigning considerable weight to nuances in ceramic temper can lead to the appearance of marked dissimilarities between McKern's Upper Mississippian and Middle Mississippian, or Phillips's (1970) Late Mississippi period Parkin and Nodena phases, notwithstanding numerous and obvious similarities between artifact assemblages. It would not be far off the mark to suggest that in both instances the selection and weights given to specific traits were conditioned by preconceived notions of hierarchical taxonomic structure in the archaeological record (cf. Brown, this volume).

Do taxonomic units *really* influence our conceptions of the prehistoric archaeological record? Absolutely. An excellent example is provided by the phenomenon of truncated rectangular Middle Woodland mounds in the eastern United States. Prior to 1960, no unequivocal examples of pre-Mississippian flat-topped mounds had been recognized, notwithstanding a number of early Weeden Island (and related) examples reported by C. B. Moore (1894, 1896, 1902) around the turn of the century. With the inception of the Midwestern Taxonomic Method, if not a bit before, however, truncated rectangular mounds became inextricably linked with late prehistoric Mississippian cultures. By no means did this come about by capriciousness. Rather, extensive excavations during the Depression era, coupled with earlier investigations, produced no examples to the contrary.

In a 1962 *American Antiquity* paper, Kellar, Kelly, and McMichael published information, including radiocarbon assays, about a truncated rectangular Middle Woodland mound at Mandeville, Georgia (Kellar et al. 1962). Professional attention, however, gravitated toward the Hopewellian artifacts from an adjacent burial mound, while evidence from the flat-topped mound was largely ignored or dismissed. Thus, over a decade later, when Kurjack (1975) reported on the flat-topped rectangular Shorter Mound, located near Mandeville and excavated at the same time, the entire mound was attributed to the Mississippi period, despite the exclusively Middle Woodland ceramic assemblage in the primary mound stages.

Since the 1970s, of course, a number of unequivocal Middle Woodland flat-topped mounds have been identified in the Southeast (Knight 1990: 166–172; Mainfort 1986:82–83, 1988, 1996), and there is now a credible radiocarbon date for the Capitolium Mound at Marietta, Ohio (Pickard 1996), confirming Prufer's (1964a:51) earlier interpretation. Truncated rectangular mounds are no longer regarded as exclusively Mississippian, and Middle Woodland examples are no longer considered unusual. Still unexplained, however, is the developmental relationship (if any) between Middle Woodland and Mississippian flat-topped mounds.

Confronting the Issues

Beginning with Squier and Davis (1848:301), early researchers emphasized similarity, if not unity, within the diversity exhibited by Woodland archaeological sites throughout the Middle Ohio Valley. Today, as the chapters in this volume show, more research centers on exploring local diversity rather than on the unity emphasized by Webb (e.g., Webb and Snow 1945) and others.

The chapter by Greber, an outgrowth of her earlier work (Greber 1991b), is to date perhaps the clearest and most explicit attempt to define and compare the two nebulous taxonomic units that are central to this volume—Adena and Hopewell. What could be more sensible than to use the type sites, conveniently located in relative proximity to each other in Ross County, Ohio, as the basis for comparing the two taxonomic entities at the local level?

One key to Greber's success is her emphasis on making comparisons between sites within geographic boundaries appropriate to the questions being asked. Although this is hardly a profound revelation, most of the taxonomic problems noted throughout this volume exist due to inadequate consideration of geographic scale by previous researchers. Thus, comparisons between contemporary sites and artifacts dating between A.D. 1 and 400 in Ross County and the Hocking River valley must be approached with caution, as a Hopewellian florescence did not occur in the latter area. Moreover, researchers must take into account the time-transgressive nature of attributes used to describe archaeological remains when attempting comparisons.

Greber neatly demonstrates that "Adena" and "Hopewell" are useful taxonomic entities in Ross County, Ohio. Outside this area, their utility diminishes, and new taxonomic units to encompass local expressions of Adena and Hopewell would be more appropriate. As discussed below, Sieg (this volume) makes a step in this direction.

In advocating a multiscalar approach to analysis, Rafferty (this volume) calls attention to the fall off in the material expressions of Early and Middle Woodland mortuary ritual north and east of the Ohio Valley, especially with regard to earthen architecture. Clearly, we have here a phenomenon of some social and political importance, but this has been overshadowed by continued research emphasis on the Adena and Hopewell "heartland." Rafferty is well aware that local and regional scales are coextensive and that conceptualization of these scales has the potential to become mired in the essentialist thinking that characterizes existing taxonomic units.

As Rafferty notes, rituals are programmatic, goal-oriented, repetitive social practices. The last is especially important in that formal rigidity and serial repetitions are qualities that distinguish ritual from other human activities. Following Rappaport (1979) and Lewis (1979), in performing rituals according to traditional guidelines, participants not only are acknowledging duties to those no longer present but also are publicly demonstrating acceptance of the authority of these individuals. Although many features of rituals can vary from one performance to the next, some—what Rappaport (1979:182) calls "liturgies"—do not vary in the short term and must be performed in the course of a given ritual or set of rituals. In the case of disposal of the dead, alternative liturgies are available. Although still subject to traditional regulation, variability can be based on social position, conspicuous display on the part of a living political leader, and other factors in combination with these.

One could postulate that smaller, less complex "Adena" burial mounds, such as Morgan Stone in Kentucky, represent loci of local-scale ritual performance. In contrast, larger mounds such as Wright may reflect periodic ritual performance on a regional scale and over a longer period of time. One implication is that within any specified area, the archaeological remains of both local-scale and regional-scale mortuary rituals may be present, and this should be taken into account when undertaking multiscalar comparisons of mortuary sites. Such an approach ties in nicely with Rafferty's comments regarding the false dichotomy between local versus regional patterns and his observation, mirroring Greber (this volume), that within the lower Scioto River valley, for example, the case can be made for numerous related, but distinct, "Adenas" and "Hopewells."

Brown's (this volume) observation that archaeological taxons can be "gerrymandered to fulfill certain culture-historical expectations" is particularly well illustrated by Adena. Emblematic of this practice is the statement by Webb and Snow (1945:14) that "only traits have been listed, which in the opinion of the authors, are sufficient to justify the classification of the site as Adena, since the purpose was only to justify the use of the site in plotting the 'distribution of Adena.'" For Webb and Snow, "Adena"—

whatever it was—existed. Their task was simply to provide justification for assigning specific sites that they *knew* were Adena to the taxon "Adena," a construct that remained undefined. To their credit, Webb and Snow were honest about what they were doing, although they did not explicitly state they regarded as Adena any site that exhibited two or more of their Adena traits (cf. Greenman 1932; Webb and Snow 1945:12). Remarkably, Willey and Phillips (1958:158) took the view that "Adena is a reasonably well-defined archaeological unit," presumably on the basis of *The Adena People*. To this day Adena has not been "reasonably well defined."

I agree with Clay and Brown (this volume) that we would be better off without "Adena," save for in the very restrictive sense proposed by Greber. For masking variation in the archaeological record, Adena is a taxonomic entity with few equals, as even a cursory review of differences in mortuary treatment between river drainages makes evident. As one of the last of the trait-based "cultures," Adena is something of an anathema in the twenty-first century, as it was even several decades earlier (Brown 1986). As shown by Greber, research directed toward examining the remains known as Adena within local cultural sequences has great potential.

Moving beyond taxonomic considerations, Clay (this volume) provides a fascinating historical perspective on how the original concept of Adena was coopted and transformed into something rather more than ever was intended. At a tender age Adena was appropriated by influential archaeologists who had only marginal interests in Ohio Valley archaeology, but their explicit developmental implications produced for Adena a historical interpretation with a vengeance. Clay's chapter should lay to rest any notion that archaeology exists totally independent of politics.

The notion of Ohio Hopewell as a cohesive grouping of sites (called a phase, a culture, or something else) seems fairly common among archaeologists *not* familiar with the actual data, and this is the impression given in classic North American archaeology textbooks (e.g., Jennings 1974; Willey 1966). The contributors to this volume, in contrast, understand that variability is central to the concept of Ohio Hopewell (see also Seeman 1992b: 27–29). For instance, Sieg's (this volume) discussion of the unique materials in the Turner collections highlights a key characteristic of Ohio Hopewell, namely, that each of the large sites is unique. As such, these sites are ill suited to the imposition of traditional taxonomic units.

Looking at variation among Middle Woodland sites within individual river drainages certainly is a step in the right direction, but creating associated archaeological phases may be a bit premature, if not unnecessary. Willey and Phillips's (1958) concept of the archaeological phase is not so far removed from the systematics of the Midwestern Taxonomic Method and, if judged by the most ambitious application (Phillips 1970), is seriously flawed. The utility of archaeological phases is in part a function of the extent to which certain kinds of material culture vary normatively in time and space (see Plog 1974). I am not convinced that it is desirable or appropriate to accept this assumption in attempting to organize taxonomically the contextually rich data from Ohio Hopewell sites.

Although I will concede that formulation of explicitly defined, localized phases offers some promise, I urge researchers not to fall into the essentialist thinking that has led to a hodgepodge of phases in the lower Mississippi valley, virtually none of which are analytically defensible (e.g., Mainfort 2003a, 2003b). They are not classes, as the members do not share a unique set of traits. Nor are they groups, as the members of a phase cannot be judged to be more similar to each other than to any member of another phase. These intuitively derived phase constructs have had an enervating effect on systematic investigations of variability in the archaeological record of the region for more than three decades. Parenthetically, it is disturbing that, since the publication of Phillips's (1970) landmark study, attempts to group archaeological sites into culture-historical units (phases) have not been accompanied by either theoretical or methodological advances.

Several contributors to this volume comment on Hopewell habitation sites. Obviously, it is important to identify and understand such sites (see, for example, Dancey and Pacheco, eds. 1997), but I have some reservations about creating archaeological units, whether phases or something else, that subsume both enclosure and mound sites and habitation sites. By definition, these two classes of sites share few similarities in material culture—a situation that creates taxonomic problems. If, for example, utilitarian ceramics become the basis for phase designations, where does that leave Hopewell, the élan of which is ceremonialism? Phases, per se, are not necessary to the study of settlements associated with Hopewell ceremonial sites.

That said, Sieg's (this volume) focus on Hopewellian phenomena within the Little Miami valley provides a useful perspective on variability within a manageable study area and holds much promise. The use of limestone in the construction of enclosure walls at all excavated localities in the region is intriguing. Also of interest are the recent excavation data that suggest that domestic occupations occurred within and/or immediately adjacent to the enclosures. Both features seem to be unique to the Little Miami locality, a finding that should provide stimulus for similarly focused studies. Although such an approach has obvious analytical and operational utility, as Burks (this volume) points out, it is important for researchers not to allow their thinking to be dominated by modern concepts of appropriate geographic areas.

On a larger geographical scale, the distinction between geometric enclosures and so-called hilltop enclosures (those that conform to upland topographic features), which has a strong geographic component, clearly warrants more attention, as does the spatial distribution of specific enclosure forms and embankment-ditch variants (no ditch, interior ditch, exterior ditch). Byers (1987) has offered some provocative thoughts regarding the structural principles that underlie variation in enclosures.

The three Kentucky case studies not only provide specific examples of the inadequacies of Adena and Hopewell as taxonomic entities but also contribute important new data. At the Walker-Noe Mound, reported by Pollack et al. (this volume), both Adena Plain pottery and Adena Stemmed points (some evidently produced specifically for use in mortuary ritual) were found in undisturbed contexts, leading the authors to view the mound as an Adena phenomenon. The artifact type names themselves contribute in no small measure to the taxonomic quandary confronted by Pollack et al. If artifact types inextricably linked to Adena by their very names are found at a site, how could the site not be Adena?

Perhaps matters would be a bit different if the limestone-tempered plain sherds were typed as Mulberry Creek Plain, characteristic of Woodland occupations along the Tennessee River (Haag 1942a:516; see also Griffin 1945:244–245), rather than Adena Plain. This is not as unreasonable as it might seem, as Pollack et al. identify a single limestone-tempered check-stamped sherd as Wright Check Stamped, a surface-decorated companion type of Mulberry Creek Plain with essentially the same geographic distribution. Similarly, the Adena Stemmed points could be considered variants of the Gary type, which has a long history in the Tennessee River valley, the lower Mississippi valley, and Texas (Cambron and Hulse 1969:57). Unlike the two "Adena" types, neither Mulberry Creek Plain pottery nor Gary points are at odds with a date of circa A.D. 1, such as that for Walker-Noe, nor does either of the types carry as much additional cultural baggage.

The relative abundance of Adena (setting aside the issue of what precisely Adena is) in the Bluegrass region of Kentucky and the virtual absence of anything that might be called Hopewell in the same region is an extraordinarily interesting culture-historical problem. The Hopewellian copper ear spools reported by Richmond and Kerr (this volume) at the Amburgey site represent only the second documented case of these typically Hopewellian artifacts in Kentucky. Two radiocarbon assays place the site squarely within the Middle Woodland period. Some artifacts (copper artifacts and a nonlocal ceramic vessel), as well as the presence of an oval arrangement of post molds and thermal features, suggest a ritual function, but no human burials were located, and no mound was present. Appropriately conservative in their interpretation, Richmond and Kerr note that Amburgey is not Adena and that the site does not conform to traditional notions of Hopewell. This situation should be no cause for taxonomic concern. Amburgey and the essentially contemporary Camargo Mound are local Middle Woodland expressions that differ from Ohio Hopewell.

Schlarb's (this volume) summary of the previously unreported Bullock Mound excavations also provides important documentation of Woodland variability in the Bluegrass region of Kentucky. The artifact assemblage from the Bullock Mound suggests an age within several centuries of A.D. 1, despite the lack of corroborating radiocarbon assays. Bladelets of Flint Ridge chert seem to be one of the best Hopewell horizon markers. At Bullock, the fact that a bladelet was found in a context suggesting general contemporaneity with Adena Plain pottery (or Mulberry Creek Plain, as suggested above) need not imply interaction between contemporary "Adena" and "Hopewell" groups. A more parsimonious scenario is simply that some bladelets and some Adena Plain (or Mulberry Creek Plain) pottery were roughly contemporary. The rectangular structure beneath the Bullock Mound clearly is at odds with Webb's concept of Adena, and Schlarb appropriately notes a general similarity between this structure and the one uncovered at the base of the Middle Woodland Riley Mound (Webb 1943). Schlarb may be correct in his suggestion that Webb's failure to prepare a report on the Bullock Mound may have been influenced by the fact that the site clearly does not represent what Webb would have considered typical Adena.

I applaud the reluctance of Dancey and Seeman (this volume) to create a Late Woodland period Cole phase (or other taxon) on the basis of existing data. Their reasoning parallels my own in refusing to create a "Pinson phase" to encompass the dozens of small recorded Middle Woodland habitation sites and several mound groups within a ten-mile radius of the Pinson Mounds site. Would such a construct contribute to understanding the processes that led to massive earthen construction at Pinson Mounds? No. Would such a construct create the impression that these sites all were in some sense similar to each other? Definitely, even in the absence of excavated data from any of them. Moreover, a Pinson phase would mask variation among sites that presently are known only via relatively small surface-collected artifact samples. If our taxonomic units do not contribute in some way to explaining variability in the archaeological record (the only justifiable reason for creating and retaining such units), they should be abandoned or, in the case of a "Pinson phase," not created in the first place. As suggested by Dancey and Seeman, by maintaining a "loose" approach to taxonomy, "we are less likely to mask the processes pertaining to the major questions we are likely to ask of these materials in the future."

Concluding Remarks

The taxonomic concerns expressed by Phillips et al. (1951:437), noted earlier, are easily overcome. That they often are not is in no small part due to the simple fact that archaeologists tend to forget that their taxonomic units, whether potsherd types or "cultures" (in the 1920s–1930s sense), are arbitrary constructs that should be retained only so long as they prove to be useful *tools* for explaining the archaeological record (cf. Ford 1951:13). As tools, they are subject to modification and refinement, and if they are no longer useful, to discard. Research questions should dictate appropriate taxonomy, and, at the very least, existing taxonomy should not constrain research questions. Flexibility and awareness of appropriate geographic scale are both critical to the utility of taxonomic units at any level. Moreover, as suggested by Brown (this volume), "there needs to be more, different kinds of classification."

The contributions to this volume not only make the case for moving beyond, if not eschewing, long-entrenched taxonomic inadequacies but also provide important direction in sharpening the focus of archaeological inquiry within one of the most vibrant regions in pre-Columbian North America.

References Cited

Abrams, Elliot M.
   1989   The Boudinot #4 Site (33AT521): An Early Woodland Habitation Site in Athens County, Ohio. *West Virginia Archaeologist* 41(2):16–26.
   1992a   Archaeological Investigation of the Armitage Mound (33-At-434), The Plains, Ohio. *Midcontinental Journal of Archaeology* 17:80–111.
   1992b   Woodland Settlement Patterns in the Southern Hocking River Valley, Southeastern Ohio. In *Cultural Variability in Context: Woodland Settlements of the Mid-Ohio Valley,* edited by M. F. Seeman, pp. 19–23. Midcontinental Journal of Archaeology Special Paper Number 7. Kent State University, Kent, Ohio.

Adams, William R.
   1949   *Archaeological Notes on Posey County, Indiana.* Indiana Historical Bureau, Indianapolis.

Ahler, Steven R.
   1988   *Excavations at the Hansen Site.* Program for Cultural Resource Assessment Archaeological Report 173. University of Kentucky, Lexington.

Allman, John C.
   1967   A New Late Woodland Culture for Ohio: The Lichliter Village Site Near Dayton. *Ohio Archaeologist* 7(2):59–68.

Anderson, David G., and Robert C. Mainfort Jr.
   2002a   An Introduction to Woodland Archaeology in the Southeast. In *The Woodland Southeast,* edited by D. G. Anderson and R. C. Mainfort Jr., pp. 1–19. University of Alabama Press, Tuscaloosa.
   2002b   Epilogue: Future Directions for Woodland Archaeology in the Southeast. In *The Woodland Southeast,* edited by D. G. Anderson and R. C. Mainfort Jr., pp. 540–542. University of Alabama Press, Tuscaloosa.

Anderson, David G., and Robert C. Mainfort Jr. (editors)
   2002   *The Woodland Southeast.* University of Alabama Press, Tuscaloosa.

Anderson, J. L.
   1981   History and Climate: Some Economic Models. In *Climate and History: Studies in Past Climates and their Impact on Man,* edited by T. M. L. Wigley,

M. J. Ingram, and G. Farmer, pp. 337–355. Cambridge University Press, Cambridge.

Anderson, Warren H.
1994   *Rocks and Minerals of Kentucky.* Kentucky Geological Survey Special Publication 20, Series XI. University of Kentucky, Lexington.

Andrews, E. B.
1877   Report of Explorations of Mounds in Southeastern Ohio. *Peabody Museum of Archaeology and Ethnology, Harvard University Tenth Annual Report* 11(1):48–74. Harvard University, Cambridge.

Applegate, Darlene
2000   The Watkins Site (15Lo12) Revisited: Previous Research, New Interpretations, and Recent Artifact Analysis. In *Current Archaeological Research in Kentucky: Volume Six,* edited by D. Pollack and K. J. Gremillion, pp. 121–143. Kentucky Heritage Council, Frankfort.

Aristotle
1955   [325 B.C.E.] The Organon [Prior and Posterior Analytics]. In *Basic Works of Aristotle,* edited and translated by R. McKeon. Modern Library Classics, New York.

Arnold, Philip J., III
2003   Ethnoarchaeology: Timing Change in These Changing Times. In *Time in Archaeology: Time Perspectivism Twenty Years Later,* organized by S. Holdaway and L. Wandsnider. Electronic symposium for the Annual Meeting of the Society for American Archaeology, Milwaukee, April 9–13, 2003, www.anthro.Washington.edu/saa.

Asch, Nancy B., Richard. I. Ford, and David L. Asch
1972   *Paleoethnobotany of the Koster Site: The Archaic Horizons.* Reports of Investigations 24. Illinois State Museum, Springfield.

Atwater, Caleb
1820   *A Description of the Antiquities Discovered in Ohio and Other Western States.* Transactions and Collections I, Archaeologica Americana. American Antiquarian Society, Worcester, Massachusetts.
1833   *The Writings of Caleb Atwater.* Scott and Wright, Columbus, Ohio.

Baby, Raymond S.
1947   Unpublished field notes, W. S. Cole Site. Manuscript on file, Ohio Historical Society, Columbus.
1952   Unpublished field notes, Orange Township Works. Manuscript on file, Ohio Historical Society, Columbus.
1971   Prehistoric Architecture: A Study of House Types in the Ohio Valley. *Ohio Journal of Science* 71(4):193–198.

Baby, Raymond S., and Asa Mays Jr.
1959   Exploration of the William H. Davis Mound. *Museum Echoes 32.* (December):95–96.

Baby, Raymond S., and Martha A. Potter
1965   *The Cole Complex: A Preliminary Analysis of Late Woodland Ceramics in*

Ohio and Their Relationship to the Ohio Hopewell Phase. Papers in Archaeology Number 2. Ohio Historical Society, Columbus.

Baby, Raymond S., Martha A. Potter, and Asa Mays Jr.
- 1966 *Exploration of the O. C. Voss Mound, Big Darby Reservoir Area, Franklin County, Ohio.* Ohio Historical Society, Columbus.

Baby, Raymond S., Martha A. Potter, and Barbara S. Saurborn
- 1967 Exploration of the O. C. Voss Site, Big Darby Reservoir Area, Franklin County, Ohio. Manuscript on file at the Ohio Historical Society, Columbus.
- 1968 Excavation of the Enos Holmes Mound and Robert McMullen Site, Paint Creek Reservoir Area, Highland County, Ohio. Manuscript on file at the Ohio Historical Society, Columbus.

Baby, Raymond S., and J. W. Shaffer
- 1957 Exploration of the Zencor Village Site. *Museum Echoes* 30(11):87. Ohio Historical Society, Columbus.

Baca, Keith A.
- 2002 Correspondence between James A. Ford and Henry B. Collins: Selected Letters 1927–1941. *Mississippi Archaeology* 37(2):99–158.

Baerreis, David A.
- 1994 [1949] Some Comments on Trait Lists and the Hopewellian Culture. *Wisconsin Archeologist* 75(1–2):19–26.

Baker, F. C., J. B. Griffin, R. G. Morgan, G. K. Neumann, and J. L. B. Taylor
- 1941 *Contributions to the Archaeology of the Illinois River Valley.* American Philosophical Society, Transactions 32, Part 1.

Barkes, B. M.
- 1978 The Ufferman Site in Delaware County, Ohio: A Brief Report. Manuscript on file, Ohio Historical Society, Columbus.
- 1983 An Analysis of Late Woodland Ceramics from the DECCO (33DL28), Ufferman (33DL12), and W. S. Cole (33DL11) Sites: The Cole Complex Reconsidered. M.A. thesis, Department of Anthropology, The Ohio State University, Columbus.

Beck, Lane Anderson
- 1995 Regional Cults and Ethnic Boundaries in "Southern Hopewell." In *Regional Approaches to Mortuary Analysis,* edited by L. A. Beck, pp. 167–187. Plenum Press, New York.

Bender, Barbara
- 1985a Emergent Tribal Formations in the American Midcontinent. *American Antiquity* 50(1):52–62.
- 1985b Prehistoric Developments in the American Midcontinent and in Brittany, Northwest France. In *Prehistoric Hunter-Gatherers: The Emergence of Cultural Complexity,* edited by T. D. Price and J. A. Brown, pp. 21–57. Academic Press, Orlando, Florida.

Binford, Lewis R.
- 1968 Post-Pleistocene Adaptations. In *New Perspectives in Archeology,* edited by S. R. Binford and L. R. Binford, pp. 313–341. Aldine, Chicago.

1972   *An Archaeological Perspective.* Seminar Press, New York.
1983   *In Pursuit of the Past.* Thames and Hudson, London.

Black, Deborah Bush
  1979   Adena and Hopewell Relations in the Lower Hocking Valley. In *Hopewell Archaeology,* edited by D. S. Brose and N. Greber, pp. 19–26. Kent State University Press, Kent, Ohio.

Blosser, J. K.
  1996   The 1984 Excavation at 12D295: A Middle Woodland Village in Southeastern Indiana. In *A View from the Core,* edited by P. J. Pacheco, pp. 54–69. Ohio Archaeological Council, Columbus.

Braun, David P.
  1977   Middle Woodland–Early Late Woodland Social Change in the Prehistoric Central Midwestern U.S. Unpublished Ph.D. dissertation, Department of Anthropology, University of Michigan, Ann Arbor.
  1986   Midwestern Hopewellian Exchange and Supralocal Interaction. In *Peer Polity Interaction and Socio-Political Change,* edited by C. Renfrew and J. F. Cherry, pp. 117–126. Cambridge University Press, Cambridge.

Braun, David P., and Stephen Plog
  1982   Evolution of "Tribal" Social Networks: Theory and Prehistoric North American Evidence. *American Antiquity* 47(3):504–525.

Brew, Junius O.
  1946   *Archaeology of Alkali Ridge, Southeastern Utah.* Peabody Museum of American Archaeology and Ethnology Papers, Volume 21. Harvard University, Cambridge.

Brose, David S.
  1972   The Development of Archaeology in Northeastern America. In *The Development of North American Archaeology,* edited by J. E. Fitting, pp. 116–139. Natural History Press, New York.
  1979   A Speculative Model of the Role of Exchange in the Prehistory of the Eastern Woodlands. In *Hopewell Archaeology,* edited by D. S. Brose and N. Greber, pp. 3–8. Kent State University Press, Kent, Ohio.
  1982   *The Archaeological Investigation of a Fort Ancient Community near Ohio Brush Creek, Adams County, Ohio.* Kirtlandia 34. Cleveland Museum of Natural History, Cleveland.
  1992   Changing Paradigms in the Explanation of Southeastern Prehistory. In *The Development of Southeastern Archaeology,* edited by J. K. Johnson, pp. 1–17. University of Alabama Press, Tuscaloosa.
  1994a Trade and Exchange in the Midwestern United States. *Prehistoric Exchange Systems in North America,* edited by J. Erikson and T. Baugh, pp. 215–240. Plenum Press, New York.
  1994b *The South Park Site and the Whittlesey Tradition of Northeast Ohio.* Monographs in World Prehistory 20. Prehistory Press, Madison, Wisconsin.
  2001   Introduction to Eastern North America at the Dawn of European Colonization. In *Societies in Eclipse,* edited by D. S. Brose, C. W. Cowan, and

R. C. Mainfort Jr., pp. 1–8. Smithsonian Institution Press, Washington, D.C.
2002 Museum Paradigms and the History of Southeastern Archaeology. In *Histories of Southeastern Archaeology*, edited by S. Tushingham, J. Hill, and C. McNutt, pp. 13–25. University of Alabama Press, Tuscaloosa.

Brose, David S., and N'omi Greber (editors)
1979 *Hopewell Archaeology*. Kent State University Press, Kent, Ohio.

Brown, James A.
1977 Current Directions in Midwestern Archaeology. *Annual Reviews of Anthropology* 6: 161–179.
1979 Charnel Houses and Mortuary Crypts: Disposal of the Dead in the Middle Woodland Period. In *Hopewell Archaeology*, edited by D. S. Brose and N. Greber, pp. 211–219. Kent State University Press, Kent, Ohio.
1986 Early Ceramics and Culture: A Review of Interpretations. In *Early Woodland Archeology*, edited by K. B. Farnsworth and T. E. Emerson, pp. 598–608. Center for American Archeology Kampsville Seminars in Archaeology, No. 2. Center for American Archeology Press, Kampsville, Illinois.

Buikstra, Jane E., and Douglas K. Charles
1999 Centering the Ancestors: Cemeteries, Mounds, and Sacred Landscapes of the Ancient North American Midcontinent. In *Archaeologies of Landscape: Contemporary Perspectives*, edited by W. Ashmore and A. B. Knapp, pp. 201–228. Blackwell Publishers, Oxford, U.K.

Buikstra, Jane E., and Mark Swegle
1989 Bone Modification Due to Burning: Experimental Evidence. In *Bone Modification*, edited by R. Bonnichsen and M. Sorg, pp. 247–258. Center for the Study of the First Americans, Orono, Maine.

Buikstra, Jane E., and Douglas H. Ubelaker (editors)
1994 *Standards for Data Collection from Human Skeletal Remains*. Research Series 44. Arkansas Archeological Survey, Fayetteville.

Burks, Jarrod
2001 Strait Site Radiocarbon Dates Revealed. *Ohio Archaeological Council Newsletter* 13(1):7.
2004 Identifying Household Cluster and Refuse Disposal Patterns at the Strait Site: A Third Century A.D. Nucleated Settlement in the Middle Ohio River Valley. Ph.D. dissertation. Department of Anthropology, Ohio State University, Columbus.

Burks, Jarrod, and William S. Dancey
1999 Documenting Terminal Middle Woodland Community Pattern Change in Central Ohio: Aggregated Households at the Strait Site. Paper Presented at the 45th Annual Midwest Archaeological Conference, East Lansing, Michigan.

Bybee, Alexandra D., and Michael D. Richmond
2003 *Data Recovery at a Nineteenth Century Cemetery (15Mm137) in Montgomery*

County, Kentucky. Contract Publication Series 02–256. Cultural Resource Analysts, Inc., Lexington, Kentucky.

Byers, A. Martin
- 1987 The Earthwork Enclosures of the Central Ohio Valley. Unpublished Ph.D. dissertation, Department of Anthropology, State University of New York at Albany, Albany.

Caldwell, Joseph R.
- 1958 *Trend and Tradition in the Prehistory of the Eastern United States.* Memoirs of the American Anthropological Association Number 88. American Anthropological Association, Washington, D.C.
- 1962 Eastern North America. In *Courses toward Urban Life,* edited by R. J. Braidwood and G. R. Willey, pp. 288–308. Viking Fund Publications in Anthropology 32. Aldine, Chicago.
- 1964 Interaction Spheres in Prehistory. In *Hopewellian Studies,* edited by J. R. Caldwell and R. L. Hall, pp. 133–143. Scientific Papers, Volume 12, Number 2. Illinois State Museum, Springfield.

Callender, C.
- 1971 Comments. In *Adena: The Seeking of an Identity,* edited by B. K. Swartz, pp. 179–182. Ball State University, Muncie, Indiana.

Cambron, James W., and David C. Hulse
- 1969 *Handbook of Alabama Archaeology: Part 1, Point Types.* Archaeological Research Association of Alabama, Birmingham.

Cameron, Catherine
- 1998 Coursed Adobe Architecture, Style, and Social Boundaries in the American Southwest. In *The Archaeology of Social Boundaries,* edited by M. T. Stark, pp. 183–207. Smithsonian Institution Press, Washington, D.C.

Carr, Christopher
- 1995 A Unified, Middle-Range Theory of Artifact Design. In *Style, Society and Person,* edited by C. Carr and J. Neitzel, pp. 171–258. Plenum Press, New York.

Carr, Christopher, and Herbert Haas
- 1996 Beta-Count and AMS Radiocarbon Dates of Woodland and Fort Ancient Period Occupations in Ohio 1350 B.C.-A.D. 1650. *West Virginia Archeologist* 48(1–2):19–53.

Carskadden, Jeff, and Larry Edmister
- 1992 Excavation of Henderson Mound 1, Muskingum County, Ohio. *Ohio Archaeologist* 42(1):6–9.

Carskadden, Jeff, and James F. Morton
- 1996 The Middle–Late Woodland Transition in the Central Muskingum Valley of Eastern Ohio: A View from the Philo Archaeological District. In *A View from the Core,* edited by P. J. Pacheco, pp. 316–338. Ohio Archaeological Council, Columbus.
- 1997 Living on the Edge: A Comparison of Adena and Hopewell Communities in the Central Muskingum Valley of Eastern Ohio. In *Ohio Hope-*

well Community Organization, edited by W. S. Dancey and P. J. Pacheco, pp. 365–401. Kent State University Press, Kent, Ohio.

2000 Fort Ancient in the Central Muskingum Valley of Eastern Ohio: A View from the Philo II Site. In *Cultures before Contact: The Late Prehistory of Ohio and Surrounding Regions,* edited by R. A. Genheimer, pp. 158–194. Ohio Archaeological Council, Columbus.

Chapman, Jefferson, and Bennie C. Keel
 1979 Candy Creek–Connestee Components in Eastern Tennessee and Western North Carolina and Their Relationship with Adena-Hopewell. In *Hopewell Archaeology,* edited by D. S. Brose and N. Greber, pp. 157–161. Kent State University Press, Kent, Ohio.

Charles, Douglas K., Steven R. Leigh, and Jane E. Buikstra (editors)
 1988 *The Archaic and Woodland Cemeteries at the Elizabeth Site in the Lower Illinois Valley.* Research Series Volume 7. Center for American Archaeology, Kampsville, Illinois.

Clarke, David L.
 1968 *Analytical Archaeology.* Methuen, London.

Clay, R. Berle
 1980 The Cultural Placement of Fayette Phick Ceramics in Central Kentucky. Tennessee Anthropologist 5:166–178.
 1983 Pottery and Graveside Ritual in Kentucky Adena. *Midcontinental Journal of Archaeology* 8(2):109–126.
 1985 Peter Village 164 Years Later: A Summary of 1983 Excavations. In *Woodland Period Archaeology in Kentucky,* edited by D. Pollack, T. N. Sanders and C. D. Hockensmith, pp. 1–41. Kentucky Heritage Council, Frankfort.
 1986 Adena Ritual Spaces. In *Early Woodland Archaeology,* edited by K. B. Farnsworth and T. E. Emerson, pp. 581–595. Center for American Archaeology, Kampsville, Illinois.
 1987 Circles and Ovals: Two Types of Adena Space. *Southeastern Archaeology* 6(1):46–56.
 1989 Peter Village: An Adena Enclosure. In *Middle Woodland Settlement and Ceremonialism in the Mid-South and Lower Mississippi Valley,* edited by R. C. Mainfort Jr., pp. 19–30. Archaeological Report No. 22. Mississippi Department of Archives and History, Jackson.
 1991a Adena Ritual Development: An Organizational Type in a Temporal Perspective. In *The Human Landscape in Kentucky's Past,* edited by C. Stout and C. K. Hensley, pp. 30–39. Kentucky Heritage Council, Frankfort.
 1991b *Essential Features of Adena Ritual: A Lecture Delivered at Angel Mounds National Historic Landmark, Evansville, Indiana on 3 April 1990.* Research Reports Number 13. Glenn A. Black Laboratory of Archaeology, Indiana University, Bloomington.
 1992 Chiefs, Big Men, or What? Economy, Settlement Patterns, and Their Bearing on Adena Political Models. In *Cultural Variability in Context,* edited by M. F. Seeman, pp. 77–80. Midcontinental Journal of Archaeology Special Paper Number 7. Kent State University Press, Kent, Ohio.

1998a Adena. In *Archaeology of Prehistoric Native America: An Encyclopedia,* edited by G. Gibbon, pp. 5–7. Garland Publishing, New York.

1998b The Essential Features of Adena Ritual and Their Implications. *Southeastern Archaeology* 17(1):1–21.

2002 Deconstructing the Woodland Sequence from the Heartland: A Review of Recent Research Directions in the Upper Ohio Valley. In *The Woodland Southeast,* edited by D. G. Anderson and R. C. Mainfort Jr., pp. 162–184. University of Alabama Press, Tuscaloosa.

Clay, R. Berle, and Steven D. Creasman

1999 Middle Ohio Valley Late Woodland Nucleated Settlements: "Where's the Beef." *West Virginia Archeologist* 51(1–2):1–10.

Clay, R. Berle, and Charles M. Niquette

1989 *Phase III Excavations at the Niebert Site (46MS103) in the Gallipolis Locks and Dam Replacement Project Mason County, West Virginia.* Cultural Resource Analysts, Inc., Lexington, Kentucky.

1992 Middle Woodland Mortuary Ritual in the Gallipolis Locks and Dam Vicinity, West Virginia. *West Virginia Archeologist* 44(1–2):1–25.

Cleland, Charles E.

1976 The Focal-Diffuse Model: An Evolutionary Perspective on the Prehistoric Cultural Adaptations of the Eastern United States. *Midcontinental Journal of Archaeology* 1:59–75.

Cobb, Charles R., and Patrick H. Garrow

1996 Woodstock Culture and the Question of Mississippian Emergence. *American Antiquity* 61(1):21–37.

Cochran, Donald R.

1996 The Adena/Hopewell Convergence in East Central Indiana. In *A View from the Core,* edited by P. J. Pacheco, pp. 340–353. Ohio Archaeological Council, Columbus.

Cole, Fay Cooper

1951 *Kincaid: A Prehistoric Illinois Metropolis.* University of Chicago Press, Chicago.

Cole, Fay Cooper, and Thorne Deuel

1937 *Rediscovering Illinois.* University of Chicago Publications in Anthropology. University of Chicago Press, Chicago.

Connolly, Robert P.

1995 Middle Woodland Hilltop Enclosures: The Built Environment, Construction and Function. Unpublished Ph.D. dissertation, Department of Anthropology, University of Illinois, Urbana-Champaign.

1996 Prehistoric Land Modification at the Fort Ancient Hilltop Enclosure: A Model of Formal and Accretive Development. In *A View from the Core,* edited by P. J. Pacheco, pp. 258–273. Ohio Archaeological Council, Columbus.

Connolly, Robert P., and Lauren E. Sieg

1996 1995 Report of Investigations at the Fort Ancient State Memorial, Volume 1: Museum Expansion and Garden Zones. Report submitted to the Ohio Historical Society, Columbus.

Coughlin, Sean, and Mark F. Seeman
 1997 Hopewellian Settlements at the Liberty Earthworks, Ross County, Ohio. In *Ohio Hopewell Community Organization,* edited by W. S. Dancey and P. J. Pacheco, pp. 231–250. Kent State University Press, Kent, Ohio.

Cowan, C. Wesley
 1996 Social Implications of Ohio Hopewell Art. In *A View from the Core,* edited by Paul J. Pacheco, pp. 128–148. Ohio Archaeological Council, Columbus.

Cowan, Frank L., and Ted S. Sunderhaus
 2002 Dating the Stubbs "Woodworks." *Ohio Archaeological Council Newsletter* 14(1):11–16.

Cowan, Frank L., Ted S. Sunderhaus, and Robert A. Genheimer
 1999 Notes from the Field, 1999: More Hopewell "Houses" at the Stubbs Earthworks Site. *Ohio Archaeological Council Newsletter* 11(2):11–16.

Crane, Howard R., and James B. Griffin
 1959 University of Michigan Radiocarbon Dates IV. *Radiocarbon* 1:173–198.
 1972 University of Michigan Radiocarbon Dates XIV. *Radiocarbon* 14(1): 155–194.

Creamer, Winifred, and Jonathan Haas
 1985 Tribe Versus Chiefdom in Lower Central America. *American Antiquity* 50(4):738–754.

Crites, Gary D.
 1992 Plant Remains from the Winfield Locks Site (46PU4). In *The Winfield Locks Site: A Phase III Excavation in the Lower Kanawha Valley, Putnam County, West Virginia,* edited by M. A. Hughes and C. M. Niquette, pp. 183–192. Contract Publication Series 92–81. Cultural Resource Analysts, Inc., Lexington, Kentucky.

Crites, Gary D., and Jonathan P. Kerr
 1991 The Late Woodland Paleoethnobotanical Record at Parkline. In *Late Woodland Archeology at the Parkline Site (46PU99) Putnam County, West Virginia,* edited by C. M. Niquette and M. A. Hughes, pp. 160–176. Cultural Resource Analysts, Inc., Contract Publication Series 90–93. Lexington, Kentucky.

Dancey, William S.
 1988 The Community Plan of an Early Late Woodland Village in the Middle Scioto River Valley. *Midcontinental Journal of Archaeology* 13:223–258.
 1992 Village Origins in Central Ohio: The Results and Implications of Recent Middle and Late Woodland Research. In *Cultural Variability in Context,* edited by M. F. Seeman, pp. 24–29. Midcontinental Journal of Archaeology Special Paper Number 7. Kent State University Press, Kent, Ohio.

1996 Putting an End to Ohio Hopewell. In *A View from the Core,* edited by P. J. Pacheco, pp. 394–405. Ohio Archaeological Council, Columbus.

1998 The Value of Surface Archaeological Data in Exploring the Dynamics of Community Evolution in the Middle Ohio Valley. In *Surface Archaeology,* edited by A. P. Sullivan III, pp. 3–19. University of New Mexico Press, Albuquerque.

Dancey, William S., and Paul J. Pacheco

1997 A Community Model of Ohio Hopewell Settlement. In *Ohio Hopewell Community Organization,* edited by W. S. Dancey and P. J. Pacheco, pp. 3–40. Kent State University Press, Kent, Ohio.

Dancey, William S., and Paul J. Pacheco (editors)

1997 *Ohio Hopewell Community Organization.* Kent State University Press, Kent, Ohio.

Dancey, William S., Mary Lou Fricke, and Flora Church

1987 The Water Plant Site and Other Sites in Southeastern Hamilton Township, Franklin County, Ohio. Report submitted to the Ohio Historic Preservation Office, Columbus.

Davis, Christine E., and David A. Anderson

1997 Summary Report, Phase III Data Recovery: CDC Site #1, North Putnam Regional Wastewater Facility Kanawha County, West Virginia. Christine Davis Consultants, Inc., Verona, Pennsylvania.

Davis, Watson (editor)

1934 *The Advance of Science.* Doubleday, Doran & Co., Inc., Garden City, New York.

Deuel, Thorne

1935 Basic Cultures of the Mississippi Valley. *American Anthropologist* 37:429–445.

1937 The Application of a Classificatory Method to Mississippi Valley Archaeology. In *Rediscovering Illinois,* edited by Fay Cooper Cole and Thorne Deuel, Appendix 1, pp. 207–219. University of Chicago Publications in Anthropology. University of Chicago Press, Chicago.

Dragoo, Don W.

1963 *Mounds for the Dead.* Annals of the Carnegie Museum Volume 37. Carnegie Museum, Pittsburgh.

1964 The Development of Adena and Its Role in the Formation of Ohio Hopewell. In *Hopewellian Studies,* edited by J. R. Caldwell and R. L. Hall, pp. 2–34. Illinois State Museum Scientific Papers 12. Illinois State Museum, Springfield.

1976a Adena and the Eastern Burial Cult. *Archaeology of Eastern North America* 4:1–9.

1976b Some Aspects of Eastern North American Prehistory: A Review 1975. *American Antiquity* 41(1):3–27.

Dunnell, Robert C.

1971 *Systematics in Prehistory.* Free Press, New York.

1982 Science, Social Science and Common Sense: The Agonizing Dilemma of Modern Archaeology. *Journal of Anthropological Research* 38:1–25.

East, Thomas C., Phillip T. Fitzgibbons, Christopher Espenshade, Linda Espenshade, Margaret Sams, Jeffrey A. Drobney, and Albert T. Vish
 1998 Putnam County, West Virginia, Lower Buffalo Development Site Bridge, Archaeological Studies, Volumes 1 and 2. Skelly and Loy, Inc., Harrisburg, Pennsylvania.

Espenshade, Christopher T., Gerald M. Kuncio, Deborah R. Langer, Albert T. Vish, Linda K. Espenshade, and Margaret G. Sams
 2001 Boone and Kanawha Counties, West Virginia Orgas to Chelyan Connector Improvement Project, Phase I/II Archaeology. Skelly and Loy, Inc., Monroeville, Alabama.

Essenpreis, Patricia S., and Michael E. Moseley
 1984 Fort Ancient: Citadel or Coliseum? *Field Museum of Natural History Bulletin* 55(6):5–10, 20–26.

Farnsworth, Kenneth B., and David L. Asch
 1986 Early Woodland Chronology, Artifact Styles, and Settlement Distribution in the Lower Illinois Valley Region. In *Early Woodland Archeology*, edited by K. B. Farnsworth and T. E. Emerson, pp. 326–457. Kampsville Seminars in Archeology No. 2, Center for American Archeology, CAA Press, Kampsville, Illinois.

Fenneman, Nevin M.
 1938 *Physiography of Eastern United States.* McGraw-Hill, New York.

Fenton, James P., and Richard W. Jefferies
 1991 The Camargo Mound and Earthworks: Preliminary Findings. In *The Human Landscape in Kentucky's Past,* edited by C. Stout and C. K. Hensley, pp. 40–55. Kentucky Heritage Council, Frankfort.

Fetzer, E. W., and W. J. Mayer-Oakes
 1951 Excavation of an Adena Burial Mound at the Half-Moon Site. *West Virginia Archaeologist* 4:1–25.

Feyerabend, Paul
 1999 *Conquest of Abundance: A Tale of Abstraction Versus the Richness of Being,* posthumous writings edited by Bert Terpstra. University of Chicago Press, Chicago.

Fisher, Alton K.
 1997 Origins of the Midwestern Taxonomic Method. *Midcontinental Journal of Archaeology* 22:117–122.

Fisher, David H.
 1970 *Historians' Fallacies: Toward a Logic of Historical Thought.* Harper and Row, New York.

Fitting, James E., and David S. Brose
 1971 The Northern Periphery of Adena. In *Adena: The Seeking of an Identity,* edited by B. K. Swartz, pp. 29–55. Ball State University, Muncie, Indiana.

Flannery, Kent V.
- 1968 Archaeological Systems Theory and Early Mesoamerica. In *Anthropological Archaeology in the Americas,* edited by B. Meggers, pp. 67–88. Anthropological Society of Washington, Washington, D.C.

Ford, James A.
- 1936 *Analysis of Indian Village Site Collections from Louisiana and Mississippi.* Anthropological Study Number 2. Louisiana Department of Conservation, Baton Rouge.
- 1951 *Greenhouse: A Troyville-Coles Creek Period Site in Avoyelles Parrish, Louisiana.* American Museum of Natural History, Anthropological Papers 44(1). American Museum of Natural History, New York.
- 1963 *Hopewell Culture Burial Mounds Near Helena, Arkansas.* Anthropological Papers of the American Museum of Natural History 50(1). American Museum of Natural History, New York.
- 1969 *A Comparison of Formative Cultures in the Americas.* Smithsonian Contributions to Anthropology 11. Smithsonian Institution Press, Washington, D.C.

Ford, James A., and James B. Griffin
- 1938 Report of the Conference on Southeastern Pottery Typology. Manuscript on file at The Ceramic Repository for the Eastern United States, Museum of Anthropology, University of Michigan, Ann Arbor. Reprinted in *Americanist Culture History,* edited by R. L. Lyman, M. J. O'Brien, and R. C. Dunnell, pp. 171–183. Plenum Press, New York.

Ford, James A., and George Quimby
- 1945 *The Tchefuncte Culture, An Early Occupation of the Lower Mississippi Valley.* Society for American Archaeology Memoir Number 2. Washington, D.C.

Ford, James A., and Gordon R. Willey
- 1940 *Crooks Site, A Marksville Period Burial Mound in La Salle Parish, Louisiana.* Anthropological Study Number 3. Department of Conservation, Louisiana Geological Survey, Baton Rouge.
- 1941 An Interpretation of the Prehistory of the Eastern United States. *American Anthropologist* 43(3:1):325–363.

Ford, Richard I.
- 1974 Northeastern Archaeology: Past and Future Directions. *Annual Review of Anthropology* 3:385–413.
- 1977 Evolutionary Ecology and the Evolution of Human Ecosystems: A Case Study from the Midwestern U.S.A. In *Explanation of Prehistoric Change,* edited by J. N. Hill, pp. 153–184. University of New Mexico Press, Albuquerque.

Fowke, Gerard
- 1902 *Archaeological History of Ohio.* Ohio State Archaeological and Historical Society, Columbus.

Fowler, Daniel B., E. Thomas Hemmings, and Gary R. Wilkins
  1976 Some Recent Additions to Adena Archaeology in West Virginia. *Archeology of Eastern North America* 4:110–121.
Fowler, Melvin L.
  1957 *Rutherford Mound: Hardin County, Illinois.* Illinois State Museum Scientific Papers 1:1–44. Illinois State Museum, Springfield.
Froedge, Ronnie B.
  1986 *Soil Survey of Montgomery County, Kentucky.* United States Department of Agriculture, Soil Conservation Service, Washington, D.C.
Fuller, John W.
  1981 The Development of Sedentary Village Communities in Northern West Virginia: The Test of a Model. In *Plowzone Archaeology,* edited by M. J. O'Brien and D. E. Lewarch, pp. 187–214. Vanderbilt University Publications in Anthropology Number 27. Vanderbilt University, Nashville.
Funkhouser, William D., and William S. Webb
  1935 *The Ricketts Site in Montgomery County, Kentucky.* Reports in Anthropology and Archaeology 3(3). University of Kentucky, Lexington.
Gardin, Jean-Claude, and Christopher S. Peebles
  1992 *Representations in Archaeology.* Indiana University Press, Bloomington.
Genheimer, Robert A.
  1996 Bladelets Are Tools Too: The Predominance of Bladelets among Formal Tools at Ohio Hopewell Sites. In *A View from the Core,* edited by P. J. Pacheco, pp. 92–107. Ohio Archaeological Council, Columbus.
  1997 Stubbs Cluster: Hopewellian Site Dynamics at a Forgotten Little Miami River Valley Settlement. In *Ohio Hopewell Community Organization,* edited by W. S. Dancey and P. J. Pacheco, pp. 283–309. Kent State University Press, Kent, Ohio.
Gladwin, Harold S.
  1936 Methodology in the Southwest. *American Antiquity* 1(4):256–259.
Gladwin, Winifred, and Harold S. Gladwin
  1934 *A Method for the Designation of Cultures and Their Variations.* Medallion Papers, Number 15. Globe, Arizona.
Goslin, R. M.
  1957 Food of the Adena People. In *The Adena People No. 2,* by W. S. Webb and R. S. Baby, pp. 41–46. Ohio Historical Society, Columbus.
Greber, N'omi B.
  1976 Within Ohio Hopewell: Analysis of Burial Patterns from Several Classic Sites. Ph.D. dissertation, Department of Anthropology, Case Western Reserve University.
  1979a Comparative Study of Site Morphology and Burial Patterns at Edwin Harness Mound and Seip Mounds 1 and 2. In *Hopewell Archaeology,* edited by D. S. Brose and N. Greber, pp. 27–38. Kent State University Press, Kent, Ohio.

1979b Variations in Social Structure of Ohio Hopewell Peoples. *Midcontinental Journal of Archaeology* 4(1):35–78.
1983   Recent Excavations at the Edwin Harness Mound, Liberty Works, Ross County, Ohio. *Kirtlandia* 19. Cleveland Museum of Natural History, Cleveland, Ohio.
1991a Preliminary Report on the 1990 Excavations at Capitolium Mound, Marietta Earthworks, Ohio. Report submitted to National Geographic Society, Washington, D.C.
1991b A Study of Continuity and Contrast between Central Scioto Adena and Hopewell Sites. *West Virginia Archaeologist* 43(1–2):1–26.
1996   A Commentary on the Contexts and Contents of Large to Small Ohio Hopewell Deposits. In *A View from the Core,* edited by P. J. Pacheco, pp. 150–172. Ohio Archaeological Council, Columbus.
1997   Two Geometric Enclosures in the Paint Creek Valley: An Estimate of Possible Changes in Community Patterns through Time. In *Ohio Hopewell Community Organization,* edited by W. S. Dancey and P. J. Pacheco, pp. 207–229. Kent State University Press, Kent, Ohio.
1998   Ohio Hopewell. In *Archaeology of Prehistoric America: An Encyclopedia,* edited by G. Gibbon, pp. 601–604. Garland, New York.
2000   Enclosures and Communities in Ohio Hopewell. Paper presented at Hopewell at the Millennium, a conference sponsored by the Center for American Archeology, Grafton, Illinois, July.
2002   A Preliminary Comparison of 1997 and 2002 Limited Excavations in the Great Circle Wall, High Bank Works, Ross County, Ohio. *Hopewell Archaeology: The Newsletter of Hopewell Archaeology in the Ohio River Valley* 5(2):1–6.
2003   Chronological Relationships among Ohio Hopewell Sites: Few Dates and Much Complexity. In *Archaeological Method and Theory,* edited by R. Jeske and D. K. Charles, pp. 88–113. Praeger Press, Westport, Connecticut.

Greber, N'omi B., and Katharine C. Ruhl
2000   *The Hopewell Site: A Contemporary Analysis Based on the Work of Charles C. Willoughby.* Eastern National, Washington, Pennsylvania.

Green, William
1999   Integrative Taxa in Midwestern Archaeology. In *Taming the Taxonomy,* edited by R. F. Williamson and C. M. Watts, pp. 25–36. Eastendbooks, Toronto.

Greenman, Emerson F.
1932   Excavation of the Coon Mound and an Analysis of the Adena Culture. *Ohio Archaeological and Historical Quarterly* 41:366–523.
1938   Hopewellian Traits in Florida. *American Antiquity* 3(4):327.

Gregg, Susan A.
1991   Introduction. In *Between Bands and States,* edited by Susan A. Gregg, pp. xvii–xix. Occasional Paper 9, Center for Archaeological Investigations. Southern Illinois University, Carbondale.

Griffin, James B.
- 1943a Adena Village Pottery from Fayette County, Kentucky. *University of Kentucky Reports in Anthropology and Archaeology* 5(7):667–672. University of Kentucky, Lexington.
- 1943b *The Fort Ancient Aspect.* University of Michigan Press, Ann Arbor.
- 1945 The Ceramic Affiliations of the Ohio Valley Adena Culture. In *The Adena People,* by W. S. Webb and C. E. Snow, pp. 220–246. Reports in Anthropology and Archaeology 6. University of Kentucky, Lexington.
- 1946 Cultural Change and Continuity in Eastern U.S. Archaeology. In *Man in Northeastern North America,* edited by F. Johnson, pp. 37–95. Papers of the Robert S. Peabody Foundation for Archaeology 3. Phillips Academy, Andover, Massachusetts.
- 1952a Cultural Periods in Eastern United States Archaeology. In *Archeology of Eastern United States,* edited by J. B. Griffin, pp. 352–364. University of Chicago Press, Chicago.
- 1952b The Late Prehistoric Cultures of the Ohio Valley. *Ohio State Archaeological and Historical Quarterly* 61:186–195.
- 1958 *The Chronological Position of Hopewellian Culture in the Eastern United States.* Anthropological Papers Number 12. Museum of Anthropology, University of Michigan, Ann Arbor.
- 1959 Review of "Trend and Tradition in the Prehistory of the Eastern United States," by J. Caldwell. *American Journal of Archaeology* 63:414–416.
- 1961 Review of "The Eastern Dispersal of Adena," by William A. Ritchie and Don W. Dragoo. *American Antiquity* 26:572–573.
- 1964 The Northeast Woodlands Area. In *Prehistoric Man in the New World,* edited by J. D. Jennings and E. Norbeck, pp. 223–257. University of Chicago Press, Chicago.
- 1967 Eastern North American Archaeology: A Summary. *Science* 156:175–191.
- 1971 General Discussion. In *Adena: The Seeking of an Identity,* edited by B. K. Swartz, pp. 158–178. Ball State University, Muncie, Indiana.
- 1973 Review of "Archaeological Survey in the Lower Yazoo Basin, Mississippi, 1949–1955," by Philip Phillips. *American Antiquity* 38(3):374–380.
- 1974 Forward to the New Edition. In *The Adena People,* by W. S. Webb and C. Snow, pp. v–xix. University of Tennessee Press, Knoxville.
- 1978a Eastern United States. In *Chronologies in New World Archaeology,* edited by R. E. Taylor and C. W. Meighan, pp. 51–70. Academic Press, New York.
- 1978b Late Prehistory of the Ohio Valley. In *Handbook of North American Indians, Volume 15, Northeast,* edited by B. Trigger, pp. 547–559. Smithsonian Institution, Washington, D.C.
- 1978c The Midlands and Northeastern United States. In *Ancient Native Americans,* edited by J. D. Jennings, pp. 221–280. W. H. Freeman and Company, San Francisco.
- 1986 Comments on the Kampsville Early Woodland Conference. In *Early*

Woodland Archeology, edited by K. B. Farnsworth and T. E. Emerson, pp. 609–620. Kampsville Seminars in Archeology No. 2, Center for American Archaeology, CAA Press, Kampsville, Illinois.

1996   The Hopewell Housing Shortage in Ohio, A.D. 1–350. In *A View from the Core*, edited by P. J. Pacheco, pp. 4–15. Ohio Archaeological Council, Columbus.

1997   Interpretations of Ohio Hopewell 1845–1984 and the Recent Emphasis on the Study of Dispersed Hamlets. In *Ohio Hopewell Community Organization*, edited by W. S. Dancey and P. J. Pacheco, pp. 405–426. Kent State University Press, Kent, Ohio.

Guthe, Carl

1952   Twenty-five Years of Archeology in the Eastern United States. In *Archeology of Eastern United States*, edited by James B Griffin, pp. 1–12. University of Chicago Press, Chicago.

Haag, William G.

1940   A Description of the Wright Site Pottery. In *The Wright Mounds, Sites 6 and 7, Montgomery County, Kentucky*, by W. S. Webb, pp. 75–82. Reports in Anthropology and Archaeology 5(1). University of Kentucky, Lexington.

1941   The Pottery from the Morgan Stone Mound. In *The Morgan Stone Mound, Site 15, Bath County, Kentucky*, by W. S. Webb, pp. 263–267. Reports in Anthropology and Archaeology 5(3). University of Kentucky, Lexington.

1942a A Description and Analysis of the Pickwick Pottery. In *An Archaeological Survey of the Pickwick Basin in the Adjacent Portions of the States of Alabama, Mississippi, and Tennessee*, by W. S. Webb and D. L. DeJarnette, pp. 509–529. Bulletin Number 129, Bureau of American Ethnology. Government Printing Office, Washington, D.C.

1942b The Pottery from the C and O Mounds at Paintsville. In *The C. and O. Mounds at Paintsville, Sites Jo 2 and Jo 9, Johnson County, Kentucky*, by W. S. Webb, pp. 341–349. Reports in Anthropology and Archaeology 5(4). Department of Anthropology and Archaeology, University of Kentucky, Lexington.

1947a Preliminary Appraisal of the Archaeological Resources of Wolf Creek Dam Reservoir. Manuscript on file, Office of State Archaeology, University of Kentucky, Lexington.

1947b Unpublished Field Records from Bullock Mound Excavations, Woodford County, Kentucky. Manuscript on file at the William S. Webb Museum of Anthropology, University of Kentucky, Lexington.

1974   The Adena Culture. In *Archaeological Researches in Retrospect*, edited by G. R. Willey, pp. 119–145. Winthrop Publishers, Cambridge, Massachusetts.

1985   Federal Aid to Archaeology in the Southeast, 1933–1942. *American Antiquity* 50(2):272–280.

Hall, Robert L.

1979   In Search of the Ideology of the Adena-Hopewell Climax. In *Hopewell*

Archaeology, edited by D. S. Brose and N. Greber, pp. 258–265. Kent State University Press, Kent, Ohio.

1997 *An Archaeology of the Soul: North American Indian Belief and Ritual.* University of Illinois Press, Chicago.

Hawkins, Rebecca A.

1996 Revising the Ohio Middle Woodland Ceramic Typology: New Information from the Twin Mounds West Site. In *A View from the Core,* edited by P. J. Pacheco, pp. 70–91. Ohio Archaeological Council, Columbus.

Hays, Christopher Tinsley

1994 Adena Mortuary Patterns and Ritual Cycles in the Upper Scioto Valley, Ohio. Ph.D. dissertation, Department of Anthropology, State University of New York, Binghamton.

Hegmon, Michelle

2003 Setting Theoretical Egos Aside: Issues and Theory in North American Archaeology. *American Antiquity* 68(2):213–244.

Hemmings, E. Thomas

1985 Virginia Radiocarbon Dates and Prehistory. *West Virginia Archeologist* 37(2): 33–45.

Henderson, A. Gwynn, and David Pollack

1985 The Late Woodland Occupation of the Bentley Site. In *Woodland Period Research in Kentucky,* edited by D. Pollack, T. N. Sanders, and C. D. Hockensmith, pp. 140–165. Kentucky Heritage Council, Frankfort.

Henderson, A. Gwynn, David Pollack, and Dwight R. Cropper

1988 The Old Fort Earthworks, Greenup County, Kentucky. In *New Deal Archaeology and Current Research in Kentucky,* edited by D. Pollack and M. L. Powell, pp. 64–81. Kentucky Heritage Council, Frankfort.

Hollinger, R. Eric, and David W. Benn (editors)

1998 Oneota Taxonomy: Papers from the Oneota Symposium of the 54th Plains Anthropological Conference, 1996. *Wisconsin Archeologist* 79(2).

Hooge, Paul

1986– From the Director. *Newsletter* Fall/Winter:3. Licking County Archae-
1987 ology and Landmarks Society, Newark, Ohio.

Hughes, Myra A., Jonathan P. Kerr, and Albert M. Pecora

1992 *The Winfield Locks Site: A Phase III Excavation in the Lower Kanawha Valley, Putnam County, West Virginia.* Contract Publication Series 92–81. Cultural Resource Analysts, Inc., Lexington, Kentucky.

Hume, David

1963 [1779] *A Treatise on Human Understanding.* Oxford University Press, London.

Hunt, Charles B.

1967 *Physiography of the United States.* W. H. Freeman and Company, San Francisco.

Hurley, William M.

1979 *Prehistoric Cordage: Identifications of Impressions on Pottery.* Tarazcum Press, Washington, D.C.

Jefferies, Richard W.
- 1976 *The Tunacunnhee Site.* Anthropological Papers of the University of Georgia, Number 1. University of Georgia, Athens.
- 1987 The Green Mound Archaeological Project: Investigations of Off-Mound Activity at a Kentucky Adena Site. In *Current Archaeological Research in Kentucky: Volume 1,* edited by D. Pollack, pp. 13–32. Kentucky Heritage Council, Frankfort.
- 1991 Kentucky Adena Mounds in Retrospect: New Insights from Old Collections. In *Studies in Kentucky Archaeology,* edited by C. D. Hockensmith, pp. 45–65. Kentucky Heritage Council, Frankfort.

Jefferson, Thomas
- 1984 [1787] *Notes on the State of Virginia: Query II: The Aboriginies.* Literary Classics of the United States. Viking Press, New York.

Jennings, Jesse D.
- 1941 Chickasaw and Earlier Indian Cultures of Northeast Mississippi. *Journal of Mississippi History* 3(3):155–227.
- 1974 *Prehistory of North America.* 2nd ed. McGraw-Hill, New York.

Johnson, Alfred E.
- 1979 Kansas City Hopewell. In *Hopewell Archaeology,* edited by D. S. Brose and N. Greber, pp. 86–93. Kent State University Press, Kent, Ohio.

Johnson, William C.
- 1982 Ceramics. In *The Prehistory of the Paintsville Reservoir, Johnson and Morgan Counties, Kentucky,* compiled by J. M. Adovasio, pp. 752–845. Ethnology Monographs Number 6. Department of Anthropology, University of Pittsburgh, Pittsburgh, Pennsylvania.

Justice, Noel D.
- 1987 *Stone Age Spear and Arrow Points of the Midcontinental and Eastern United States.* Indiana University Press, Bloomington.

Keel, Bennie C.
- 1976 *Cherokee Archaeology.* University of Tennessee Press, Knoxville.

Keener, Craig S., and Stephen M. Biehl
- 1999 Examination and Distribution of Woodland Period Sites along the Twin Creek Drainage in Southwestern Ohio. *North American Archaeologist* 20:319–346.

Keener, Craig S., and Albert M. Pecora III
- 2003 Phase II Archaeological Assessment of Site 33Ms29 Located at the Proposed Ohio River Boat Access in Racine, Sutton Township, Meigs County, Ohio. Report 235. Professional Archaeological Services Team. Report on file, Ohio Historic Preservation Office, Columbus.

Kehoe, Alice B.
- 1990 The Monumental Midwestern Taxonomic Method. In *The Woodland Tradition in the Western Great Lakes: Papers Presented to Elden Johnson,* edited by G. E. Gibbon, pp. 31–36. Publications in Anthropology Number 4. University of Minnesota, Minneapolis.

1998   *The Land of Prehistory.* Routledge, New York.

Kellar, James H., A. R. Kelly, and Edward V. McMichael
1962   The Mandeville Site in Southwest Georgia. *American Antiquity* 27(3): 336–355.

Kerr, Jonathan P.
1995   Prehistoric Ceramic Analysis. In *Upper Cumberland Archaic and Woodland Period Archeology at the Main Site (15Bl35), Bell County, Kentucky, Volume II,* by S. D. Creasman, pp. C1–C13. Contract Publication Series 94–56. Cultural Resource Analysts, Inc., Lexington, Kentucky.

Knapp, A. Bernard, and Wendy Ashmore
1999   Archaeological Landscapes: Constructed, Conceptualized, Ideational. In *Archaeologies of Landscape,* edited by W. Ashmore and A. B. Knapp, pp. 1–30. Blackwell Publishers, Oxford, U.K.

Knight, Vernon J., Jr.
1990   *Excavation of the Truncated Mound at the Walling Site.* Report of Investigations 56. Alabama State Museum of Natural History, Division of Archaeology, Tuscaloosa.

Konigsberg, Lyle W.
1988   Demography and Mortuary Practice at Seip Mound One. *Midcontinental Journal of Archaeology* 10(1):123–148.

Krieger, Alex D.
1944   The Typological Concept. *American Antiquity* 9(3):271–288.
1953   Basic Stages of Cultural Evolution. In *An Appraisal of Anthropology Today,* edited by S. Tax, pp. 247–250. University of Chicago Press, Chicago.
1960   Archaeological Typology in Theory and Practice. In *Men and Cultures: Selected Papers from the Proceedings of the Fifth International Congress of Anthropological and Ethnological Sciences,* edited by A.D. Wallace, pp. 141–151. University of Pennsylvania Press, Philadelphia.

Kurjack, Edward B.
1975   Archaeological Investigations in the Walter F. George Basin. In *Archaeological Salvage in the Walter F. George Basin of the Chattahoochee River in Alabama,* by D. L. DeJarnette, pp. 87–198. University of Alabama Press, Tuscaloosa.

Lazzazera, Adrienne
1997   Preliminary Report of 1995 Winter and 1996 Summer Investigations at the Fort Ancient State Memorial: Hopewell Habitation on the North Fort Interior. Report on file at the Ohio Historical Society, Columbus, Ohio.

Leader, Jonathan M.
1988   Technological Continuities and Specialization in Prehistoric Metalwork in the Eastern United States. Ph.D. Dissertation, Department of Anthropology, University of Florida.

Lepper, Bradley T.
1996   The Newark Earthworks and the Geometric Enclosures of the Scioto

Valley: Connections and Conjectures. In *A View from the Core,* edited by P. J. Pacheco, pp. 224–241. Ohio Archaeological Council, Columbus.

1998 The Archaeology of the Newark Earthworks. In *Ancient Earthen Enclosures of the Eastern Woodlands,* edited by R. C. Mainfort Jr. and L. P. Sullivan, pp. 114–134. University Press of Florida, Gainesville.

Lepper, Bradley T., and Richard W. Yerkes

1997 Hopewellian Occupation at the Northern Periphery of the Newark Earthworks: The Newark Expressway Sites Revisited. In *Ohio Hopewell Community Organization,* edited by W. S. Dancey and P. J. Pacheco, pp. 175–205. Kent State University Press, Kent, Ohio.

Lewis, Gilbert L.

1979 *Day of Shining Red.* Cambridge University Press, Cambridge.

Lewis, R. Barry

1986a Early Woodland Adaptations to the Illinois Prairie. In *Early Woodland Archeology,* edited by K. B. Farnsworth and T. E. Emerson, pp. 171–178. Kampsville Seminars in Archeology No. 2, Center for American Archeology, CAA Press, Kampsville, Illinois.

1986b Why are Early Woodland Base Camps So Rare? In *Early Woodland Archeology,* edited by K. B. Farnsworth and T. E. Emerson, pp. 596–597. Kampsville Seminars in Archeology No. 2, Center for American Archeology, CAA Press, Kampsville, Illinois.

Linton, Ralph

1955 *The Tree of Culture.* Knopf, New York.

Lyman, R. Lee, and Michael J. O'Brien

2003 *W. C. McKern and the Midwestern Taxonomic Method.* University of Alabama Press, Tuscaloosa.

Lyman, R. Lee., Michael J. O'Brien, and Robert C. Dunnell (editors)

1997 *Americanist Culture History: Fundamentals of Time, Space, and Form.* Plenum Press, New York.

Lynott, Mark J.

2004 Earthwork Construction and the Organization of Hopewell Society. Paper presented at the 69th Annual Meeting of the Society for American Archaeology, Montreal, Canada.

Mainfort, Robert C., Jr.

1986 *Pinson Mounds: A Middle Woodland Ceremonial Center.* Research Series Number 7. Tennessee Department of Conservation, Division of Archaeology, Nashville.

1988 Middle Woodland Ceremonialism at Pinson Mounds, Tennessee. *American Antiquity* 53(1):158–173.

1989 Adena Chiefdoms? Evidence from the Wright Mound. *Midcontinental Journal of Archaeology* 14(2):164–178.

1996 Pinson Mounds and the Middle Woodland Period in the Midsouth and Lower Mississippi Valley. In *A View from the Core,* edited by P. J. Pacheco, pp. 370–391. Ohio Archaeological Council, Columbus.

2003a Late Period Ceramic Rim Attribute Variation in the Central Mississippi Valley. *Southeastern Archaeology* 22(1):33–46.
2003b An Ordination Approach to Assessing Late Period Phases in the Central Mississippi Valley. *Southeastern Archaeology* 22(2):176–184.

Mainfort, Robert C., Jr., and Lynne P. Sullivan
1998 Explaining Earthen Enclosures. In *Ancient Earthen Enclosures of the Eastern Woodlands,* edited by R. C. Mainfort, Jr. and L. P. Sullivan, pp. 1–16. University Press of Florida.

Marquardt, William H.
1992 Dialectical Archaeology. *Archaeological Method and Theory,* Volume 4, edited by M. B. Schiffer, pp. 101–140. Academic Press, New York.

Marquardt, William H., and Carole L. Crumley
1987 Theoretical Issues in the Analysis of Spatial Patterning. In *Regional Dynamics in Historical Perspective,* edited by C. L. Crumley and W. H. Marquardt, pp. 1–18. Academic Press, New York.

Martin, Alexander C., and William D. Barkley
2000 *Seed Identification Manual.* Blackburn Press, Caldwell, New Jersey.

Maslowski, Robert F.
1985 Woodland Settlement Patterns in the Mid and Upper Ohio Valley. *West Virginia Archeologist* 37:23–34.

Maslowski, Robert F., Charles M. Niquette, and Derek M. Wingfield
1995 The Kentucky, Ohio, and West Virginia Radiocarbon Data Base. *West Virginia Archaeologist* 47(1–2):1–75.

Maslowski, Robert F., and Mark F. Seeman
1992 Woodland Archaeology in the Mid-Ohio Valley: Setting Parameters for Ohio Main Stem/Tributary Comparisons. In *Cultural Variability in Context,* edited by M. F. Seeman, pp. 10–14. Midcontinental Journal of Archaeology Special Paper Number 7. Kent State University Press, Kent, Ohio.

McCollough, Mark
1972 *National Register of Historic Places Nomination Form for Highbank Park Works (and/or Historic: Orange Township Works).* National Park Service, Washington, D.C.

McConaughy, Mark A.
1990 Early Woodland Mortuary Practices in Western Pennsylvania. *West Virginia Archaeologist* 42(2):1–10

McDowell, Robert C.
1978 *Geologic Map of the Levee Quadrangle, East-Central Kentucky.* Kentucky Geological Survey, Lexington.

McElrath, Dale L., Thomas E. Emerson, and Andrew C. Fortier
2000 Social Evolution or Social Response? A Fresh Look at the "Good Gray Cultures" after Four Decades of Midwest Research. In *Late Woodland Societies,* edited by T. E. Emerson, D. L. McElrath, and A. C. Fortier, pp. 3–36. University of Nebraska Press, Lincoln.

McGrain, Preston, and James C. Currens
- 1978 *Topography of Kentucky.* Special Publication Number 25. University of Kentucky, Kentucky Geological Survey, Lexington.

McKern, Will C.
- 1931 A Wisconsin Variant of the Hopewell Culture. *Bulletin of the Public Museum of the City of Milwaukee* 10(2):185–328.
- 1934 Certain Culture Classification Problems in Middle Western Archaeology. Paper presented at the 11th Annual Meeting of the American Anthropological Association, Central Section, Indianapolis.
- 1936 Indianapolis Conference. *American Antiquity* 1(4):329–330.
- 1937 A Hypothesis for the Asiatic Origins of the Woodland Culture Pattern. *American Antiquity* 3(2):138.
- 1939 The Midwestern Taxonomic Method as an Aid to Archaeological Culture Study. *American Antiquity* 4(4):301–313.
- 1943 Regarding Midwestern Archaeological Taxonomy. *American Anthropologist* 45: 313–315.
- 1945 *Preliminary Report on the Upper Mississippi Phase in Wisconsin.* Bulletin of the Public Museum of the City of Milwaukee, Volume 16, Number 3. Milwaukee.

McMichael, Edward V.
- 1962 Preliminary Report on Mount Carbon Village Excavations 46-Fa-7. *West Virginia Archeologist* 14:46–51.
- 1965 *Archaeological Survey of Nicholas County, W. Va.* Archaeological Series Number 1. West Virginia Geological and Economic Survey, Morgantown.
- 1968 *Introduction to West Virginia Archeology.* 2nd ed. West Virginia Geological and Economic Survey, Morgantown.
- 1971 Adena-East: An Appraisal of the More Easterly Extensions of the Spread of the Adena Phenomenon. In *Adena: The Seeking of an Identity,* edited by B. K. Swartz Jr., pp. 87–99. Ball State University Press, Muncie, Indiana.

McMichael, Edward V., and Oscar L. Mairs
- 1963 Salvage Excavations of the Leslie Mound (46-Pu-3) Putnam County, West Virginia. *West Virginia Archeologist* 15:23–40.
- 1965 Archaeological Salvage and Analysis of Two Kanawha Valley Mounds. *West Virginia Archeologist* 18:30–43.
- 1969 *Excavation of the Murad Mound, Kanawha County, West Virginia and an Analysis of Kanawha Valley Mounds.* Report of Investigations, Number 1. West Virginia Geological and Economic Survey, Morgantown.

Metz, Charles L.
- 1878 The Prehistoric Monuments of the Little Miami Valley. *Journal of the Cincinnati Society of Natural History* 1(3):119–128.
- 1881 The Prehistoric Monuments of Anderson Township, Hamilton County, Ohio. *Journal of the Cincinnati Society of Natural History* 4(4):293–305.

Mills, Lisa
- 2003 Mitochondrial DNA Analysis of the Ohio Hopewell of the Hopewell

Mound Group. Unpublished Ph.D. Dissertation, Department of Anthropology, Ohio State University.

Mills, William C.
- 1901–1902 Excavations of the Adena Mound. *Ohio Archaeological and Historical Quarterly* 10:451–479. [Reprinted 1907 in *Certain Mounds and Village Sites* 1(1).]
- 1906 Explorations of the Baum Prehistoric Village Site. *Ohio Archaeological and Historical Quarterly* 15:5–96.
- 1907 Explorations of the Edwin Harness Mound. *Ohio Archaeological and Historical Quarterly* 16:113–193.
- 1909 Explorations of the Seip Mound. *Ohio Archaeological and Historical Quarterly* 18:269–321.
- 1916 Exploration of the Tremper Mound. *Ohio Archaeological and Historical Quarterly* 25:262–398.
- 1917 Exploration of the Westenhaver Mound. *Ohio Archaeological and Historical Quarterly* 26:226–266.
- 1922 Exploration of the Mound City Group. *Ohio Archaeological and Historical Quarterly* 31:423–584.

Milner, George R., and Richard W. Jefferies
- 1987 A Reevaluation of the WPA Excavation of the Robbins Mound in Boone County, Kentucky. In *Current Archaeological Research in Kentucky: Volume 1*, edited by D. Pollack, pp. 33–42. Kentucky Heritage Council, Frankfort.

Miroff, Laurie E., and Timothy Knapp
- 2004 *Tipping the Scale: Levels of Analysis in Iroquoian Archaeology.* University of Oklahoma Press, Norman.

Moerman, Daniel E.
- 1998 *Native American Ethnobotany.* Timber Press, Portland, Oregon.

Moore, Clarence B.
- 1894 Certain Sand Mounds on the St. Johns River, Florida. *Journal of the Academy of Natural Sciences of Philadelphia* 10:130–246.
- 1896 Certain River Mounds of Duvall County, Florida. *Journal of the Academy of Natural Sciences of Philadelphia* 10:449–516.
- 1902 Certain Aboriginal Mounds of the Northwest Florida Coast. *Journal of the Academy of Natural Sciences of Philadelphia* 12(2):125–335.

Moore, David G.
- 1982 Test Excavations at Indian Fort Mountain, Berea, Kentucky. Paper presented at the 39th annual meeting of the Southeastern Archaeological Conference, Memphis.

Moorehead, Warren K.
- 1890 *Fort Ancient: The Great Prehistoric Earthwork of Warren County, Ohio.* Robert Clarke, Cincinnati.
- 1892 *Primitive Man in Ohio.* Knickerbocker Press, G. P. Putnam's Sons, New York.

1897– The Hopewell Group. *Antiquarian* 1:114–120, 153–158, 178–184, 208–
1898 214, 236–244, 254–264, 291–295, 312–316.
1898– Report of Field Work in Various Portions of Ohio. *Ohio State Archaeologi-*
1899 *cal and Historical Quarterly* 7:110–203.
1909 A Study of Primitive Culture in Ohio. Putnam Anniversary Volume. Putnam, New York.
1922 The Hopewell Mound Group of Ohio. *Field Museum of Natural History Anthropological Series* 6:73–184.

Morgan, Richard G.
1946 Review of "The Adena People," by W. S. Webb and C. E. Snow. *American Antiquity* 12(1):54–58.
1952 Outline of Cultures in the Ohio Region. In *Archeology of Eastern United States*, edited by J. B. Griffin, pp. 83–98. University of Chicago Press, Chicago.

Morton, James F.
1977 Excavations of Mound B, a Hopewellian Site in the Muskingum Valley. *Ohio Archaeologist* 27(1):22–24.
1984a The Longacre Sites: Cole/Baldwin-like and Philo Phase Interaction in the Central Muskingum Valley. *Ohio Archaeologist* 34(4):7–11.
1984b Toward a Late Woodland Taxonomy for the Central Muskingum Valley. *Ohio Archaeologist* 34(1):41–47.
1989 Middle and Late Woodland Components at the Philo II Site, Muskingum County, Ohio. *Ohio Archaeologist* 39(2): 61–69.

Muller, Jon
1986 *Archaeology of the Lower Ohio River Valley*. Academic Press, Orlando, Florida.

Murphy, James L.
1975 *An Archaeological History of the Hocking Valley*. Ohio University Press, Athens.
1989 *An Archaeological History of the Hocking Valley*. Revised ed. Ohio University Press, Athens.

Nassaney, Michael S., and Kenneth E. Sassaman (editors)
1995 *Native American Interactions*. University of Tennessee Press, Knoxville.

Niquette, Charles M., and Myra A. Hughes (editors)
1991 *Late Woodland Archeology at the Parkline Site (46PU99) Putnam County, West Virginia*. Contract Publication Series 90–93. Cultural Resource Analysts, Inc., Lexington, Kentucky.

Niquette, Charles M., and Jonathan P. Kerr
1993 Late Woodland Archeology at the Parkline Site, Putnam County, West Virginia. *West Virginia Archeologist* 45 (1–2):43–59.

Norris, Rae
1985 Excavation of the Toephner Mound. *Archaeology of Eastern North America* 13:128–137.

Norris, Rae, and Shaune M. Skinner
   1985   Excavation of the Connett Mound 3, The Wolf Plains National Register District, The Plains, Ohio. *Ohio Archaeologist* 35(1):21–26.
O'Brien, Michael J., and T. D. Holland
   1990   Variation, Selection, and the Archaeological Record. In *Archaeological Method and Theory*, Volume 2, edited by M. B. Schiffer, pp. 31–80. University of Arizona Press, Tucson.
O'Brien, Michael J., and R. Lee Lyman (editors)
   1998   *James A. Ford and the Growth of Americanist Archaeology*. University of Missouri Press, Columbia
   1999   *Measuring the Flow of Time*. University of Alabama Press, Tuscaloosa.
   2001   *Setting the Agenda for American Archaeology*. University of Alabama Press, Tuscaloosa.
O'Brien, Michael J., R. Lee Lyman, and J. W. Cogswell
   2002   Culture-Historical Units and the Woodland Southeast: A Case Study from Southeastern Missouri. In *The Woodland Southeast*, edited by D. G. Anderson and R. C. Mainfort Jr., pp. 421–443. University of Alabama Press, Tuscaloosa.
O'Malley, Nancy
   1988   Adena Mound Ceramics in Retrospective. In *New Deal Era Archaeology and Current Research in Kentucky*, edited by D. Pollack and M. L. Powell, pp. 46–62. Kentucky Heritage Council, Frankfort.
O'Malley, Nancy, Teresa W. Tune, and Melinda S. Blustain
   1983   Technological Examination of Fayette Thick Ceramics: A Petrographic Analysis and Review. *Southeastern Archaeology* 2(2):145–154.
Otto, Martha Potter
   1979   Hopewell Antecedents in the Adena Heartland. In *Hopewell Archaeology*, edited by D. S. Brose and N. Greber, pp. 9–14. Kent State University Press, Kent, Ohio.
   1983   Archaeological Dig Links Late Woodland Indians with Hopewells. *Echoes* 22(1):2. Ohio Historical Society, Columbus.
Pacheco, Paul J.
   1996   Ohio Hopewell Regional Settlement Patterns. In *A View from the Core*, edited by P. J. Pacheco, pp. 16–35. Ohio Archaeological Council, Columbus.
   1997   Ohio Middle Woodland Intracommunity Settlement Variability: A Case Study from the Licking Valley. In *Ohio Hopewell Community Organization*, edited by W. S. Dancey and P. J. Pacheco, pp. 41–84. Kent State University Press, Kent, Ohio.
Pacheco, Paul J. (editor)
   1996   *A View from the Core*. Ohio Archaeological Council, Columbus.
Pecora, Albert M., and Jarrod Burks
   2004   The Bremen Site: A Terminal Late Archaic Period Upland Occupation in Fairfield County, Ohio. In *The Emergence of the Moundbuilders: The Ar-*

chaeology of Tribal Societies in Southeastern Ohio, edited by E. M. Abrams and A. Freter, pp. 39–58. Ohio University Press, Athens.

Pederson, Jennifer, Jarrod Burks, and William Dancey
    2002   Hopewell Mound Group: Data Collection in 2001. *Ohio Archaeological Council Newsletter* 14(1):17–19.

Phagan, C. J.
    1977   Intensive Archaeological Survey of the S.R. 315 Wastewater Treatment Facility Location Known as the DECCO-1 Site (33DL28). Progress Report to the Board of County Commissioners, Delaware County, Ohio.

Phillips, Philip
    1955   American Archaeology and General Anthropological Theory. *Southwestern Journal of Anthropology* 11:246–250.
    1970   *Archaeological Survey in the Lower Yazoo Basin, Mississippi: 1949–1955*. Papers of the Peabody Museum of American Archaeology and Ethnology, Harvard University, Volume 60, Parts 1 and 2. Cambridge.

Phillips, Philip, James A. Ford, and James B. Griffin
    1951   *Archaeological Survey in the Lower Mississippi Alluvial Valley, 1940–1947*. Papers of the Peabody Museum of American Archaeology and Ethnology, Harvard University, Volume 25. Cambridge.

Phillips, Philip, and Gordon R. Willey
    1953   Method and Theory in American Archaeology: An Operational Basis for Culture-Historical Integration. *American Anthropologist* 55:615–633.

Pickard, William H.
    1996   1990 Excavations at Capitolium Mound (33WN13), Marietta, Washington County, Ohio: A Working Evaluation. In *A View from the Core*, edited by P. J. Pacheco, pp. 274–285. Ohio Archaeological Council, Columbus.

Pickard, William H., and Laura Pahdopony
    1995   Paradise Regained and Lost Again; The Anderson Earthwork, Ross County, Ohio (33Ro551). *Hopewell Archaeology: The Newsletter of Hopewell Archaeology in the Ohio River Valley* 1(2):3–6.

Piotrowski, Leonard R.
    1985   Flourine and Nitrogen Skeletal Dating: An Example from Two Ohio Adena Burial Mounds. Ph.D. dissertation, Department of Anthropology, Ohio State University, Columbus.

Plog, Fred T.
    1974   *The Study of Prehistoric Change*. Academic Press, New York.

Pollack, David, and A. Gwynn Henderson
    2000   Late Woodland Cultures in Kentucky. In *Late Woodland Societies*, edited by T. E. Emerson, D. L. McElrath, and A. C. Fortier, pp. 613–641. University of Nebraska Press, Lincoln.

Potter, Martha
    1966   Cole Ceramics: A Study of Late Woodland Pottery. Anthropology. M.A. thesis, Department of Anthropology, Ohio State University, Columbus.
    1968   *Ohio's Prehistoric Peoples*. Ohio Historical Society, Columbus.

Prufer, Olaf H.
- 1964a The Hopewell Complex of Ohio. In *Hopewellian Studies,* edited by J. R. Caldwell and R. L. Hall, pp. 35–83. Scientific Papers 12(2). Illinois State Museum, Springfield.
- 1964b The Hopewell Cult. *Scientific American* 211:90–102.
- 1965 *The McGraw Site.* Cleveland Museum of Natural History Scientific Publications, Volume 4. Cleveland Museum of Natural History, Cleveland.
- 1967 Chesser Cave: A Late Woodland Phase in Southeastern Ohio. In *Studies in Ohio Archaeology,* edited by O. H. Prufer and D. H. McKenzie, pp. 1–62. Kent State University Press, Kent, Ohio.
- 1968 *Ohio Hopewell Ceramics.* Anthropological Papers 33. University of Michigan, Museum of Anthropology, Ann Arbor.
- 1975 The Scioto Valley Archaeological Survey. In *Studies in Ohio Archaeology,* revised ed., edited by O. H. Prufer and D. H. McKenzie, pp. 267–328. Kent State University Press, Kent, Ohio.
- 1997 Fort Hill 1964: New Data and Reflections on Hopewell Hilltop Enclosures in Southern Ohio. In *Ohio Hopewell Community Organization,* edited by W. S. Dancey and P. J. Pacheco, pp. 311–327. Kent State University Press, Kent, Ohio.

Prufer, Olaf H., and Douglas H. McKenzie
- 1965 Ceramics. In *The McGraw Site,* by Olaf H. Prufer, pp. 16–57. Cleveland Museum of Natural History Scientific Publications, Volume 4. Cleveland Museum of Natural History, Cleveland.
- 1966 Peters Cave: Two Woodland Occupations in Ross County, Ohio. *Ohio Journal of Science* 66(3):233–253.

Prufer, Olaf H., and Orrin C. Shane III
- 1970 *Blain Village and the Fort Ancient Tradition in Ohio.* Kent State University Press, Kent, Ohio.

Putnam, Frederick W.
- 1882 Notes on Copper Objects from North and South America. *Peabody Museum of Archaeology and Ethnology, Fifteenth Annual Report* 3:83–148.
- 1884 Report of the Curator. *Seventeenth Annual Report of the Peabody Museum of Archaeology and Ethnology* 3:339–346.
- 1885 Explorations of the Harness Mounds in the Scioto Valley, Ohio. *18th and 19th Annual Reports of the Peabody Museum, 1884–1885* bound in Peabody Museum Reports 3:405–407.
- 1886 Explorations in Ohio: The Marriott Mound, No. 1 and its Contents. *18th and 19th Annual Reports of the Peabody Museum, 1884–1885,* bound in Peabody Museum Reports 3:449–466.

Rafferty, Sean M.
- 1995 Tubular Pipes as Evidence of Regional Belief System. Presented at the annual meeting of the Southeastern Archaeological Conference, Knoxville, Tennessee.
- 2001 They Pass Their Lives in Smoke, and at Death, Fall into the Fire: Smoking Pipes and Mortuary Ritual During the Early Woodland Period. Ph.D.

dissertation, Department of Anthropology, Binghamton University, Binghamton, New York.

2004 They Pass Their Lives in Smoke, and at Death, Fall into the Fire: Smoking Pipes and Mortuary Ritual During the Early Woodland Period. In *Smoking and Culture: Recent Developments in the Archaeology of Smoking Pipes,* edited by S. M. Rafferty and R. B. Mann. University of Tennessee Press, Knoxville.

Rafinesque, Constantine S.

1824 *Ancient History, or Annals of Kentucky; with a Survey of the Ancient Monuments of North America, and a Tabular View of the Principal Languages and Primitive Nations of the Whole Earth.* Printed for the Author. Frankfort, Kentucky.

Railey, Jimmy A.

1984 *The Pyles Site (15Ms28), a Newtown Village in Mason County Kentucky.* Occasional Paper Number 1. William S. Webb Archaeological Society, Lexington, Kentucky.

1990 Woodland Period. In *The Archaeology of Kentucky: Past Accomplishments and Future Directions,* edited by D. Pollack, pp. 247–374. State Historic Preservation Comprehensive Plan Report Number 1. Kentucky Heritage Council, Frankfort.

1991 Woodland Settlement Trends and Symbolic Architecture in the Kentucky Bluegrass. In *The Human Landscape in Kentucky's Past,* edited by C. Stout and C. K. Hensley, pp. 56–77. Kentucky Heritage Council, Frankfort.

1996 Woodland Cultivators. In *Kentucky Archaeology,* edited by R. B. Lewis, pp. 79–126. The University Press of Kentucky, Lexington.

Ramenofsky, Ann F.

1998 The Illusion of Time. In *Unit Issues in Archaeology,* edited by A. F. Ramenofsky and A. Steffen, pp. 74–84. University of Utah Press, Salt Lake City.

Ramenofsky, Ann F., and Anastasia Steffen

1998 Units As Tools of Measurement. In *Unit Issues in Archaeology,* edited by A. F. Ramenofsky and A. Steffen, pp. 3–17. University of Utah Press, Salt Lake City.

Rappaport, Roy A.

1979 *Ecology, Meaning, and Religion.* North Atlantic Books, Richmond, Virginia.

Ray, Jack H.

2000 Chert Resource Availability, Procurement, and Use in the Upper Rolling Fork River Valley, Marion County, Kentucky. In *Current Archaeological Research in Kentucky: Volume Six,* edited by D. Pollack and K. J. Gremillion, pp. 94–116. Kentucky Heritage Council, Frankfort.

Redfield, Robert

1955 The Social Organization of Tradition. *Far Eastern Quarterly* 15(1):13–21.

Renfrew, Colin, and John F. Cherry (editors)

1986 *Peer Polity Interaction and Socio-Political Change.* Cambridge University Press, Cambridge.

Richmond, Michael D.
- 2000   *A National Register Evaluation of Sites 15Mm137, 15Mm139 and 15Mm140 and Deep Testing Along Sycamore Creek in Montgomery County, Kentucky.* Contract Publication Series 01–106. Cultural Resource Analysts, Inc., Lexington, Kentucky.
- 2002   A Geochemical Analysis of Select Copper Artifacts from the Midcontinental United States. M.A. thesis, Department of Anthropology, Kent State University, Kent, Ohio.

Richmond, Michael D., and Jonathan P. Kerr
- 2002   Archaeological Investigations at 15Mm137: Evidence for Middle Woodland Ritualism in the Central Bluegrass? Presented at the 48th Annual Midwest Archaeological Conference, Columbus, Ohio.

Riggs, Rodney
- 1998   Ceramics, Chronology and Cultural Change in the Lower Little Miami River Valley, Southwestern Ohio, Circa 100 B.C. to Circa A.D. 1650. Unpublished Ph.D. dissertation, Department of Anthropology, University of Wisconsin, Madison.

Riordan, Robert V.
- 1995   A Construction Sequence for a Middle Woodland Hilltop Enclosure. *Midcontinental Journal of Archaeology* 20(1):62–104.
- 1996   The Enclosed Hilltops of Southern Ohio. In *A View from the Core,* edited by P. J. Pacheco, pp. 242–257. Ohio Archaeological Council, Columbus.

Ritchie, William A.
- 1937   Culture Influence from Ohio in New York Archaeology. *American Antiquity* 2(3):187.
- 1965   *The Archaeology of New York State.* Natural History Press, Garden City, New York.

Ritchie, William A., and Don W. Dragoo
- 1960   *The Eastern Dispersal of Adena.* New York State Museum and Science Service Bulletin Number 379. University of the State of New York, Albany.

Robinson, Gilbert de B.
- 1946   *The Foundations of Geometry.* University of Toronto Press, Toronto.

Rossen, Jack
- 1991   Kentucky Landscapes: The Role of Environmental Reconstruction in Settlement Pattern Studies. In *The Human Landscape in Kentucky's Past: Site Structure and Settlement Patterns,* edited by C. Stout and C. K. Hensley, pp. 1–8. Kentucky Heritage Council, Frankfort.
- 1997   Botanical Remains from Site 46Bx73. In *Phase III Archaeological Data Recovery for the Mitigation of the OSB Two Site (46BX73) in Braxton County, West Virginia,* by S. A. Stathakis, J. B. Harrison, and J. Blake, pp. 4.1–4.6. Big Blue Archaeological Research, Inc., Morgantown, West Virginia.

Rouse, Irving
- 1960   The Classification of Artifacts in Archaeology. *American Antiquity* 25(3):313–323.

Ruby, Bret J.
  1997 Research at the Hopeton Earthworks. *Hopewell Archeology: The Newsletter of Hopewell Archaeology in the Ohio River Valley* 2(2):2–5.
Ruhl, Katharine C.
  1992 Copper Earspools from Ohio Hopewell Sites. *Midcontinental Journal of Archaeology* 17(1): 46–79.
  1996 Copper Earspools in the Hopewell Interaction Sphere: The Temporal and Social Implications. M.A. thesis, Department of Anthropology, Kent State University, Kent, Ohio.
Ruhl, Katharine C., and Mark F. Seeman
  1998 The Temporal and Social Implications of Ohio Hopewell Copper Earspool Design. *American Antiquity* 63: 651–662.
Sahlins, Marshall D.
  1968 *Tribesmen.* Prentice-Hall, Englewood Cliffs, New Jersey.
Sanger, David
  2002 Archaeological Taxonomy: Beyond Typology to Behavior. *Review of Archaeology* 23:5–11.
Santayana, George
  1968 [1905] *The Life of Reason.* Prometheus Books, New York.
Saunders, J. W., R. D. Mandel, R. T. Saucier, E. T. Allen, C. T. Hallmark, J. K. Johnson, E. H. Jackson, C. M. Allen, G. L. Stringer, D. S. Frink, J. K. Feathers, S. Williams, K. J. Gremillion, M. F. Vidrine, and R. Jones
  1997 A Mound Complex in Louisiana at 5400–5000 Years before the Present. *Science* 277(5333):1796.
Schiffer, Michael B.
  1976 *Behavioral Archaeology.* Academic Press, New York.
Schlarb, Eric, and Leon Lane
  1999 An Early Archaic Hunting Camp in Garrard County, Kentucky. Paper presented at the Sixteenth Annual Kentucky Heritage Council Archaeological Conference, Lexington.
Schweikart, John F.
  2002 Coming Together at the Crossroads: Aggregated Settlement at the Swinehart Village, Fairfield County, Ohio. Paper presented at the Midwest Archaeological Conference, Columbus, Ohio.
Seeman, Mark F.
  1977 The Hopewell Interaction Sphere: The Evidence for Inter-Regional Trade and Structural Complexity. Ph.D. dissertation, Department of Anthropology, Indiana University, Bloomington.
  1979 *The Hopewell Interaction Sphere.* Prehistory Research Series 5(2). Indiana Historical Society, Indianapolis.
  1980 A Taxonomic Review of Southern Ohio Late Woodland. Paper presented at the Midwest Archaeological Conference, Chicago.
  1985 *The Locust Site (33MU160): The 1983 Test Excavation of a Multicomponent Workshop in East Central Ohio.* Kent State University Press, Kent, Ohio.

1986 Adena "Houses" and Their Implications for Early Woodland Settlement Models in the Ohio Valley. In *Early Woodland Archeology*, edited K. B. Farnsworth and T. E. Emerson, pp. 564–580. Kampsville Seminars in Archeology Number 2. Center for American Archeology, CAA Press, Kampsville, Illinois.

1992a The Bow and Arrow, the Intrusive Mound Complex, and a Late Woodland Jack's Reef Horizon in the Mid-Ohio Valley. In *Cultural Variability in Context*, edited by M. F. Seeman, pp. 41–51. Midcontinental Journal of Archaeology Special Paper Number 7. Kent State University Press, Kent, Ohio.

1992b Woodland Traditions in the Midcontinent: A Comparison of Three Regional Sequences. In *Long Term Subsistence Change in Prehistoric North America*, edited by D. R. Cross, R. A. Hawkins, and B. L. Isaac, pp. 3–46. Research in Economic Anthropology, Supplement 6. JAI Press, Greenwich, Connecticut.

1995 When Words Are Not Enough: Hopewell Interregionalism and the Use of Material Symbols at the GE Mound. In *Native American Interactions*, edited by M. S. Nassaney and K. E. Sassaman, pp. 122–143. University of Tennessee Press, Knoxville.

1996 The Ohio Hopewell Core and Its Many Margins: Deconstructing Upland and Hinterland Relations. In *A View from the Core*, edited by P. J. Pacheco, pp. 304–315. Ohio Archaeological Council, Columbus.

Seeman, Mark F., and William S. Dancey
2000 The Late Woodland Period in Southern Ohio: Basic Issues and Prospects. In *Late Woodland Societies*, edited by T. E. Emerson, D. L. McElrath, and A. C. Fortier, pp. 583–611. University of Nebraska Press, Lincoln.

Setzler, Frank M.
1933a Hopewell Type Pottery From Louisiana. *Journal of the Washington Academy of Sciences* 23(3):149–153.

1933b Pottery of the Hopewell Type from Louisiana. *United States National Museum Proceedings* 82(2963), Article 22:1–21. United States National Museum, Washington, D.C.

1935 A Prehistoric Cave Culture in Southwestern Texas. *American Anthropologist* 37:104–110.

1960 Welcome Mound and the Effigy Pipes of the Adena People. *Proceedings of the United States National Museum* 112 (3441):451–458. United States National Museum, Washington, D.C.

Shane, Orrin C.
1975 The Mixter Site: A Multicomponent Hunting Station in Erie County, Ohio. In *Studies in Ohio Archaeology*, revised ed., edited by O. H. Prufer and D. H. McKenzie, pp. 121–186. Kent State University Press, Kent, Ohio.

Shane, Orrin C., and James L. Murphy
1975 A Survey of the Hocking Valley, Ohio. In *Studies in Ohio Archaeology*, re-

vised ed., edited by O. H. Prufer and D. H. McKenzie, pp. 329–356. Kent State University Press, Kent, Ohio.

Sheets, Charlynn J., and Mark D. Kozar
- 2000 *Ground-Water Quality in the Appalachian Plateaus, Kanawha River Basin, West Virginia*. Water Resources Investigations Report 99–4269. U.S. Department of the Interior, U.S. Geological Survey. Charleston, West Virginia.

Sherratt, Andrew
- 1982 What Can Archaeologists Learn from Annalistes? In *Archaeology, Annales, and Ethnohistory*, edited by A. B. Knapp, pp. 135–142. Cambridge University Press, New York.

Shetrone, Henry C.
- 1920 The Culture Problem in Ohio Archaeology. *American Anthropologist* 22(2):142–172.
- 1923 The Spetnagel Cache of Flint Spear Points. *Ohio Archaeological and Historical Quarterly* 32:638–640.
- 1926 Exploration of the Hopewell Group of Prehistoric Earthworks. *Ohio Archaeological and Historical Quarterly* 35:1–277.
- 1930a *The Mound Builders*. D. Appleton and Company, New York.
- 1937 The Newark Earthworks. *Museum Echoes* 10:1.

Shetrone, Henry C., and Emerson F. Greenman
- 1931 Explorations of the Seip Group of Prehistoric Earthworks. *Ohio Archaeological and Historical Society Quarterly* 40:343–509.

Shott, Michael J.
- 1989 Childers, Woods, and Late Woodland Chronology in the Upper Ohio Valley. *West Virginia Archaeologist* 41(2): 27–39.

Shott, Michael J. (editor)
- 1990 *Childers and Woods: Two Late Woodland Sites in the Upper Ohio Valley, Mason County, West Virginia*. Archaeological Report 200. Program for Cultural Resource Assessment, University of Kentucky, Lexington.

Shott, Michael J. and Richard W. Jefferies
- 1992 Late Woodland Economy and Settlement in the Mid-Ohio Valley: Recent Results from the Childers/Woods Project. In *Cultural Variability in Context*, edited by M. F. Seeman, pp. 52–64. Midcontinental Journal of Archaeology Special Paper No. 7. Kent State University Press, Kent, Ohio.

Shott, Michael J., Richard W. Jefferies, Gerald Oetelaar, Nancy O'Malley, Mary Lucas Powell, and Dee Ann Wymer
- 1993 The Childers Site and Early Late Woodland Cultures of the Upper Ohio Valley. *West Virginia Archeologist* 45(1–2):1–30.

Sieg, Lauren E.
- 1999 Report on Radiocarbon Testing of the Charcoal Samples from the Gateway Embankment Wall at the Fort Ancient Site, Ohio. Submitted to the Ancient Technologies and Archaeology Materials Program, University of Illinois at Urbana-Champaign.

Sieg, Lauren E., and Robert P. Connolly
　1997　1995 Report of Investigations at the Fort Ancient State Memorial, Ohio (33WA2), Volume II: The Gateway 84 Embankment Wall. Submitted to the Ohio Historical Society, Columbus.
Sieg, Lauren E., and Priya Sankalia
　1997　The 1995 Ceramic Assemblage. In 1995 Report of Investigations at Fort Ancient State Memorial: Volume 4, Artifact Analysis and Project Summary, edited by L. E. Sieg, C. A. Yokell, and R. P. Connolly, pp. 65–92. Report submitted to the Ohio Historical Society, Columbus.
Sieg, Lauren E., and Ted S. Sunderhaus
　2004　The Fort Ancient Middle Woodland Ceramic Assemblage. In *The Fort Ancient Earthworks: Prehistoric Lifeways of the Hopewell Culture in Southwestern Ohio*, edited by R. P. Connolly and B. T. Lepper, pp. 147–166. Ohio Historical Society, Columbus.
Silverberg, Robert S.
　1968　*Mound Builders of Ancient America*. New York Graphic Society, Greenwich, Connecticut.
Skinner, Shaune M.
　1985　Preliminary Results of the 1983 Excavations at the Connett Mounds #3 and #4, the Wolf Plains National Register District Athens County, Ohio. *Archaeology of Eastern North America* 13:138–152.
Skinner, Shaune M., and Rae Norris
　1981　Archaeological Assessment of Six Sites in the Central Hocking River Valley for the Proposed Relocation of Route 33 through Athens and Hocking Counties, Ohio. Report submitted by Donald R. Bier, Ohio Historical Society, to the Ohio Department of Transportation, Bureau of External Contracts, Columbus.
　1984a　Archaeological Investigations in the Adena Park Subdivision Including Excavations of the Connett Mounds 3 and 4, The Wolf Plains National Historic District, The Plains, Ohio. Report submitted by Donald R. Bier, Ohio Historical Society to the Ohio Historic Preservation Office, Columbus.
　1984b　Excavation of the Connett Mound 4, The Wolf Plains National Register District, The Plains, Ohio. *Ohio Archaeologist* 34(4):225–26.
Smith, Betty A.
　1979　The Hopewell Connection in Southwest Georgia. In *Hopewell Archaeology*, edited by D. S. Brose and N. Greber, pp. 181–187. Kent State University Press, Kent, Ohio.
Smith, Bruce D.
　1992　*Rivers of Change*. Smithsonian Institution Press, Washington, D.C.
Solecki, Ralph
　1953　Exploration of an Adena Mound at Natrium, West Virginia. *Bureau of American Ethnology Bulletin* 151:313–395. Government Printing Office, Washington, D.C.

Spaulding, Albert C.
- 1952 The Origin of Adena Culture of the Ohio Valley. *Southwestern Journal of Archaeology* 8:260–268.
- 1955 Prehistoric Cultural Development in the Eastern United States. In *New Interpretations of Aboriginal American Culture History*, pp. 12–27. Anthropological Society of Washington, Washington, D.C.
- 1960 The Dimensions of Archaeology. In *Essays in the Science of Culture in Honor of Leslie A. White*, edited by G. E. Dole and R. L. Carniero, pp. 437–456. Cromwell, New York.
- 1977 On Growth and Form in Archaeology: Multivariate Analysis. *Journal of Anthropological Research* 33:1–15.
- 1983 Archaeological Theory: 1936. In *Lulu Linear Punctated*, edited by R. C. Dunnell and D. K. Grayson, pp. 19–25. Anthropological Papers Number 72. Museum of Anthropology, University of Michigan, Ann Arbor.
- 1985 Fifty Years of Theory. *American Antiquity* 50(2):301–308.

Spier, Leslie
- 1921 The Sun Dance of the Plains Indians: Its Development and Diffusion. *American Museum of Natural History, Anthropological Papers* 16:451–527.

Squier, George Ephraim, and Edwin H. Davis
- 1848 *Ancient Monuments of the Mississippi Valley*. Smithsonian Contributions to Knowledge 1. Smithsonian Institution, Washington, D.C.
- 1998 [1848] *Ancient Monuments of the Mississippi Valley*. Smithsonian Institution Press, Washington, D.C.

Stallings, Richard, and Nancy Ross-Stallings
- 1996 A Phase I Cultural Resource Survey of the Proposed US460 Realignment Corridor, Camargo to Jeffersonville, Montgomery County, Kentucky. Project 94-12. Cultural Horizons, Inc., Harrodsburg, Kentucky.

Stark, Miriam T., Mark D. Elson, and Jeffrey J. Clark
- 1998 Social Boundaries and Technical Choices in Tonto Basin Prehistory. In *The Archaeology of Social Boundaries*, edited by M. T. Stark, pp. 208–231. Smithsonian Institution Press, Washington, D.C.

Stathakis, Steven A., J. Brian Harrison, and Jerrell Blake
- 1997 Phase III Archaeological Data Recovery for the Mitigation of the OSB Two Site (46BX73) in Braxton County, West Virginia. Big Blue Archaeological Research, Inc., Morgantown, West Virginia.

Steward, Julian, and Frank M. Setzler
- 1938 Function and Configuration in Archaeology. *American Antiquity* 4(1):4–10.

Stoltman, James B.
- 1978 Temporal Models in Prehistory: An Example from Eastern North America. *Current Anthropology* 19:703–746.

Stoltman, James B., and George W. Christiansen
- 2000 The Late Woodland Stage in the Driftless Area of the Upper Mississippi Valley. In *Late Woodland Societies*, edited by T. E. Emerson, D. L. McElrath, and A. C. Fortier, pp. 497–524. University of Nebraska Press, Lincoln.

Stothers, David M.
  1999 Comments: Taxonomic Classification and Related Prerequisites of Scientific Research. In *Taming the Taxonomy,* edited by R. F. Williamson and C. M. Watts, pp. 283–288. Eastendbooks, Toronto.
Stothers, David M., G. Michael Pratt, and Orrin C. Shane III
  1979 The Western Basin Middle Woodland: Non-Hopewellians in a Hopewellian World. In *Hopewell Archaeology,* edited by D. S. Brose and N. Greber, pp. 47–58. Kent State University Press, Kent, Ohio.
Strong, William Duncan
  1935 *An Introduction to Nebraska Archaeology.* Smithsonian Miscellaneous Collections, Volume 93, Number 10. Smithsonian Institution, Washington D.C.
Struever, Stuart
  1964 The Hopewell Interaction Sphere in Riverine-Western Great Lakes Culture History. In *Hopewellian Studies,* edited by J. R. Caldwell and R. L. Hall, pp. 85–106. Illinois State Museum Scientific Papers Volume 12. Illinois State Museum, Springfield.
Struever, Stuart, and Gail L. Houart
  1972 An Analysis of the Hopewell Interaction Sphere. In *Social Exchange and Interaction,* edited by E. N. Wilmsen, pp. 47–79. University of Michigan, Ann Arbor.
Stuiver, Minze, and G. W. Pearson
  1993 High-precision Bidecadal Calibration of the Radiocarbon Time Scale, A.D. 1950–500 B.C. and 2500–6000 B.C. *Radiocarbon* 35:1–23.
Stuiver, Minze, Paula J. Reimer, Edouard Bard, J. Warren Beck, G. S. Burr, Konrad A. Hughen, Bernd Kromer, Gerry McCormac, Johannes van der Plicht, and Marco Spurk
  1998 INTCAL98 Radiocarbon Age Calibration, 24,000–0 cal B.P. *Radiocarbon* 40(3):1041–1083.
Sunderhaus, Ted S., Rodney Riggs, and Frank L. Cowan
  2001 The Smith Site: A Small Hopewell Site Overlooking the Stubbs Earthwork. *Ohio Archaeological Council Newsletter* 13(2):5–12.
Swartz, B. K., Jr. (editor)
  1971 *Adena: The Seeking of an Identity.* Ball State University Press, Muncie, Indiana.
Taylor, Walter W.
  1948 *A Study of Archaeology.* American Anthropological Association Memoir Number 69. Washington, D.C.
Terrell, John
  1990 Storytelling and Prehistory. *Archaeological Method and Theory* 2:1–29.
Thomas, Cyrus
  1894 *Report on the Mound Explorations of the Bureau of Ethnology.* Smithsonian Institution, Bureau of Ethnology, Annual Report 12:3–742.
Thomas, Julian
  1991 *Rethinking the Neolithic.* Cambridge University Press, Cambridge.

Thucydides
  1923   [431 B.C.E.] *History of the Peloponnesian War,* translated by Charles F. Smith. Harvard University Press Cambridge.
Tiffany, Joseph A.
  1986   The Early Woodland Period in Iowa. In *Early Woodland Archeology,* edited by K. B. Farnsworth and T. E. Emerson, pp. 159–170. Kampsville Seminars in Archeology No. 2, Center for American Archeology, CAA Press, Kampsville, Illinois.
Tomak, Curtis H., and Frank N. Burkett
  1996   Decorated Leather Objects from the Mount Vernon Site, a Hopewell Site in Posey County, Indiana. In *A View from the Core,* edited by P. J. Pacheco, pp. 354–369. Ohio Archaeological Council, Columbus.
Townsend, Thomas, and Delf Norona
  1962   Grave Creek Mound. *West Virginia Archaeologist* 14:10–18.
Trigger, Bruce G.
  1978   *Time and Traditions.* Columbia University Press, New York.
  1989   *A History of Archaeological Thought.* Cambridge University Press, Cambridge.
  1999   Master and Servant: A Conference Overview. In *Taming the Taxonomy,* edited by R. F. Williamson and C. M. Watts, pp. 303–322. Eastendbooks, Toronto.
Tune, Teresa W.
  1985   Fayette Thick: A New Vessel Form for an Old Ceramic Type. In *Woodland Period Research in Kentucky,* edited by D. Pollack, T. N. Sanders, and C. D. Hockensmith, pp. 43–61. Kentucky Heritage Council, Frankfort.
Turff, Gina M.
  1997   A Synthesis of Middle Woodland Panpipes in Eastern North America. M.A. thesis, Department of Anthropology, Trent University, Peterborough, Ontario.
van Dommelen, Peter
  1999   Exploring Everyday Places and Cosmologies. In *Archaeologies of Landscape,* edited by W. Ashmore and A. B. Knapp, pp. 277–285. Blackwell Publishers, Oxford, U.K.
Vickery, Kent D.
  1979   "Reluctant" or "Avant-Garde" Hopewell?: Suggestions of Middle Woodland Culture Change in East-central Indiana and South-central Ohio. In *Hopewell Archaeology,* edited by D. S. Brose and N. Greber, pp. 59–64. Kent State University Press, Kent, Ohio.
  1996   Flint Raw Material Use in Ohio Hopewell. In *A View from the Core,* edited by P. J. Pacheco, pp. 108–127. Ohio Archaeological Council, Columbus.
Voigt, Eric E., Mary Ann Owac, Carol S. Weed, E. G. Harris, Patrick M. Bennett, and A. Sassi
  1998   Archaeological Data Recovery at Coco Station (46KA294): A Stratified

Late Archaic, Terminal Archaic, and Early Woodland Site in Kanawha County, West Virginia. Report Prepared for Columbia Gas Transmission Corporation. Gray and Pape, Inc., Richmond, Virginia.

Waldron, John, and Elliot M. Abrams
    1999   Adena Burial Mounds and Inter-hamlet Visibility: A GIS Approach. *Midcontinental Journal of Archaeology* 24:1:97–111.

Wandsnider, LuAnn
    1998   Regional Scale Processes and Archaeological Landscape Units. In *Unit Issues in Archaeology*, edited by A. F. Ramenofsky and A. Steffen, pp. 87–102. University of Utah Press, Salt Lake City.
    2003   *Time in Archaeology: Time Perspectivism Twenty Years Later.* Electronic symposium for the Annual Meeting of the Society for American Archaeology, Milwaukee, April 9–13, 2003, www.anthro.Washington.edu/saa

Ward, Herbert Henry
    1980   Selected Studies of the Osteology of the Ufferman Site, 33DL12. Manuscript on file at the Ohio Historical Center, Columbus.

Webb, Clarence H.
    1968   The Extent and Content of Poverty Point Culture. *American Antiquity* 33:297–321.

Webb, William S.
    1940   *The Wright Mounds, Sites 6 and 7, Montgomery County, Kentucky* Reports in Anthropology and Archaeology 5(1). University of Kentucky, Lexington.
    1941a   *Mount Horeb Earthworks, Site 1, and the Drake Mound, Site 11, Fayette County, Kentucky.* University of Kentucky Reports in Anthropology and Archaeology 5(2). University of Kentucky, Lexington.
    1941b   *The Morgan Stone Mound, Site 15, Bath County, Kentucky.* Reports in Anthropology and Archaeology 5(3). University of Kentucky, Lexington.
    1943   *The Riley Mound, Site Be15, and the Landing Mound, Site Be17, Boone County, Kentucky.* Reports in Anthropology and Archaeology 5(7). University of Kentucky, Lexington.

Webb, William S., and Raymond S. Baby
    1957   *The Adena People No. 2.* Ohio Historical Society, Columbus.

Webb, William S., and John B. Elliott
    1942   *The Robbins Mounds, Site Be3 and Be14, Boone County Kentucky.* Reports in Anthropology and Archaeology 5(5), University of Kentucky, Lexington.

Webb, William S., and William D. Funkhouser
    1940   *Ricketts Site Revisited. Site 3, Montgomery County, Kentucky.* Reports in Archaeology and Anthropology 3(6). University of Kentucky, Lexington.

Webb, William S., and William G. Haag
    1947   *The Fischer Site, Fayette County, Kentucky.* University of Kentucky Reports in Anthropology and Archaeology 7(2). University of Kentucky, Lexington.

Webb, William S., and Charles E. Snow
- 1943 *The Crigler Mounds, Sites Be20 and Be27 and the Hartman Mound Site Be32, Boone County, Kentucky.* Reports in Anthropology and Archaeology 5(6). University of Kentucky, Lexington.
- 1945 *The Adena People.* Reports in Anthropology and Archaeology 6. University of Kentucky, Lexington.
- 1974 *The Adena People.* University of Tennessee Press, Knoxville.

Wedel, Waldo R.
- 1938 *The Direct-Historical Approach in Pawnee Archaeology.* Smithsonian Miscellaneous Collections, Volume 97. Smithsonian Institution, Washington, D.C.

Weir, Gordon W.
- 1969 *Geologic Map of the Paint Lick Quadrangle East-Central Kentucky.* U.S. Geological Survey Washington D.C.
- 1976 *Geological Map of the Means Quadrangle, East-Central Kentucky.* Kentucky Geological Survey, Lexington.

Wendorf, Fred, and Raymond H. Thompson
- 2002 The Committee for the Recovery of Archaeological Remains: Three Decades of Service to the Archaeological Profession. *American Antiquity* 67(2):317–330.

Wilkins, Gary R.
- 1977 Salvage Excavations of the Gore Mound (46 Bo 26). *West Virginia Archeologist* 26:1–12.
- 1979 The Kanawha Tradition: A Review and Re-evaluation. *Tennessee Anthropologist* 4(1):63–81.

Willey, Gordon R.
- 1941 Review of "The Wright Mounds," by William S. Webb. *American Antiquity* 7:651–653.
- 1949a Review of "Archaic Sites in McLean County, Kentucky," by William S. Webb and William G. Haag. *American Antiquity* 15(1):68–70.
- 1949b Review of "The Fischer Site, Fayette County, Kentucky," by William S. Webb and William G. Haag, *American Antiquity* 15(1):68–70.
- 1949c *Archaeology of the Florida Gulf Coast.* Smithsonian Miscellaneous Collections, Volume 113. Smithsonian Institution, Washington, D.C.
- 1953 Archaeological Theories and Interpretation: New World. In *Anthropology Today*, edited by A. L. Kroeber, pp. 361–385. University of Chicago Press, Chicago.
- 1966 *Introduction to American Archaeology. Volume 1: North and Middle America.* Prentice-Hall, Englewood Cliffs, New Jersey.
- 1969 James Alfred Ford. *American Antiquity* 34(1):62–71.
- 1985 Some Continuing Problems in New World Culture History. *American Antiquity* 50(2):351–363.
- 1999 Foreword. In *Measuring the Flow of Time*, edited by M. J. O'Brien and R. L. Lyman, pp. vi–xx. University of Alabama Press, Tuscaloosa.

Willey, Gordon R., and Robert Braidwood
  1962 *Courses toward Urban Life*. Viking Fund Publications in Anthropology 32. Aldine, Chicago.
Willey, Gordon R., and Philip Phillips
  1955 Method and Theory in American Archaeology, II: Historical-Developmental Interpretation. *American Anthropologist* 57:723–819.
  1958 *Method and Theory in American Archaeology*. University of Chicago Press, Chicago.
  2001 *Method and Theory in American Archaeology*, edited by R. L. Lyman and M. J. O'Brien. University of Alabama Press, Tuscaloosa.
Willey, Gordon R., and Jeremy A. Sabloff
  1974 *A History of American Archaeology*. W. H. Freeman, San Francisco.
  1980 *A History of American Archaeology*, 2nd ed. W. H. Freeman and Company, New York.
Williamson, Ronald F., and Christopher M. Watts (editors)
  1999 *Taming the Taxonomy*. Eastendbooks, Toronto.
Willoughby, Charles C., and Earnest A. Hooton
  1922 The Turner Group of Earthworks, Hamilton County, Ohio. *Papers of the Peabody Museum* 8(3). Harvard University, Cambridge.
Winters, Howard D.
  1963 *An Archaeological Survey of the Wabash Valley in Illinois*. Reports of Investigations Number 10. Illinois State Museum, Springfield.
Wylie, Alison
  2002 *Thinking from Things: Essays in the Philosophy of Archaeology*. University of California Press, Berkeley.
Wymer, Dee Anne
  1989 The Paleoethnobotanical Record at Niebert. In *Phase III Excavations at the Niebert Site (46MS103) in the Gallipolis Locks and Dam Replacement Project Mason County, West Virginia*, edited by R. Berle Clay and Charles M. Niquette, pp. 130–158. Cultural Resource Analysts, Inc., Contract Publication Series 89-06. Lexington, Kentucky.
  1992 Trends and Disparities: The Woodland Paleoethnobotanical Record of the Mid-Ohio Valley. In *Cultural Variability in Context*, edited by M. F. Seeman, pp. 65–76. Midcontinental Journal of Archaeology Special Paper Number 7. Kent State University Press, Kent, Ohio.
  1996 The Ohio Hopewell Econiche: Human-Land Interaction in the Core Area. In *A View from the Core*, edited by P. J. Pacheco, pp. 36–53. Ohio Archaeological Council, Columbus.
Yellen, John, and Mary W. Greene
  1985 Archaeology and the National Science Foundation. *American Antiquity* 50(2):332–341.
Yerkes, Richard W.
  1988 Woodland and Mississippian Traditions in the Prehistory of Midwestern North America. *Journal of World Prehistory* 2:307–353.

1992 Vertebrate Remains. In *The Winfield Locks Site: A Phase III Excavation in the Lower Kanawha Valley, Putnam County, West Virginia,* edited by M. A. Hughes and C. M. Niquette, pp. 193–197. Contract Publication Series 92–81. Cultural Resource Analysts, Inc., Lexington, Kentucky.

Yokell, Carol A.

1997 Faunal Analysis. In *1995 Report of Investigations at Fort Ancient State Memorial, Ohio (22WA2), Volume IV: Artifact Analysis and Project Summary,* edited by L. E. Sieg, C. A. Yokell and R. P. Connolly, pp. 94–115. Report submitted to the Ohio Historical Society, Columbus.

Youse, Hillis J.

1969 Excavations of the Young Mound and Identification of Other Mounds in Dunbar, West Virginia. *West Virginia Archeologist* 22:5–29.

1980 Excavation of Ennis Mound 46KA108. Unpublished manuscript on file, West Virginia Division of Culture and History, State Historic Preservation Office, Charleston.

Zabecki, Melissa

2001 *A Report on the Human Skeletal Remains Recovered from the Bullock Site (15Wd10).* Report submitted to the Kentucky Archaeological Survey. Research notes on file, William S. Webb Museum of Anthropology, University of Kentucky, Lexington.

Contributors

Darlene Applegate is associate professor of anthropology at Western Kentucky University. Her research interests include rockshelter and cave archaeology, mortuary archaeology, bioarchaeology, lithic studies, and site formation processes.

Director of the Cranbrook Institute of Science in Bloomfield Hills, Michigan, **David S. Brose** has been chief curator and director at museums in Ohio; Ontario, Canada; and North Carolina. He has taught prehistory, history, and museum management at Case Western Reserve University, Cleveland State University, the University of Toronto, and the University of North Carolina–Charlotte and has written and edited numerous publications on the archaeology of the midcontinent.

James A. Brown is a professor of anthropology at Northwestern University with experience in many periods of Eastern Woodlands archaeology. His current interests lie in the social and religious interpretation of precontact material culture.

Jarrod Burks currently divides his time among Ohio Valley Archaeological Consultants, for whom he conducts geophysical surveys on sites mostly in Ohio, Hopewell Culture National Historical Park, and Hocking College. He recently completed his doctoral dissertation on changes in Middle–Late Woodland period community settlement patterns in the Middle Ohio Valley.

R. Berle Clay lives in Lexington, Kentucky. He is a senior archaeologist at Cultural Resource Analysts, Inc., of Lexington and has long been concerned with Woodland and late prehistoric archaeology in the mid-South.

Contributors

William S. Dancey is associate professor of anthropology at The Ohio State University in Columbus. He is coeditor, with Paul Pacheco, of *Ohio Hopewell Community Organization*.

N'omi B. Greber is curator of archaeology at the Cleveland Museum of Natural History and adjunct associate professor of anthropology at Case Western Reserve University. She has joined new fieldwork in southern Ohio with renewed analyses of archived materials in her long-term study of Ohio Hopewell. Her latest publication concerns the chronological relationships among sites; current fieldwork is at High Bank Works.

R. Eric Hollinger is a research scientist at the Smithsonian Institution's National Museum of Natural History in Washington, D.C. He has edited a volume on taxonomy issues in the Late Prehistoric Midwest and eastern Plains and published reports and articles on lithics, paleoethnobotany, osteology, domestic architecture, social organization, prehistoric conflict, and repatriation.

Jonathan P. Kerr is a principal investigator with Cultural Resource Analysts, Inc., in Lexington, Kentucky. His research interests include ceramic analysis, site structure and function, and geophysical survey.

Robert C. Mainfort Jr. is series editor and sponsored research administrator, Arkansas Archeological Survey, and professor of anthropology, University of Arkansas.

David Pollack received his Ph.D. in anthropology from the University of Kentucky in 1998. He is currently a staff archaeologist with the Kentucky Heritage Council and co-director of the Kentucky Archaeological Survey. His research focuses on the Woodland and Late Prehistoric cultures of the lower and middle Ohio Valley.

Sean M. Rafferty is assistant professor of anthropology at the University at Albany, New York. His interests include Early and Middle Woodland period mortuary practices and archaeometry.

Michael D. Richmond currently lives in Davenport, Iowa, where he works as an archaeological consultant. His research interests include Woodland ritualism, lithic analysis, and provenance studies, specifically concerning the geological origin of protohistoric and prehistoric copper artifacts.

Contributors / 273

Eric J. Schlarb is a staff archaeologist with the Kentucky Archaeological Survey in Lexington. Primary research interests include lithic technology and experimental archaeology, as well as the Archaic and Middle Woodland periods of Kentucky's Bluegrass region. He is coauthor of *Prehistoric Hunters and Gatherers: Kentucky's First Pioneers*.

Mark F. Seeman is a professor of anthropology at Kent State University in Ohio. Much of his research has focused on the Woodland periods of the Ohio Valley region.

William E. Sharp is an archaeologist with the U.S. Department of Agriculture. He earned baccalaureate and master's degrees in anthropology from the University of Kentucky. His research interests include Fort Ancient archaeology in Kentucky.

Lauren E. Sieg has published reports and articles on Middle Woodland ceramics, excavations at the Fort Ancient site, and repatriation. Her research interests include Hopewell horizon art, Middle Woodland settlement patterns, patterns and variability in the archaeological record of the prehistoric Ohio Valley, and the ethical practice of archaeology.

Patrick D. Trader is currently acting director at the University of Kentucky's Program for Archaeological Research. His research interests include Middle and Late Woodland settlement patterns.

Teresa W. Tune received a baccalaureate degree from Transylvania University and a master's degree from the University of Kentucky. Her research interests include faunal analysis and historic pottery traditions in eastern and central Kentucky.

Index

Abrams, Elliot M., 50, 108
abstract validity, 3, 4, 8
acorn, 72, 206, 210, 211, 213, 215, 217
adaptation, 3, 4, 5, 138, 146, 148, 152, 170
Adena, xiii, xiv, xv, xvi, xvii, xviii, xix, 1, 2, 5, 7–8, 9, 10, 17, 18, 20, 21, 22, 24, 31, 32, 34, 35, 37, 38, 39, 40, 45, 46, 48, 49, 50, 51, 52, 53, 54, 59, 61, 62, 64, 68, 72, 73, 74, 75, 76, 87, 88, 90, 91, 93, 94–98, 100–110, 118–19, 122, 126, 151, 153, 154–62, 164–67, 183, 191, 195, 196, 199, 202, 208, 216, 218, 220n, 221, 224, 225–26, 228, 229; aspect, 8; complex, 8, 9, 34, 37, 39, 104, 151; cult, 8; culture, 7, 8, 9, 18n, 52, 104, 112, 118–19, 152, 153, 158; Mound site, Ohio, 4, 23, 24–30, 35–36, 38, 110, 118–19, 161, 183; Plain pottery, 58, 60, 62, 68–69, 72, 73, 74, 88, 193, 195, 208, 216, 228, 229; phase, 8, 105, 157, 193–94; Stemmed point, 69–70, 72, 73, 74, 88, 155, 162, 208, 216, 228; people, 20, 24, 25, 37, 49, 60, 62, 102, 158, 174; population, 44, 45, 46, 51, 61, 151, 158. *See also* Central Scioto Adena; Early Adena; Late Adena; Middle Adena; Scioto Adena
affinis Snyders point. *See* Snyders point
age-area approach, xviii, 96, 98, 99, 118, 119
aggregation, xvii, 44, 45, 47

Amburgey site, Kentucky, xii, xvii, 34, 35, 76–93, 228, 229
analogy, 168, 174
Anderson site, Ohio, xii, 23
Andrews, E. B., 32
Appalachian Plateau, xiii
archaeological: context, 4, 103, 105, 106, 115; culture, 2, 3, 6, 44, 145, 151, 152, 172; type section, 174; unit, xv, 1, 2, 3, 4, 6, 10, 11, 125, 126, 127, 129, 131, 134, 178, 193, 197, 214, 215, 219, 222, 223, 226, 227
Archaic, 13, 24, 70, 98, 100, 103, 167, 209, 215; culture, 100; period, 11, 37, 219; stage, 11, 100. *See also* Early Archaic period; Late Archaic period; Middle Archaic period; Terminal Archaic period
area, 126
Aristotle, 177n
Armitage Mound site, Ohio, 33, 49, 184
Armstrong: complex, 216; phase, 201; series ceramics, 216
Arnold, Philip J., III, 168–69
aspect, xv, 2, 6, 8, 124
Atwater, Caleb, 120–21
Auvergne Mound site, Kentucky, xii, 6
Aztalan site, Wisconsin, 113

Baby, Raymond S., 7, 21, 135–38, 141, 148, 161, 162, 163

Baldwin site, Ohio, 138
band, 122
Barkes, B. M., 138–39, 144
base, 2, 123, 124
Basic Hopewell, 124. *See also* Hopewell
bast fiber, 85
Baum pottery, 139
bedstraw, 81, 83, 90, 208
behavioral archaeology, 4
Bentley site, Kentucky, 84
bicymbal ear spool. *See* ear spool
Big Coal River, West Virginia, 211
Big Sandy River, Kentucky, xii, 21
Big Walnut Creek, Ohio, 138
Binford, Lewis R., 102, 168
binomial, 4, 9, 10, 97
Blacklick Park site, Ohio, 135
black locust, 208
Black Sand tradition, 174
black walnut, 72, 206, 208, 211, 213, 215
blade, 91, 156, 159, 161, 162, 208, 209. *See also* bladelet; lamellar blade; prismatic blade
bladelet, 14, 32, 33, 47, 48, 50, 58, 62, 70, 91, 192, 229
Blanton site, 84
Blue Creek, West Virginia, 203
Bluegrass region, xiii, 24, 52, 53, 61, 62, 64, 73, 74, 75, 88, 109, 228, 229
boatstone, 31, 100, 192
boundary criterion/criteria, xix, 10, 11, 13, 14, 15, 16, 17, 18, 113, 202, 215, 216, 217, 218
box turtle, 206, 212, 215
Boyle chert, 58, 69, 70, 77
Braidwood, Robert, 101, 102
Brannon chert, 58
Brew, Junius O., 119
Brose, David S., xi, xix, 9, 105, 106
Brown Heirs Mound site, West Virginia, 197
Brown, James A., xvii, xviii, 6, 38, 225, 226, 230
Buck Garden, 214, 217–18; Buck Garden phase, 201, 202, 214, 215, 218; Buck Garden Run Shelter site, West Virginia, xii, 217; Buck Garden Series ceramics, 217
Buikstra, Jane E., 38
Bullock Mound site, Kentucky, xii, xvii, 52–63, 91, 229
Burial Mound I, 11, 98, 103, 125; II, 11, 98, 125
Burks, Jarrod, xvi, 227
Burning Springs Branch Creek, West Virginia, 211; site, West Virginia, 211, 215
butternut, 72, 208, 209
Byers, A. Martin, 228

cache, 21, 24, 81, 89, 90, 174; blade, 208
Caldwell, Joseph R., 6, 9, 101, 126–27, 129, 169, 180
Camargo site, Kentucky, xii, 34, 35, 84–85, 89–90, 91–93, 229
Camden Works site, Ohio, xii, 184–86
Cameron, Catherine, 36
Capitolium Mound (at Marietta site, Ohio), 224. *See also* Marietta site, Ohio
Carr, Christopher, 87
Carriage Factory (Miller Mound) site, Ohio, 27, 28, 30
Carskadden, Jeff, 47, 50, 108
CDC #1 site, West Virginia, 207, 215
Cedar Banks site, Ohio, 183
celt, 29, 31, 59, 71, 76, 82, 87–88, 127, 209, 217
Central Muskingum locality/valley, 129, 140, 183, 184
Central Scioto: Adena, xvi, 25, 32, 39; Hopewell, 32, 39; locality/valley, 20, 21, 23, 24, 31, 109, 138, 146, 153, 183, 84, 19, 192, 193, 194. *See also* Scioto Adena; Scioto Hopewell; Scioto River, Ohio
ceremonialism, 6, 13, 14, 15, 43, 44, 45, 50, 51, 75, 88, 135, 193, 227. *See also* ritual

Charles, Douglas K., 38
Charleston Mound Group site, West Virginia, xii, 37, 199
charnel house, 61, 62, 74, 154, 193
chenopod, 71. *See also* goosefoot
Cherry Valley Mounds site, Ohio, 23
Chesser: Cave site, Ohio, 137; Notched point, 15, 48, 203, 206, 207, 211, 213, 217; phase, 137
Childers: phase, 202–3, 206–7, 212, 213, 217, 218, 219; Series pottery, 203, 206, 213, 217; site, xii, 203, 212, 213, 214, 216
Chillicothe, Ohio 22, 25, 109, 161, 183; Northwest Group site, Ohio 25, 28, 34, 36
chokeberry, 83
chronological unit, xvi, xix, 2, 8–10, 202. *See also* temporal unit
chronology, 8, 12, 96, 104, 108, 118, 125, 139, 164, 177n, 222; construction, 10–11, 16
civilization, 3, 99, 107, 129, 130
cladistics, 169
Clarke, David L., 117
class, xiv, xv, 5, 9, 10, 17, 114, 116, 177n
Classic state, 100
classification, xiv, 2, 9, 10, 17, 18, 53, 72, 97, 101, 105, 106, 109, 119, 120, 121, 123, 128, 170, 171, 177n, 197, 199, 201, 202, 215, 218, 221, 223, 225, 230. *See also* taxonomic classification
Clay, R. Berle, xi, xvii, 8, 30, 60, 61, 69, 74, 88, 89, 157, 158, 163, 202, 207–8, 215, 216, 218, 219, 226
climax, 6, 126, 129
Cochran, Don R., 108
Coco Station site, West Virginia, xii, 203–6, 215
Cogswell point, 206
Cole, 17, 134–49; complex, xvi, xviii, 134–49; horizon, 134, 137, 138, 146; phase, 146, 229; Series pottery, 135,
137, 139, 141, 145, 146, 148. *See also* W. S. Cole site, Ohio
Cole, Fay Cooper, 5, 6, 124
Cole, W. S. site, Ohio. *See* W. S. Cole site, Ohio
Collins, Henry B., 98
Committee for the Recovery of Archaeological Remains, 101
Committee on State Archaeological Surveys (of the National Research Council), 123, 124
complex, xviii, 5, 6, 7, 8, 9, 10, 34, 36, 37, 39, 40, 44, 53, 84, 89, 95, 103, 104, 106, 118, 123, 129, 132, 151–52, 161, 177n, 199. *See also* Adena complex; Armstrong complex; Cole complex; Eastern Agricultural Complex; Hopewell complex.
component, 2, 3, 7, 9, 24, 34, 43, 58, 64, 70, 76, 78, 84, 88, 90, 111, 112, 113, 118, 119, 124, 125, 126, 128, 139, 140, 165, 206, 207, 208, 209, 210, 211, 222, 223, 228
Conference on Midwestern Archaeology, 123, 171
Conference on Southern Pre-History, 124, 172
Connestee series pottery, xvii, 34, 76, 84, 89, 90
Connett Mounds site, Ohio, 32–33, 49, 184
Coon Mound site, Ohio, 33, 38, 95, 109
Copeland Island site, Ohio, 140, 148
copper, 14, 23, 29, 30, 31–33, 34, 44, 55, 57, 59, 60, 71, 76, 81, 82, 83, 85–88, 90, 91, 95, 100, 126–27, 132, 157, 158, 159, 160, 162, 163, 179, 180, 186, 192, 228
C. & O. Mounds site, Kentucky, 84
core: lithic, 70; spatial unit, 4, 43, 47, 48, 51, 118, 123
corn. *See* maize
cottontail. *See* eastern cottontail
Cowan, C. Wesley, 127

Crab Orchard: chert, 69–70; tradition, 126, 180
cremation, xvii, 29, 32, 55, 59, 60, 61, 64, 66, 67, 69, 71, 72, 73, 74, 75, 89, 90, 156, 157, 159, 160, 161, 162–63, 164, 186, 209, 216
crematorium, 74
Cresap Mound site, West Virginia, xii, 8, 33, 105, 107, 154–58, 159, 160, 164; point, 156
Crigler Mound site, Kentucky, 91
critical historical approach, 197
Crystal River region, 181
c-transform, 4
cult, xv, 7, 8, 118, 167
cultural evolution, 99, 114, 169. *See also* evolution
cultural-historical, 13, 95
culture, xv, xviii, 3, 5, 6, 7, 8, 9, 12, 40, 43, 45, 62, 72, 73, 95, 98, 100, 101, 103, 104, 108, 109, 112, 113, 114, 117–18, 121, 122, 124, 125, 128, 129, 130, 133, 146, 151, 153, 158, 172, 174, 177n, 179, 199, 222, 226, 230; area, 5, 116; historical, 45, 115, 222, 225, 227, 228; history, 3, 4, 5, 11–12, 13, 94, 96–97, 100, 102–3, 106, 107, 151, 199. *See also* Adena culture; Archaic culture; Hopewell culture; Mississippi culture; Woodland culture
culture, archaeological. *See* archaeological culture
culture, ethnographic. *See* ethnographic culture
Cumberland River, Kentucky, 53

Dancey, William S., xviii, 43, 46, 138, 229–30
Davis, Edwin H., 89, 121, 128, 140, 224
Davis, William H. Mound site, Ohio, xii, 154, 161–62, 163–64, 165
DECCO site, Ohio, 139, 140, 144–45, 148
deconstruct/deconstruction, xviii, 107

deer, 36, 82, 90, 192, 206, 210, 212, 215, 217
depositional environment, 174
determinant/determinant trait, 2, 5, 11–12, 40, 124
Deuel, Thorne, 5, 6, 123, 124
diagnostic trait, 8, 15, 52, 124
diffusion, 3, 4, 13, 21, 99, 118, 131, 151, 199
direct historical method, 11, 124
ditch, 46, 140, 157, 186, 193, 228
dock, 80
Dominion Thick point, 162
Dragoo, Don W., xiii, 7–8, 21, 62, 103, 105, 155, 157
Drake Mound site, Kentucky, xii, 52, 53, 61, 73
Dunnell, Robert C., xiv, xv, 114, 170–71

Eagle Mound (at Newark Earthworks site, Ohio), 36
Early Adena, 35, 155, 162; phase, 8, 157
Early Archaic period, 11, 70, 76, 78, 206, 210
Early Middle Woodland subperiod, 17, 64, 89, 90, 216, 218
Early phase, 215
Early Woodland: period, xv, xvi, 11, 13–14, 15, 16, 17, 20, 34, 38, 40, 43–44, 45, 46, 50, 53, 61, 72–73, 103, 107, 166, 201, 202, 203, 206, 207, 210, 211, 213–14, 215–16, 218, 219; tradition, 5, 8
ear spool, xvii, 29, 30, 76, 81, 83, 85–87, 90, 91, 228; bicymbal ear spool, 86
earthwork, 5, 7, 11, 12, 13, 15, 23, 44, 52, 53, 72, 78, 100, 120, 122, 128, 132, 140, 181, 184, 186, 191, 194. *See also* enclosure; mound
Eastern Agricultural Complex, 211, 212, 213, 217
eastern cottontail, 206
Eastern Maize Area, 99
eastern redbud, 83, 208

Eastern Woodlands, xiii, 1, 5, 11, 12, 14, 15, 39, 90, 101, 118, 166, 171
ecology, 4
Edwin Harness Mound site, Ohio, xii, 30, 46, 61, 122, 191
Elemental Hopewellian, 125. *See also* Hopewell
Elkhorn Creek, Kentucky, 52, 53, 81
Elliott, John B., 73
elm, 210
emic, 153
empirical validity, 2, 4
enclosure, 23, 24, 25, 30, 31, 33, 44, 45, 47, 52, 61, 89, 90, 103, 106, 109, 121–22, 128, 135, 140, 157, 179, 183, 184, 186, 191, 193, 194, 195, 221, 227, 228. *See also* earthwork; mound
Ennis Mound site, West Virginia, 202
Enos Holmes site, Ohio, 137, 139
era, 12, 23, 31, 33, 116, 175, 221
erect knotweed, 71, 212, 213
Erp site, Ohio, 135, 138
Esch site, Ohio, 87
esker, 141, 144
Essenpreis, Patricia, 195; phase, 195
essentialist, 3, 12, 94, 152, 153, 225, 227
ethnoarchaeology, 4
ethnography/ethnographic, 81, 124, 168, 171, 174, 175, 177n; analogy, 174; culture, 3, 6, 7, 9
etic, 153
Ety site, Ohio, xii, 46
evolution, 107, 172–74. *See also* cultural evolution
exotic/exotica, 23, 24, 39, 30, 44, 126, 127, 174, 181
experimental archaeology, 4
extended burial, 28, 32, 60–61, 64, 68, 73, 75, 156, 157, 159, 160, 162, 163, 186

facies, 8–9, 174
Fairchance phase, 107–8
Fayette Thick pottery, 69
Fenton, James P. 84, 89

Fischer site, Kentucky, 52, 73
Fishinger Road site, Ohio, 135
Fitting, James E., xi, 9, 105, 106
flexed burial, 68, 163
Flint Ridge (of Ohio) chert, 33, 58, 229
Fluted Point period, 11
focal, 4
focus, 2, 4, 113, 123–24, 222
Ford, James A., xvi, 12, 96–100, 101, 102, 103, 107, 109, 125, 132, 221–22
Ford, Richard I., 8
form/formal: attribute, 1, 2, 3, 7, 10, 11, 20, 29, 31, 33, 111–12, 114, 116, 119, 120, 121, 123, 124, 125, 127, 128, 129, 130–31, 132, 133, 150, 179, 180, 181, 182, 193, 194, 196, 215; unit, xvi, xix, 2–10, 11, 17–18, 112, 125–26, 127, 215
formation process, 3–4
Formative stage, 5, 100, 102, 104
Fort Ancient, 122, 135, 137–38, 139, 146, 148, 217; culture, 121; period, 64, 135, 202; site, xii, 23, 31, 175, 184, 186, 191, 192, 194, 195; tradition, 134, 139
Fosters site, Ohio, xii, 184, 186, 194
Fowke, Gerard, 5, 96, 121
Fryman site, Ohio, 138
Fuller, John W., 46
function, 3, 16, 121, 128
Funkhouser, William D., 53, 57, 159–60

Garden Creek site, Tennessee, 85
Gary point, 228
Gauley: phase, 217–18, 219; River, West Virginia, 217–18
G. E. Mound (Mount Vernon) site, Indiana, 27
geometric enclosure. *See* enclosure
Glacial Kame, 4. *See also* kame
Glacial Till Plain, xiii
Glaciated Plateau, 135
Golf Course Mound site, West Virginia, 197

goosefoot, 80, 81, 83, 90, 192, 208, 212, 213. *See also* chenopod
Gore Mound site, West Virginia, 199
gorget, 29, 59, 71, 88, 127, 163, 209, 217
gourd, 102, 211
grape, 72, 206, 215
Grave Creek Mound site, West Virginia, 154
great house, 44, 191
Great Miami: locality, 183, 184; River, Ohio, xiii, 23, 31, 108, 184
Greber, N'omi B., xvi, 14, 61, 88, 108, 109, 127, 153, 193, 195, 224, 225, 226
Green Camp site, Ohio, 138
Greenman, Emerson F., xiii, 7, 21, 29, 38, 39, 95, 106, 109, 118–19
Green, William, 180
Griffin, James B., xvi, 5, 6, 8, 11, 13, 14, 15, 18n, 101, 102, 103–4, 105, 106, 110, 119, 123, 126, 221–22
Grimes site, Ohio, 84
Grimes Village site, Kentucky, 60
group, xiv, xv, 2, 4, 5, 9, 10, 17
grouping, xiv, 17
Gulf Coast region, 95

Haag, William G., 8, 53–54, 55, 57, 58, 59, 62, 68, 100
Half-Moon Cordmarked pottery, 206, 207, 215
Hall, Robert L., 126, 127, 180
hamlet, 4, 50
Hansen site, Kentucky, 46, 84
Hardin point, 70
Harness 28 site, Ohio, 46
Harness, Edwin Mound site, Ohio. *See* Edwin Harness Mound site, Ohio
Harness Mound (at Liberty site, Ohio), 122, 191. *See also* Liberty site, Ohio
Harris site, West Virginia, 209–10, 211, 216
Havana tradition, 126, 180
Hays, Christopher Tinsley, 153, 162, 163
hazelnut, 206, 209, 210, 215

Hegmon, Michelle, 20
Hemmings, E. Thomas, 198, 199–200, 201, 215, 218
Henderson Mound 2 site, Ohio, 44, 51n
Henderson Road site, Ohio, 135, 138
hickory, 72, 83, 90, 206, 208, 209, 210, 211, 213
High Banks Works site, Ohio, xii, 183
Highbank Park site, Ohio. *See* Orange Township Works site, Ohio
hilltop enclosure. *See* enclosure
hinterland, 23, 50
historical integration, 107, 222
historiography, 107, 109
Hocking locality, 183, 184; River, Ohio, xii, 14, 21, 23, 31–33, 39, 45, 49, 50, 108, 109, 138, 184, 224
Hollinger, R. Eric, xviii, 6, 7
Holmes, Enos site, Ohio. *See* Enos Holmes site, Ohio
Hopeton (Hopetown) site, Ohio, xii, 23, 183
Hopetown site, Ohio. *See* Hopeton site, Ohio
Hopewell, xiii, xiv, xv, xvi, xvii, xviii, xix, 1, 5–7, 8, 10, 14, 17, 18, 20, 21, 22, 23, 24, 31, 33, 34, 35, 37, 38, 39, 40, 43, 45, 46, 47, 48, 49, 50, 51, 52, 53, 61, 62, 72, 76, 85, 86, 87, 88, 89, 90, 91, 93, 94–95, 96, 98, 99, 100, 103, 104, 105, 107, 108, 109, 116, 120–33, 144, 151, 153, 154, 172, 175, 178–79, 183, 191, 192, 196, 199, 201, 202, 216, 218, 221, 223, 224, 225, 227, 228, 229; climax, 6, 126; complex, 6, 104, 151; cult, 7, 174; culture, 6, 7, 17, 53, 62, 94–95, 104, 122, 124, 125, 129, 132, 152, 153, 179; episode, 174; era, 23; horizon, 6, 120, 126, 130–33, 178–81, 183–90, 192–96, 229; Interaction Sphere, 6, 43, 112, 122–23, 126–27, 201; network, 6; people, 7, 20, 22, 25, 37, 122, 129; phase, 6, 124, 126, 131, 193–94; phenomenon, 7, 43, 126;

population, 7, 44, 51; pottery, 47, 48–49, 124, 131, 186; site, Ohio, xii, 6, 24–31, 32, 35, 36, 38, 87, 109, 122, 175, 183, 191; tradition, 6, 105, 126. *See also* Basic Hopewell; Elemental Hopewellian; Mound 25; Ohio Hopewell

horizon, xiv, xv, xviii, xix, 3, 4, 6, 9, 116, 120, 125, 126, 178–79; marker, 2, 130, 131, 132, 179, 180, 184, 186, 192, 195, 229; style, 112, 130, 131, 132, 135, 179, 184, 186, 192. *See also* Cole horizon; Hopewell horizon; style; style zone

Horticultural-Pottery Base, 124

Houart, Gail L., 6, 14, 126–27, 128, 179

huckleberry, 208

Hudson Mound site, Ohio, 135

Hughes, Myra A., 206

Icehouse Bottom site, Tennessee, 85

idealism/idealist, 173, 177n

Illinois River Valley region, 37–39, 132, 181

index function, 111

Indianapolis Archaeological Conference, 172

integrative approach, xvi, 2–3

interactional archaeology, 4

interaction sphere, xviii, 4, 126, 127, 131. *See also* Hopewell Interaction Sphere

Interior Low Plateau, xiii

Intrusive Mound, xvi, 4, 17, 138

Iroquoian, 153, 172, 175

Jack's Reef point, 207, 211

Jefferies, Richard W., 84, 89

Jefferson, Thomas, 169

Jenkins House site, West Virginia, 212

Jennings, Jesse D., 5

Jonathan Creek, Ohio, 50

kame, 141, 146. *See also* Glacial Kame

Kanawha: phase, 217, 218, 219; River, West Virginia, xii, xix, 14, 106, 181, 197, 199, 201–3, 206–19; tradition, xvi, 8, 199, 201, 214, 218

Keel, Bennie C., 84

Kehoe, Alice B., 170

Kellar, James H., 223

Kelly, A. R., 223

Kentucky River, Kentucky, xii, 52, 64

Kerr, Jonathan P., xvii, 24, 213, 218, 228–29

Kincaid site, Illinois, 96

Kirk Corner Notched point, 58, 70

Kirk Mound site, West Virginia, 208–9, 216

Knife River flint, 132, 186

knotweed, erect. *See* erect knotweed

Krebbs site, Ohio, 46

Kroeber, Alfred, 96–101

Kurjack, Edward B., 223

Knobs province, Kentucky, xii, 64, 77

Lake Ellensmere, Ohio, 25, 28

lamellar blade, 179, 192, 193. *See also* blade; bladelet; prismatic blade

Landing Mound site, Kentucky, 52

Late Adena, 35, 50, 62, 91, 135, 155; phase, 8, 157, 193

Late Archaic period, 11, 58, 70, 78, 165, 206, 207, 214

Late Middle Woodland subperiod, 144, 211, 216, 218, 219

Late Prehistoric period, 12, 47, 78, 116, 139, 144–45, 148, 172, 207, 208, 210, 211, 214, 223

Late Woodland: period, xv, xvi, xviii, 11, 13, 15, 17, 40, 42–43, 44, 45, 46, 47, 50, 111, 115–18, 134, 135, 137, 138, 139, 141, 142, 148, 174, 201, 202, 203, 206, 208, 209, 210, 211, 212, 213, 214, 215, 216–18, 219, 229; stage, 137; tradition, 5

Leslie Mound site, West Virginia, 197, 208, 216

Levanna point, 211

Lewis, Gilbert L., 225

Lexington Plain, xiii
Liberty site, Ohio, 44, 183, 191. *See also* Harness Mound
Lichliter site, Ohio, xii, 46, 47, 135, 138, 139, 148
Licking River, Kentucky, xii, 154, 164
Licking: locality, Ohio, 183; River, Ohio, 23, 24, 139, 140, 147, 183
linked trait, 113, 124
Linn 7 site, Ohio, xii, 49
Linton, Ralph, 117
Lithic stage, 106
little barley, 192
Little Kanawha River, West Virginia, xii
Little Miami: locality, 178, 181, 184–96, 227; River, Ohio, xii, 23, 31, 122, 178, 183, 184, 227
Little Tennessee River region, 181
liturgy, 225
locality, xiv, 126, 131, 178, 181, 183, 193, 194
Locust site, Ohio, 49, 139, 140, 148
log tomb, 32, 60, 64, 68, 73, 75, 88, 158, 159, 160, 161, 162, 163, 164, 165, 193
Longacre: I site, Ohio, 140, 148; II site, Ohio, 140, 148
Lowe: Cluster points, 47, 48, 50, 211, 217; Flared Base point, 203, 206
Lower Mississippi Valley, xix, 98–99, 103, 104, 106, 181, 222, 227, 288
Lower Muskingum locality, 23, 183, 184. *See also* Muskingum River, Ohio
Lower Scioto locality, 183. *See also* Scioto River, Ohio
Lower Shawnee Town site, Kentucky, 44
Lower Wabash region, 181
Lower Yazoo Basin, 222
Lyman, R. Lee, 3

Madison point, 211
Mainfort, Robert C., Jr., xix
Main site, Kentucky, 84

Mairs, Oscar L., 8, 197–98, 201, 208, 215, 218
maize, 14, 15, 46, 99, 104, 116, 117, 118, 134, 148, 212, 213, 217
Mandeville site, Georgia, 223
maple, 207, 210
Marietta site, Ohio, xii, 31, 87, 122, 184, 224
Marksville site, 94–5, 96, 97, 98
marsh elder, 80
Maslowski, Robert F., xiii
maygrass, 71, 192, 206, 207, 208, 209, 211, 212, 213
Mays, Asa, Jr., 161
McConaughy, Mark A., 107–8
McGraw: Plain pottery, 192, 193, 194; site, Ohio, 105
McKenzie, Douglas H., 137
McKern, Will C., xvi, 2, 5, 6, 8, 112–13, 117, 123–24, 133, 171, 177n, 223
McMichael, Edward V., xix, 8, 37, 105, 106, 197–98, 201–2, 208, 214, 215, 216, 217, 218, 220n, 223
McWhinney Heavy Stemmed point, 58
Merom Cluster points, 210
Meso-Indian Era, 12
meteoric iron, 127, 186
Metz, Charles, 195; Metz phase, 195
Miami Fort site, Ohio, xii, 23, 184
Miamisburg Mound site, Ohio, xii, 31
mica, 14, 23, 29, 30, 31, 44, 82, 83, 87, 88, 90, 91, 127, 132, 179, 186, 192, 208
micro-stratigraphy, 169
Middle Adena, 157, 162. *See also* Adena
Middle Archaic period, 11, 210. *See also* Archaic
Middle Mississippian focus, 113, 117, 223. *See also* Mississippi; Upper Mississippian focus
Middle Ohio Valley, xi, xii, xv, xvi, xviii, 1, 2, 4, 5, 6, 8, 9, 10, 13, 14, 15, 16, 17, 20, 21, 22, 35, 37, 38, 39, 40, 44, 45, 46, 52, 61, 62, 64, 70, 72, 74, 76, 84,

Index / 283

87, 90, 105, 125, 139, 154, 178, 181, 183, 191, 192, 193, 194, 196, 224. *See also* Upper Ohio Valley

Middle Tennessee region, 173, 181

Middle Woodland period, xv, xvi, xvii, xix, 5, 11, 12, 13, 14, 15, 16, 17, 20, 31, 34, 35, 38, 42, 44, 45, 53, 58, 60, 61, 62, 70, 72, 73, 74, 75, 76, 78, 80, 81, 84, 85, 86, 87, 88, 89, 90, 91, 103, 107, 116, 120, 126, 129, 132, 134, 135, 140, 144, 151, 152, 173, 175, 178, 179, 180, 181, 183, 186, 192, 193, 194, 195, 196, 201, 202, 208, 209, 210, 211, 212, 214, 215, 216, 218, 219, 220n, 223, 224, 225, 226, 228, 229. *See also* Early Middle Woodland subperiod; Late Middle Woodland subperiod

middle-range theory, 3

Midwestern Taxonomic Method (MTM), xvi, 2–3, 6, 8, 112–13, 115–18, 123–25, 177n, 223, 226. *See also* Midwestern Taxonomic System

Midwestern Taxonomic System (MTS), 97–98, 105, 112, 116, 146, 177n. *See also* Midwestern Taxonomic Method

migration/migrationism/migrationist, xvii, 13, 103, 105, 129, 151, 171, 198

Milford site, Ohio, xii, 184–86

Miller Mound site, Ohio. *See* Carriage Factory site, Ohio

Mills, William C., xiii, 6, 7, 21, 95, 118, 121–22

Mississippi/an, 5, 98, 100, 137, 146, 153, 174, 223, 224; Basic Culture, 124; culture, 116, 223; pattern, 124; period, 11, 98, 118, 222, 223; River valley, 5, 94–95, 96, 98, 99, 103, 104, 121, 181; tradition, 12. *See also* Lower Mississippi Valley; Middle Mississippian focus; Upper Mississippian focus

model, 10, 17, 22, 75, 87, 105, 117, 119, 127, 151, 70, 174, 177n

Montgomery Incised pottery, 88, 216

Moore, Clarence B., 223

Moorehead, Warren K., xiii, 5–6, 25, 96, 121–22

Morgan, Richard G., 103, 106, 141

Morgan Stone Mound site, Kentucky, 47, 50, 51n, 108, 139

mound, 5, 7, 15, 22 24, 25, 27, 28, 30, 31, 32, 33, 34, 35, 36, 37, 38, 43, 44, 45, 48, 49, 51, 52, 53–62, 64–75, 84, 87, 88, 89, 90, 91, 93, 96, 97, 98, 99, 100, 101, 102, 103, 104, 105, 106, 108, 109, 110, 118, 199, 120, 121, 122, 128, 135, 144, 151, 153–65, 167, 174, 179, 183, 184, 186, 191, 193, 194, 197, 198, 201, 202, 208, 209, 214, 215, 216, 220, 221, 223, 224, 225, 227, 228, 229. *See also* earthwork; enclosure

Mound 25 (at Hopewell site, Ohio), 25, 28–31, 36, 38, 175, 191. *See also* Hopewell site, Ohio

mound builder, 94–95, 97–98, 101, 121, 128; myth, 129, 197

Mound City site, Ohio, xii, 25, 30, 35, 44, 61, 183

Moundsville site, West Virginia, 154, 157

Mount Carbon Village site, West Virginia, xii, 197, 216, 217–18

Mount Horeb Earthwork site, Kentucky, 52

Mount Vernon site, Indiana. *See* G. E. Mound site, Indiana

Mountain View site, West Virginia, 211, 216

MTM. *See* Midwestern Taxonomic Method

MTS. *See* Midwestern Taxonomic System

mulberry. *See* red mulberry

Mulberry Creek Plain pottery, 228–29

Muldraugh chert, 69, 70

multi-scalar approach, xviii, 152, 224, 225

Murad Mound site, West Virginia, xii, 197, 208

Murphy, James L., 8 138

Muskingum River, Ohio, xii, 23–24, 31, 39, 45, 47, 49, 50, 108, 109, 134, 135, 139, 140, 146, 183, 184. *See also* Central Muskingum locality; Lower Muskingum locality
mussel, 27, 213

narrative, 102, 114–15, 197, 201, 219
National Research Council (NRC), 94–95, 96, 101–2, 123, 124
National Science Foundation (NSF), 94
Natrium Mound site, West Virginia, xii, 7, 33, 154, 157–58, 160, 164
Neo-Indian era, 12
New Archaeology, 102
Newark Earthworks site, Ohio, xii, 23, 24, 31, 36, 122, 183
Newman Mound site, West Virginia, 208, 209, 216
Newtown: phase, xvi, 4, 17, 40, 44, 45, 138–39; pottery, 139
Niebert site, West Virginia, 90, 207–8
Niquette, Charles M., 89, 202, 207, 208, 213, 215, 216, 218, 220n
Nodena phase, 222, 223
Norris, Rae, 33
North American Formative stage, 99
n-transform, 4
nucleation, 24, 40–51
Nu-Way site, Ohio, 140

oak, 208, 209, 210, 213
obsidian, 14, 22, 23, 36, 44, 127, 132, 186
O. C. Voss Mound site, Ohio, 135–39, 148
Ohio Historical Society, 141
Ohio Hopewell, xix, 6, 7, 22, 23, 25, 30, 31, 34, 37, 38, 61, 85, 90, 91, 106, 107, 120, 121, 124, 125, 126, 179, 226, 227, 229. *See also* Hopewell
Ohio State Museum, 137, 140, 141
Olen Corporation site, Ohio, 135, 138
Olentangy River, Ohio, 138, 140, 144
Orange Township Works (Highbank Park) site, Ohio, 135, 140, 144

Orient Fishtail point, 206
Osborn Mound site, Ohio, 49
OSB Two site, West Virginia, 210–11, 216
Otto, Martha Potter, 138
oxalis, 80

Paint Creek, Ohio, 25, 137, 183
Paint Lick Creek, Kentucky, 64
paleoanthropology, 172–74, 176
paleoethnography, 173, 176
paleoethnology, 173
Paleo-Indian era, 12
Paleoindian period, 11, 64, 208
panpipe, 32, 33, 132, 179, 186. *See also* pipe
paradigm, xiv, 3, 4, 8, 12, 13, 151, 170, 171, 172, 198
paradigmatic classification, xiv
Parkin phase, 223
Parkline: phase, 203, 210, 212, 213, 214, 217, 218; series pottery, 203, 210, 217; site, West Virginia, xii, 203, 213, 216
parsimony, xiv, xv
pattern, 2, 5, 6, 124. *See also names of specific patterns*
peer polity, 4
period, xiv, xvi, xviii, 11–13, 15–16, 39, 40, 45, 115, 118, 126, 129, 130, 131, 150, 151, 215. *See also names of specific periods*
periphery, 4, 43, 210
Peter Village site, Kentucky, xii, 52, 60, 61, 69
Peters: Cave site, Ohio, 137, 138; phase, 137; pottery, 139
Phagan, Carl J., 138–39, 142, 144
phase, xv, xviii, xix, 2–3, 4, 5, 9, 40, 45, 107, 108, 115, 124–26, 129–30, 132, 137, 146, 148, 150, 151, 157, 164, 178, 179, 180, 181, 183, 193–96, 198, 201, 202, 203, 211, 213, 214, 215, 217, 219, 222, 223, 226, 227. *See also names of specific phases*
phenomenological unit, 10

Phillips, Phillip, xvi, xiii, 2–3, 5, 6, 8, 100–101, 104, 112, 118, 120, 123, 125–26, 129–31, 133, 137, 146, 178
Philo: II site, Ohio, 140, 148; II Lower Village site, Ohio, 47, 51; Mound Group site, Ohio, 51
phylogeny, 117
pine, 208, 209, 213
Pinson Mounds site, Tennessee, 33, 229
pipe, 11, 14, 32, 71, 88, 91, 100, 127, 132, 157, 160, 163, 179, 186, 209. *See also* panpipe
Plains, The, Ohio, xii, 31–33, 50, 184
pokeweed, 83
Point Peninsula tradition, 180
Pollack, David, xvii, 228
Pollock site, Ohio, xii, 23
Post-Classic stage, 100
Potter, Martha A., 135–37, 148
prismatic blade, 127. *See also* blade; bladelet; lamellar blade
processual archaeology, 3, 151
Prufer, Olaf H., 6, 137–38, 192, 195, 224
purslane, 80, 81, 90
Putnam, Frederick W., 5, 121–22
Pyles site, Kentucky, 46

Raddatz Side Notched point, 58
radiocarbon, 11, 21, 22, 30, 33, 34, 43, 47, 49, 51n, 57, 66, 67, 72, 73, 78, 80, 84, 103, 104, 105, 118, 139, 142, 144, 148, 151, 155, 157, 158, 160, 161, 162, 186, 191–92, 194–95, 198, 201, 202, 203, 206, 207, 208, 209, 210, 212, 213, 215, 216, 218, 223, 224, 228, 229
Rafferty, Sean M., xviii, 224–25
Rafinesque, Constantine, 52, 89
Railey, Jimmy A., 51n
Ramenofsky, Ann F., xiv, xv, 16
Rappaport, Roy A., 225
realism/realist, 173, 177n
redbud. *See* eastern redbud
Redfield, Robert, 180
red mulberry, 208

red ochre, 57–59
region, 121, 216, 131, 178, 180–81, 183, 193, 227
reliability, 4, 12, 16, 18, 132, 133, 201
Richmond, Michael D., xvii, 34, 228–29
Ricketts site, Kentucky, xii, 34, 59, 73, 88, 154, 160–61, 164
Riggs, Rodney, 194
Right Fork, West Virginia, 210
Riley Mound site, Kentucky, 52, 58, 61, 91, 229
Ritchie, William A., 7, 105, 137
ritual, 9, 20, 21, 22, 24, 25, 28–31, 35–38, 72, 76, 81, 83, 88–91, 108, 127, 153–65, 167, 191, 193, 196, 202, 208, 214, 225, 228. *See also* ceremonialism
Robbins: Mound site, Kentucky, xii, 73–74; phase, 107, 157; point, 50, 88, 156, 157, 162, 193, 208, 209
Ross County, Ohio, xvi, 24, 28, 29, 31, 35, 36, 38, 39, 44, 49, 50, 140, 183, 224
R. P. Swartz Mound site, Ohio, 27, 28
Ruhl, Katharine C., 30, 85–87, 90
rush, 208

Sabloff, Jeremy A., 131
scale, xv, xix, xx, 1, 21, 128, 151–54, 169, 176, 224–25, 228, 230
scatter, 4
Schlarb, Eric, xvii, 229
Scioto: Adena, 25, 30, 39; Hopewell, xvi, 25, 32, 39; River, Ohio, xii, 6, 23, 25, 31, 33, 44, 88, 110, 122, 135, 153, 154, 161, 162, 173, 180, 193, 192, 193, 195; tradition, 8, 105, 126, 131, 135, 180; Trail (Zencor) site, Ohio, xii, 46, 138. *See also* Central Scioto; Lower Scioto locality; Upper Scioto locality
Seeman, Mark F., xiii, xviii, 5, 8, 38, 46, 86–87, 126–28, 131, 138–39, 180, 193–96, 229–30
Seip, 44, 61, 122; Conjoined Mounds site, Ohio, xii, 36; Pricer Mound site, Ohio, xii, 25, 30, 36

settlement archaeology, 4, 142
settlement pattern, 4, 24, 50, 158, 194, 198, 201, 202, 215, 217, 219
settlement system, 4, 9, 108
Setzler, Frank M., 94–98, 101–2, 104, 123
Shane, Orrin C., III, 8, 105, 137, 138
Shawnee, 174
Shetrone, Henry C., xiii, 7, 95–96, 98, 121–22
Shipley site, Ohio, 135
Shorter Mound site, Georgia, 223
Shott, Michael J., 134–35, 139, 214, 217, 218
Shriver Circle site, Ohio, 30
Sieg, Lauren E., xviii, xix, 6, 7, 224, 226–27
Skinner, Shaune M., 32
Smith, Harlan I., 170
Smith site, Ohio, 186, 191
Smithsonian Institution, 86, 94, 97–98, 99, 100, 197
Snow, Charles E., 7, 21, 22, 60, 106, 225–26
Snyders point, 70, 82, 174, 179, 192, 207, 216; *affinis* Snyders point, 70, 73, 210, 216
sociocultural unit, 3, 5, 10, 12, 17, 132
Solecki, Ralph, 7, 157
Southeast Ceremonial Complex, 118
Southeastern Ceramic Typology, 4
South Elkhorn Creek, Kentucky, 52, 53, 61
space transgression/transgressive, 33. *See also* time transgression/transgressive
Spaulding, Albert C., 97–98, 101–2, 114
Spetnagel cache, 27
Spier, Leslie, 118
squash, 81, 90, 208, 209, 211, 212, 213
Squier, George Ephriam, 89, 121, 128, 140, 224
stage unit, xvi, 3, 5, ,11, 13, 16, 17, 98, 100, 101, 103, 107, 110, 112, 125, 137, 152. *See also names of specific stages*
Stathakis, Steven A., 210

status, 60, 158, 159, 165
Steffen, Anastasia, xiv, xv
Steward, Julian, 97, 101
sticky catchfly, 81, 90
St. Johns: River region, 181; wort, 83
St. Joseph Cemetery site, Ohio, 135
stockade, 46
Stoltman, James B., 12, 22, 39, 83–85, 170
Story Mound site, Ohio, 27
Stothers, David M., xv
Strait site, Ohio, xii, 46–47, 50
Strong, William Duncan, 124
Stubbs site, Ohio, xii, 184, 186, 191
Struever, Stuart, 6, 14, 126–27, 128, 179
style, xviii, 3, 6, 87, 118, 126, 129, 139, 141, 178, 198; zone, xviii, 9. *See also* horizon style
subperiod, 12, 40, 43, 50, 216
subphase, 130
sumac, 72, 206, 208, 211
sumpweed, 192, 206, 207, 208, 212
sunflower, 71–72, 206, 208, 209, 212, 215
Susquehanna Broad point, 210
Swartz, R. P. Mound site, Ohio. *See* R. P. Swartz Mound site, Ohio
Swift Creek region, 180, 181
Swinehart site, Ohio, xii, 46, 138
sycamore, 210
Sycamore Creek, Kentucky, 77
system, 3, 4, 117, 127, 130, 132, 170
systematics, xiii, xiv, xv, xviii, 3, 6, 8, 17, 111, 112, 117, 118, 120, 123, 129, 130, 135, 137, 146, 198, 214, 226
systemic context, 4

tablet, 88
taphonomy, 169
Tarlton Mound site, Kentucky, 59, 61
taxa/taxon, xiv, xv, xviii, xix, 1, 40, 44, 45, 50, 51, 54, 91, 111, 113, 115, 116, 118, 120, 124, 131, 134, 146, 148, 153, 170, 176, 196, 212, 226, 229
taxonomic: classification, xiv, 2, 111–12, 150, 151, 173, 223; system, 43, 120,

Index / 287

123, 127–28, 130, 133, 171, 180, 196; units, 40, 44, 45, 46, 50, 51, 72, 76, 125, 126, 127, 129, 130, 132–33, 134, 135, 138, 148, 153, 169, 173, 175, 176, 178–79, 180, 181, 193, 195, 221, 222, 223, 224, 225, 226, 228, 229, 230. See also specific names of taxonomic systems; taxonomic units

taxonomy, xiv, xx, 40, 43, 44, 45, 51, 106, 111–15, 120, 125–30, 134, 148, 150, 169, 173, 174, 175, 176, 178, 179, 181, 192, 196, 221, 230. See also specific names of taxonomies

Taylor, Walter W., 97, 104, 107, 109
Tchefuncte site, Louisiana, 98, 103
Temple Mound I/II, 11, 98
temporal modeling, 17
temporal unit, xviii, 43, 113, 126. See also chronological unit
Terminal Archaic period, 161, 211. See also Archaic
territory, 22, 45, 50
Thomas, Cyrus, 97
Thomas Earthwork site, Ohio, 46
Thomas, Julian, 107
Thucydides, 169
Tiffany, Joseph A., 16
Till Plain, 135, 148
time transgression/transgressive, xviii, 14, 15, 16, 17, 22, 29, 33, 224
tobacco, 102, 212
Toephner Mound site, Ohio, xii, 44, 154, 162–63, 165
Tombigbee region, 181
Trader, Patrick D., xix, 14
tradition, xiv, xv, xviii,, 3, 4, 5, 6, 9, 37, 40, 44, 103, 125–26, 130, 131, 132, 137, 165, 167, 180. See also specific names of traditions
trait list, xiv, xvii, 2, 7, 52, 61–62, 105–6, 118–19, 123, 127–29, 153, 179
transgression/transgressive, 13. See also space transgression/transgressive; time transgression/transgressive

Transitional I/II period, 12
Tremper site, Ohio, xii, 23, 61, 86, 122, 183
Trempealeau, 37
tribe/tribal, 6, 18, 74, 75, 122, 132, 172, 177n
tulip tree, 208
turkey, 192, 206, 212, 217
Turkey-tail point, 27, 28
turtle, box. See box turtle
Turner site, Ohio, xii, 5, 31, 32, 36, 87, 184, 186, 191–92, 194–95, 226
type, xiv, 2, 5, 6, 11, 12, 27, 48, 50, 106, 107, 114, 122, 139, 170, 175, 177n, 179, 193, 195, 202, 219, 221, 223, 228; section, 174, 175; site, 4, 20, 24–25, 30, 109, 110, 138, 140, 212, 213, 224; specimen, 119
type-variety system, 12
typology, 105, 106, 120, 128, 202

Ufferman site, Ohio, 138–40, 144, 148
Unglaciated Allegheny Plateau, xiii
unit, xii, xiv, xv, xvi, xvii, xviii, xix, xx, 1; application, xvi, xvii, 2, 5, 9, 10, 17, 128, 129–30, 170, 175, 227; construction, xiii, xvi, xix, 1, 2, 3, 10–11, 17, 40, 115, 174, 201, 215; evaluation, xiii, xv, xvi, xvii, 1, 2, 4, 18, 120, 141, 146, 150, 193, 198. See also archaeological unit; chronological unit; chronology construction; formal unit; phenomenological unit; sociocultural unit; temporal unit
Upper Mississippi River region, 181. See also Lower Mississippi valley
Upper Mississippian focus, 113, 117, 181, 223. See also Middle Mississippian focus; Mississippi
Upper Ohio Valley region, 33, 107, 181, 202, 210. See also Middle Ohio Valley
Upper Scioto locality, 134, 135

validity, abstract. See abstract validity
validity, empirical. See empirical validity

variant, 94, 124, 132, 180
vector analysis, 170
vetch, 208
Voss phase, 138
Voss, O. C. Mound site, Ohio. *See* O. C. Voss Mound site, Ohio
Voss Village site, Ohio, 135, 137

Walker Branch, Kentucky, 64, 70
Walker-Noe Mound site, Kentucky, xii, xvii, 64–75, 228
walnut, 72, 83, 90, 138, 206, 208, 209, 210, 211, 213, 215
Wandsnider, LuAnn, 169
Water Plant site, Ohio, 46, 138
Watkins site, Kentucky, 84
Watson Ware pottery, 210
Watts, Christopher M., xi
Webb, William S., xiii, 2, 7, 21, 22, 34, 37, 39, 52–54, 55, 59–62, 73, 91, 95, 98, 100, 101–2, 106, 108, 109, 159, 160, 224–26, 229
Weeden Island region, 223
Welcome Mound site, West Virginia, 96
Western Basin region, 181
white-tail deer. *See* deer
Wilkins, Gary R., 197–98, 201, 214, 215, 218, 220
Willey, Gordon R., xvi, xviii, 2–3, 5, 6, 8, 11, 22, 96–104, 107, 109, 112, 118, 120, 123, 125–26, 129–32, 137, 146, 178–81, 193, 196, 198, 222–23, 226
William H. Davis Mound site, Ohio. *See* Davis, William H. Mound site, Ohio
Williamson, Ronald F., xi
William S. Webb Museum of Anthropology, 57
willow, 210
Winfield Locks site, West Virginia, xii, 206–7, 215
Wolf Creek Dam and Reservoir, 53, 54, 101

Wolf Plains archaeological district. *See* Plains, The, Ohio
Wolf Rockshelter site, Ohio, 135
Woodland, xvi, xviii, 2, 4, 5, 6, 8, 9, 10, 15, 17, 20, 39, 45, 46, 72, 116, 119, 124, 125, 135, 146, 153, 167, 197, 198, 201, 202, 213, 214, 215, 219, 224, 226, 228, 229; Basic Culture, 5, 124; Basic Pattern, 5; cultural pattern, 125; culture, 4, 20, 108, 121; pattern, 5, 6, 11, 124, 125; period, xvii, xix, 1, 15, 20, 40, 42, 43, 45, 46, 50, 51, 51n, 52, 53, 61, 62, 98, 105, 148, 180, 197, 202, 214, 215, 218, 219, 220, 221, 228; tradition, 5, 8, 12. *See also* Early Middle Woodland subperiod; Early Woodland period; Early Woodland tradition; Eastern Woodlands; Late Middle Woodland subperiod; Late Woodland period; Middle Woodland period
Woods phase, 203, 207, 208, 212, 217, 218; series pottery, 203, 208, 217; site, West Virginia, xii, 203, 212–13, 214, 216
Works Progress Administration (WPA), 52, 89, 171
Worthington Mounds site, Ohio, 27, 36
Wright: Check Stamped pottery, 69, 228; Mounds site, Kentucky, xii, 34, 35, 52, 68–69, 73, 88, 91, 102, 154, 158–61, 164, 225
W. S. Cole site, Ohio, 135, 138–39, 140, 141–42, 144, 148
Wyandotte chert, 27, 58
Wylie, Alison, 111, 114

Yazoo Basin, 222
Yerkes, Richard W., 12–13
Young Mound site, West Virginia, 197, 216

Zencor site, Ohio. *See* Scioto Trail site, Ohio